Introduction to Language

Syracuse University

Victoria Fromkin | Robert Rodman | Nina Hyams

CENGAGE
Learning™

Australia • Brazil • Japan • Korea • Mexico • Singapore • Spain • United Kingdom • United States

Introduction to Language: Syracuse University

An Introduction to Language, Ninth Edition
Victoria Fromkin | Robert Rodman | Nina Hyams

Executive Editors:
 Maureen Staudt
 Michael Stranz

Senior Project Development Manager:
 Linda deStefano

Marketing Specialist:
 Courtney Sheldon

Senior Production/Manufacturing Manager:
 Donna M. Brown

PreMedia Manager:
 Joel Brennecke

Sr. Rights Acquisition Account Manager:

 Todd Osborne

Cover Image:
Getty Images*

*Unless otherwise noted, all cover images used by Custom
Solutions, a part of Cengage Learning, have been supplied
courtesy of Getty Images with the exception of the Earthview
cover image, which has been supplied by the National
Aeronautics and Space Administration (NASA).

For product information and technology assistance, contact us at
Cengage Learning Customer & Sales Support, 1-800-354-9706

For permission to use material from this text or product,
submit all requests online at **cengage.com/permissions**
Further permissions questions can be emailed to
permissionrequest@cengage.com

This book contains select works from existing Cengage Learning resources and was produced by Cengage Learning Custom Solutions for collegiate use. As such, those adopting and/or contributing to this work are responsible for editorial content accuracy, continuity and completeness.

Compilation © 2010 Cengage Learning
ISBN-13: 978-1-111-46847-7

ISBN-10: 1-111-46847-8

Cengage Learning
5191 Natorp Boulevard
Mason, Ohio 45040
USA
Cengage Learning is a leading provider of customized learning solutions with office locations around the globe, including Singapore, the United Kingdom, Australia, Mexico, Brazil, and Japan. Locate your local office at:
international.cengage.com/region.

Cengage Learning products are represented in Canada by Nelson Education, Ltd.
For your lifelong learning solutions, visit **www.cengage.com/custom.**
Visit our corporate website at **www.cengage.com.**

Printed in the United States of America

Contents

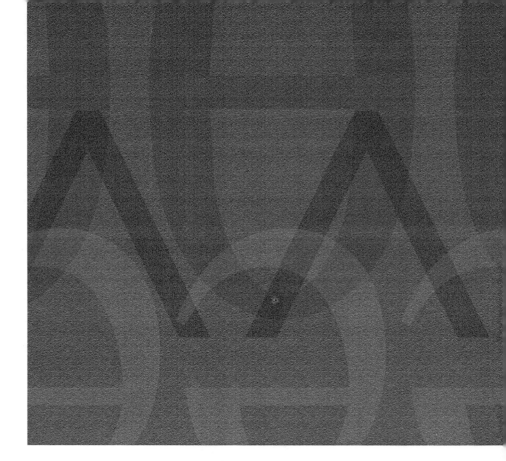

1

The Nature of Human Language

Reflecting on Noam Chomsky's ideas on the innateness of the fundamentals
of grammar in the human mind, I saw that any innate features of the language
capacity must be a set of biological structures, selected in the course of the
evolution of the human brain.

S. E. LURIA, *A Slot Machine, a Broken Test Tube, an Autobiography,* 1984

The nervous systems of all animals have a number of basic functions in common, most notably the control of movement and the analysis of sensation. What distinguishes the human brain is the variety of more specialized activities it is capable of learning. The preeminent example is language.

NORMAN GESCHWIND, 1979

Linguistics shares with other sciences a concern to be objective, systematic, consistent, and explicit in its account of language. Like other sciences, it aims to collect data, test hypotheses, devise models, and construct theories. Its subject matter, however, is unique: at one extreme it overlaps with such "hard" sciences as physics and anatomy; at the other, it involves such traditional "arts" subjects as philosophy and literary criticism. The field of linguistics includes both science and the humanities, and offers a breadth of coverage that, for many aspiring students of the subject, is the primary source of its appeal.

DAVID CRYSTAL, *The Cambridge Encyclopedia of Language,* 1987

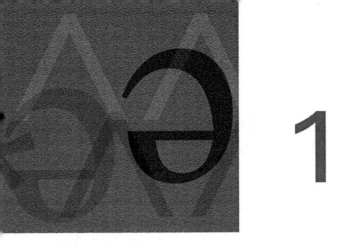

1

What Is Language?

> When we study human language, we are approaching what some might call the "human essence," the distinctive qualities of mind that are, so far as we know, unique to man.
>
> **NOAM CHOMSKY,** *Language and Mind*, 1968

Whatever else people do when they come together—whether they play, fight, make love, or make automobiles—they talk. We live in a world of language. We talk to our friends, our associates, our wives and husbands, our lovers, our teachers, our parents, our rivals, and even our enemies. We talk to bus drivers and total strangers. We talk face-to-face and over the telephone, and everyone responds with more talk. Television and radio further swell this torrent of words. Hardly a moment of our waking lives is free from words, and even in our dreams we talk and are talked to. We also talk when there is no one to answer. Some of us talk aloud in our sleep. We talk to our pets and sometimes to ourselves.

The possession of language, perhaps more than any other attribute, distinguishes humans from other animals. To understand our humanity, one must understand the nature of language that makes us human. According to the philosophy expressed in the myths and religions of many peoples, language is the source of human life and power. To some people of Africa, a newborn child is a *kintu*, a "thing," not yet a *muntu*, a "person." Only by the act of learning language does the child become a human being. According to this tradition, we all become "human" because we all know at least one language. But what does it mean to "know" a language?

Linguistic Knowledge

> Do we know only what we see, or do we see what we somehow already know?
>
> **CYNTHIA OZICK,** "What Helen Keller Saw," *New Yorker*, June 16 & 23, 2003

When you know a language, you can speak and be understood by others who know that language. This means you have the capacity to produce sounds that signify certain meanings and to understand or interpret the sounds produced by others. But language is much more than speech. Deaf people produce and understand sign languages just as hearing persons produce and understand spoken languages. The languages of the deaf communities throughout the world are equivalent to spoken languages, differing only in their modality of expression.

Most everyone knows at least one language. Five-year-old children are nearly as proficient at speaking and understanding as their parents. Yet the ability to carry out the simplest conversation requires profound knowledge that most speakers are unaware of. This is true for speakers of all languages, from Albanian to Zulu. A speaker of English can produce a sentence having two relative clauses without knowing what a relative clause is, such as

> My goddaughter who was born in Sweden and who now lives in Iowa is named Disa, after a Viking queen.

In a parallel fashion, a child can walk without understanding or being able to explain the principles of balance and support or the neurophysiological control mechanisms that permit one to do so. The fact that we may know something unconsciously is not unique to language.

What, then, do speakers of English or Quechua or French or Mohawk or Arabic know?

Knowledge of the Sound System

"B.C." © 1994 Creators Syndicate, Inc. Reprinted by permission of John L. Hart FLP and Creators Syndicate, Inc.

Part of knowing a language means knowing what sounds (or signs[1]) are in that language and what sounds are not. One way this unconscious knowledge is revealed is by the way speakers of one language pronounce words from another

---

[1]The sign languages of the deaf will be discussed throughout the book. A reference to "language," then, unless speech sounds or spoken languages are specifically mentioned, includes both spoken and signed languages.

language. If you speak only English, for example, you may substitute an English sound for a non-English sound when pronouncing "foreign" words like French *ménage à trois*. If you pronounce it as the French do you are using sounds outside the English sound system.

French people speaking English often pronounce words like *this* and *that* as if they were spelled *zis* and *zat*. The English sound represented by the initial letters *th* in these words is not part of the French sound system, and the French mispronunciation reveals the speaker's unconscious knowledge of this fact.

Knowing the sound system of a language includes more than knowing the inventory of sounds. It means also knowing which sounds may start a word, end a word, and follow each other. The name of a former president of Ghana was *Nkrumah*, pronounced with an initial sound like the sound ending the English word *sink*. While this is an English sound, no word in English begins with the *nk* sound. Speakers of English who have occasion to pronounce this name often mispronounce it (by Ghanaian standards) by inserting a short vowel sound, like *Nekrumah* or *Enkrumah*. Children who learn English recognize that *nk* cannot begin a word, just as Ghanaian children learn that words in their language can and do begin with the *nk* sound.

We will learn more about sounds and sound systems in chapters 6 and 7.

Knowledge of Words

Knowing the sounds and sound patterns in our language constitutes only one part of our linguistic knowledge. Knowing a language means also knowing that certain sequences of sounds signify certain concepts or **meanings**. Speakers of English know what *boy* means, and that it means something different from *toy* or *girl* or *pterodactyl*. You also know that *toy* and *boy* are words, but *moy* is not. When you know a language, you know words in that language, that is, which sequences of sounds are related to specific meanings and which are not.

Arbitrary Relation of Form and Meaning

> The minute I set eyes on an animal I know what it is. I don't have to reflect a moment; the right name comes out instantly. I seem to know just by the shape of the creature and the way it acts what animal it is. When the dodo came along he [Adam] thought it was a wildcat. But I saved him. I just spoke up in a quite natural way and said, "Well, I do declare if there isn't the dodo!"
>
> **MARK TWAIN,** *Eve's Diary,* 1906

If you do not know a language, the words (and sentences) of that language will be mainly incomprehensible, because the relationship between speech sounds and the meanings they represent is, for the most part, an **arbitrary** one. When you are acquiring a language you have to learn that the sounds represented by the letters *house* signify the concept 🏠; if you know French, this same meaning is represented by *maison*; if you know Russian, by *dom*; if you know Spanish, by *casa*. Similarly, ✋ is represented by *hand* in English, *main* in French, *nsa* in Twi, and *ruka* in Russian.

The following are words in some different languages. How many of them can you understand?

a. kyinii
b. doakam
c. odun
d. asa
e. toowq
f. bolna
g. wartawan
h. inaminatu
i. yawwa

People who know the languages from which these words are taken understand that they have the following meanings:

a. a large parasol (in Twi, a Ghanaian language)
b. living creature (in Tohono O'odham, an American Indian language)
c. wood (in Turkish)
d. morning (in Japanese)
e. is seeing (in Luiseño, a California Indian language)
f. to speak (in Hindi-Urdu); aching (in Russian)
g. reporter (in Indonesian)
h. teacher (in Warao, a Venezuelan Indian language)
i. right on! (in Hausa, a Nigerian language)

These examples show that the words of a particular language have the meanings they do only by convention. Despite what Eve says in Mark Twain's satire *Eve's Diary*, a pterodactyl could have been called *ron*, *blick*, or *kerplunkity*.

As Juliet says in Shakespeare's *Romeo and Juliet*:

> What's in a name? That which we call a rose
> By any other name would smell as sweet.

This **conventional** and arbitrary relationship between the **form** (sounds) and **meaning** (concept) of a word is also true in sign languages. If you see someone using a sign language you do not know, it is doubtful that you will understand the message from the signs alone. A person who knows Chinese Sign Language (CSL) would find it difficult to understand American Sign Language (ASL), and vice versa, as illustrated in Figure 1.1.

Many signs were originally like miming, where the relationship between form and meaning is not arbitrary. Bringing the hand to the mouth to mean "eating," as in miming, would be nonarbitrary as a sign. Over time these signs may change, just as the pronunciation of words changes, and the miming effect is lost. These signs become conventional, so that knowing the shape or movement of the hands does not reveal the meaning of the gestures in sign languages, as also shown in Figure 1.1.

FATHER (ASL)   FATHER (CSL)

SUSPECT (ASL)   SUSPECT (CSL)

FIGURE 1.1 | Arbitrary relation between gestures and meanings of the signs for *father* and *suspect* in ASL and CSL.[2]

Copyright © 1987 Massachusetts Institute of Technology, by permission of The MIT Press.

---

[2]From Poizner, Howard, Edward Klima, and Ursula Bellugi. "What the Hands Reveal about the Brain" figure: "Arbitrary relationship between gestures and meanings in ASL and CSL," Copyright © 1987 Massachusetts Institute of Technology, by permission of The MIT Press.

There is some **sound symbolism** in language—that is, words whose pronunciation suggests the meaning. Most languages contain **onomatopoeic** words like *buzz* or *murmur* that imitate the sounds associated with the objects or actions they refer to. But even here, the sounds differ from language to language, reflecting the particular sound system of the language. In English *cock-a-doodle-doo* is an onomatopoeic word whose meaning is the crow of a rooster, whereas in Finnish the rooster's crow is *kukkokiekuu*. Forget *gobble gobble* when you're in Istanbul; a turkey in Turkey goes *glu-glu*.

Sometimes particular sound sequences seem to relate to a particular concept. In English many words beginning with *gl* relate to sight, such as *glare, glint, gleam, glitter, glossy, glaze, glance, glimmer, glimpse,* and *glisten*. However, *gl* words and their like are a very small part of any language, and *gl* may have nothing to do with "sight" in another language, or even in other words in English, such as *gladiator, glucose, glory, glutton, globe,* and so on.

English speakers know the *gl* words that relate to sight and those that do not; they know the onomatopoeic words and all the words in the basic vocabulary of the language. No speaker of English knows all 472,000 entries in *Webster's Third New International Dictionary*. And even if someone did know all the words in *Webster's*, that person would still not know English. Imagine trying to learn a foreign language by buying a dictionary and memorizing words. No matter how many words you learned, you would not be able to form the simplest phrases or sentences in the language, or understand a native speaker. No one speaks in isolated words. Of course, you could search in your traveler's dictionary for individual words to find out how to say something like "car—gas—where?" After many tries, a native might understand this question and then point in the direction of a gas station. If he answered you with a sentence, however, you probably would not understand what was said or be able to look it up, because you would not know where one word ended and another began. Chapter 4 will discuss how words are put together to form phrases and sentences, and chapter 5 will explore word and sentence meanings.

The Creativity of Linguistic Knowledge

ALBERT: So are you saying that you were the best friend of the woman who was married to the man who represented your husband in divorce?

ANDRÉ: In the history of speech, that sentence has never been uttered before.

NEIL SIMON, *The Dinner Party,* 2000

Knowledge of a language enables you to combine sounds to form words, words to form phrases, and phrases to form sentences. You cannot buy a dictionary or phrase book of any language with all the sentences of the language. No dictionary can list all the possible sentences, because the number of sentences in a language is infinite. Knowing a language means being able to produce new sentences never spoken before and to understand sentences never heard before. The linguist Noam Chomsky, one of the people most responsible for the modern revolution in language and cognitive science, refers to this ability as part of the **creative aspect** of language use. Not every speaker of a language can create great literature, but everybody who knows a language can and does create new sentences when speaking and understands new sentences created by others, a fact expressed more than 400 years ago by Huarte de San Juan (1530–1592): "Normal human minds are such that . . . without the help of anybody, they will produce 1,000 (sentences) they never heard spoke of . . . inventing and saying such things as they never heard from their masters, nor any mouth."

In pointing out the creative aspect of language, Chomsky made a powerful argument against the behaviorist view of language that prevailed in the first half of the twentieth century, which held that language is a set of learned responses to stimuli. While it is true that if someone steps on your toes you may automatically respond with a scream or a grunt, these sounds are not part of language. They are involuntary reactions to stimuli. After we reflexively cry out, we can then go on to say: "Thank you very much for stepping on my toe, because I was afraid I had elephantiasis and now that I can feel the pain I know I don't," or any one of an infinite number of sentences, because the particular sentences we produce are not controlled by any stimulus.

Even some involuntary cries like "ouch" are constrained by our own language system, as are the filled pauses that are sprinkled through conversational speech, such as *er*, *uh*, and *you know* in English. They contain only the sounds found in the language. French speakers, for example, often fill their pauses with the vowel sound that starts their word for egg—*oeuf*—a sound that does not occur in English.

Our creative ability is reflected not only in what we say but also includes our understanding of new or novel sentences. Consider the following sentence: "Daniel Boone decided to become a pioneer because he dreamed of pigeon-toed giraffes and cross-eyed elephants dancing in pink skirts and green berets on the wind-swept plains of the Midwest." You may not believe the sentence; you may question its logic; but you can understand it, although you have probably never heard or read it before now.

Knowledge of a language, then, makes it possible to understand and produce new sentences. If you counted the number of sentences in this book that you have seen or heard before, the number would be small. Next time you write an essay or a letter, see how many of your sentences are new. Few sentences are stored in your brain, to be pulled out to fit some situation or matched with some sentence that you hear. Novel sentences never spoken or heard before cannot be stored in your memory.

Simple memorization of all the possible sentences in a language is impossible in principle. If for every sentence in the language a longer sentence can be formed, then there is no limit to the number of sentences. In English you can say:

This is the house.

or

This is the house that Jack built.

or

This is the malt that lay in the house that Jack built.

or

> This is the dog that worried the cat that killed the rat that ate the malt that lay in the house that Jack built.

And you need not stop there. How long, then, is the longest sentence? A speaker of English can say:

> The old man came.

or

> The old, old, old, old, old man came.

How many "olds" are too many? Seven? Twenty-three?

It is true that the longer these sentences become, the less likely we would be to hear or to say them. A sentence with 276 occurrences of "old" would be highly unusual in either speech or writing, even to describe Methuselah. But such a sentence is theoretically possible. If you know English, you have the knowledge to add any number of adjectives as modifiers to a noun and to form sentences with an indefinite number of clauses, as in "the house that Jack built."

All human languages permit their speakers to increase the length and complexity of sentences in these ways; creativity is a universal property of human language.

Knowledge of Sentences and Nonsentences

To memorize and store an infinite set of sentences would require an infinite storage capacity. However, the brain is finite, and even if it were not, we could not store novel sentences, which are, well, novel. When you learn a language you must learn something finite—your vocabulary is finite (however large it may be)—and that can be stored. If sentences were formed simply by placing one word after another in any order, then a language could be defined simply as a set of words. But you can see that knowledge of words is not enough by examining the following strings of words:

1. a. John kissed the little old lady who owned the shaggy dog.
   b. Who owned the shaggy dog John kissed the little old lady.
   c. John is difficult to love.
   d. It is difficult to love John.
   e. John is anxious to go.
   f. It is anxious to go John.
   g. John, who was a student, flunked his exams.
   h. Exams his flunked student a was who John.

If you were asked to put an asterisk or star before the examples that seemed ill formed or ungrammatical or "no good" to you, which ones would you mark? Our intuitive knowledge about what is or is not an allowable sentence in English convinces us to star *b*, *f*, and *h*. Which ones did you star?

Would you agree with the following judgments?

2. a. What he did was climb a tree.
    b. *What he thought was want a sports car.[3]
    c. Drink your beer and go home!
    d. *What are drinking and go home?
    e. I expect them to arrive a week from next Thursday.
    f. *I expect a week from next Thursday to arrive them.
    g. Linus lost his security blanket.
    h. *Lost Linus security blanket his.

If you find the starred sentences unacceptable, as we do, you see that not every string of words constitutes a well-formed sentence in a language. Our knowledge of a language determines which strings of words are well-formed sentences and which are not. Therefore, in addition to knowing the words of the language, linguistic knowledge includes *rules* for forming sentences and making the kinds of judgments you made about the examples in (1) and (2). These rules must be finite in length and finite in number so that they can be stored in our finite brains. Yet, they must permit us to form and understand an infinite set of new sentences. They are not rules determined by a judge or a legislature, or even rules taught in a grammar class. They are unconscious rules that we acquire as young children as we develop language.

A language, then, consists of all the sounds, words, and infinitely many possible sentences. When you know a language, you know the sounds, the words, and the rules for their combination.

Linguistic Knowledge and Performance

"What's one and one and one and one and one and one and one and one and one and one?" "I don't know," said Alice. "I lost count." "She can't do Addition," the Red Queen interrupted.

LEWIS CARROLL, *Through the Looking-Glass,* 1871

Our linguistic knowledge permits us to form longer and longer sentences by joining sentences and phrases together or adding modifiers to a noun. Whether we stop at three, five, or eighteen adjectives, it is impossible to limit the number we could add if desired. Very long sentences are theoretically possible, but they are highly improbable. Evidently, there is a difference between having the knowledge necessary to produce sentences of a language and applying this knowledge. It is a difference between what we know, which is our **linguistic competence**, and how we use this knowledge in actual speech production and comprehension, which is our **linguistic performance**.

Speakers of all languages have the knowledge to understand or produce sentences of any length. Here is an example from the ruling of a federal judge:

---

[3]The asterisk is used before examples that speakers find ungrammatical. This notation will be used throughout the book.

We invalidate the challenged lifetime ban because we hold as a matter of federal constitutional law that a state initiative measure cannot impose a severe limitation on the people's fundamental rights when the issue of whether to impose such a limitation on these rights is put to the voters in a measure that is ambiguous on its face and that fails to mention in its text, the proponent's ballot argument, or the state's official description, the severe limitation to be imposed.

However, there are physiological and psychological reasons that limit the number of adjectives, adverbs, clauses, and so on that we actually produce and understand. Speakers may run out of breath, lose track of what they have said, or die of old age before they are finished. Listeners may become confused, tired, bored, or disgusted.

When we speak, we usually wish to convey some message. At some stage in the act of producing speech, we must organize our thoughts into strings of words. Sometimes the message is garbled. We may stammer, or pause, or produce **slips of the tongue**. We may even sound like Hattie in the cartoon, who illustrates the difference between linguistic knowledge and the way we use that knowledge in performance.

"The Born Loser" © Newspaper Enterprise Association, Inc.

For the most part, linguistic knowledge is unconscious knowledge. The linguistic system—the sounds, structures, meanings, words, and rules for putting them all together—is acquired with no conscious awareness. Just as we may not be conscious of the principles that allow us to stand or walk, we are unaware of the rules of language. Our ability to speak, to understand, and to make judgments about the grammaticality of sentences reveals our knowledge of the rules of our language. This knowledge represents a complex cognitive system. The nature of this system is what this book is all about.

What Is Grammar?

We use the term "grammar" with a systematic ambiguity. On the one hand, the term refers to the explicit theory constructed by the linguist and proposed as a description of the speaker's competence. On the other hand, it refers to this competence itself.

NOAM CHOMSKY AND MORRIS HALLE, *The Sound Pattern of English*, 1968

Descriptive Grammars

There are no primitive languages. The great and abstract ideas of Christianity can be discussed even by the wretched Greenlanders.

JOHANN PETER SUESSMILCH, in a paper delivered before the Prussian Academy, 1756

The way we are using the word *grammar* differs from most common usages. In our sense, the grammar is the knowledge speakers have about the units and rules of their language—rules for combining sounds into words (called phonology), rules of word formation (called morphology), rules for combining words into phrases and phrases into sentences (called syntax), as well as the rules for assigning meaning (called semantics). The grammar, together with a mental dictionary (called a lexicon) that lists the words of the language, represents our linguistic competence. To understand the nature of language we must understand the nature of grammar.

Every human being who speaks a language knows its grammar. When linguists wish to describe a language, they make explicit the rules of the grammar of the language that exist in the minds of its speakers. There will be some differences among speakers, but there must be shared knowledge too. The shared knowledge—the common parts of the grammar—makes it possible to communicate through language. To the extent that the linguist's description is a true model of the speakers' linguistic capacity, it is a successful description of the grammar and of the language itself. Such a model is called a **descriptive grammar**. It does not tell you how you *should* speak; it describes your basic linguistic knowledge. It explains how it is possible for you to speak and understand and make judgments about well-formedness, and it tells what you know about the sounds, words, phrases, and sentences of your language.

When we say in later chapters that a sentence is **grammatical** we mean that it conforms to the rules of the mental grammar (as described by the linguist); when we say that it is **ungrammatical,** we mean it deviates from the rules in some way. If, however, we posit a rule for English that does not agree with your intuitions as a speaker, then the grammar we are describing differs in some way from the mental grammar that represents your linguistic competence; that is, your language is not the one described. No language or variety of a language (called a **dialect**) is superior to any other in a linguistic sense. Every grammar is equally complex, logical, and capable of producing an infinite set of sentences to express any thought. If something can be expressed in one language or one dialect, it can be expressed in any other language or dialect. It might involve different means and different words, but it can be expressed. We will have more to say about dialects in chapter 10. This is true as well for languages of technologically underdeveloped cultures. The grammars of these languages are not primitive or ill formed in any way. They have all the richness and complexity of the grammars of languages spoken in technologically advanced cultures.

Prescriptive Grammars

It is certainly the business of a grammarian to find out, and not to make, the laws of a language.

JOHN FELL, *Essay towards an English Grammar,* 1784

Just read the sentence aloud, Amanda, and listen to how it sounds. If the sentence sounds OK, go with it. If not, rearrange the pieces. Then throw out the rule books and go to bed.

JAMES KILPATRICK, "Writer's Art" (syndicated newspaper column), 1998

Any fool can make a rule
And every fool will mind it

HENRY DAVID THOREAU, journal entry, 1860

Not all grammarians, past or present, share the view that all grammars are equal. Language "purists" of all ages believe that some versions of a language are better than others, that there are certain "correct" forms that all educated people should use in speaking and writing, and that language change is corruption. The Greek Alexandrians in the first century, the Arabic scholars at Basra in the eighth century, and numerous English grammarians of the eighteenth and nineteenth centuries held this view. They wished to *prescribe* rather than *describe* the rules of grammar, which gave rise to the writing of **prescriptive grammars.**

In the Renaissance a new middle class emerged who wanted their children to speak the dialect of the "upper" classes. This desire led to the publication of many prescriptive grammars. In 1762 Bishop Robert Lowth wrote *A Short Introduction to English Grammar with Critical Notes.* Lowth prescribed a number of new rules for English, many of them influenced by his personal taste. Before the publication of his grammar, practically everyone—upper-class, middle-class, and lower-class—said *I don't have none* and *You was wrong about that.* Lowth, however, decided that "two negatives make a positive" and therefore one should say *I don't have any*; and that even when *you* is singular it should be followed by the plural *were*. Many of these prescriptive rules were based on Latin grammar and made little sense for English. Because Lowth was influential and because the rising new class wanted to speak "properly," many of these new rules were legislated into English grammar, at least for the **prestige dialect**—that variety of the language spoken by people in positions of power.

The view that dialects that regularly use double negatives are inferior cannot be justified if one looks at the standard dialects of other languages in the world. Romance languages, for example, use double negatives, as the following examples from French and Italian show:

| *French*: | Je | ne | veux | parler | avec | personne. |
| | I | not | want | speak | with | no-one. |

| *Italian*: | Non | voglio | parlare | con | nessuno. |
| | not | I-want | speak | with | no-one. |

English translation: "I don't want to speak with anyone."

Prescriptive grammars such as Lowth's are different from the descriptive grammars we have been discussing. Their goal is not to describe the rules people know, but to tell them what rules they should follow. The great British Prime Minister Winston Churchill is credited with this response to the "rule" against ending a sentence with a preposition: "This is the sort of nonsense up with which I will not put."

Today our bookstores are populated with books by language purists attempting to "save the English language." They criticize those who use *enormity* to mean "enormous" instead of "monstrously evil." But languages change in the course of time and words change meaning. Language change is a natural process, as we discuss in chapter 11. Over time *enormity* was used more and more in the media to mean "enormous," and we predict that now that President Barack Obama has used it that way (in his victory speech of November 4, 2008), that usage will gain acceptance. Still, the "saviors" of the English language will never disappear. They will continue to blame television, the schools, and even the National Council of Teachers of English for failing to preserve the standard language, and are likely to continue to dis (oops, we mean disparage) anyone who suggests that African American English (AAE)[4] and other dialects are viable, complete languages.

In truth, human languages are without exception fully expressive, complete, and logical, as much as they were two hundred or two thousand years ago. Hopefully (another frowned-upon usage), this book will convince you that all languages and dialects are rule-governed, whether spoken by rich or poor, powerful or weak, learned or illiterate. Grammars and usages of particular groups

---

[4]AAE is also called African American Vernacular English (AAVE), Ebonics, and Black English (BE). It is spoken by some (but by no means all) African Americans. It is discussed in chapter 10.

in society may be dominant for social and political reasons, but from a linguistic (scientific) perspective they are neither superior nor inferior to the grammars and usages of less prestigious members of society.

Having said all this, it is undeniable that the **standard** dialect (defined in chapter 10) may indeed be a better dialect for someone wishing to obtain a particular job or achieve a position of social prestige. In a society where "linguistic profiling" is used to discriminate against speakers of a minority dialect, it may behoove those speakers to learn the prestige dialect rather than wait for social change. But linguistically, prestige and standard dialects do not have superior grammars.

Finally, all of the preceding remarks apply to *spoken* language. Writing (see chapter 12) is not acquired naturally through simple exposure to others speaking the language (see chapter 8), but must be taught. Writing follows certain prescriptive rules of grammar, usage, and style that the spoken language does not, and is subject to little, if any, dialectal variation.

Teaching Grammars

> I don't want to talk grammar. I want to talk like a lady.
>
> **G. B. SHAW,** *Pygmalion,* 1912

The descriptive grammar of a language attempts to describe the rules internalized by a speaker of that language. It is different from a **teaching grammar,** which is used to learn another language or dialect. Teaching grammars can be helpful to people who do not speak the standard or prestige dialect, but find it would be advantageous socially and economically to do so. They are used in schools in foreign language classes. This kind of grammar gives the words and their pronunciations, and explicitly states the rules of the language, especially where they differ from the language of instruction.

It is often difficult for adults to learn a second language without formal instruction, even when they have lived for an extended period in a country where the language is spoken. (Second language acquisition is discussed in more detail in chapter 8.) Teaching grammars assume that the student already knows one language and compares the grammar of the target language with the grammar of the native language. The meaning of a word is provided by a **gloss**—the parallel word in the student's native language, such as *maison,* "house" in French. It is assumed that the student knows the meaning of the gloss "house," and so also the meaning of the word *maison.*

Sounds of the target language that do not occur in the native language are often described by reference to known sounds. Thus the student might be aided in producing the French sound *u* in the word *tu* by instructions such as "Round your lips while producing the vowel sound in *tea.*"

The rules on how to put words together to form grammatical sentences also refer to the learner's knowledge of their native language. For example, the teaching grammar *Learn Zulu* by Sibusiso Nyembezi states that "The difference between singular and plural is not at the end of the word but at the beginning of it," and warns that "Zulu does not have the indefinite and definite articles 'a' and 'the.'" Such statements assume students know the rules of their own grammar, in this case English. Although such grammars might be considered prescriptive in the sense that they attempt to teach the student what is or is not a grammatical construction in the new language, their aim is different from grammars that attempt to change the rules or usage of a language that is already known by the speaker.

This book is not primarily concerned with either prescriptive or teaching grammars. However, these kinds of grammars are considered in chapter 10 in the discussion of standard and nonstandard dialects.

Language Universals

In a grammar there are parts that pertain to all languages; these components form what is called the general grammar. In addition to these general (universal) parts, there are those that belong only to one particular language; and these constitute the particular grammars of each language.

CÉSAR CHESNEAU DU MARSAIS, c. 1750

There are rules of particular languages, such as English, Swahili, and Zulu, that form part of the individual grammars of these languages, and then there are rules that hold in all languages. Those rules representing the universal properties that all languages share constitute a universal grammar. The linguist attempts to uncover the "laws" of particular languages, and also the laws that pertain to all languages. The universal laws are of particular interest because they give us a window into the workings of the human mind in this cognitive domain.

In about 1630, the German philosopher Johann Heinrich Alsted first used the term *general grammar* as distinct from *special grammar*. He believed that the function of a general grammar was to reveal those features "which relate to the method and etiology of grammatical concepts. They are common to all languages." Pointing out that "general grammar is the pattern 'norma' of every particular grammar whatsoever," he implored "eminent linguists to employ their insight in this matter." Three and a half centuries before Alsted, the scholar Robert Kilwardby held that linguists should be concerned with discovering the nature of language in general. So concerned was Kilwardby with Universal Grammar that he excluded considerations of the characteristics of particular languages, which he believed to be as "irrelevant to a science of grammar as the material of the measuring rod or the physical characteristics of objects were to geometry." Kilwardby was perhaps too much of a universalist. The particular properties of individual languages are relevant to the discovery of language universals, and they are of interest for their own sake.

People attempting to study Latin, Greek, French, or Swahili as a second language are so focused on learning those aspects of the second language that are different from their native language that they may be skeptical of assertions that there are universal laws of language. Yet the more we investigate this question, the more evidence accumulates to support Chomsky's view that there is a **Universal Grammar (UG)** that is part of the biologically endowed human language faculty. We can think of UG as the basic blueprint that all languages follow. It specifies the different components of the grammar and their relations, how the different rules of these components are constructed, how they interact, and so on. It is a major aim of **linguistic theory** to discover the nature of UG. The linguist's goal is to reveal the "laws of human language" as the physicist's goal is to reveal the "laws of the physical universe." The complexity of language, a product of the human brain, undoubtedly means this goal will never be fully achieved. All scientific theories are incomplete, and new hypotheses must be proposed to account for new data. Theories are continually changing as new discoveries are made. Just as physics was enlarged by Einstein's theories of relativity, so grows the linguistic theory of UG as new discoveries shed new light on the nature of human language. The comparative study of many different languages is of central importance to this enterprise.

The Development of Grammar

> How comes it that human beings, whose contacts with the world are brief and personal and limited, are nevertheless able to know as much as they do know?
>
> **BERTRAND RUSSELL,** *Human Knowledge: Its Scope and Limits,* 1948

Linguistic theory is concerned not only with describing the knowledge that an adult speaker has of his or her language, but also with explaining how that knowledge is acquired. All normal children acquire (at least one) language in a relatively short period with apparent ease. They do this despite the fact that parents and other caregivers do not provide them with any specific language instruction. Indeed, it is often remarked that children seem to "pick up" language just from hearing it spoken around them. Children are language learning virtuosos—whether a child is male or female, from a rich family or a disadvantaged one, grows up on a farm or in the city, attends day care or has home care—none of these factors fundamentally affects the way language develops. Children can acquire any language they are exposed to with comparable ease— English, Dutch, French, Swahili, Japanese—and even though each of these languages has its own peculiar characteristics, children learn them all in very much the same way. For example, all children go through a babbling stage; their babbles gradually give way to words, which then combine into simple sentences. When children first begin to produce sentences, certain elements may be missing. For example, the English-speaking two-year-old might say *Cathy build house* instead of *Cathy is building the house.* On the other side of the world, a Swahili-speaking child will say *mbuzi kula majani,* which translates as "goat eat grass," and which also lacks many required elements. They pass through other linguistic stages on their way to adultlike competence, and by about age five children speak a language that is almost indistinguishable from the language of the adults around them.

In just a few short years, without the benefit of explicit guidance and regardless of personal circumstances, the young child—who may be unable to tie her shoes or do even the simplest arithmetic computation—masters the complex grammatical structures of her language and acquires a substantial lexicon. Just how children accomplish this remarkable cognitive feat is a topic of intense interest to linguists. The child's inexorable path to adult linguistic knowledge and the uniformity of the acquisition process point to a substantial innate component to language development. Chomsky, following the lead of the early rationalist philosophers, proposed that human beings are born with an innate "blueprint" for language, what we referred to earlier as Universal Grammar. Children acquire language as quickly and effortlessly as they do because they do not have to figure out all the grammatical rules, only those that are specific to their particular language. The universal properties—the laws of language—are part of their biological endowment. Linguistic theory aims to uncover those principles that characterize all human languages and to reveal the innate component of language that makes language acquisition possible. In chapter 8 we will discuss language acquisition in more detail.

Sign Languages: Evidence for the Innateness of Language

> It is not the want of organs that [prevents animals from making] . . . known their thoughts . . . for it is evident that magpies and parrots are able to utter words just like ourselves, and yet they cannot speak as we do, that is, so as to give evidence that they think of what they say. On the other hand, men who, being born deaf and mute . . . are destitute of the organs which serve the others for talking, are in the habit of themselves inventing certain signs by which they make themselves understood.
>
> **RENÉ DESCARTES,** *Discourse on Method*, 1637

The sign languages of deaf communities provide some of the best evidence to support the notion that humans are born with the ability to acquire language, and that all languages are governed by the same universal properties.

Because deaf children are unable to hear speech, they do not acquire spoken languages as hearing children do. However, deaf children who are exposed to sign languages acquire them just as hearing children acquire spoken languages. Sign languages do not use sounds to express meanings. Instead, they are visual-gestural systems that use hand, body, and facial gestures as the forms used to represent words and grammatical rules. Sign languages are fully developed languages, and signers create and comprehend unlimited numbers of new sentences, just as speakers of spoken languages do. Current research on sign languages has been crucial to understanding the biological underpinnings of human language acquisition and use.

About one in a thousand babies is born deaf or with a severe hearing deficiency. Deaf children have difficulty learning a spoken language because normal speech depends largely on auditory feedback. To learn to speak, a deaf child requires extensive training in special schools or programs designed especially for deaf people.

Although deaf people can be taught to speak a language intelligibly, they can never understand speech as well as a hearing person. Seventy-five percent of spoken English words cannot be read on the lips accurately. The ability of many deaf individuals to comprehend spoken language is therefore remarkable; they combine lip reading with knowledge of the structure of language, the meaning redundancies that language has, and context.

If, however, human language is a biologically based ability and all human beings have the innate ability (or as Darwin suggested, instinct) to acquire a language, it is not surprising that nonspoken languages have developed among nonhearing individuals. The more we learn about the human linguistic knowledge, the clearer it becomes that language acquisition and use are not dependent on the ability to produce and hear sounds, but on a far more abstract cognitive capacity that accounts for the similarities between spoken and sign languages.

American Sign Language

The major language of the deaf community in the United States is **American Sign Language (ASL)**. ASL is an outgrowth of the sign language used in France and brought to the United States in 1817 by the great educator Thomas Hopkins Gallaudet.

Like all languages, ASL has its own grammar with phonological, morphological, syntactic, and semantic rules, and a mental lexicon of signs, all of which is encoded through a system of gestures, and is otherwise equivalent to spoken languages.

Signers communicate ideas at a rate comparable to spoken communication. Moreover, language arts are not lost to the deaf community. Poetry is composed in sign language, and stage plays such as Richard Brinsley Sheridan's *The Critic* have been translated into sign language and acted by the National Theatre of the Deaf.

Deaf children acquire sign language much in the way that hearing children acquire a spoken language, going through the same linguistic stages including the babbling stage. Deaf children babble with their hands, just as hearing children babble with their vocal tract. Deaf children often sign themselves to sleep just as hearing children talk themselves to sleep. Deaf children report that they dream in sign language as French-speaking children dream in French and Hopi-speaking children dream in Hopi. Deaf children sign to their dolls and stuffed animals. Slips of the hand occur similar to slips of the tongue; finger fumblers amuse signers as tongue twisters amuse speakers. Sign languages resemble spoken languages in all major aspects, showing that there truly are universals of language despite differences in the modality in which the language is performed. This universality is predictable because regardless of the modality in which it is expressed, language is a biologically based ability.

In the United States there are several signing systems that educators have created in an attempt to represent spoken and/or written English. Unlike ASL, these languages are artificial, consisting essentially in the replacement of each spoken English word (and grammatical elements such as the -s ending for plurals and the -ed ending for past tense) by a sign. So the syntax and semantics of these manual codes for English are approximately the same as those of spoken English. The result is unnatural—similar to trying to speak French by translating every English word or ending into its French counterpart. Difficulties arise because there are not always corresponding forms in the two languages. The problem is even greater with sign languages because they use multidimensional space while spoken languages are sequential.

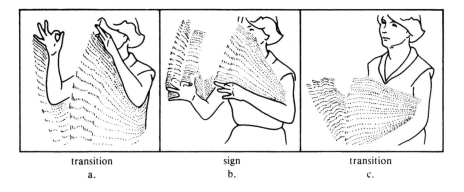

transition   sign   transition

a.   b.   c.

FIGURE 1.2 | The ASL sign DECIDE: (a) and (c) show transitions from the sign; (b) illustrates the single downward movement of the sign.

Reprinted by permission of the publisher from THE SIGNS OF LANGUAGE by Edward Klima and Ursula Bellugi, p. 62, Cambridge, Mass.: Harvard University Press, Copyright © 1979 by the President and Fellows of Harvard College.

There are occasions when signers need to represent a word or concept for which there is no sign. New coinages, foreign words, acronyms, certain proper nouns, technical vocabulary, or obsolete words as might be found in a signed interpretation of a play by Shakespeare are among some of these. For such cases ASL provides a series of hand shapes and movements that represent the letters of the English alphabet, permitting all such words and concepts to be expressed through finger spelling.

Signs, however, are produced differently from finger-spelled words. As Klima and Bellugi observe, "The sign DECIDE cannot be analyzed as a sequence of distinct, separable configurations of the hand. Like all other lexical signs in ASL, but unlike the individual finger-spelled letters in D-E-C-I-D-E taken separately, the ASL sign DECIDE does have an essential movement but the hand shape occurs simultaneously with the movement. In appearance, the sign is a continuous whole."[5] This sign is shown in Figure 1.2.

Animal "Languages"

A dog cannot relate his autobiography; however eloquently he may bark, he cannot tell you that his parents were honest though poor.

BERTRAND RUSSELL, *Human Knowledge: Its Scope and Limits,* 1948

Is language the exclusive property of the human species? The idea of talking animals is as old and as widespread among human societies as language itself. All cultures have legends in which some animal plays a speaking role. All over West Africa, children listen to folktales in which a "spider-man" is the hero. "Coyote" is a favorite figure in many Native American tales, and many an animal takes

[5]Klima, E. S., and U. Bellugi. 1979. *The signs of language.* Cambridge, MA: Harvard University Press.

the stage in Aesop's famous fables. The fictional Doctor Doolittle's forte was communicating with all manner of animals, from giant snails to tiny sparrows.

If language is viewed only as a system of communication, then many species communicate. Humans also use systems other than language to relate to each other and to send and receive "messages," like so-called body language. The question is whether the communication systems used by other species are at all like human linguistic knowledge, which is acquired by children with no instruction, and which is used creatively rather than in response to internal or external stimuli.

"Talking" Parrots

Words learned by rote a parrot may rehearse; but talking is not always to converse.

WILLIAM COWPER, *Poems by William Cowper, of the Inner Temple, Esq.,* 1782

Most humans who acquire language use speech sounds to express meanings, but such sounds are not a necessary aspect of language, as evidenced by the sign languages. The use of speech sounds is therefore not a basic part of what we have been calling language. The chirping of birds, the squeaking of dolphins, and the dancing of bees may potentially represent systems similar to human languages. If animal communication systems are not like human language, it is not because of a lack of speech.

Conversely, when animals vocally imitate human utterances, it does not mean they possess language. Language is a system that relates sounds or gestures to meanings. Talking birds such as parrots and mynahs are capable of faithfully reproducing words and phrases of human language that they have heard, but their utterances carry no meaning. They are speaking neither English nor their own language when they sound like us.

Talking birds do not dissect the sounds of their imitations into discrete units. *Polly* and *Molly* do not rhyme for a parrot. They are as different as *hello* and *good-bye*. One property of all human languages (which will be discussed further in chapter 6) is the discreteness of the speech or gestural units, which are ordered and reordered, combined and split apart. Generally, a parrot says what it is taught, or what it hears, and no more. If Polly learns "Polly wants a cracker" and "Polly wants a doughnut" and also learns to imitate the single words *whiskey* and *bagel*, she will not spontaneously produce, as children do, "Polly wants whiskey" or "Polly wants a bagel" or "Polly wants whiskey and a bagel." If she learns *cat* and *cats*, and *dog* and *dogs*, and then learns the word *parrot*, she will not be able to form the plural *parrots* as children do by the age of three; nor can a parrot form an unlimited set of utterances from a finite set of units, or understand utterances never heard before. Reports of an African gray parrot named Alex suggest that new methods of training animals may result in more learning than was previously believed possible. When the trainer uses words in context, Alex seems to relate some sounds with their meanings. This is more than simple imitation, but it is not how children acquire the complexities of the grammar of any language. It is more like a dog learning to associate certain sounds with meanings, such as *heel*, *sit*, *fetch*, and so on. Indeed, a recent study in Germany reports on a nine-year-old border collie named Rico who has acquired a 200-word vocabulary (containing both German and English words). Rico did not require intensive training but was able to learn many of these words quite quickly.

However impressive these feats, the ability of a parrot to produce sounds similar to those used in human language, even if meanings are related to these sounds, and Rico's ability to understand sequences of sounds that correspond to specific objects, cannot be equated with the child's ability to acquire the complex grammar of a human language.

The Birds and the Bees

The birds and animals are all friendly to each other, and there are no disputes about anything. They all talk, and they all talk to me, but it must be a foreign language for I cannot make out a word they say.

MARK TWAIN, *Eve's Diary*, 1906

Most animals possess some kind of "signaling" communication system. Among certain species of spiders there is a complex system for courtship. The male spider, before he approaches his ladylove, goes through an elaborate series of gestures to inform her that he is indeed a spider and a suitable mate, and not a crumb or a fly to be eaten. These gestures are invariant. One never finds a creative spider changing or adding to the courtship ritual of his species.

A similar kind of gestural language is found among the fiddler crabs. There are forty species, and each uses its own claw-waving movement to signal to another member of its "clan." The timing, movement, and posture of the body never change from one time to another or from one crab to another within the particular variety. Whatever the signal means, it is fixed. Only one meaning can be conveyed.

The imitative sounds of talking birds have little in common with human language, but the natural calls and songs of many species of birds do have a communicative function. They also resemble human languages in that there are "regional dialects" within the same species, and as with humans, these dialects are transmitted from parents to offspring. Indeed, researchers have noted that dialect differences may be better preserved in songbirds than in humans because there is no homogenization of regional accents due to radio or TV.

Birdcalls (consisting of one or more short notes) convey messages associated with the immediate environment, such as danger, feeding, nesting, flocking, and so on. **Bird songs** (more complex patterns of notes) are used to stake out territory and to attract mates. There is no evidence of any internal structure to these songs, nor can they be segmented into independently meaningful parts as words of human language can be. In a study of the territorial song of the European robin, it was discovered that the rival robins paid attention only to the alternation between high-pitched and low-pitched notes, and which came first did not matter. The message varies only to the extent of how strongly the robin feels about his possession and to what extent he is prepared to defend it and start a family in that territory. The different alternations therefore express intensity and nothing more. The robin is creative in his ability to sing the same thing in many ways, but not creative in his ability to use the same units of the system to express many different messages with different meanings.

As we will discuss in chapter 2, some species of birds can only acquire their song during a specific period of development. In this respect bird songs are similar to human language, for which there is also a critical period for acquisition. Although this is an important aspect of both bird song and human language, birdcalls and songs are fundamentally different kinds of communicative systems. The kinds of messages that birds can convey are limited, and messages are stimulus controlled.

This distinction is also true of the system of communication used by honeybees. A forager bee is able to return to the hive and communicate to other bees where a source of food is located. It does so by performing a dance on a wall of the hive that reveals the location and quality of the food source. For one species of Italian honeybee, the dancing behavior may assume one of three possible patterns: *round* (which indicates locations near the hive, within 20 feet or so); *sickle* (which indicates locations at 20 to 60 feet from the hive); and *tail-wagging* (for distances that exceed 60 feet). The number of repetitions per minute of the basic pattern in the tail-wagging dance indicates the precise distance; the slower the repetition rate, the longer the distance.

The bees' dance is an effective system of communication for bees. It is capable, in principle, of infinitely many different messages, like human language; but unlike human language, the system is confined to a single subject—food source. An experimenter who forced a bee to walk to the food source showed the inflexibility. When the bee returned to the hive, it indicated a distance twenty-five times farther away than the food source actually was. The bee had no way of communicating the special circumstances in its message. This absence of creativity makes the bee's dance qualitatively different from human language.

In the seventeenth century, the philosopher and mathematician René Descartes pointed out that the communication systems of animals are qualitatively different from the language used by humans:

> It is a very remarkable fact that there are none so depraved and stupid, without even excepting idiots, that they cannot arrange different words together, forming of them a statement by which they make known their thoughts; while, on the other hand, there is no other animal, however perfect and fortunately circumstanced it may be, which can do the same.

Descartes goes on to state that one of the major differences between humans and animals is that human use of language is not just a response to external, or even internal, stimuli, as are the sounds and gestures of animals. He warns against confusing human use of language with "natural movements which betray passions and may be . . . manifested by animals."

To hold that animals communicate by systems qualitatively different from human language systems is not to claim human superiority. Humans are not inferior to the one-celled amoeba because they cannot reproduce by splitting in two; they are just different sexually. They are not inferior to hunting dogs, whose sense of smell is far better than that of human animals. As we will discuss in the next chapter, the human language ability is rooted in the human brain, just as the communication systems of other species are determined by their biological structure. All the studies of animal communication systems, including those of primates, provide evidence for Descartes' distinction between other animal communication systems and the linguistic creative ability possessed by the human animal.

Can Chimps Learn Human Language?

It is a great baboon, but so much like man in most things. . . . I do believe it already understands much English; and I am of the mind it might be taught to speak or make signs.

ENTRY IN SAMUEL PEPYS'S DIARY, 1661

In their natural habitat, chimpanzees, gorillas, and other nonhuman primates communicate with each other through visual, auditory, olfactory, and tactile signals. Many of these signals seem to have meanings associated with the animals' immediate environment or emotional state. They can signal danger and can communicate aggressiveness and subordination. However, the natural sounds and gestures produced by all nonhuman primates are highly stereotyped and limited in the type and number of messages they convey, consisting mainly of emotional responses to particular situations. They have no way of expressing the anger they felt yesterday or the anticipation of tomorrow.

Even though the natural communication systems of these animals are quite limited, many people have been interested in the question of whether they have the latent capacity to acquire complex linguistic systems similar to human language. Throughout the second half of the twentieth century, there were a number of studies designed to test whether nonhuman primates could learn human language.

In early experiments researchers raised chimpanzees in their own homes alongside their children, in order to recreate the natural environment in which human children acquire language. The chimps were unable to vocalize words despite the efforts of their caretakers, though they did achieve the ability to understand a number of individual words.

One disadvantage suffered by primates is that their vocal tracts do not permit them to pronounce many different sounds. Because of their manual dexterity, primates might better be taught sign language as a test of their cognitive linguistic ability. Starting with a chimpanzee named Washoe, and continuing over the years with a gorilla named Koko and another chimp ironically named Nim Chimpsky (after Noam Chomsky), efforts were made to teach them American Sign Language. Though the primates achieved small successes such as the ability to string two signs together, and to occasionally show flashes of creativity, none achieved the qualitative linguistic ability of a human child.

Similar results were obtained in attempting to teach primates artificial languages designed to resemble human languages in some respects. Sarah, Lana, Sherman, Austin, and other chimpanzees were taught languages whose "words" were plastic chips, or keys on a keyboard, that could be arranged into "sentences." The researchers were particularly interested in the ability of primates to communicate using such abstract symbols.

These experiments also came under scrutiny. Questions arose over what kind of knowledge Sarah and Lana were showing with their symbol manipulations. The conclusion was that the creative ability that is so much a part of human language was not evidenced by the chimps' use of the artificial languages.

More recently, psychologists Patricia Greenfield and Sue Savage-Rumbaugh studied a different species of chimp, a male bonobo (or pygmy chimpanzee) named Kanzi. They used the same plastic symbols and computer keyboard that were used with Lana. They claimed that Kanzi not only learned, but also invented, grammatical rules. One rule they described is the use of a symbol designating an object such as "dog" followed by a symbol meaning "go." After combining these symbols, Kanzi would then go to an area where dogs were located to play with them. Greenfield and Savage-Rumbaugh claimed that this "ordering" rule was not an imitation of his caretakers' utterances, who they said used an opposite ordering, in which "go" was followed by "dogs."

Kanzi's acquisition of grammatical skills was slower than that of children, taking about three years (starting when he was five and a half years old). Most of Kanzi's "sentences" are fixed formulas with little if any internal structure. Kanzi has not yet exhibited the linguistic knowledge of a human three-year-old, whose complexity level includes knowledge of sentence structure. Moreover, unlike Kanzi's use of a different word order from his caretakers, children rapidly adopt the correct word order of the surrounding language.

As often happens in science, the search for the answers to one kind of question leads to answers to other questions. The linguistic experiments with primates have led to many advances in our understanding of primate cognitive ability. Researchers have gone on to investigate other capacities of the chimp mind, such as causality; Savage-Rumbaugh and Greenfield are continuing to study the ability of chimpanzees to use symbols. These studies also point out how remarkable it is that human children, by the ages of three and four, without explicit teaching or overt reinforcement, create new and complex sentences never spoken and never heard before.

In the Beginning:
The Origin of Language

Nothing, no doubt, would be more interesting than to know from historical documents the exact process by which the first man began to lisp his first words, and thus to be rid forever of all the theories on the origin of speech.

MAX MÜLLER, *Lectures on the Science of Language*, 1874

All religions and mythologies contain stories of language origin. Philosophers through the ages have argued the question. Scholarly works have been written on the subject. Prizes have been awarded for the "best answer" to this eternally perplexing problem. Theories of divine origin, language as a human invention, and evolutionary development have all been put forward.

Linguistic history suggests that spoken languages of the kind that exist today have been around for tens of thousands of years at the very least, but the earliest deciphered written records are barely six thousand years old. (The origin of writing is discussed in chapter 12.) These records appear so late in the history of the development of language that they provide no clue to its origin.

Despite the difficulty of finding scientific evidence, speculations on language origin have provided valuable insights into the nature and development of language, which prompted the great Danish linguist Otto Jespersen to state that "linguistic science cannot refrain forever from asking about the whence (and about the whither) of linguistic evolution." A brief look at some of these speculative notions will reveal this point.

Divine Gift

And out of the ground the Lord God formed every beast of the field, and every fowl of the air; and brought them unto Adam to see what he would call them: and whatsoever Adam called every living creature, that was the name thereof.

GENESIS 2:19, *The Bible*, King James Version

According to Judeo-Christian beliefs, the one deity gave Adam the power to name all things. Similar beliefs are found throughout the world. According to the Egyptians, the creator of speech was the god Thoth. Babylonians believed that the language giver was the god Nabu, and the Hindus attributed our unique language ability to a female god: Brahma was the creator of the universe, but his wife Sarasvati gave language to us. Plato held that at some ancient time, a "legislator" gave the correct, natural name to everything, and that words echoed the essence of their meanings.

Belief in the divine origin of language is intertwined with the supernatural properties that have been associated with the spoken word. In many religions only special languages may be used in prayers and rituals, such as Latin in the Catholic Church for many centuries. The Hindu priests of the fifth century B.C.E. believed that the original pronunciation of Vedic Sanskrit was sacred and must be preserved. This led to important linguistic study because their language had already changed greatly since the hymns of the Vedas had been written. The first linguist known to us is Panini, who wrote a descriptive grammar of Sanskrit in the fourth century B.C.E. that revealed the earlier pronunciation, which could then be used in religious worship. Even today Panini's deep insights into the workings of language are highly revered by linguists.

Although myths, customs, and superstitions do not tell us very much about language origin, they do tell us about the importance ascribed to language. There is no way to prove or disprove the divine origin of language, just as one cannot argue scientifically for or against the existence of deities.

The First Language

Imagine the Lord talking French! Aside from a few odd words in Hebrew, I took it completely for granted that God had never spoken anything but the most dignified English.

CLARENCE DAY, *Life with Father*, 1935

For millennia, "scientific" experiments have reportedly been devised to verify particular theories of the first language. The Egyptian pharaoh Psammetichus (664–610 B.C.E.) sought to determine the most primitive language by isolating two infants in a mountain hut, to be cared for by a mute servant, in the belief that their first words would be in the original language. They weren't! History is replete with similar stories, but as we shall see in chapter 2, all such "experimentation" on children is unspeakably cruel and utterly worthless.

Nearly all "theories" of language origin, however silly and superstitious, contain the implicit belief that all languages originated from a single source—the **monogenetic theory of language origin**. Opposing this is the proposition that language arose in several places, or at several times, in the course of history. Which of these is true is still debated by linguists.

Human Invention or the Cries of Nature?

Language was born in the courting days of mankind; the first utterances of speech I fancy to myself like something between the nightly love lyrics of puss upon the tiles and the melodious love songs of the nightingale.

OTTO JESPERSEN, *Language, Its Nature, Development, and Origin,* 1922

Despite all evidence to the contrary, the idea that the earliest form of language was imitative, or echoic, was proposed up to the twentieth century. A parallel view states that language at first consisted of emotional ejaculations of pain, fear, surprise, pleasure, anger, and so on. French philosopher Jean-Jacques Rousseau proposed that the earliest manifestations of language were "cries of nature."

Other hypotheses suggested that language arose out of the rhythmical grunts of men and women working together, or more charming, that language originated from song as an expressive rather than a communicative need. Just as with the beliefs in a divine origin of language, these proposed origins are not verifiable by scientific means.

Language most likely evolved with the human species, possibly in stages, possibly in one giant leap. Research by linguists, evolutionary biologists, and neurologists support this view and the view that from the outset the human animal was genetically equipped to learn language. We'll have more to say on this topic in chapter 2.

Language and Thought

It was intended that when Newspeak had been adopted once and for all and Oldspeak forgotten, a heretical thought—that is, a thought diverging from the principles of IngSoc—should be literally unthinkable, at least so far as thought is dependent on words.

GEORGE ORWELL, appendix to *1984,* 1949

Many people are fascinated by the question of how language relates to thought. It is natural to imagine that something as powerful and fundamental to human nature as language would influence how we think about or perceive the world around us. This is clearly reflected in the appendix of George Orwell's masterpiece *1984,* quoted above. Over the years there have been many claims made regarding the relationship between language and thought. The claim that the structure of a language influences how its speakers perceive the world around them is most closely associated with the linguist Edward Sapir and his student Benjamin Whorf, and is therefore referred to as the **Sapir-Whorf hypothesis**. In 1929 Sapir wrote:

> Human beings do not live in the objective world alone, nor in the world of social activity as ordinarily understood, but are very much at the mercy of the particular language which has become the medium of expression for their society . . . we see and hear and otherwise experience very largely as we do because the language habits of our community predispose certain choices of interpretation.[6]

Whorf made even stronger claims:

> The background linguistic system (in other words, the grammar) of each language is not merely the reproducing instrument for voicing ideas but rather is itself the shaper of ideas, the program and guide for the individual's mental activity, for his analysis of impressions, for his synthesis of his mental stock in trade . . . We dissect nature along lines laid down by our native languages.[7]

The strongest form of the Sapir-Whorf hypothesis is called **linguistic determinism** because it holds that the language we speak *determines* how we perceive and think about the world. On this view language acts like a filter on reality. One of Whorf's best-known claims in support of linguistic determinism was that the Hopi Indians do not perceive time in the same way as speakers of European languages because the Hopi language does not make the grammatical distinctions of tense that, for example, English does with words and word endings such as *did, will, shall, -s, -ed,* and *-ing.*

A weaker form of the hypothesis is **linguistic relativism**, which says that different languages encode different categories and that speakers of different languages therefore think about the world in different ways. For example, languages break up the color spectrum at different points. In Navaho, blue and green are one word. Russian has different words for dark blue (*siniy*) and light blue (*goluboy*), while in English we need to use the additional words *dark* and *light* to express the difference. The American Indian language Zuni does not distinguish between the colors yellow and orange. Languages also differ in how they express locations. For example, in Italian you ride "in" a bicycle and you go "in" a country while in English you ride "on" a bicycle and you go "to" a country. In English we say that a ring is placed "on" a finger and a finger is placed "in" the ring. Korean, on the other hand, has one word for both situations, *kitta*, which expresses the idea of a tight-fitting relation between the two objects. Spanish has two different words for the inside of a corner (*esquina*) and the outside of a corner (*rincon*). The Whorfian claim that is perhaps most

---

[6]Sapir, E. 1929. *Language.* New York: Harcourt, Brace & World, p. 207.

[7]Whorf, B. L., and J. B. Carroll. 1956. *Language, thought, and reality: Selected writings.* Cambridge, MA: MIT Press.

familiar is that the Eskimo language Inuit has many more words than English for snow and that this affects the world view of the Inuit people.

"At the store today, the computer wasn't ON line, we stood IN line, and Billy was OUT of line."

"Family Circus" © 1999 Bil Keane, Inc. Reprinted with permission of King Features Syndicate.

That languages show linguistic distinctions in their lexicons and grammar is certain, and we will see many examples of this in later chapters. The question is to what extent—if at all—such distinctions determine or influence the thoughts and perceptions of speakers. The Sapir-Whorf hypothesis is controversial, but it is clear that the strong form of this hypothesis is false. Peoples' thoughts and perceptions are not determined by the words and structures of their language. We are not prisoners of our linguistic systems. If speakers were unable to think about something for which their language had no specific word, translations would be impossible, as would learning a second language. English may not have a special word for the inside of a corner as opposed to the outside of a corner, but we are perfectly able to express these concepts using more than one word. In fact, we just did. If we could not think about something for which we do not have words, how would infants ever learn their first word, much less a language?

Many of the specific claims of linguistic determinism have been shown to be wrong. For example, the Hopi language may not have words and word endings for specific tenses, but the language has other expressions for time, including words for the days of the week, parts of the day, yesterday and tomorrow, lunar phases, seasons, etc. The Hopi people use various kinds of calendars and various devices for time-keeping based on the sundial. Clearly, they have a sophisticated concept of time despite the lack of a tense system in the language. The Munduruku, an indigenous people of the Brazilian Amazon, have no words in their language for triangle, square, rectangle, or other geometric concepts, except circle. The only terms to indicate direction are words for upstream, downstream, sunrise, and sunset. Yet Munduruku children understand many principles of geometry as well as American children, whose language is rich in geometric and spatial words.

Similarly, though languages differ in their color words, speakers can readily perceive colors that are not named in their language. Grand Valley Dani is a language spoken in New Guinea with only two color words, black and white (dark and light). In experimental studies, however, speakers of the language showed recognition of the color red, and they did better with fire-engine red than off-red. This would not be possible if their color perceptions were fixed by their language. Our perception of color is determined by the structure of the human eye, not by the structure of language. A source of dazzling linguistic creativity is to be found at the local paint store where literally thousands of colors are given names like *soft pumpkin*, *Durango dust*, and *lavender lipstick*.

Anthropologists have shown that Inuit has no more words for snow than English does: around a dozen, including *sleet*, *blizzard*, *slush*, and *flurry*. But even if it did, this would not show that language conditions the Inuits' experience of the world, but rather that experience with a particular world creates the need for certain words. In this respect the Inuit speaker is no different from the computer programmer, who has a technical vocabulary for Internet protocols, or the linguist, who has many specialized words regarding language. In this book we will introduce you to many new words and linguistic concepts, and surely you will learn them! This would be impossible if your thoughts about language were determined by the linguistic vocabulary you now have.

These studies show that our perceptions and thoughts are not determined by the words or word endings of our language. But what about the linguistic structures we are accustomed to using? Could these be a strong determinant? In a recent study, psychologist Susan Goldin-Meadow and colleagues asked whether the word order of a particular language influences the way its speakers describe an event nonverbally, either with gestures or with pictures. Languages differ in how they encode events, such as a person twisting a knob. Speakers of languages like English, Chinese, and Spanish typically use the word order *actor—action—object* (person—twist—knob), whereas speakers of languages like Turkish and Japanese use the order *actor—object—action* (person—knob—twist). Word order is one of the earliest aspects of language structure that children acquire and it is a fundamental aspect of our linguistic knowledge. Therefore if language structure strongly influences how we interpret events, then these ordering patterns might show up in the way we describe events even when we are not talking. Goldin-Meadow and colleagues asked adult speakers of English, Turkish, and Chinese (Mandarin) to describe vignettes shown on a computer screen using only their hands, and also using a set of pictures. Their results showed that all the speakers—irrespective of their language—used the same order in the non-verbal tasks. The predominant gesture order was *actor—action—object*, and the same results were found in the picture-ordering task. Goldin-Meadow and colleagues suggest that there is a universal, natural order in which people cognitively represent events, and that this is not affected by the language they happen to speak.

Similar results have been observed between English and Greek speakers. These languages differ in how their verbs encode motion. When describing movement, English speakers will commonly use verbs that focus on the *manner* of motion such as *slide*, *skip*, and *walk*. Greek speakers, on the other hand, use verbs that focus on the *direction* of the motion, as in *approach* and *ascend*. Measurements of eye movements of these speakers as they verbally describe an event show that they focus on the aspect of the event encoded by their language. However, when freely observing an event but not describing it verbally, they attend to the event in the same ways regardless of what language they speak. These results show that speakers' attention to events is not affected by their language except as they are preparing to speak.

In our understanding of the world we are certainly not "at the mercy of whatever language we speak," as Sapir suggested. However, we may ask whether the language we speak *influences* our cognition in some way. In the domain of color categorization, for example, it has been shown that if a language lacks a word for *red*, say, then it's harder for speakers to reidentify red objects. In other words, having a label seems to make it easier to store or access information in memory. Similarly, experiments show that Russian speakers are better at discriminating light blue (*goluboy*) and dark blue (*siniy*) objects than English speakers, whose language does not make a lexical distinction between these categories. These results show that words can influence simple perceptual tasks in the domain of color discrimination. Upon reflection, this may not be a surprising finding. Colors exist on a continuum, and the way we segment into "different" colors happens at arbitrary points along this spectrum. Because there is no physical motivation for these divisions, this may be the kind of situation where language could show an effect.

The question has also been raised regarding the possible influence of grammatical gender on how people think about objects. Many languages, such as Spanish and German, classify nouns as masculine or feminine; Spanish "key" is *la llave* (feminine) and "bridge" is *el puente* (masculine). Some psychologists have suggested that speakers of gender-marking languages think about objects as having gender, much like people or animals have. In one study, speakers of German and Spanish were asked to describe various objects using English adjectives (the speakers were proficient in English). In general, they used more masculine adjectives—independently rated as such—to describe objects that are grammatically masculine in their language. For example, Spanish speakers described bridges (el puente) as *big*, *dangerous*, *long*, *strong*, and *sturdy*. In German the word for bridge is feminine (die Brücke) and German speakers used more feminine adjectives such as *beautiful*, *elegant*, *fragile*, *peaceful*, *pretty*, and *slender*. Interestingly, it has been noted that English speakers, too, make consistent judgments about the gender of objects (ships are "she") even though English has no grammatical gender on common nouns. It may be, then, that regardless of the language spoken, humans have a tendency to anthropomorphize objects and this tendency is somehow enhanced if the language itself has grammatical gender. Though it is too early to come to any firm conclusions, the results of these and similar studies seem to support a weak version of linguistic relativism.

Politicians and marketers certainly believe that language can influence our thoughts and values. One political party may refer to an inheritance tax as the "estate tax," while an opposing party refers to it as the "death tax." One politician may refer to "tax breaks for the wealthy" while another refers to "tax relief." In the abortion debate, some refer to the "right to choose" and others to the "right to life." The terminology reflects different ideologies, but the choice of expression is primarily intended to sway public opinion. Politically correct (PC) language also reflects the idea that language can influence thought. Many people believe that by changing the way we talk, we can change the way we think; that if we eliminate racist and sexist terms from our language, we will become a less racist and sexist society. As we will discuss in chapter 10, language itself is not sexist or racist, but people can be, and because of this particular words take on negative meanings. In his book *The Language Instinct*, Steven Pinker uses the expression *euphemism treadmill* to describe how the euphemistic terms that are created to replace negative words often take on the negative associations of the words they were coined to replace. For example, *handicapped* was once a euphemism for the offensive term *crippled*, and when *handicapped* became politically incorrect it was replaced by the euphemism *disabled*. And as we write, *disabled* is falling into disrepute and is often replaced by yet another euphemism, *challenged*. Nonetheless, in all such cases, changing language has not resulted in a new world view of the speakers.

Prescient as Orwell was with respect to how language could be used for social control, he was more circumspect with regard to the relation between language and thought. He was careful to qualify his notions with the phrase "at least so far as thought is dependent on words." Current research shows that language does not determine how we think about and perceive the world. Future research should show the extent to which language influences other aspects of cognition such as memory and categorization.

What We Know about Human Language

Much is unknown about the nature of human languages, their grammars and use. The science of linguistics is concerned with these questions. Investigations of linguists and the analyses of spoken languages date back at least to 1600 B.C.E. in Mesopotamia. We have learned a great deal since that time. A number of facts pertaining to all languages can be stated.

1. Wherever humans exist, language exists.
2. There are no "primitive" languages—all languages are equally complex and equally capable of expressing any idea. The vocabulary of any language can be expanded to include new words for new concepts.

3. All languages change through time.
4. The relationships between the sounds and meanings of spoken languages and between the gestures and meanings of sign languages are for the most part arbitrary.
5. All human languages use a finite set of discrete sounds or gestures that are combined to form meaningful elements or words, which themselves may be combined to form an infinite set of possible sentences.
6. All grammars contain rules of a similar kind for the formation of words and sentences.
7. Every spoken language includes discrete sound segments, like *p*, *n*, or *a*, that can all be defined by a finite set of sound properties or features. Every spoken language has both vowel sounds and consonant sounds.
8. Similar grammatical categories (for example, noun, verb) are found in all languages.
9. There are universal semantic properties like *entailment* (one sentence inferring the truth of another) found in every language in the world.
10. Every language has a way of negating, forming questions, issuing commands, referring to past or future time, and so on.
11. All languages permit abstractions like *goodness*, *spherical*, and *skillful*.
12. All languages have slang, epithets, taboo words, and euphemisms for them, such as *john* for "toilet."
13. All languages have hypothetical, counterfactual, conditional, unreal, and fictional utterances; e.g., "If I won the lottery, I would buy a Ferrari," or "Harry Potter battled Voldemort with his wand by Hogwarts castle."
14. All languages exhibit freedom from stimulus; a person can choose to say anything at any time under any circumstances, or can choose to say nothing at all.
15. Speakers of all languages are capable of producing and comprehending an infinite set of sentences. Syntactic universals reveal that every language has a way of forming sentences such as:

    Linguistics is an interesting subject.
    I know that linguistics is an interesting subject.
    You know that I know that linguistics is an interesting subject.
    Cecelia knows that you know that I know that linguistics is an interesting subject.
    Is it a fact that Cecelia knows that you know that I know that linguistics is an interesting subject?

16. The ability of human beings to acquire, know, and use language is a biologically based ability rooted in the structure of the human brain, and expressed in different modalities (spoken or signed).
17. Any normal child, born anywhere in the world, of any racial, geographical, social, or economic heritage, is capable of learning any language to which he or she is exposed. The differences among languages are not due to biological reasons.

It seems that the universalists from all ages were not spinning idle thoughts. We all possess human language.

Summary

We are all intimately familiar with at least one language, our own. Yet few of us ever stop to consider what we know when we know a language. No book contains, or could possibly contain, the English or Russian or Zulu language. The words of a language can be listed in a dictionary, but not all the sentences can be; and a language consists of these sentences as well as words. Speakers use a finite set of rules to produce and understand an infinite set of possible sentences.

These rules are part of the **grammar** of a language, which develops when you acquire the language and includes the sound system (the **phonology**), the structure and properties of words (the **morphology** and **lexicon**), how words may be combined into phrases and sentences (the **syntax**), and the ways in which sounds and meanings are related (the **semantics**). The sounds and meanings of individual words are related in an **arbitrary** fashion. If you had never heard the word *syntax* you would not know what it meant by its sounds. The gestures used by signers are also arbitrarily related to their meanings. Language, then, is a system that relates sounds (or hand and body gestures) with meanings. When you know a language, you know this system.

This knowledge (**linguistic competence**) is different from behavior (**linguistic performance**). If you woke up one morning and decided to stop talking (as the Trappist monks did after they took a vow of silence), you would still have knowledge of your language. This ability or competence underlies linguistic behavior. If you do not know the language, you cannot speak it; but if you know the language, you may choose not to speak.

There are different kinds of "grammars." The **descriptive grammar** of a language represents the unconscious linguistic knowledge or capacity of its speakers. Such a grammar is a model of the **mental grammar** every speaker of the language knows. It does not teach the rules of the language; it describes the rules that are already known. A grammar that attempts to legislate what your grammar should be is called a **prescriptive grammar**. It prescribes. It does not describe, except incidentally. **Teaching grammars** are written to help people learn a foreign language or a dialect of their own language.

The more that linguists investigate the thousands of languages of the world and describe the ways in which they differ from each other, the more they discover that these differences are limited. There are linguistic universals that pertain to each of the parts of grammars, the ways in which these parts are related, and the forms of rules. These principles compose **Universal Grammar**, which provides a blueprint for the grammars of all possible human languages. Universal Grammar constitutes the innate component of the human language faculty that makes normal language development possible.

Strong evidence for Universal Grammar is found in the way children acquire language. Children learn language by exposure. They need not be deliberately taught, though parents may enjoy "teaching" their children to speak or sign. Children will learn any human language to which they are exposed, and they learn it in definable stages, beginning at a very early age. By four or five years of age, children have acquired nearly the entire adult grammar. This suggests that children are born with a genetically endowed faculty to learn and use human language, which is part of the Universal Grammar.

The fact that deaf children learn **sign language** shows that the ability to hear or produce sounds is not a prerequisite for language learning. All the sign languages in the world, which differ as spoken languages do, are visual-gestural systems that are as fully developed and as structurally complex as spoken languages. The major sign language used in the United States is **American Sign Language (ASL)**.

If language is defined merely as a system of communication, or the ability to produce speech sounds, then language is not unique to humans. There are, however, certain characteristics of human language not found in the communication systems of any other species. A basic property of human language is its **creativity**—a speaker's ability to combine the basic linguistic units to form an infinite set of "well-formed" grammatical sentences, most of which are novel, never before produced or heard.

For many years researchers were interested in the question of whether language is unique to the human species. There have been many attempts to teach nonhuman primates communication systems that are supposed to resemble human language in certain respects. Overall, results have been disappointing: Chimpanzees like Sarah and Lana learned to manipulate symbols for rewards, and others, like Washoe and Nim Chimpsky, learned a number of ASL signs. But a careful examination of their multisign utterances reveals that unlike in children, the language of the chimps shows little spontaneity, is highly imitative (echoic), and has little syntactic structure. It has been suggested that the pygmy chimp Kanzi shows grammatical ability greater than the other chimps studied, but he still does not have the ability of even a three-year-old child.

At present we do not know if there was a single original language—the **monogenetic** hypothesis—or whether language arose independently in several places, or at several times, in human history. Myths of language origin abound; divine origin and various modes of human invention are the source of these myths. Language most likely evolved with the human species, possibly in stages, possibly in one giant leap.

The **Sapir-Whorf hypothesis** holds that the particular language we speak determines or influences our thoughts and perceptions of the world. Much of the early evidence in support of this hypothesis has not stood the test of time. More recent experimental studies suggest that the words and grammar of a language may affect aspects of cognition, such as memory and categorization.

References for Further Reading

Anderson, S. R. 2008. The logical structure of linguistic theory. *Language* (December): 795–814.

Bickerton, D. 1990. *Language and species*. Chicago: Chicago University Press.

Chomsky, N. 1986. *Knowledge of language: Its nature, origin, and use*. New York and London: Praeger.

_____. 1975. *Reflections on language*. New York: Pantheon Books.

_____. 1972. *Language and mind*. Enlarged ed. New York: Harcourt Brace Jovanovich.

Gentner, D., and S. Goldin-Meadow. 2003. *Language in mind*. Cambridge, MA: MIT Press.

Hall, R. A. 1950. *Leave your language alone.* Ithaca, NY: Linguistica.

Jackendoff, R. 1997. *The architecture of the language faculty.* Cambridge, MA: MIT Press.

_____. 1994. *Patterns in the mind: Language and human nature.* New York: Basic Books.

Klima, E. S., and U. Bellugi. 1979. *The signs of language.* Cambridge, MA: Harvard University Press.

Lane, H. 1989. *When the mind hears: A history of the deaf.* New York: Vintage Books (Random House).

Milroy, J., and L. Milroy. 1998. *Authority in language: Investigating standard English,* 3rd edn. New York: Routledge.

Napoli, D. J. 2003. *Language matters: A guide to everyday thinking about language.* New York: Oxford University Press.

Pinker, S. 1999. *Words and rules: The ingredients of language.* New York: HarperCollins.

_____. 1994. *The language instinct.* New York: William Morrow.

Premack, A. J., and D. Premack. 1972. Teaching language to an ape. *Scientific American* (October): 92–99.

Terrace, H. S. 1979. *Nim: A chimpanzee who learned sign language.* New York: Knopf.

Stam, J. 1976. *Inquiries into the origin of language: The fate of a question.* New York: Harper & Row.

Stokoe, W. 1960. *Sign language structure: An outline of the visual communication system of the American deaf.* Silver Spring, MD: Linstok Press.

Exercises

1. An English speaker's knowledge includes the sound sequences of the language. When new products are put on the market, the manufacturers have to think up new names for them that conform to the allowable sound patterns. Suppose you were hired by a manufacturer of soap products to name five new products. What names might you come up with? List them.

   We are interested in how the names are pronounced. Therefore, describe in any way you can how to say the words you list. Suppose, for example, you named one detergent *Blick.* You could describe the sounds in any of the following ways:

   bl as in *blood, i* as in *pit, ck* as in *stick*
   bli as in *bliss, ck* as in *tick*
   b as in *boy, lick* as in *lick*

2. Consider the following sentences. Put a star (*) after those that do not seem to conform to the rules of your grammar, that are ungrammatical for you. State, if you can, why you think the sentence is ungrammatical.

   a. Robin forced the sheriff go.
   b. Napoleon forced Josephine to go.
   c. The devil made Faust go.
   d. He passed by a large pile of money.
   e. He came by a large sum of money.
   f. He came a large sum of money by.

    g. Did in a corner little Jack Horner sit?

    h. Elizabeth is resembled by Charles.

    i. Nancy is eager to please.

    j. It is easy to frighten Emily.

    k. It is eager to love a kitten.

    l. That birds can fly amazes.

    m. The fact that you are late to class is surprising.

    n. Has the nurse slept the baby yet?

    o. I was surprised for you to get married.

    p. I wonder who and Mary went swimming.

    q. Myself bit John.

    r. What did Alice eat the toadstool with?

    s. What did Alice eat the toadstool and?

3. It was pointed out in this chapter that a small set of words in languages may be onomatopoeic; that is, their sounds "imitate" what they refer to. *Ding-dong, tick-tock, bang, zing, swish,* and *plop* are such words in English. Construct a list of ten new onomatopoeic words. Test them on at least five friends to see if they are truly nonarbitrary as to sound and meaning.

4. Although sounds and meanings of most words in all languages are arbitrarily related, there are some communication systems in which the "signs" unambiguously reveal their "meaning."

    a. Describe (or draw) five different signs that directly show what they mean. *Example*: a road sign indicating an S curve.

    b. Describe any other communication system that, like language, consists of arbitrary symbols. *Example*: traffic signals, where red means stop and green means go.

5. Consider these two statements: I learned a new word today. I learned a new sentence today. Do you think the two statements are equally probable, and if not, why not?

6. What do the barking of dogs, the meowing of cats, and the singing of birds have in common with human language? What are some of the basic differences?

7. A wolf is able to express subtle gradations of emotion by different positions of the ears, the lips, and the tail. There are eleven postures of the tail that express such emotions as self-confidence, confident threat, lack of tension, uncertain threat, depression, defensiveness, active submission, and complete submission. This system seems to be complex. Suppose that there were a thousand different emotions that the wolf could express in this way. Would you then say a wolf had a language similar to a human's? If not, why not?

8. Suppose you taught a dog to *heel, sit up, roll over, play dead, stay, jump,* and *bark* on command, using the italicized words as cues. Would you be teaching it language? Why or why not?

9. State some rule of grammar that you have learned is the correct way to say something, but that you do not generally use in speaking. For example, you may have heard that *It's me* is incorrect and that the correct form is *It's I*. Nevertheless, you always use *me* in such sentences; your friends do also, and in fact *It's I* sounds odd to you.

   Write a short essay presenting arguments against someone who tells you that you are wrong. Discuss how this disagreement demonstrates the difference between descriptive and prescriptive grammars.

10. Noam Chomsky has been quoted as saying:

    > It's about as likely that an ape will prove to have a language ability as that there is an island somewhere with a species of flightless birds waiting for human beings to teach them to fly.

    In the light of evidence presented in this chapter, comment on Chomsky's remark. Do you agree or disagree, or do you think the evidence is inconclusive?

11. Think of song titles that are "bad" grammar, but that, if corrected, would lack effect. For example, the 1929 "Fats" Waller classic "Ain't Misbehavin'" is clearly superior to the bland "I am not misbehaving." Try to come up with five or ten such titles.

12. Linguists who attempt to write a descriptive grammar of linguistic competence are faced with a difficult task. They must understand a deep and complex system based on a set of sparse and often inaccurate data. (Children learning language face the same difficulty.) Albert Einstein and Leopold Infeld captured the essence of the difficulty in their book *The Evolution of Physics*, written in 1938:

    > In our endeavor to understand reality we are somewhat like a man trying to understand the mechanism of a closed watch. He sees the face and the moving hands, even hears its ticking, but he has no way of opening the case. If he is ingenious he may form some picture of a mechanism which could be responsible for all the things he observes, but he may never be quite sure his picture is the only one which could explain his observations. He will never be able to compare his picture with the real mechanism and he cannot even imagine the possibility of the meaning of such a comparison.

    Write a short essay that speculates on how a linguist might go about understanding the reality of a person's grammar (the closed watch) by observing what that person says and doesn't say (the face and moving hands). For example, a person might never say *the sixth sheik's sixth sheep is sick as a dog*, but the grammar should specify that it is a well-formed sentence, just as it should somehow indicate that *Came the messenger on time* is ill-formed.

13. View the motion picture *My Fair Lady* (drawn from the play *Pygmalion* by George Bernard Shaw). Write down every attempt to teach grammar (pro-

nunciation, word choice, and syntax) to the character of Eliza Doolittle. This is an illustration of a "teaching grammar."

14. Many people are bilingual or multilingual, speaking two or more languages with very different structures.

   a. What implications does bilingualism have for the debate about language and thought?
   b. Many readers of this textbook have some knowledge of a second language. Think of a linguistic structure or word in one language that does not exist in the second language and discuss how this does or does not affect your thinking when you speak the two languages. (If you know only one language, ask this question of a bilingual person you know.)
   c. Can you find an example of an untranslatable word or structure in one of the languages you speak?

15. The South American indigenous language Pirahã is said to lack numbers beyond two and distinct words for colors. Research this language—Google would be a good start—with regard to whether Pirahã supports or fails to support linguistic determinism and/or linguistic relativism.

16. English (especially British English) has many words for woods and woodlands. Here are some:

   woodlot, carr, fen, firth, grove, heath, holt, lea, moor, shaw, weald, wold, coppice, scrub, spinney, copse, brush, bush, bosquet, bosky, stand, forest, timberland, thicket

   a. How many of these words do you recognize?
   b. Look up several of these words in the dictionary and discuss the differences in meaning. Many of these words are obsolete, so if your dictionary doesn't have them, try the Internet.
   c. Do you think that English speakers have a richer concept of woodlands than speakers whose language has fewer words? Why or why not?

17. English words containing *dge* in their spelling (*trudge*, *edgy*) are said mostly to have an unfavorable or negative connotation. Research this notion by accumulating as many *dge* words as you can and classifying them as unfavorable (*sludge*) or neutral (*bridge*). What do you do about *budget*? Unfavorable or not? Are there other questionable words?

18. With regard to the "euphemism treadmill": Identify three other situations in which a euphemism evolved to be as offensive as the word it replaced, requiring yet another euphemism. *Hint*: Sex, race, and bodily functions are good places to start.

19. **Research project**: Read the Cratylus Dialogue—it's online. In it is a discussion (or "dialogue") of whether names are "conventional" (i.e., what we have called *arbitrary*) or "natural." Do you find Socrates' point of view sufficiently well argued to support the thesis in this chapter that the relationship between form and meaning is indeed arbitrary? Argue your case in either direction in a short (or long, if you wish) essay.

20. **Research project:** (Cf. exercise 15) It is claimed that Pirahã—an indigenous language of Brazil—violates some of the universal principles hypothesized by linguists. Which principles are in question? Is the evidence persuasive? Conclusive? Speculative? (*Hint:* Use the journal *Language*, Volume 85, Number 2, June 2009.)

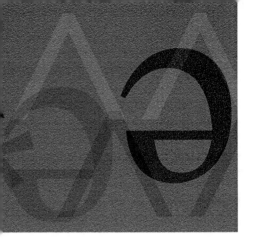

2

Brain and Language

> The functional asymmetry of the human brain is unequivocal, and so is its anatomical asymmetry. The structural differences between the left and the right hemispheres are visible not only under the microscope but to the naked eye. The most striking asymmetries occur in language-related cortices. It is tempting to assume that such anatomical differences are an index of the neurobiological underpinnings of language.
>
> **ANTONIO AND HANNA DAMÁSIO,** University of Southern California, Brain and Creativity Institute and Department of Neuroscience

Attempts to understand the complexities of human cognitive abilities and especially the acquisition and use of language are as old and as continuous as history itself. What is the nature of the brain? What is the nature of human language? And what is the relationship between the two? Philosophers and scientists have grappled with these questions and others over the centuries. The idea that the brain is the source of human language and cognition goes back more than two thousand years. The philosophers of ancient Greece speculated about the brain/mind relationship, but neither Plato nor Aristotle recognized the brain's crucial function in cognition or language. However, others of the same period showed great insight, as illustrated in the following quote from the Hippocratic Treatises on the Sacred Disease, written c. 377 B.C.E.:

> [The brain is] the messenger of the understanding [and the organ whereby] in an especial manner we acquire wisdom and knowledge.

The study of language has been crucial to understanding the brain/mind relationship. Conversely, research on the brain in humans and other primates is helping to answer questions concerning the neurological basis for language. The study of the biological and neural foundations of language is called **neurolinguistics**. Neurolinguistic research is often based on data from atypical or impaired language and uses such data to understand properties of human language in general.

The Human Brain

"Rabbit's clever," said Pooh thoughtfully.

"Yes," said Piglet, "Rabbit's clever."

"And he has Brain."

"Yes," said Piglet, "Rabbit has Brain."

There was a long silence.

"I suppose," said Pooh, "that that's why he never understands anything."

A. A. MILNE, *The House at Pooh Corner*, 1928

The brain is the most complex organ of the body. It lies under the skull and consists of approximately 100 billion nerve cells (neurons) and billions of fibers that interconnect them. The surface of the brain is the **cortex**, often called "gray matter," consisting of billions of neurons. The cortex is the decision-making organ of the body. It receives messages from all of the sensory organs, initiates all voluntary and involuntary actions, and is the storehouse of our memories. Somewhere in this gray matter resides the grammar that represents our knowledge of language.

The brain is composed of **cerebral hemispheres**, one on the right and one on the left, joined by the **corpus callosum**, a network of more than 200 million fibers (see Figure 2.1). The corpus callosum allows the two hemispheres of the brain to communicate with each other. Without this system of connections, the

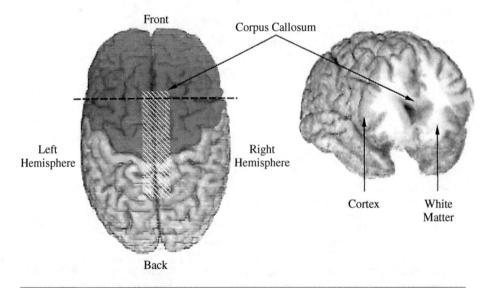

FIGURE 2.1 | Three-dimensional reconstruction of the normal living human brain. The images were obtained from magnetic resonance data using the Brainvox technique. *Left panel* = view from top. *Right panel* = view from the front following virtual coronal section at the level of the dashed line.

Courtesy of Hanna Damásio.

two hemispheres would operate independently. In general, the left hemisphere controls the right side of the body, and the right hemisphere controls the left side. If you point with your right hand, the left hemisphere is responsible for your action. Similarly, sensory information from the right side of the body (e.g., right ear, right hand, right visual field) is received by the left hemisphere of the brain, and sensory input to the left side of the body is received by the right hemisphere. This is referred to as **contralateral** brain function.

The Localization of Language in the Brain

"Peanuts" copyright © 1984 United Feature Syndicate, Inc. Reprinted by permission.

An issue of central concern has been to determine which parts of the brain are responsible for human linguistic abilities. In the early nineteenth century, Franz Joseph Gall proposed the theory of **localization**, which is the idea that different human cognitive abilities and behaviors are localized in specific parts of the brain. In light of our current knowledge about the brain, some of Gall's particular views are amusing. For example, he proposed that language is located in the frontal lobes of the brain because as a young man he had noticed that the most articulate and intelligent of his fellow students had protruding eyes, which he believed reflected overdeveloped brain material. He also put forth a pseudoscientific theory called "organology" that later came to be known as **phrenology**, which is the practice of determining personality traits, intellectual capacities, and other matters by examining the "bumps" on the skull. A disciple of Gall's, Johann Spurzheim, introduced phrenology to America, constructing elaborate maps and skull models such as the one shown in Figure 2.2, in which language is located directly under the eye.

Gall was a pioneer and a courageous scientist in arguing against the prevailing view that the brain was an unstructured organ. Although phrenology has long been discarded as a scientific theory, Gall's view that the brain is not a uniform mass, and that linguistic and other cognitive capacities are functions of localized

FIGURE 2.2 | Phrenology skull model.

brain areas, has been upheld by scientific investigation of brain disorders, and, over the past two decades, by numerous studies using sophisticated technologies.

Aphasia

The study of **aphasia** has been an important area of research in understanding the relationship between brain and language. Aphasia is the neurological term for any language disorder that results from brain damage caused by disease or trauma. In the second half of the nineteenth century, significant scientific advances were

FIGURE 2.3 | Lateral (*external*) view of the left hemisphere of the human brain, showing the position of Broca's and Wernicke's areas—two key areas of the cortex related to language processing.

made in localizing language in the brain based on the study of people with aphasia. In the 1860s the French surgeon Paul Broca proposed that language is localized to the left hemisphere of the brain, and more specifically to the front part of the left hemisphere (now called **Broca's area**). At a scientific meeting in Paris, he claimed that we speak with the left hemisphere. Broca's finding was based on a study of his patients who suffered language deficits after brain injury to the left frontal lobe. A decade later Carl Wernicke, a German neurologist, described another variety of aphasia that occurred in patients with lesions in areas of the left hemisphere temporal lobe, now known as **Wernicke's area**. Language, then, is lateralized to the left hemisphere, and the left hemisphere appears to be the language hemisphere from infancy on. **Lateralization** is the term used to refer to the localization of function to one hemisphere of the brain. Figure 2.3 is a view of the left side of the brain that shows Broca's and Wernicke's areas.

The Linguistic Characterization of Aphasic Syndromes

Most aphasics do not show total language loss. Rather, different aspects of language are selectively impaired, and the kind of impairment is generally related to the location of the brain damage. Because of this damage-deficit correlation, research on patients with aphasia has provided a great deal of information about how language is organized in the brain.

Patients with injuries to Broca's area may have **Broca's aphasia**, as it is often called today. Broca's aphasia is characterized by labored speech and certain kinds of word-finding difficulties, but it is primarily a disorder that affects a person's ability to form sentences with the rules of syntax. One of the most notable characteristics of Broca's aphasia is that the language produced is often **agrammatic**, meaning that it frequently lacks articles, prepositions, pronouns, auxiliary verbs, and other grammatical elements that we will call "function words" for now. Broca's aphasics also typically omit inflections such as the past tense suffix -*ed* or the third person singular verb ending -*s*. Here is an excerpt of a conversation between a patient with Broca's aphasia and a doctor:

DOCTOR: Could you tell me what you have been doing in the hospital?
PATIENT: Yes, sure. Me go, er, uh, P.T. [physical therapy] none o'cot, speech . . . two times . . . read . . . r . . . ripe . . . rike . . . uh write . . . practice . . . get . . . ting . . . better.
DOCTOR: And have you been going home on weekends?
PATIENT: Why, yes . . . Thursday uh . . . uh . . . uh . . . no . . . Friday . . . Bar . . . ba . . . ra . . . wife . . . and oh car . . . drive . . . purpike . . . you know . . . rest . . . and TV.

Broca's aphasics (also often called **agrammatic aphasics**) may also have difficulty understanding complex sentences in which comprehension depends exclusively on syntactic structure and where they cannot rely on their real-world knowledge. For example, an agrammatic aphasic may have difficulty knowing who kissed whom in questions like:

Which girl did the boy kiss?

where it is equally plausible for the boy or the girl to have done the kissing; or might be confused as to who is chasing whom in passive sentences such as:

The cat was chased by the dog.

where it is plausible for either animal to chase the other. But they have less difficulty with:

Which book did the boy read?

or

The car was chased by the dog.

where the meaning can be determined by nonlinguistic knowledge. It is implausible for books to read boys or for cars to chase dogs, and aphasic people can use that knowledge to interpret the sentence.

Unlike Broca's patients, people with **Wernicke's aphasia** produce fluent speech with good intonation, and they may largely adhere to the rules of syntax. However, their language is often semantically incoherent. For example, one patient replied to a question about his health with:

I felt worse because I can no longer keep in mind from the mind of the minds to keep me from mind and up to the ear which can be to find among ourselves.

Another patient described a fork as "a need for a schedule" and another, when asked about his poor vision, replied, "My wires don't hire right."

People with damage to Wernicke's area have difficulty naming objects presented to them and also in choosing words in spontaneous speech. They may make numerous lexical errors (word substitutions), often producing **jargon** and **nonsense words,** as in the following example:

The only thing that I can say again is madder or modder fish sudden fishing sewed into the accident to miss in the purdles.

Another example is from a patient who was a physician before his aphasia. When asked if he was a doctor, he replied:

Me? Yes sir. I'm a male demaploze on my own. I still know my tubaboys what for I have that's gone hell and some of them go.

Severe Wernicke's aphasia is often referred to as **jargon aphasia.** The linguistic deficits exhibited by people with Broca's and Wernicke's aphasia point to a **modular** organization of language in the brain. We find that damage to different parts of the brain results in different kinds of linguistic impairment (e.g., syntactic versus semantic). This supports the hypothesis that the mental grammar, like the brain itself, is not an undifferentiated system, but rather consists of distinct components or modules with different functions.

The kind of word substitutions that aphasic patients produce also tell us about how words are organized in the mental lexicon. Sometimes the substituted words are similar to the intended words in their sounds. For example, *pool* might be substituted for *tool, sable* for *table,* or *crucial* for *crucible.* Sometimes they are similar in meaning (e.g., *table* for *chair* or *boy* for *girl*). These errors resemble the speech errors that anyone might make, but they occur far more frequently in people with aphasia. The substitution of semantically or phonetically related words tells us that neural connections exist among semantically related words and among words that sound alike. Words are not mentally represented in a simple list but rather in an organized network of connections.

Similar observations pertain to reading. The term dyslexia refers to reading disorders. Many word substitutions are made by people who become dyslexic after brain damage. They are called **acquired dyslexics** because before their brain lesions they were normal readers (unlike developmental dyslexics, who have difficulty learning to read). One group of these patients, when reading words printed on cards aloud, produced the kinds of substitutions shown in the following examples.

Stimulus	Response 1	Response 2
act	*play*	*play*
applaud	*laugh*	*cheers*
example	*answer*	*sum*
heal	*pain*	*medicine*
south	*west*	*east*

The omission of function words in the speech of agrammatic aphasics shows that this class of words is mentally distinct from content words like nouns. A similar phenomenon has been observed in acquired dyslexia. The patient who produced the semantic substitutions cited previously was also agrammatic and was not able to read function words at all. When presented with words like *which* or *would*, he just said, "No" or "I hate those little words." However, he could read homophonous nouns and verbs, though with many semantic mistakes, as shown in the following:

Stimulus	Response	Stimulus	Response
witch	*witch*	which	*no!*
hour	*time*	our	*no!*
eye	*eyes*	I	*no!*
hymn	*bible*	him	*no!*
wood	*wood*	would	*no!*

All these errors provide evidence that the mental dictionary has content words and function words in different compartments, and that these two classes of words are processed in different brain areas or by different neural mechanisms, further supporting the view that both the brain and language are structured in a complex, modular fashion.

Additional evidence regarding hemispheric specialization is drawn from Japanese readers. The Japanese language has two main writing systems. One system, *kana*, is based on the sound system of the language; each symbol corresponds to a syllable. The other system, *kanji*, is ideographic; each symbol corresponds to a word. (More about this in chapter 12 on writing systems.) *Kanji* is not based on the sounds of the language. Japanese people with left-hemisphere damage are impaired in their ability to read *kana*, whereas people with right-hemisphere damage are impaired in their ability to read *kanji*. Also, experiments with unimpaired Japanese readers show that the right hemisphere is better and faster than the left hemisphere at reading *kanji*, and vice versa.

Most of us have experienced word-finding difficulties in speaking if not in reading, as Alice did in "Wonderland" when she said:

"And now, who am I? I will remember, if I can. I'm determined to do it!"
But being determined didn't help her much, and all she could say, after a great deal of puzzling, was "L, I know it begins with L."

This **tip-of-the-tongue phenomenon** (often referred to as **TOT**) is not uncommon. But if you could *rarely* find the word you wanted, imagine how frustrated you would be. This is the fate of many aphasics whose impairment involves severe **anomia**—the inability to find the word you wish to speak.

It is important to note that the language difficulties suffered by aphasics are not caused by any general cognitive or intellectual impairment or loss of motor or sensory controls of the nerves and muscles of the speech organs or hearing apparatus. Aphasics can produce and hear sounds. Whatever loss they suffer has to do only with the language faculty (or specific parts of it).

Deaf signers with damage to the left hemisphere show aphasia for sign language similar to the language breakdown in hearing aphasics, even though sign language is a visual-spatial language. Deaf patients with lesions in Broca's area show language deficits like those found in hearing patients, namely severely dysfluent, agrammatic sign production. Likewise, those with damage to Wernicke's area have fluent but often semantically incoherent sign language, filled with made-up signs. Although deaf aphasic patients show marked sign language deficits, they have no difficulty producing nonlinguistic gestures or sequences of nonlinguistic gestures, even though both nonlinguistic gestures and linguistic signs are produced by the same "articulators"—the hands and arms. Deaf aphasics also have no difficulty in processing nonlinguistic visual-spatial relationships, just as hearing aphasics have no problem with processing nonlinguistic auditory stimuli. These findings are important because they show that the left hemisphere is lateralized for language—an abstract system of symbols and rules—and not simply for hearing or speech. Language can be realized in different modalities, spoken or signed, but will be lateralized to the left hemisphere regardless of modality.

The kind of selective impairments that we find in people with aphasia has provided important information about the organization of different language and cognitive abilities, especially grammar and the lexicon. It tells us that language is a separate cognitive module—so aphasics can be otherwise cognitively normal—and also that within language, separate components can be differentially affected by damage to different regions of the brain.

Historical Descriptions of Aphasia

Interest in aphasia has a long history. Greek Hippocratic physicians reported that loss of speech often occurred simultaneously with paralysis of the right side of the body. Psalm 137 states: "If I forget thee, Oh Jerusalem, may my right hand lose its cunning and my tongue cleave to the roof of my mouth." This passage also shows that a link between loss of speech and paralysis of the right side was recognized.

Pliny the Elder (C.E. 23–79) refers to an Athenian who "with the stroke of a stone fell presently to forget his letters only, and could read no more; otherwise, his memory served him well enough." Numerous clinical descriptions of patients like the Athenian with language deficits, but intact nonlinguistic cognitive systems, were published between the fifteenth and eighteenth centuries. The language difficulties were not attributed to either general intellectual deficits or loss of memory, but to a specific impairment of language.

Carl Linnaeus in 1745 published a case study of a man suffering from jargon aphasia, who spoke "as if it were a foreign language, having his own names for all words." Another physician of that century reported on a patient's word substitution errors:

> After an illness, she was suddenly afflicted with a forgetting, or, rather, an incapacity or confusion of speech. . . . If she desired a *chair*, she would ask for a *table*. . . . Sometimes she herself perceived that she misnamed objects; at other times, she was annoyed when a *fan*, which she had asked for, was brought to her, instead of the *bonnet*, which she thought she had requested.

Physicians of the day described other kinds of linguistic breakdown in detail, such as a priest who, following brain damage, retained his ability to read Latin but lost the ability to read German.

The historical descriptions of language loss following brain damage fore-shadow the later controlled scientific studies of aphasia that have provided substantial evidence that language is predominantly and most frequently a left-hemisphere function. In most cases lesions to the left hemisphere result in apha-sia, but injuries to the right do not (although such lesions result in deficits in facial recognition, pattern recognition, and other cognitive abilities). Still, cau-tion must be taken. The ability to understand intonation connected with various emotional states and also to understand metaphors (e.g., *The walls have ears*), jokes, puns, double entendres, and the like can be affected in patients with right hemisphere damage. If such understanding has a linguistic component, then we may have to attribute some language cognition to the right hemisphere.

Studies of aphasia have provided not only important information regard-ing where and how language is localized in the brain, but also data bearing on the properties and principles of grammar that have been hypothesized for non-brain-damaged adults. For example, the study of aphasia has provided empirical evidence concerning theories of word structure (chapter 3), sentence formation (chapter 4), meaning (chapter 5), and sound systems (chapters 6 and 7).

Brain Imaging Technology

The historical descriptions of aphasia illustrate that people have long been fasci-nated by the brain-language connection. Today we no longer need to rely on sur-gery or autopsy to locate brain lesions or to identify the language regions of the brain. Noninvasive brain recording technologies such as computer tomography (CT) scans and **magnetic resonance imaging (MRI)** can reveal lesions in the liv-ing brain shortly after the damage occurs. In addition, **positron emission tomog-raphy (PET)** scans, functional MRI (fMRI) scans, and single photon emission CT (SPECT) scans provide images of the brain in action. It is now possible to detect changes in brain activity and to relate these changes to localized brain damage and specific linguistic and nonlinguistic cognitive tasks.

Figures 2.4 and 2.5 show MRI scans of the brains of a Broca's aphasic patient and a Wernicke's aphasic patient. The black areas show the sites of the lesions. Each diagram represents a slice of the left side of the brain.

A variety of scanning techniques permit us to measure metabolic activity in particular areas of the brain. Areas of greater activity are those most involved in the mental processes at the moment of the scan. Supplemented by magnetic encephalography (MEG), which measures magnetic fields in the living brain, these techniques can show us how the healthy brain reacts to particular linguis-tic stimuli. For example, the brains of normal adults are observed when they are asked to listen to two or more sounds and determine if they are the same. Or they may be asked to listen to strings of sounds or read a string of letters and determine if they are real or possible words, or listen to or read sequences of words and say whether they form grammatical or ungrammatical sentences. The results of these studies reaffirm the earlier findings that language resides in specific areas of the left hemisphere.

Dramatic evidence for a differentiated and structured brain is also provided by studies of both normal individuals and patients with lesions in regions of the brain other than Broca's and Wernicke's areas. Some patients have difficulty speaking a person's name; others have problems naming animals; and still oth-

FIGURE 2.4 | Three-dimensional reconstruction of the brain of a living patient with Broca's aphasia. Note area of damage in left frontal region (*dark gray*), which was caused by a stroke.
Courtesy of Hanna Damásio.

FIGURE 2.5 | Three-dimensional reconstruction of the brain of a living patient with Wernicke's aphasia. Note area of damage in left posterior temporal and lower parietal region (*dark gray*), which was caused by a stroke.
Courtesy of Hanna Damásio.

ers cannot name tools. fMRI studies have revealed the shape and location of the brain lesions in each of these types of patients. The patients in each group had brain lesions in distinct, nonoverlapping regions of the left temporal lobe. In a follow-up PET scan study, normal subjects were asked to name persons, animals, or tools. Experimenters found that there was differential activation in the normal brains in just those sites that were damaged in the aphasics who were unable to name persons, animals, or tools.

Further evidence for the separation of cognitive systems is provided by the neurological and behavioral findings that follow brain damage. Some patients lose the ability to recognize sounds or colors or familiar faces while retaining all other functions. A patient may not be able to recognize his wife when she walks into the room until she starts to talk. This suggests the differentiation of many aspects of visual and auditory processing.

Brain Plasticity and Lateralization in Early Life

It takes only one hemisphere to have a mind.

A. L. WIGAN, *The Duality of the Mind,* 1844

Lateralization of language to the left hemisphere is a process that begins very early in life. Wernicke's area is visibly distinctive in the left hemisphere of the fetus by the twenty-sixth gestational week. Infants as young as one week old show a greater electrical response in the left hemisphere to language and in the right hemisphere to music. A recent study videotaped the mouths of babies between the ages of five and twelve months when they were smiling and when they were babbling in syllables (producing sequences like *mamama* or *gugugu*). The study found that during smiling, the babies had a greater opening of the left side of the mouth (the side controlled by the right hemisphere), whereas during babbling, they had a greater opening of the *right* side (controlled by the left hemisphere). This indicates more left hemisphere involvement even at this very early stage of productive language development (see chapter 8).

While the left hemisphere is innately predisposed to specialize for language, there is also evidence of considerable *plasticity* (i.e., flexibility) in the system during the early stages of language development. This means that under certain circumstances, the right hemisphere can take over many of the language functions that would normally reside in the left hemisphere. An impressive illustration of plasticity is provided by children who have undergone a procedure known as **hemispherectomy,** in which one hemisphere of the brain is surgically removed. This procedure is used to treat otherwise intractable cases of epilepsy. In cases of left hemispherectomy after language acquisition has begun, children experience an initial period of aphasia and then reacquire a linguistic system that is virtually indistinguishable from that of normal children. They also show many of the developmental patterns of normal language acquisition. UCLA professor Susan Curtiss and colleagues have studied many of these children. They hypothesize that the latent linguistic ability of the right hemisphere is "freed" by the removal of the diseased left hemisphere, which may have had a strong inhibitory effect before the surgery.

In adults, however, surgical removal of the left hemisphere inevitably results in severe loss of language function (and so is done only in life-threatening circumstances), whereas adults (and children who have already acquired language) who have had their right hemispheres removed retain their language abilities. Other cognitive losses may result, such as those typically lateralized to the right hemisphere. The plasticity of the brain decreases with age and with the increasing specialization of the different hemispheres and regions of the brain.

Despite strong evidence that the left hemisphere is predetermined to be the language hemisphere in most humans, some evidence suggests that the right hemisphere also plays a role in the earliest stages of language acquisition. Children with prenatal, perinatal, or childhood brain lesions in the right hemisphere can show delays and impairments in babbling and vocabulary learning, whereas children with early left hemisphere lesions demonstrate impairments in their ability to form phrases and sentences. Also, many children who undergo right hemispherectomy before two years of age do not develop language, even though they still have a left hemisphere.

Various findings converge to show that the human brain is essentially designed to specialize for language in the left hemisphere but that the right hemisphere is involved in early language development. They also show that, under the right circumstances, the brain is remarkably resilient and that if brain damage or surgery occurs early in life, normal left hemisphere functions can be taken over by the right hemisphere.

Split Brains

© Scott Adams/Dist. by United Feature Syndicate, Inc.

People suffering from intractable epilepsy may be treated by severing communication between their two hemispheres. Surgeons cut through the corpus callosum (see Figure 2.1), the fibrous network that connects the two halves. When this pathway is severed, there is no communication between the "two brains." Such **split-brain** patients also provide evidence for language lateralization and for understanding contralateral brain functions.

The psychologist Michael Gazzaniga states:

> With [the corpus callosum] intact, the two halves of the body have no secrets from one another. With it sectioned, the two halves become two different conscious mental spheres, each with its own experience base and

control system for behavioral operations. . . . Unbelievable as this may seem, this is the flavor of a long series of experimental studies first carried out in the cat and monkey.[1]

When the brain is surgically split, certain information from the left side of the body is received only by the right side of the brain, and vice versa. To illustrate, suppose that a monkey is trained to respond with both its hands to a certain visual stimulus, such as a flashing light. After the training is complete, the brain is surgically split. The stimulus is then shown only to the left visual field (the right hemisphere). Because the right hemisphere controls the left side of the body, the monkey will perform only with the left hand.

In humans who have undergone split-brain operations, the two hemispheres appear to be independent, and messages sent to the brain result in different responses, depending on which side receives the message. For example if a pencil is placed in the left hand of a split-brain person whose eyes are closed, the person can use the pencil appropriately but cannot name it because only the left hemisphere can speak. The right brain senses the pencil but the information cannot be relayed to the left brain for linguistic naming because the connections between the two halves have been severed. By contrast, if the pencil is placed in the right hand, the subject is immediately able to name it as well as to describe it because the sensory information from the right hand goes directly to the left hemisphere, where the language areas are located.

Various experiments of this sort have provided information on the different capabilities of the two hemispheres. The right brain does better than the left in pattern-matching tasks, in recognizing faces, and in spatial tasks. The left hemisphere is superior for language, rhythmic perception, temporal-order judgments, and arithmetic calculations. According to Gazzaniga, "the right hemisphere as well as the left hemisphere can emote and while the left can tell you why, the right cannot."

Studies of human split-brain patients have also shown that when the interhemispheric visual connections are severed, visual information from the right and left visual fields becomes confined to the left and right hemispheres, respectively. Because of the crucial endowment of the left hemisphere for language, written material delivered to the right hemisphere cannot be read aloud if the brain is split, because the information cannot be transferred to the left hemisphere. An image or picture that is flashed to the right visual field of a split-brain patient (and therefore processed by the left hemisphere) can be named. However, when the picture is flashed in the left visual field and therefore "lands" in the right hemisphere, it cannot be named.

Other Experimental Evidence of Brain Organization

Dichotic listening is an experimental technique that uses auditory signals to observe the behavior of the individual hemispheres of the human brain. Subjects hear two different sound signals simultaneously through earphones. They may hear *curl* in one ear and *girl* in the other, or a cough in one ear and a laugh in the other. When asked to state what they heard in each ear, subjects are more fre-

---

[1]Gazzaniga, M. S. 1970. *The bisected brain.* New York: Appleton-Century-Crofts.

quently correct in reporting linguistic stimuli (words, nonsense syllables, and so on) delivered directly to the right ear, but are more frequently correct in reporting nonverbal stimuli (musical chords, environmental sounds, and so on) delivered to the left ear. Such experiments provide strong evidence of lateralization.

Both hemispheres receive signals from both ears, but the contralateral stimuli prevail over the **ipsilateral** (same-side) stimuli because they are processed more robustly. The contralateral pathways are anatomically thicker (think of a four-lane highway versus a two-lane road) and are not delayed by the need to cross the corpus callosum. The accuracy with which subjects report what they hear is evidence that the left hemisphere is superior for linguistic processing, and the right hemisphere is superior for nonverbal information.

These experiments are important because they show not only that language is lateralized, but also that the left hemisphere is not superior for processing all sounds; it is only better for those sounds that are linguistic. The left side of the brain is specialized for language, not sound, as we also noted in connection with sign language research discussed earlier.

Other experimental techniques are also being used to map the brain and to investigate the independence of different aspects of language and the extent of the independence of language from other cognitive systems. Even before the advances in imaging technology of the 1980s and more recently, researchers were taping electrodes to different areas of the skull and investigating the electrical activity of the brain related to perceptual and cognitive information. In such experiments scientists measure **event-related brain potentials (ERPs)**, which are the electrical signals emitted from the brain in response to different stimuli.

For example, ERP differences result when the subject hears speech sounds versus nonspeech sounds, with a greater response from the left hemisphere to speech. ERP experiments also show variations in timing, pattern, amplitude, and hemisphere of response when subjects hear sentences that are meaningless, such as

The man admired Don's headache of the landscape.

as opposed to meaningful sentences such as

The man admired Don's sketch of the landscape.

Such experiments show that neuronal activity varies in location within the brain according to whether the stimulus is language or nonlanguage, with a left hemisphere preference for language. Even jabberwocky sentences—sentences that are grammatical but contain nonsense words, such as Lewis Carroll's 'Twas brillig, and the slithy toves—elicit an asymmetrical left hemisphere ERP response, demonstrating that the left hemisphere is sensitive to grammatical structure even in the absence of meaning. Moreover, because ERPs also show the timing of neuronal activity as the brain processes language, they can provide insight into the mechanisms that allow the brain to process language quickly and efficiently, on the scale of milliseconds.

ERP and imaging studies of newborns and very young infants show that from birth onward, the left hemisphere differentiates between nonlinguistic acoustic processing and linguistic processing of sounds, and does so via the same neural pathways that adults use. These results indicate that at birth the left hemisphere is primed to process language, and to do so in terms of the specific localization of language functions we find in the adult brain.

What is more, these studies have shown that early stages of phonological and syntactic processing do not require attentional resources but are automatic, very much like reflexes. For example, even *sleeping* infants show the asymmetrical and distinct processing of phonological versus equally different but nonlinguistic acoustic signals; and adults are able to perform a completely unrelated task, one that takes up considerable attentional resources, at the same time they are listening to sentences, without affecting the nature or degree of the brain activity that is the neural reflex of automatic, mandatory early syntactic processing.

Experimental evidence from these various neurolinguistic techniques has provided empirical confirmation for theories of language structure. For example, ERP, fMRI, PET, and MEG studies provide measurable confirmation of discrete speech sounds and their phonetic properties. These studies also substantiate linguistic evidence that words have an internal structure consisting of *morphemes* (chapter 3) and belong to categories such as nouns and verbs. Neurolinguistic experiments also support the mental reality of many of the syntactic structures proposed by linguists. Thus neurolinguistic experimentation provides data for both aspects of neurolinguistics: for helping to determine where and how language is represented and processed in the brain, and for providing empirical support for concepts and hypotheses in linguistic theory.

The results of neurolinguistic studies, which use different techniques and different subject populations, both normal and brain damaged, are converging to provide the information we seek on the relationship between the brain and various language and nonlanguage cognitive systems. However, as pointed out by Professors Colin Phillips and Kuniyoshi Sakai,

> . . . knowing where language is supported in the human brain is just one step on the path to finding what are the special properties of those brain regions that make language possible. . . . An important challenge for coming years will be to find whether the brain areas implicated in language studies turn out to have distinctive properties at the neuronal level that allow them to explain the special properties of human language.[2]

The Autonomy of Language

In addition to brain-damaged individuals who have lost their language ability, there are children without brain lesions who nevertheless have difficulties in acquiring language or are much slower than the average child. They show no other cognitive deficits, they are not autistic or retarded, and they have no perceptual problems. Such children are suffering from **specific language impairment**

---

[2]Phillips, C., and K. L. Sakai. 2005. Language and the brain. *Yearbook of science and technology 2005*. Boston: McGraw-Hill Publishers.

(SLI). Only their linguistic ability is affected, and often only specific aspects of grammar are impaired.

Children with SLI have problems with the use of function words such as articles, prepositions, and auxiliary verbs. They also have difficulties with inflectional suffixes on nouns and verbs such as markers of tense and agreement. Several examples from a four-year-old boy with SLI illustrate this:

> Meowmeow chase mice.
> Show me knife.
> It not long one.

An experimental study of several SLI children showed that they produced the past tense marker on the verb (as in *danced*) about 27 percent of the time, compared with 95 percent by the normal control group. Similarly, the SLI children produced the plural marker -*s* (as in *boys*) only 9 percent of the time, compared with 95 percent by the normal children.

Other studies of children with SLI reveal broader grammatical impairments, involving difficulties with many grammatical structures and operations. However, most investigations of SLI children show that they have particular problems with verbal inflection, especially with producing tensed verbs (*walks, walked*), and also with syntactic structures involving certain kinds of word reorderings such as *Mother is hard to please*, a rearrangement of *It is hard to please Mother*. In many respects these difficulties resemble the impairments demonstrated by aphasics. Recent work on SLI children also shows that the different components of language (phonology, syntax, lexicon) can be selectively impaired or spared. As is the case with aphasia, these studies of SLI provide important information about the nature of language and help linguists develop theories about the underlying properties of language and its development in children.

SLI children show that language may be impaired while general intelligence stays intact, supporting the view of a grammatical faculty that is separate from other cognitive systems. But is it possible for language to develop normally when general intelligence is impaired? If such individuals can be found, it argues strongly for the view that language does not derive from some general cognitive ability.

Other Dissociations of Language and Cognition

> [T]he human mind is not an unstructured entity but consists of components which can be distinguished by their functional properties.
>
> **NEIL SMITH AND IANTHI-MARIA TSIMPLI,** *The Mind of a Savant: Language, Learning, and Modularity,* 1995

There are numerous cases of intellectually handicapped individuals who, despite their disabilities in certain spheres, show remarkable talents in others. There are superb musicians and artists who lack the simple abilities required to take care of themselves. Such people are referred to as **savants.** Some of the most famous savants are human calculators who can perform arithmetic computations at phenomenal speed, or calendrical calculators who can tell you without pause on which day of the week any date in the last or next century falls.

Until recently, most such savants have been reported to be linguistically handicapped. They may be good mimics who can repeat speech like parrots, but they show meager creative language ability. Nevertheless, the literature reports cases of language savants who have acquired the highly complex grammar of their language (as well as other languages in some cases) but who lack nonlinguistic abilities of equal complexity. Laura and Christopher are two such cases.

Laura

Laura was a retarded young woman with a nonverbal IQ of 41 to 44. She lacked almost all number concepts, including basic counting principles, and could draw only at a preschool level. She had an auditory memory span limited to three units. Yet, when at the age of sixteen she was asked to name some fruits, she responded with *pears, apples,* and *pomegranates.* In this same period she produced syntactically complex sentences like *He was saying that I lost my battery-powered watch that I loved,* and *She does paintings, this really good friend of the kids who I went to school with and really loved,* and *I was like 15 or 19 when I started moving out of home . . .*

Laura could not add 2 + 2. She didn't know how old she was or how old she was when she moved away from home, nor whether 15 is before or after 19. Nevertheless, Laura produced complex sentences with multiple phrases and sentences with other sentences inside them. She used and understood passive sentences, and she was able to inflect verbs for number and person to agree with the subject of the sentence. She formed past tenses in accord with adverbs that referred to past time. She could do all this and more, but she could neither read nor write nor tell time. She did not know who the president of the United States was or what country she lived in. Her drawings of humans resembled potatoes with stick arms and legs. Yet, in a sentence imitation task, she both detected and corrected grammatical errors.

Laura is but one of many examples of children who display well-developed grammatical abilities, less-developed abilities to associate linguistic expressions with the objects they refer to, and severe deficits in nonlinguistic cognition.

In addition, any notion that linguistic competence results simply from communicative abilities, or develops to serve communicative functions, is belied by studies of children with good linguistic skills, but nearly no or severely limited communicative skills. The acquisition and use of language seem to depend on cognitive skills different from the ability to communicate in a social setting.

Christopher

Christopher has a nonverbal IQ between 60 and 70 and must live in an institution because he is unable to take care of himself. The tasks of buttoning a shirt, cutting his fingernails, or vacuuming the carpet are too difficult for him. However, his linguistic competence is as rich and as sophisticated as that of any native speaker. Furthermore, when given written texts in some fifteen to twenty languages, he translates them quickly, with few errors, into English. The languages include Germanic languages such as Danish, Dutch, and German; Romance languages such as French, Italian, Portuguese, and Spanish; as well as Polish, Finnish, Greek,

Hindi, Turkish, and Welsh. He learned these languages from speakers who used them in his presence, or from grammar books. Christopher loves to study and learn languages. Little else is of interest to him. His situation strongly suggests that his linguistic ability is independent of his general intellectual ability.

The question as to whether the language faculty is a separate cognitive system or whether it is derivative of more general cognitive mechanisms is controversial and has received much attention and debate among linguists, psychologists, neuropsychologists, and cognitive scientists. Cases such as Laura and Christopher argue against the view that linguistic ability derives from general intelligence because these two individuals (and others like them) developed language despite other pervasive intellectual deficits. A growing body of evidence supports the view that the human animal is biologically equipped from birth with an autonomous language faculty that is highly specific and that does not derive from general human intellectual ability.

Genetic Basis of Language

Studies of genetic disorders also reveal that one cognitive domain can develop normally along with abnormal development in other domains, and they also underscore the strong biological basis of language. Children with Turner syndrome (a chromosomal anomaly) have normal language and advanced reading skills along with serious nonlinguistic (visual and spatial) cognitive deficits. Similarly, studies of the language of children and adolescents with Williams syndrome reveal a unique behavioral profile in which certain linguistic functions seem to be relatively preserved in the face of visual and spatial cognitive deficits and moderate retardation. In addition, developmental dyslexia and SLI also appear to have a genetic basis. And recent studies of Klinefelter syndrome (another chromosomal anomaly) show quite selective syntactic and semantic deficits alongside intact intelligence.

Epidemiological and familial aggregation studies show that SLI runs in families. One such study is of a large multigenerational family, half of whom are language impaired. The impaired members of this family have a very specific grammatical problem: They do not reliably use word-endings or "irregular" verbs correctly. In particular, they often fail to indicate the tense of the verb. They routinely produce sentences such as the following:

She remembered when she hurts herself the other day.
He did it then he fall.
The boy climb up the tree and frightened the bird away.

These and similar results show that a large proportion of SLI children have language-impaired family members, pointing to SLI as a heritable disorder. Studies also show that monozygotic (identical) twins are more likely to both suffer from SLI than dizygotic (fraternal) twins. Thus evidence from SLI and other genetic disorders, along with the asymmetry of abilities in linguistic savants, strongly supports the view that the language faculty is an autonomous, genetically determined module of the brain.

Language and Brain Development

"Jump Start" copyright © United Feature Syndicate. Reprinted with permission.

Language and the brain are intimately connected. Specific areas of the brain are devoted to language, and injury to these areas disrupts language. In the young child, injury to or removal of the left hemisphere has severe consequences for language development. Conversely, increasing evidence shows that normal brain development depends on early and regular exposure to language. (See chapter 8.)

The Critical Period

Under normal circumstances, a child is introduced to language virtually at the moment of birth. Adults talk to him and to each other in his presence. Children do not require explicit language instruction, but they do need exposure to language in order to develop normally. Children who do not receive linguistic input during their formative years do not achieve nativelike grammatical competence. Moreover, behavioral tests and brain imaging studies show that late exposure to language alters the fundamental organization of the brain for language.

The **critical-age hypothesis** assumes that language is biologically based and that the ability to learn a native language develops within a fixed period, from birth to middle childhood. During this **critical period**, language acquisition proceeds easily, swiftly, and without external intervention. After this period, the acquisition of grammar is difficult and, for most individuals, never fully achieved. Children deprived of language during this critical period show atypical patterns of brain lateralization.

The notion of a critical period is true of many species and seems to pertain to species-specific, biologically triggered behaviors. Ducklings, for example, during the period from nine to twenty-one hours after hatching, will follow the first moving object they see, whether or not it looks or waddles like a duck. Such behavior is not the result of conscious decision, external teaching, or intensive practice. It unfolds according to what appears to be a maturationally determined schedule that is universal across the species. Similarly, as discussed in a later section, certain species of birds develop their bird song during a biologically determined window of time.

Instances of children reared in environments of extreme social isolation constitute "experiments in nature" for testing the critical-age hypothesis. The most dramatic cases are those described as "wild" or "feral" children. A celebrated case, documented in François Truffaut's film *The Wild Child*, is that of Victor, "the wild boy of Aveyron," who was found in 1798. It was ascertained that he had been left in the woods when very young and had somehow survived. In 1920 two children, Amala and Kamala, were found in India, supposedly having been reared by wolves.

Other children have been isolated because of deliberate efforts to keep them from normal social intercourse. In 1970, a child called Genie in the scientific reports was discovered. She had been confined to a small room under conditions of physical restraint and had received only minimal human contact from the age of eighteen months until nearly fourteen years.

None of these children, regardless of the cause of isolation, was able to speak or knew any language at the time they were reintroduced into society. This linguistic inability could simply be caused by the fact that these children received no linguistic input, showing that language acquisition, though an innate, neurologically based ability, must be triggered by input from the environment. In the documented cases of Victor and Genie, however, these children were unable to acquire grammar even after years of exposure, and despite the ability to learn many words.

Genie was able to learn a large vocabulary, including colors, shapes, objects, natural categories, and abstract as well as concrete terms, but her grammatical skills never fully developed. The UCLA linguist Susan Curtiss, who worked with Genie for several years, reported that Genie's utterances were, for the most part, "the stringing together of content words, often with rich and clear meaning, but with little grammatical structure." Many utterances produced by Genie at the age of fifteen and older, several years after her emergence from isolation, are like those of two-year-old children, and not unlike utterances of Broca's aphasia patients and people with SLI, such as the following:

Man motorcycle have.
Genie full stomach.
Genie bad cold live father house.
Want Curtiss play piano.
Open door key.

Genie's utterances lacked articles, auxiliary verbs like *will* or *can*, the third-person singular agreement marker *-s*, the past-tense marker *-ed*, question words like *who*, *what*, and *where*, and pronouns. She had no ability to form more complex types of sentences such as questions (e.g., *Are you feeling hungry?*). Genie started learning language after the critical period and was therefore never able to fully acquire the grammatical rules of English.

Tests of lateralization (dichotic listening and ERP experiments) showed that Genie's language was lateralized to the *right* hemisphere. Her test performance was similar to that found in split-brain and left hemispherectomy patients, yet Genie was not brain damaged. Curtiss speculates that after the critical period, the usual language areas functionally atrophy because of inadequate linguistic stimulation. Genie's case also demonstrates that language is not the same as communication, because Genie was a powerful nonverbal communicator, despite her limited ability to acquire language.

Chelsea, another case of linguistic isolation, is a woman whose situation also supports the critical-age hypothesis. She was born deaf but was wrongly diagnosed as retarded. When she was thirty-one, her deafness was finally diagnosed, and she was fitted with hearing aids. For years she has received extensive language training and therapy and has acquired a large vocabulary. However, like Genie, Chelsea has not been able to develop a grammar. ERP studies of the localization of language in Chelsea's brain have revealed an equal response to language in both hemispheres. In other words, Chelsea also does not show the normal asymmetric organization for language.

More than 90 percent of children who are born deaf or become deaf before they have acquired language are born to hearing parents. These children have also provided information about the critical age for language acquisition. Because most of their parents do not know sign language at the time these children are born, most receive delayed language exposure. Several studies have investigated the acquisition of American Sign Language (ASL) among deaf signers exposed to the language at different ages. Early learners who received ASL input from birth and up to six years of age did much better in the production and comprehension of complex signs and sign sentences than late learners who were not exposed to ASL until after the age of twelve, even though all of the subjects in these studies had used sign for more than twenty years. There was little difference, however, in vocabulary or knowledge of word order.

Another study compared patterns of lateralization in the brains of adult native speakers of English, adult native signers, and deaf adults who had not been exposed to sign language. The nonsigning deaf adults did not show the same cerebral asymmetries as either the hearing adults or the deaf signers. In recent years there have been numerous studies of late learners of sign language, all with similar results.

The cases of Genie and other isolated children, as well as deaf late learners of ASL, show that children cannot fully acquire language unless they are exposed to it within the critical period—a biologically determined window of opportunity during which time the brain is prepared to develop language. Moreover, the critical period is linked to brain lateralization. The human brain is primed to develop language in specific areas of the left hemisphere, but the normal process of brain specialization depends on early and systematic experience with language. Language acquisition plays a critical role in, and may even be *the* trigger for, the realization of normal cerebral lateralization for higher cognitive functions in general, not just for language.

Beyond the critical period, the human brain seems unable to acquire the grammatical aspects of language, even with substantial linguistic training or many years of exposure. However, it is possible to acquire words and various conversational skills after this point. This evidence suggests that the critical period holds for the acquisition of grammatical abilities, but not necessarily for all aspects of language.

The selective acquisition of certain components of language that occurs beyond the critical period is reminiscent of the selective impairment that occurs in various language disorders, where specific linguistic abilities are disrupted. This selectivity in both acquisition and impairment points to a strongly modularized language faculty. Language is separate from other cognitive systems and autonomous, and is itself a complex system with various components. In the chapters that follow, we will explore these different language components.

A Critical Period for Bird Song

That's the wise thrush; he sings each song twice over
Lest you should think he never could recapture
The first fine careless rapture!

ROBERT BROWNING, "Home-thoughts, from Abroad," 1845

Mutts © Patrick McDonnell, King Features Syndicate

Bird song lacks certain fundamental characteristics of human language, such as discrete sounds and creativity. However, certain species of birds show a critical period for acquiring their "language" similar to the critical period for human language acquisition.

Calls and songs of the chaffinch vary depending on the geographic area that the bird inhabits. The message is the same, but the form or "pronunciation" is different. Usually, a young bird sings a simplified version of the song shortly after hatching. Later, it undergoes further learning in acquiring the fully complex version. Because birds from the same brood acquire different chaffinch songs depending on the area in which they finally settle, part of the song must be learned. On the other hand, because the fledging chaffinch sings the song of its species in a simple degraded form, even if it has never heard it sung, some aspect of it is biologically determined, that is, innate.

The chaffinch acquires its fully developed song in several stages, just as human children acquire language. There is also a critical period in the song learning of chaffinches as well as white-crowned sparrows, zebra finches, and many other species. If these birds are not exposed to the songs of their species during certain fixed periods after their birth—the period differs from species to species—song acquisition does not occur. The chaffinch is unable to learn new song elements after ten months of age. If it is isolated from other birds before attaining the full complexity of its song and is then exposed again after ten months, its song will not develop further. If white-crowned sparrows lose their hearing during a critical period after they have learned to sing, they produce a song that differs from other white crowns. They need to hear themselves sing in order to produce particular whistles and other song features. If, however, the deafness occurs after the critical period, their songs are normal. Similarly, baby nightingales in captivity may be trained to sing melodiously by another nightingale, a "teaching bird," but only before their tail feathers are grown. After that period, they know only the less melodious calls of their parents, and nothing more can be done to further their musical development.

On the other hand, some bird species show no critical period. The cuckoo sings a fully developed song even if it never hears another cuckoo sing. These communicative messages are entirely innate. For other species, songs appear to be at least partially learned, and the learning may occur throughout the bird's lifetime. The bullfinch, for example, will learn elements of songs it is exposed to, even those of another species, and incorporate those elements into its own quiet warble. In a more recent example of unconstrained song learning, Danish ornithologists report that birds have begun to copy the ring tones of cellular phones.

From the point of view of human language research, the relationship between the innate and learned aspects of bird song is significant. Apparently, the basic nature of the songs of some species is present from birth, which means that it is biologically and genetically determined. The same holds true for human language: Its basic nature is innate. The details of bird song and of human language are both acquired through experience that must occur within a critical period.

The Development of Language in the Species

As the voice was used more and more, the vocal organs would have been strengthened and perfected through the principle of the inherited effects of use; and this would have reacted on the power of speech. But the relation between the continued use of language and the development of the brain has no doubt been far more important. The mental powers in some early progenitor of man must have been more highly developed than in any existing ape, before even the most imperfect form of speech could have come into use.

CHARLES DARWIN, *The Descent of Man,* 1871

There is much interest today among biologists as well as linguists in the relationship between the development of language and the evolutionary development of the human species. Some view language as species specific; some do not. Some view language ability as a difference in degree between humans and other primates—a continuity view; others see the onset of language ability as a qualitative leap—the discontinuity view.

In trying to understand the development of language, scholars past and present have debated the role played by the vocal tract and the ear. For example, it has been suggested that speech could not have developed in nonhuman primates because their vocal tracts were anatomically incapable of producing a large enough inventory of speech sounds. According to this hypothesis, the development of language is linked to the evolutionary development of the speech production and perception apparatus. This, of course, would be accompanied by changes in the brain and the nervous system toward greater complexity. Such a view implies that the languages of our human ancestors of millions of years ago may have been syntactically and phonologically simpler than any language known to us today. The notion "simpler" is left undefined, although it has been suggested that this primeval language had a smaller inventory of sounds.

One evolutionary step must have resulted in the development of a vocal tract capable of producing the wide variety of sounds of human language, as well as the mechanism for perceiving and distinguishing them. However, the existence of mynah birds and parrots is evidence that this step is insufficient to explain the origin of language, because these creatures have the ability to imitate human speech, but not the ability to acquire language.

More important, we know from the study of humans who are born deaf and learn sign languages that are used around them that the ability to hear speech sounds is not a necessary condition for the acquisition and use of language. In addition, the lateralization evidence from ERP and imaging studies of people using sign language, as well as evidence from sign language aphasia, show that sign language is organized in the brain like spoken language. Certain auditory locations within the cortex are activated during signing even though no sound is involved, supporting the contention that the brain is neurologically equipped for language rather than speech. The ability to produce and hear a wide variety of sounds therefore appears to be neither necessary nor sufficient for the development of language in the human species.

A major step in the development of language most probably relates to evolutionary changes in the brain. The linguist Noam Chomsky expresses this view:

> It could be that when the brain reached a certain level of complexity it simply automatically had certain properties because that's what happens when you pack 10^{10} neurons into something the size of a basketball.[3]

The biologist Stephen Jay Gould expresses a similar view:

> The Darwinist model would say that language, like other complex organic systems, evolved step by step, each step being an adaptive solution. Yet language is such an integrated "all or none" system, it is hard to imagine it evolving that way. Perhaps the brain grew in size and became capable of all kinds of things which were not part of the original properties.[4]

Other linguists, however, support a more Darwinian natural selection development of what is sometimes called "the language instinct":

> All the evidence suggests that it is the precise wiring of the brain's microcircuitry that makes language happen, not gross size, shape, or neuron packing.[5]

The attempt to resolve this controversy clearly requires more research. Another point that is not yet clear is what role, if any, hemispheric lateralization

---

[3]Chomsky, N., in Searchinger, G. 1994. The human language series, program 3. Video. New York: Equinox Film/Ways of Knowing, Inc.

[4]Gould, S. J., in Searchinger, G. 1994. The human language series, program 3. Video. New York: Equinox Film/Ways of Knowing, Inc.

[5]Pinker, S. 1995. *The language instinct.* New York: William Morrow.

played in language evolution. Lateralization certainly makes greater specialization possible. Research conducted with birds and monkeys, however, shows that lateralization is not unique to the human brain. Thus, while it may constitute a necessary step in the evolution of language, it is not a sufficient one.

We do not yet have definitive answers to the origin of language in the human brain. The search for these answers goes on and provides new insights into the nature of language and the nature of the human brain.

Summary

The attempt to understand what makes the acquisition and use of language possible has led to research on the brain-mind-language relationship. **Neurolinguistics** is the study of the brain mechanisms and anatomical structures that underlie linguistic competence and performance. Much neurolinguistic research is centered on experimental and behavioral data from people with impaired or atypical language. These results greatly enhance our understanding of language structure and acquisition.

The brain is the most complex organ of the body, controlling motor and sensory activities and thought processes. Research conducted for more than a century has shown that different parts of the brain control different body functions. The nerve cells that form the surface of the brain are called the **cortex**, which serves as the intellectual decision maker, receiving messages from the sensory organs and initiating all voluntary actions. The brain of all higher animals is divided into two parts called the **cerebral hemispheres**, which are connected by the **corpus callosum**, a network that permits the left and right hemispheres to communicate.

Each hemisphere exhibits **contralateral** control of functions. The left hemisphere controls the right side of the body, and the right hemisphere controls the left side. Despite the general symmetry of the human body, much evidence suggests that the brain is asymmetric, with the left and right hemispheres **lateralized** for different functions.

Neurolinguists have many tools for studying the brain, among them **dichotic listening** experiments and many types of scans and electrical measurements. These techniques permit the study of the living brain as it processes language. By studying **split-brain** patients and **aphasics**, localized areas of the brain can be associated with particular language functions. For example, lesions in the part of the brain called **Broca's area** may suffer from **Broca's aphasia**, which results in impaired syntax and **agrammatism**. Damage to **Wernicke's area** may result in **Wernicke's aphasia**, in which fluent speakers produce semantically anomalous utterances, or even worse, **jargon aphasia**, in which speakers produce nonsense forms that make their utterance uninterpretable. Damage to yet different areas can produce **anomia**, a form of aphasia in which the patient has word-finding difficulties.

Deaf signers with damage to the left hemisphere show aphasia for sign language similar to the language breakdown in hearing aphasics, even though sign language is a visual-spatial language.

Other evidence supports the lateralization of language. Children who undergo a left **hemispherectomy** show specific linguistic deficits, whereas other cognitive abilities remain intact. If the right brain is damaged or removed after the first two or three years, however, language is unimpaired, but other cognitive disorders may result.

The language faculty is **modular**. It is independent of other cognitive systems with which it interacts. Evidence for modularity is found in studies of aphasia, of children with **specific language impairment (SLI)**, of linguistic **savants**, and of children who learn language past the **critical period**. The genetic basis for an independent language module is supported by studies of SLI in families and twins and by studies of genetic anomalies associated with language disorders.

The **critical-age hypothesis** states that there is a window of opportunity between birth and middle childhood for learning a first language. The imperfect language learning of persons exposed to language after this period supports the hypothesis. Some songbirds also appear to have a critical period for the acquisition of their calls and songs.

References for Further Reading

Caplan, D. 2001. Neurolinguistics. *The handbook of linguistics*, M. Aronoff and J. Rees-Miller (eds.). London: Blackwell Publishers.

_____. 1992. *Language: Structure, processing, and disorders*. Cambridge, MA: MIT Press.

_____. 1987. *Neurolinguistics and linguistic aphasiology*. Cambridge, UK: Cambridge University Press.

Coltheart, M., K. Patterson, and J. C. Marshall (eds). 1980. *Deep dyslexia*. London: Routledge & Kegan Paul.

Curtiss, S. 1977. *Genie: A linguistic study of a modern-day "wild child."* New York: Academic Press.

Curtiss, S., and J. Schaeffer. 2005. Syntactic development in children with hemispherectomy: The I-, D-, and C-systems. *Brain and Language* 94: 147–166.

Damásio, H. 1981. Cerebral localization of the aphasias." *Acquired aphasia*, M. Taylor Sarno (ed.). New York: Academic Press, 27–65.

Gazzaniga, M. S. 1970. *The bisected brain*. New York: Appleton-Century-Crofts.

Geschwind, N. 1979. Specializations of the human brain. *Scientific American* 206 (September): 180–199.

Lenneberg, E. H. 1967. *Biological foundations of language*. New York: Wiley.

Obler, L. K., and K. Gjerlow. 1999. *Language and brain*. Cambridge, UK: Cambridge University Press.

Patterson, K. E., J. C. Marshall, and M. Coltheart (eds.). 1986. *Surface dyslexia*. Hillsdale, NJ: Lawrence Erlbaum.

Pinker, S. 1994. *The language instinct*. New York: William Morrow.

Poizner, H., E. S. Klima, and U. Bellugi. 1987. *What the hands reveal about the brain*. Cambridge, MA: MIT Press.

Searchinger, G. 1994. The human language series: 1, 2, 3. Videos. New York: Equinox Film/Ways of Knowing, Inc.

Smith, N. V., and I-M. Tsimpli. 1995. *The mind of a savant: Language learning and modularity*. Oxford, UK: Blackwell.

Springer, S. P., and G. Deutsch. 1997. *Left brain, right brain*, 5th edn. New York: W. H. Freeman and Company.

Stromswold, K. 2001. The heritability of language. *Language* 77(4): 647–721.

Yamada, J. 1990. *Laura: A case for the modularity of language*. Cambridge, MA: MIT Press.

Exercises

1. The Nobel Prize laureate Roger Sperry has argued that split-brain patients have two minds:

   > Everything we have seen so far indicates that the surgery has left these people with two separate minds, that is, two separate spheres of consciousness. What is experienced in the right hemisphere seems to lie entirely outside the realm of experience of the left hemisphere.

   Another Nobel Prize winner in physiology, Sir John Eccles, disagrees. He does not think the right hemisphere can think; he distinguishes between "mere consciousness," which animals possess as well as humans, and language, thought, and other purely human cognitive abilities. In fact, according to him, human nature is all in the left hemisphere.

   Write a short essay discussing these two opposing points of view, stating your opinion on how to define "the mind."

2. **A.** Some aphasic patients, when asked to read a list of words, substitute other words for those printed. In many cases, the printed words and the substituted words are similar. The following data are from actual aphasic patients. In each case, state what the two words have in common and how they differ:

	Printed Word	Word Spoken by Aphasic
i.	liberty	freedom
	canary	parrot
	abroad	overseas
	large	long
	short	small
	tall	long
ii.	decide	decision
	conceal	concealment
	portray	portrait
	bathe	bath
	speak	discussion
	remember	memory

   B. What do the words in groups (i) and (ii) reveal about how words are likely to be stored in the brain?

3. The following sentences spoken by aphasic patients were collected and analyzed by Dr. Harry Whitaker. In each case, state how the sentence deviates from normal nonaphasic language.
   a. There is under a horse a new sidesaddle.
   b. In girls we see many happy days.
   c. I'll challenge a new bike.
   d. I surprise no new glamour.
   e. Is there three chairs in this room?

    f. Mike and Peter is happy.

    g. Bill and John likes hot dogs.

    h. Proliferate is a complete time about a word that is correct.

    i. Went came in better than it did before.

4. The investigation of individuals with brain damage has been a major source of information regarding the neural basis of language and other cognitive systems. One might suggest that this is like trying to understand how an automobile engine works by looking at a damaged engine. Is this a good analogy? If so, why? If not, why not? In your answer, discuss how a damaged system can or cannot provide information about the normal system.

5. What are the arguments and evidence that have been put forth to support the notion that there are two separate parts of the brain?

6. Discuss the statement: *It only takes one hemisphere to have a mind.*

7. In this chapter, dichotic listening tests in which subjects hear different kinds of stimuli in each ear were discussed. These tests showed that there were fewer errors made in reporting linguistic stimuli such as the syllables *pa*, *ta*, and *ka* when heard through an earphone on the right ear; other nonlinguistic sounds such as a police car siren were processed with fewer mistakes if heard by the left ear. This is a result of the contralateral control of the brain. There is also a technique that permits visual stimuli to be received either by the right visual field, that is, the right eye alone (going directly to the left hemisphere), or by the left visual field (going directly to the right hemisphere). What are some visual stimuli that could be used in an experiment to further test the lateralization of language?

8. The following utterances were made either by Broca's aphasics or Wernicke's aphasics. Indicate which is which by writing a "B" or "W" next to the utterance.

    a. Goodnight and in the pansy I can't say but into a flipdoor you can see it.

    b. Well . . . sunset . . . uh . . . horses nine, no, uh, two, tails want swish.

    c. Oh, . . . if I could I would, and a sick old man disflined a sinter, minter.

    d. Words . . . words . . . words . . . two, four, six, eight, . . . blaze am he.

9. Shakespeare's Hamlet surely had problems. Some say he was obsessed with being overweight, because the first lines he speaks in the play when alone on the stage in Act II, Scene 2, are:

    O! that this too too solid flesh would melt,

    Thaw, and resolve itself into a dew;

Others argue that he may have had Wernicke's aphasia, as evidenced by the following passage from Act II, Scene 2:

    Slanders, sir: for the satirical rogue says here

    that old men have grey beards, that their faces are

wrinkled, their eyes purging thick amber and

plum-tree gum and that they have a plentiful lack of

wit, together with most weak hams: all which, sir,

though I most powerfully and potently believe, yet

I hold it not honesty to have it thus set down, for you

yourself, sir, should be old as I am, if like a crab

you could go backward.

Take up the argument. Is Hamlet aphasic? Argue either case.

10. **Research projects:**
    a. Recently, it's been said that persons born with "perfect pitch" none-theless need to exercise that ability at a young age or it goes away by adulthood. Find out what you can about this topic and write a one-page (or longer) paper describing your investigation. Begin with defining "perfect pitch." Relate your discoveries to the *critical-age hypothesis* discussed in this chapter.
    b. Consider some of the high-tech methodologies used to investigate the brain discussed in this chapter, such as PET scans and MRIs. What are the upsides and downsides of the use of these technologies on healthy patients? Consider the cost, the intrusiveness, and the ethics of explor-ing a person's brain weighed against the knowledge obtained from such studies.
    c. Investigate claims that PET scans show that reading silently and read-ing aloud involve different parts of the left hemisphere.

11. **Article review project:** Read, summarize, and critically review the article that appeared in *Science*, Volume 298, November 22, 2002, by Marc D. Hauser, Noam Chomsky, and W. Tecumseh Fitch, entitled "The Faculty of Language: What Is It, Who Has It, and How Did It Evolve?"

12. As discussed in the chapter, agrammatic aphasics may have difficulty reading function words, which are words that have little descriptive con-tent, but they can read more contentful words such as nouns, verbs, and adjectives.
    a. Which of the following words would you predict to be difficult for such a person?

ore	bee	can (be able to)	but
not	knot	may	be
may	can (metal container)	butt	or
will (future)	might (possibility)	will (willingness)	might (strength)

    b. Discuss three sources of evidence that function words and content words are stored or processed differently in the brain.

13. The traditional writing system of the Chinese languages (e.g., Mandarin, Cantonese) is ideographic (each concept or word is represented by a distinct

character). More recently, the Chinese government has adopted a spelling system called *pinyin*, which is based on the Roman alphabet, and in which each symbol represents a sound. Following are several Chinese words in their character and *pinyin* forms. (The digit following the Roman letters in *pinyin* is a tone indicator and may be ignored.)

木	mu4	tree
花	hua1	flower
人	ren2	man
家	jia1	home
狗	gou3	dog

Based on the information provided in this chapter, would the location of neural activity be the same or different when Chinese speakers read in these two systems? Explain.

14. **Research project:** Dame Margaret Thatcher, a former prime minister of the United Kingdom, has been (famously) quoted as saying: "If you want something said, ask a man . . . if you want something done, ask a woman." This suggests, perhaps, that men and women process information differently. This exercise asks you to take up the controversial question: *Are there gender differences in the brain having to do with how men and women process and use language?* You might begin your research by seeking answers (try the Internet) to questions about the incidence of SLI, dyslexia, and language development differences in boys versus girls.

15. **Research project:** Discuss the concept of *emergence* and its relevance to the quoted material of footnotes 3 and 4, as opposed to footnote 5, on page 67.

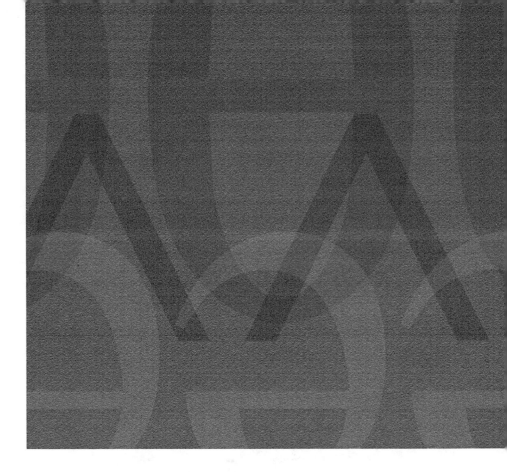

2

Grammatical Aspects of Language

The theory of grammar is concerned with the question: What is the nature of a person's knowledge of his language, the knowledge that enables him to make use of language in the normal, creative fashion? A person who knows a language has mastered a system of rules that assigns sound and meaning in a definite way for an infinite class of possible sentences.

NOAM CHOMSKY, *Language and Mind*, 1968

3

Morphology: The Words of Language

A word is dead
When it is said,
Some say.
I say it just
Begins to live
That day.

EMILY DICKINSON, "A Word Is Dead," *Complete Poems*, 1924

Reprinted by permission of the publishers and the Trustees of Amherst College from THE POEMS OF EMILY DICKINSON, Thomas H. Johnson, ed., Cambridge, Mass.: The Belknap Press of Harvard University Press, Copyright © 1951, 1955, 1979, 1983 by the President and Fellows of Harvard College.

Every speaker of every language knows tens of thousands of words. Unabridged dictionaries of English contain nearly 500,000 entries, but most speakers don't know all of these words. It has been estimated that a child of six knows as many as 13,000 words and the average high school graduate about 60,000. A college graduate presumably knows many more than that, but whatever our level of education, we learn new words throughout our lives, such as the many words in this book that you will learn for the first time.

Words are an important part of linguistic knowledge and constitute a component of our mental grammars, but one can learn thousands of words in a language and still not know the language. Anyone who has tried to communicate in a foreign country by merely using a dictionary knows this is true. On the other hand, without words we would be unable to convey our thoughts through language or understand the thoughts of others.

Someone who doesn't know English would not know where one word begins or ends in an utterance like *Thecatsatonthemat*. We separate written words by spaces, but in the spoken language there are no pauses between most words.

Without knowledge of the language, one can't tell how many words are in an utterance. Knowing a word means knowing that a particular sequence of sounds is associated with a particular meaning. A speaker of English has no difficulty in segmenting the stream of sounds into six individual words—*the*, *cat*, *sat*, *on*, *the*, and *mat*—because each of these words is listed in his or her mental dictionary, or lexicon (the Greek word for *dictionary*), that is part of a speaker's linguistic knowledge. Similarly, a speaker knows that *uncharacteristically*, which has more letters than *Thecatsatonthemat*, is nevertheless a single word.

The lack of pauses between words in speech has provided humorists with much material. The comical hosts of the show *Car Talk*, aired on National Public Radio, close the show by reading a list of credits that includes the following cast of characters:

Copyeditor:	Adeline Moore (add a line more)
Accounts payable:	Ineeda Czech (I need a check)
Pollution control:	Maury Missions (more emissions)
Purchasing:	Lois Bidder (lowest bidder)
Statistician:	Marge Innovera (margin of error)
Russian chauffeur:	Picov Andropov (pick up and drop off)
Legal firm:	Dewey, Cheetham, and Howe[1] (Do we cheat 'em? And how!)

In all these instances, you would have to have knowledge of English words to make sense of and find humor in such plays on words.

The fact that the same sound sequences (Lois Bidder—lowest bidder) can be interpreted differently shows that the relation between sound and meaning is an arbitrary pairing, as discussed in chapter 1. For example, *Un petit d'un petit* in French means "a little one of a little one," but in English the sounds resemble the name *Humpty Dumpty*.

When you know a word, you know its sound (pronunciation) and its meaning. Because the sound-meaning relation is arbitrary, it is possible to have words with the same sound and different meanings (*bear* and *bare*) and words with the same meaning and different sounds (*sofa* and *couch*).

Because each word is a sound-meaning unit, each word stored in our mental lexicon must be listed with its unique phonological representation, which determines its pronunciation, and with a meaning. For literate speakers, the spelling, or **orthography**, of most of the words we know is included.

Each word in your mental lexicon includes other information as well, such as whether it is a noun, a pronoun, a verb, an adjective, an adverb, a preposition, or a conjunction. That is, the mental lexicon also specifies the **grammatical category** or **syntactic class** of the word. You may not consciously know that a form like *love* is listed as both a verb and a noun, but as a speaker you have such knowledge, as shown by the phrases *I love you* and *You are the love of my life*. If such information were not in the mental lexicon, we would not know how to form grammatical sentences, nor would we be able to distinguish grammatical from ungrammatical sentences.

---

[1]"Car Talk"™ from National Public Radio. Dewey, Cheetham & Howe, 2006, all rights reserved.

Dictionaries

Dictionary, n. A malevolent literary device for cramping the growth of a language and making it hard and inelastic.

AMBROSE BIERCE, *The Devil's Dictionary,* 1911

The dictionaries that one buys in a bookstore contain some of the information found in our mental dictionaries. However, the aim of most early **lexicographers,** or dictionary makers, was to *prescribe* rather than *describe* the words of a language. They strove to be, as stated in *Webster's* dictionaries, the "supreme authority" of the "correct" pronunciation and meaning of a word. To Samuel Johnson, whose seminal *Dictionary of the English Language* was published in 1755, the aim of a dictionary was to "register" (describe) the language, not to "construct" (prescribe) it.

All dictionaries, from the gargantuan twenty-volume *Oxford English Dictionary* (OED) to the more commonly used "collegiate" dictionaries, provide the following information about each word: (1) spelling, (2) the "standard" pronunciation, (3) definitions to represent the word's one or more meanings, and (4) parts of speech (e.g., noun, verb, preposition). Other information may include the etymology or history of the word, whether the word is nonstandard (such as *ain't*) or slang, vulgar, or obsolete. Many dictionaries provide quotations from published literature to illustrate the given definitions, as was first done by Dr. Johnson.

Owing to the increasing specialization in science and the arts, specialty and subspecialty dictionaries are proliferating. Dictionaries of slang and jargon (see chapter 10) have existed for many years; so have multilingual dictionaries. In addition to these, the shelves of bookstores and libraries are now filled with dictionaries written specifically for biologists, engineers, agriculturists, economists, artists, architects, printers, gays and lesbians, transsexuals, runners, tennis players, and almost any group that has its own set of words to describe what they think and what they do. Our own mental dictionaries include only a small set of the entries in all of these dictionaries, but each word is in someone's lexicon.

Content Words and Function Words

"... and even ... the patriotic archbishop of Canterbury found it advisable—"
"Found what?" said the Duck.
"Found *it,*" the Mouse replied rather crossly; "of course you know what 'it' means."
"I know what 'it' means well enough, when I find a thing," said the Duck; "it's generally a frog or a worm. The question is, what did the archbishop find?"

LEWIS CARROLL, *Alice's Adventures in Wonderland,* 1865

Languages make an important distinction between two kinds of words—content words and function words. Nouns, verbs, adjectives, and adverbs are the

content words. These words denote concepts such as objects, actions, attributes, and ideas that we can think about like *children, anarchism, soar,* and *purple*. Content words are sometimes called the **open class** words because we can and regularly do add new words to these classes, such as *Bollywood, blog, dis,* and *24/7,* pronounced "twenty-four seven."

Other classes of words do not have clear lexical meanings or obvious concepts associated with them, including conjunctions such as *and, or,* and *but*; prepositions such as *in* and *of*; the articles *the* and *a/an*, and pronouns such as *it*. These kinds of words are called **function words** because they specify grammatical relations and have little or no semantic content. For example, the articles indicate whether a noun is definite or indefinite—*the* boy or *a* boy. The preposition *of* indicates possession, as in "the book of yours," but this word indicates many other kinds of relations too. The *it* in *it's raining* and *the archbishop found it advisable* are further examples of words whose function is purely grammatical—they are required by the rules of syntax, and as the cartoon suggests, we can hardly do without them.

"FoxTrot" copyright © 2000 Bill Amend. Reprinted with permission of Universal Press Syndicate. All rights reserved.

Function words are sometimes called **closed class** words. It is difficult to think of any conjunctions, prepositions, or pronouns that have recently entered the language. The small set of personal pronouns such as *I, me, mine, he, she,* and so on are part of this class. With the growth of the feminist movement, some proposals have been made for adding a genderless singular pronoun. If such a pronoun existed, it might have prevented the department head in a large university from making the incongruous statement: "We will hire the best person for the job regardless of his sex." Various proposals such as "e" have been put forward, but none are likely to gain acceptance because the closed classes are unreceptive to new membership. Rather, speakers prefer to recruit existing pronouns such as *they* and *their* for this job, as in "We will hire the best person for the job regardless of **their** sex."

The difference between content and function words is illustrated by the following test that has circulated over the Internet:

Count the number of F's in the following text without reading further:

FINISHED FILES ARE THE
RESULT OF YEARS OF SCIENTIFIC
STUDY COMBINED WITH THE
EXPERIENCE OF YEARS.

Most people come up with three, which is wrong. If you came up with fewer than six, count again, and this time, pay attention to the function word *of*.

This little test illustrates that the brain treats content and function words (like *of*) differently. A great deal of psychological and neurological evidence supports this claim. As discussed in chapter 2, some brain-damaged patients and people with specific language impairments have greater difficulty in using, understanding, or reading function words than they do with content words. Some aphasics are unable to read function words like *in* or *which*, but can read the lexical content words *inn* and *witch*.

The two classes of words also seem to function differently in **slips of the tongue** produced by normal individuals. For example, a speaker may inadvertently switch words producing "the journal of the editor" instead of "the editor of the journal," but the switching or exchanging of function words has not been observed. There is also evidence for this distinction from language acquisition (discussed in chapter 8). In the early stages of development, children often omit function words from their speech, as in for example, "doggie barking."

The linguistic evidence suggests that content words and function words play different roles in language. Content words bear the brunt of the meaning, whereas function words connect the content words to the larger grammatical context.

Morphemes: The Minimal Units of Meaning

"They gave it me," Humpty Dumpty continued, "for an un-birthday present."
"I beg your pardon?" Alice said with a puzzled air.
"I'm not offended," said Humpty Dumpty.
"I mean, what is an un-birthday present?"
"A present given when it isn't your birthday, of course."

LEWIS CARROLL, *Through the Looking-Glass,* 1871

In the foregoing dialogue, Humpty Dumpty is well aware that the prefix *un-* means "not," as further shown in the following pairs of words:

A	B
desirable	undesirable
likely	unlikely
inspired	uninspired
happy	unhappy
developed	undeveloped
sophisticated	unsophisticated

Thousands of English adjectives begin with *un-*. If we assume that the most basic unit of meaning is the word, what do we say about parts of words like *un-*, which has a fixed meaning? In all the words in the B column, *un-* means the same thing—"not." *Undesirable* means "not desirable," *unlikely* means "not likely," and so on. All the words in column B consist of at least two meaningful units: *un + desirable*, *un + likely*, *un + inspired*, and so on.

Just as *un-* occurs with the same meaning in the previous list of words, so does *phon-* in the following words. (You may not know the meaning of some of them, but you will when you finish this book.)

phone	phonology	phoneme
phonetic	phonologist	phonemic
phonetics	phonological	allophone
phonetician	telephone	euphonious
phonic	telephonic	symphony

Phon- is a minimal form in that it can't be decomposed. *Ph* doesn't mean anything; *pho*, though it may be pronounced like *foe*, has no relation in meaning to it; and *on* is not the preposition spelled *o-n*. In all the words on the list, *phon* has the identical meaning of "pertaining to sound."

Words have internal structure, which is rule-governed. *Uneaten*, *unadmired*, and *ungrammatical* are words in English, but **eatenun*, **admiredun*, and **grammaticalun* (to mean "not eaten," "not admired," "not grammatical") are not, because we form a negative meaning of a word not by suffixing *un-* but by prefixing it.

When Samuel Goldwyn, the pioneer moviemaker, announced, "In two words: im-possible," he was reflecting the common view that words are the basic meaningful elements of a language. We have seen that this cannot be so, because some words contain several distinct units of meaning. The linguistic term for the most elemental unit of grammatical form is **morpheme**. The word is derived from the Greek word *morphe*, meaning "form." If Goldwyn had taken a linguistics course, he would have said, more correctly, "In two morphemes: im-possible."

The study of the internal structure of words, and of the rules by which words are formed, is **morphology**. This word itself consists of two morphemes, *morph + ology*. The suffix *-ology* means "science of" or "branch of knowledge concerning." Thus, the meaning of *morphology* is "the science of (word) forms."

Morphology is part of our grammatical knowledge of a language. Like most linguistic knowledge, this is generally unconscious knowledge.

A single word may be composed of one or more morphemes:

one morpheme	boy
	desire
	morph ("to change form")
two morphemes	boy + ish
	desire + able
	morph + ology
three morphemes	boy + ish + ness
	desire + able + ity

four morphemes	gentle + man + li + ness
	un + desire + able + ity
more than four	un + gentle + man + li + ness
	anti + dis + establish + ment + ari + an + ism

A morpheme may be represented by a single sound, such as the morpheme *a* meaning "without" as in *amoral* and *asexual*, or by a single syllable, such as *child* and *ish* in *child* + *ish*. A morpheme may also consist of more than one syllable: by two syllables, as in *camel*, *lady*, and *water*; by three syllables, as in *Hackensack* and *crocodile*; or by four or more syllables, as in *hallucinate*, *apothecary*, and *onomatopoeia*.

A morpheme—the minimal linguistic unit—is thus an arbitrary union of a sound and a meaning (or grammatical function) that cannot be further analyzed. It is often called a **linguistic sign**, not to be confused with the *sign* of sign languages. This may be too simple a definition, but it will serve our purposes for now. Every word in every language is composed of one or more morphemes.

Internet bloggers love to point out "inconsistencies" in the English language. They observe that while singers sing and flingers fling, it is not the case that fingers "fing." However, English speakers know that *finger* is a single morpheme, or a **monomorphemic word**. The final -*er* syllable in *finger* is not a separate morpheme because a finger is not "something that fings."

The meaning of a morpheme must be constant. The agentive morpheme -*er* means "one who does" in words like *singer*, *painter*, *lover*, and *worker*, but the same sounds represent the comparative morpheme, meaning "more," in *nicer*, *prettier*, and *taller*. Thus, two different morphemes may be pronounced identically. The identical form represents two morphemes because of the different meanings. The same sounds may occur in another word and not represent a separate morpheme at all, as in *finger*. Conversely, the two morphemes -*er* and -*ster* have the same meaning, but different forms. Both *singer* and *songster* mean "one who sings." And like -*er*, -*ster* is not a morpheme in *monster* because a monster is not something that "mons" or someone that "is mon" the way *youngster* is someone who is young. All of this follows from the concept of the morpheme as a *sound* plus a *meaning* unit.

The decomposition of words into morphemes illustrates one of the fundamental properties of human language—**discreteness**. In all languages, sound units combine to form morphemes, morphemes combine to form words, and words combine to form larger units—phrases and sentences.

Discreteness is an important part of linguistic creativity. We can combine morphemes in novel ways to create new words whose meaning will be apparent to other speakers of the language. If you know that "to write" to a disk or a DVD means to put information on it, you automatically understand that a *writable* DVD is one that can take information; a *rewritable* DVD is one where the original information can be written over; and an *unrewritable* DVD is one that does not allow the user to write over the original information. You know the meanings of all these words by virtue of your knowledge of the discrete morphemes *write*, *re-*, *-able*, and *un-*, and the rules for their combination.

Bound and Free Morphemes

Prefixes and Suffixes

"LOOKS LIKE WE SPEND MOST OF OUR TIME INGING...
YOU KNOW, LIKE SLEEPING, EATING, RUNNING, CLIMBING..."

"Dennis the Menace" © Hank Ketcham. Reprinted with permission of
North America Syndicate.

Our morphological knowledge has two components: knowledge of the individual
morphemes and knowledge of the rules that combine them. One of the things we
know about particular morphemes is whether they can stand alone or whether
they must be attached to a base morpheme.

Some morphemes like *boy*, *desire*, *gentle*, and *man* may constitute words
by themselves. These are **free morphemes**. Other morphemes like *-ish*, *-ness*,
-ly, *pre-*, *trans-*, and *un-* are never words by themselves but are always parts
of words. These **affixes** are **bound morphemes**. We know whether each affix
precedes or follows other morphemes. Thus, *un-*, *pre-* (*premeditate*, *prejudge*),
and *bi-* (*bipolar*, *bisexual*) are **prefixes**. They occur before other morphemes.
Some morphemes occur only as **suffixes**, following other morphemes. English
examples of suffix morphemes are *-ing* (*sleeping*, *eating*, *running*, *climbing*),

-er (*singer, performer, reader*), *-ist* (*typist, pianist, novelist, linguist*), and *-ly* (*manly, sickly, friendly*), to mention only a few.

Many languages have prefixes and suffixes, but languages may differ in how they deploy these morphemes. A morpheme that is a prefix in one language may be a suffix in another and vice versa. In English the plural morphemes *-s* and *-es* are suffixes (*boys, lasses*). In Isthmus Zapotec, spoken in Mexico, the plural morpheme *ka-* is a prefix:

zigi	"chin"	kazigi	"chins"
zike	"shoulder"	kazike	"shoulders"
diaga	"ear"	kadiaga	"ears"

Languages may also differ in what meanings they express through affixation. In English we do not add an affix to derive a noun from a verb. We have the verb *dance* as in "I like to dance," and we have the noun *dance* as in "There's a dance or two in the old dame yet." The form is the same in both cases. In Turkish, you derive a noun from a verb with the suffix *-ak*, as in the following examples:

dur	"to stop"	durak	"stopping place"
bat	"to sink"	batak	"sinking place" or "marsh/swamp"

To express reciprocal action in English we use the phrase *each other*, as in *understand each other, love each other*. In Turkish a morpheme is added to the verb:

anla	"understand"	anlash	"understand each other"
sev	"love"	sevish	"love each other"

The reciprocal suffix in these examples is pronounced *sh* after a vowel and *ish* after a consonant. This is similar to the process in English, in which we use *a* as the indefinite article morpheme before a noun beginning with a consonant, as in *a dog*, and *an* before a noun beginning with a vowel, as in *an apple*. The same morpheme may have more than one slightly different form (see exercise 6, for example). We will discuss the various pronunciations of morphemes in more detail in chapter 7.

In Piro, an Arawakan language spoken in Peru, a single morpheme, *-kaka*, can be added to a verb to express the meaning "cause to":

cokoruha	"to harpoon"	cokoruhakaka	"cause to harpoon"
salwa	"to visit"	salwakaka	"cause to visit"

In Karuk, a Native American language spoken in the Pacific Northwest, adding *-ak* to a noun forms the locative adverbial meaning "in."

ikrivaam	"house"	ikrivaamak	"in a house"

It is accidental that both Turkish and Karuk have a suffix *-ak*. Despite the similarity in *form*, the two meanings are different. Similarly, the reciprocal suffix *-ish* in Turkish is similar in form to the English suffix *-ish* as in *greenish*.

Similarity in meaning may give rise to different forms. In Karuk the suffix *-ara* has the same meaning as the English *-y*, that is, "characterized by" (*hairy* means "characterized by hair").

aptiik   "branch"   aptikara   "branchy"

These examples illustrate again the arbitrary nature of the linguistic sign, that is, of the sound-meaning relationship, as well as the distinction between bound and free morphemes.

Infixes

Some languages also have **infixes**, morphemes that are inserted into other morphemes. Bontoc, spoken in the Philippines, is such a language, as illustrated by the following:

Nouns/Adjectives		Verbs	
fikas	"strong"	fumikas	"to be strong"
kilad	"red"	kumilad	"to be red"
fusul	"enemy"	fumusul	"to be an enemy"

In this language, the infix *-um-* is inserted after the first consonant of the noun or adjective. Thus, a speaker of Bontoc who knows that *pusi* means "poor" would understand the meaning of *pumusi*, "to be poor," on hearing the word for the first time, just as an English speaker who learns the verb *sneet* would know that *sneeter* is "one who sneets." A Bontoc speaker who knows that *ngumitad* means "to be dark" would know that the adjective "dark" must be *ngitad*.

Oddly enough, the only infixes in English are full-word obscenities, usually inserted into adjectives or adverbs. The most common infix in America is the word *fuckin'* and all the euphemisms for it, such as *friggin, freakin, flippin,* and *fuggin*, as in *in-fuggin-credible, un-fuckin-believable,* or *Kalama-flippin-zoo*, based on the city in Michigan. In Britain, a common infix is *bloody*, an obscene term in British English, and its euphemisms, such as *bloomin'*. In the movie and stage musical *My Fair Lady*, the word *abso + bloomin + lutely* occurs in one of the songs sung by Eliza Doolittle.

Circumfixes

Some languages have **circumfixes**, morphemes that are attached to a base morpheme both initially and finally. These are sometimes called **discontinuous morphemes**. In Chickasaw, a Muskogean language spoken in Oklahoma, the negative is formed with both a prefix *ik-* and the suffix *-o*. The final vowel of the affirmative is dropped before the negative suffix is added. Examples of this circumfixing are:

Affirmative		Negative	
chokma	"he is good"	ik + chokm + o	"he isn't good"
lakna	"it is yellow"	ik + lakn + o	"it isn't yellow"
palli	"it is hot"	ik + pall + o	"it isn't hot"
tiwwi	"he opens (it)"	ik + tiww + o	"he doesn't open (it)"

An example of a more familiar circumfixing language is German. The past participle of regular verbs is formed by adding the prefix *ge-* and the suffix *-t* to the verb root. This circumfix added to the verb root *lieb* "love" produces *geliebt*, "loved" (or "beloved," when used as an adjective).

Roots and Stems

Morphologically complex words consist of a morpheme **root** and one or more affixes. Some examples of English roots are *paint* in *painter*, *read* in *reread*, *ceive* in *conceive*, and *ling* in *linguist*. A root may or may not stand alone as a word (*paint* and *read* do; *ceive* and *ling* don't). In languages that have circumfixes, the root is the form around which the circumfix attaches, for example, the Chickasaw root *chokm* in *ikchokmo* ("he isn't good"). In infixing languages the root is the form into which the infix is inserted; for example, *fikas* in the Bontoc word *fumikas* ("to be strong").

Semitic languages like Hebrew and Arabic have a unique morphological system. Nouns and verbs are built on a foundation of three consonants, and one derives related words by varying the pattern of vowels and syllables. For example, the root for "write" in Egyptian Arabic is *ktb*, from which the following words (among others) are formed by infixing vowels:

katab	"he wrote"
kaatib	"writer"
kitáab	"book"
kútub	"books"

When a root morpheme is combined with an affix, it forms a **stem**. Other affixes can be added to a stem to form a more complex stem, as shown in the following:

root	Chomsky	(proper) noun
stem	Chomsky + ite	noun + suffix
word	Chomsky + ite + s	noun + suffix + suffix
root	believe	verb
stem	believe + able	verb + suffix
word	un + believe + able	prefix + verb + suffix
root	system	noun
stem	system + atic	noun + suffix
stem	un + system + atic	prefix + noun + suffix
stem	un + system + atic + al	prefix + noun + suffix + suffix
word	un + system + atic + al + ly	prefix + noun + suffix + suffix + suffix

With the addition of each new affix, a new stem and a new word are formed. Linguists sometimes use the word **base** to mean any root or stem to which an affix is attached. In the preceding example, *system, systematic, unsystematic,* and *unsystematical* are bases.

Bound Roots

> It had been a rough day, so when I walked into the party I was very chalant, despite my efforts to appear gruntled and consolate. I was furling my wieldy umbrella . . . when I saw her. . . . She was a descript person. . . . Her hair was kempt, her clothing shevelled, and she moved in a gainly way.
>
> **JACK WINTER,** "How I Met My Wife," *New Yorker*, July 25, 1994
>
> "How I Met My Wife" by Jack Winter from The New Yorker, July 25, 1994. Reprinted by permission of the Estate of Jack Winter.

Bound roots do not occur in isolation and they acquire meaning only in combination with other morphemes. For example, words of Latin origin such as *receive, conceive, perceive,* and *deceive* share a common root, *ceive;* and the words *remit, permit, commit, submit, transmit,* and *admit* share the root *mit.* For the original Latin speakers, the morphemes corresponding to *ceive* and *mit* had clear meanings, but for modern English speakers, Latinate morphemes such as *ceive* and *mit* have no independent meaning. Their meaning depends on the entire word in which they occur.

A similar class of words is composed of a prefix affixed to a bound root morpheme. Examples are *ungainly,* but no **gainly; discern,* but no **cern; nonplussed,* but no **plussed; downhearted* but no **hearted,* and others to be seen in this section's epigraph.

The morpheme *huckle,* when joined with *berry,* has the meaning of a berry that is small, round, and purplish blue; *luke* when combined with *warm* has the meaning "somewhat." Both these morphemes and others like them (*cran, boysen*) are bound morphemes that convey meaning only in combination.

Rules of Word Formation

> "I never heard of 'Uglification,'" Alice ventured to say. "What is it?" The Gryphon lifted up both its paws in surprise. "Never heard of uglifying!" it exclaimed. "You know what to beautify is, I suppose?" "Yes," said Alice doubtfully: "it means—to make—prettier." "Well, then," the Gryphon went on, "if you don't know what to uglify is, you are a simpleton."
>
> **LEWIS CARROLL,** *Alice's Adventures in Wonderland,* 1865

When the Mock Turtle listed the branches of Arithmetic for Alice as "Ambition, Distraction, Uglification, and Derision," Alice was very confused. She wasn't really a simpleton, since *uglification* was not a common word in English until Lewis Carroll used it. Still, most English speakers would immediately know the meaning of *uglification* even if they had never heard or used the word before because they would know the meaning of its individual parts—the root *ugly* and the affixes *-ify* and *-cation.*

We said earlier that knowledge of morphology includes knowledge of individual morphemes, their pronunciation, and their meaning, and knowledge of the rules for combining morphemes into complex words. The Mock Turtle added

-ify to the adjective *ugly* and formed a verb. Many verbs in English have been formed in this way: *purify, amplify, simplify, falsify.* The suffix *-ify* conjoined with nouns also forms verbs: *objectify, glorify, personify.* Notice that the Mock Turtle went even further; he added the suffix *-cation* to *uglify* and formed a noun, *uglification,* as in *glorification, simplification, falsification,* and *purification.* By using the **morphological rules** of English, he created a new word. The rules that he used are as follows:

Adjective + ify → Verb   "to make Adjective"
Verb + cation → Noun   "the process of making Adjective"

Derivational Morphology

Bound morphemes like *-ify* and *-cation* are called **derivational morphemes.** When they are added to a base, a new word with a new meaning is derived. The addition of *-ify* to *pure—purify*—means "to make pure," and the addition of *-cation—purification*—means "the process of making pure." If we invent an adjective, *pouzy,* to describe the effect of static electricity on hair, you will immediately understand the sentences "Walking on that carpet really pouzified my hair" and "The best method of pouzification is to rub a balloon on your head." This means that we must have a list of the derivational morphemes in our mental dictionaries as well as the rules that determine how they are added to a root or stem. The form that results from the addition of a derivational morpheme is called a **derived word.**

Derivational morphemes have clear semantic content. In this sense they are like content words, except that they are not words. As we have seen, when a derivational morpheme is added to a base, it adds meaning. The derived word may also be of a different grammatical class than the original word, as shown by suffixes such as *-able* and *-ly.* When a verb is suffixed with *-able,* the result is an adjective, as in *desire + able.* When the suffix *-en* is added to an adjective, a verb is derived, as in *dark + en.* One may form a noun from an adjective, as in *sweet + ie.* Other examples are:

Noun to Adjective	Verb to Noun	Adjective to Adverb
boy + -ish	acquitt + -al	exact + -ly
virtu + -ous	clear + -ance	
Elizabeth + -an	accus + -ation	
pictur + -esque	sing + -er	
affection + -ate	conform + -ist	
health + -ful	predict + -ion	
alcohol + -ic		

Noun to Verb	Adjective to Noun	Verb to Adjective
moral + -ize	tall + -ness	read + -able
vaccin + -ate	specific + -ity	creat + -ive
hast + -en	feudal + -ism	migrat + -ory
	free + -dom	run(n) + -y

Some derivational suffixes do not cause a change in grammatical class. Prefixes never do.

Noun to Noun	Verb to Verb	Adjective to Adjective
friend + -ship	un- + do	pink + -ish
human + -ity	re- + cover	red + -like
king + -dom	dis- + believe	a- + moral
New Jersey + -ite	auto- + destruct	il- + legal
vicar + -age		in- + accurate
Paul + -ine		un- + happy
America + -n		semi- + annual
humanit + -arian		dis- + agreeable
mono- + theism		sub- + minimal
dis- + advantage		
ex- + wife		
auto- + biography		

When a new word enters the lexicon by the application of morphological rules, other complex derivations may be **blocked**. For example, when *Commun + ist* entered the language, words such as *Commun + ite* (as in *Trotsky + ite*) or *Commun + ian* (as in *grammar + ian*) were not needed; their formation was blocked. Sometimes, however, alternative forms do coexist: for example, *Chomskyan* and *Chomskyist* and perhaps even *Chomskyite* (all meaning "follower of Chomsky's views of linguistics"). *Semanticist* and *semantician* are both used, but the possible word *semantite* is not.

Finally, derivational affixes appear to come in two classes. In one class, the addition of a suffix triggers subtle changes in pronunciation. For example, when we affix *-ity* to *specific* (pronounced "specifik" with a *k* sound), we get specificity (pronounced "specifisity" with an *s* sound). When deriving *Elizabeth + an* from *Elizabeth*, the fourth vowel sound changes from the vowel in *Beth* to the vowel in *Pete*. Other suffixes such as *-y*, *-ive*, and *-ize* may induce similar changes: *sane/sanity, deduce/deductive, critic/criticize*.

On the other hand, suffixes such as -er, -ful, -ish, -less, -ly, and -ness may be tacked onto a base word without affecting the pronunciation, as in baker, wishful, boyish, needless, sanely, and fullness. Moreover, affixes from the first class cannot be attached to a base containing an affix from the second class: *need + less + ity, *moral + ize + ive; but affixes from the second class may attach to bases with either kind of affix: moral + iz(e) + er, need + less + ness.

Inflectional Morphology

"Zits" © Zits Partnership. Reprinted with permission of King Features Syndicate.

Function words like to, it, and be are free morphemes. Many languages, including English, also have bound morphemes that have a strictly grammatical function. They mark properties such as tense, number, person and so forth. Such bound morphemes are called **inflectional morphemes**. Unlike derivational morphemes, they never change the grammatical category of the stems to which they are attached. Consider the forms of the verb in the following sentences:

1. I sail the ocean blue.
2. He sails the ocean blue.
3. John sailed the ocean blue.
4. John has sailed the ocean blue.
5. John is sailing the ocean blue.

In sentence (2) the -s at the end of the verb is an agreement marker; it signifies that the subject of the verb is third person and is singular, and that the verb is in the present tense. It doesn't add lexical meaning. The suffix -ed indicates past tense, and is also required by the syntactic rules of the language when verbs are used with have, just as -ing is required when verbs are used with forms of be.

Inflectional morphemes represent relationships between different parts of a sentence. For example, -s expresses the relationship between the verb and the third person singular subject; -ing expresses the relationship between the time the utterance is spoken (e.g., now) and the time of the event. If you say "John is dancing," it means John is engaged in this activity while you speak. If you say "John danced," the -ed affix places the activity before you spoke. As we will discuss in chapter 4, inflectional morphology is closely connected to the syntax of the sentence.

English also has other inflectional endings such as the plural suffix, which is attached to certain singular nouns, as in *boy/boys* and *cat/cats*. In contrast to Old and Middle English, which were more richly inflected languages, as we discuss in chapter 11, modern English has only eight bound inflectional affixes:

English Inflectional Morphemes		Examples
-s	third-person singular present	She wait-**s** at home.
-ed	past tense	She wait-**ed** at home.
-ing	progressive	She is eat-**ing** the donut.
-en	past participle	Mary has eat-**en** the donuts.
-s	plural	She ate the donut-**s**.
-'s	possessive	Disa**'s** hair is short.
-er	comparative	Disa has short-**er** hair than Karin.
-est	superlative	Disa has the short-**est** hair.

Inflectional morphemes in English follow the derivational morphemes in a word. Thus, to the derivationally complex word *commit* + *ment* one can add a plural ending to form *commit* + *ment* + *s*, but the order of affixes may not be reversed to derive the impossible *commit* + *s* + *ment* = **commitsment*.

Yet another distinction between inflectional and derivational morphemes is that inflectional morphemes are **productive**: they apply freely to nearly every appropriate base (excepting "irregular" forms such as *feet*, not **foots*). Most nouns takes an *-s* inflectional suffix to form a plural, but only some nouns take the derivational suffix *-ize* to form a verb: *idolize*, but not **picturize*.

Compared to many languages of the world, English has relatively little inflectional morphology. Some languages are highly inflected. In Swahili, which is widely spoken in eastern Africa, verbs can be inflected with multiple morphemes, as in *nimepiga* (ni + me + pig + a), meaning "he has hit something." Here the verb root *pig* meaning "hit" has two inflectional prefixes: *ni* meaning "I," and *me* meaning "completed action," and an inflectional suffix *a*, which is an object agreement morpheme.

Even the more familiar European languages have many more inflectional endings than English. In the Romance languages (languages descended from Latin), the verb has different inflectional endings depending on the subject of the sentence. The verb is inflected to agree in person and number with the subject, as illustrated by the Italian verb *parlare* meaning "to speak":

Io parlo	"I speak"	Noi parl**iamo**	"We speak"
Tu parl**i**	"You (singular) speak"	Voi parl**ate**	"You (plural) speak"
Lui/Lei parl**a**	"He/she speaks"	Loro parl**ano**	"They speak"

Russian has a system of inflectional suffixes for nouns that indicates the noun's grammatical relation—whether a subject, object, possessor, and so on—something English does with word order. For example, in English, the sentence *Maxim defends Victor* means something different from *Victor defends Maxim*. The order of the words is critical. But in Russian, all of the following sentences mean "Maxim defends Victor" (the *č* is pronounced like the *ch* in cheese; the *š* like the *sh* in shoe; the *j* like the *y* in yet):

Maksim zašiščajet Viktora.
Maksim Viktora zašiščajet.
Viktora Maksim zašiščajet.
Viktora zašiščajet Maksim.[2]

The inflectional suffix *-a* added to the name *Viktor* to derive *Viktora* shows that Victor, not Maxim, is defended. The suffix designates the object of the verb, irrespective of word order.

The grammatical relation of a noun in a sentence is called the **case** of the noun. When case is marked by inflectional morphemes, the process is referred to as **case morphology**. Russian has a rich case morphology, whereas English case morphology is limited to the one possessive *-s* and to its system of pronouns. Many of the grammatical relations that Russian expresses with its case morphology are expressed in English with prepositions.

Among the world's languages is a richness and variety of inflectional processes. Earlier we saw how German uses circumfixes to inflect a verb stem to produce a past particle: *lieb* to **geliebt**, similar to the *-ed* ending of English. Arabic infixes vowels for inflectional purposes: *kitáab* "book" but *kútub* "books." Samoan (see exercise 10) uses a process of **reduplication**—inflecting a word through the repetition of part or all of the word: *savali* "he travels," but *savavali* "they travel." Malay does the same with whole words: *orang* "person," but *orang orang* "people." Languages such as Finnish have an extraordinarily complex case morphology, whereas Mandarin Chinese lacks case morphology entirely.

Inflection achieves a variety of purposes. In English verbs are inflected with *-s* to show third person singular agreement. Languages like Finnish and Japanese have a dazzling array of inflectional processes for conveying everything from "temporary state of being" (Finnish nouns) to "strong negative intention" (Japanese verbs). English spoken 1,000 years ago had considerably more inflectional morphology than modern English, as we shall discuss in chapter 11.

In distinguishing inflectional from derivation morphemes we may summarize as follows:

Inflectional	Derivational
Grammatical function	Lexical function
No word class change	May cause word class change
Small or no meaning change	Some meaning change
Often required by rules of grammar	Never required by rules of grammar
Follow derivational morphemes in a word	Precede inflectional morphemes in a word
Productive	Some productive, many nonproductive

Figure 3.1 sums up our knowledge of how morphemes in English are classified.

---

[2]These Russian examples were provided by Stella de Bode.

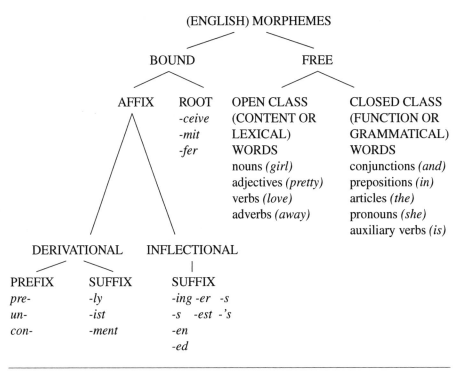

FIGURE 3.1 | Classification of English morphemes.

The Hierarchical Structure of Words

We saw earlier that morphemes are added in a fixed order. This order reflects the **hierarchical structure** of the word. A word is not a simple sequence of morphemes. It has an internal structure. For example, the word *unsystematic* is composed of three morphemes: *un-*, *system*, and *-atic*. The root is *system*, a noun, to which we add the suffix *-atic*, resulting in an adjective, *systematic*. To this adjective, we add the prefix *un-* forming a new adjective, *unsystematic*.

In order to represent the hierarchical organization of words (and sentences), linguists use **tree diagrams**. The tree diagram for *unsystematic* is as follows:

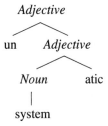

This tree represents the application of two morphological rules:

1. Noun + atic   →   Adjective
2. un + Adjective   →   Adjective

Rule 1 attaches the derivational suffix *-atic* to the root noun, forming an adjective. Rule 2 takes the adjective formed by rule 1 and attaches the derivational prefix *un-*. The diagram shows that the entire word—*unsystematic*—is an adjective that is composed of an adjective—*systematic*—plus *un*. The adjective is itself composed of a noun—*system*—plus the suffix *-atic*.

Hierarchical structure is an essential property of human language. Words (and sentences) have component parts, which relate to each other in specific, rule-governed ways. Although at first glance it may seem that, aside from order, the morphemes *un-* and *-atic* each relate to the root *system* in the same way, this is not the case. The root *system* is "closer" to *-atic* than it is to *un-*, and *un-* is actually connected to the adjective *systematic*, and not directly to *system*. Indeed, **unsystem* is not a word.

Further morphological rules can be applied to the given structure. For example, English has a derivational suffix *-al*, as in *egotistical, fantastical,* and *astronomical*. In these cases, *-al* is added to an adjective—*egotistic, fantastic, astronomic*—to form a new adjective. The rule for *-al* is as follows:

3. Adjective + al → Adjective

Another affix is *-ly*, which is added to adjectives—*happy, lazy, hopeful*—to form adverbs *happily, lazily, hopefully*. Following is the rule for *-ly*:

4. Adjective + ly → Adverb

Applying these two rules to the derived form *unsystematic*, we get the following tree for *unsystematically*:

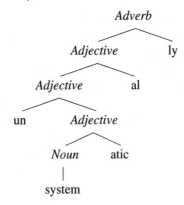

This is a rather complex word. Despite its complexity, it is well-formed because it follows the morphological rules of the language. On the other hand, a very simple word can be ungrammatical. Suppose in the above example we first added *un-* to the root *system*. That would have resulted in the nonword **unsystem*.

Unsystem is not a possible word because there is no rule of English that allows *un-* to be added to nouns. The large soft-drink company whose ad campaign promoted the *Uncola* successfully flouted this linguistic rule to capture people's attention. Part of our linguistic competence includes the ability to recognize possible versus impossible words, like **unsystem* and **Uncola*. Possible words are those that conform to the rules; impossible words are those that do not.

Tree diagrams make explicit the way speakers represent the internal structure of the morphologically complex words in their language. In speaking and writing, we appear to string morphemes together sequentially as in *un + system + atic*. However, our mental representation of words is hierarchical as well as linear, and this is shown by tree diagrams.

Inflectional morphemes are equally well represented. The following tree shows that the inflectional agreement morpheme *-s* follows the derivational morphemes *-ize* and *re-* in *refinalizes*:

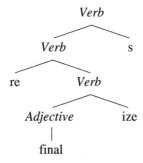

The tree also shows that *re* applies to *finalize*, which is correct as **refinal* is not a word, and that the inflectional morpheme follows the derivational morpheme.

The hierarchical organization of words is even more clearly shown by structurally ambiguous words, words that have more than one meaning by virtue of having more than one structure. Consider the word *unlockable*. Imagine you are inside a room and you want some privacy. You would be unhappy to find the door is *unlockable*—"not able to be locked." Now imagine you are inside a locked room trying to get out. You would be very relieved to find that the door is *unlockable*—"able to be unlocked." These two meanings correspond to two different structures, as follows:

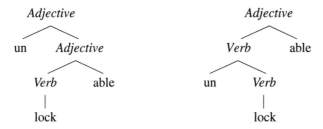

In the first structure the verb *lock* combines with the suffix *-able* to form an adjective *lockable* ("able to be locked"). Then the prefix *un-*, meaning "not,"

combines with the derived adjective to form a new adjective *unlockable* ("not able to be locked"). In the second case, the prefix *un-* combines with the verb *lock* to form a derived verb *unlock*. Then the derived verb combines with the suffix *-able* to form *unlockable*, "able to be unlocked."

An entire class of words in English follows this pattern: *unbuttonable*, *unzippable*, and *unlatchable*, among others. The ambiguity arises because the prefix *un-* can combine with an adjective, as illustrated in rule 2, or it can combine with a verb, as in *undo*, *unstaple*, *unearth*, and *unloosen*.

If words were only strings of morphemes without any internal organization, we could not explain the ambiguity of words like *unlockable*. These words also illustrate another important point, which is that structure is important to determining meaning. The same three morphemes occur in both versions of *unlockable*, yet there are two distinct meanings. The different meanings arise because of the different structures.

Rule Productivity

"Peanuts" copyright © United Feature Syndicate. Reprinted by permission.

We have noted that some morphological processes, inflection in particular, are productive, meaning that they can be used freely to form new words from the list of free and bound morphemes. Among derivational morphemes, the suffix *-able* can be conjoined with any verb to derive an adjective with the meaning of the verb and the meaning of *-able*, which is something like "able to be" as in *accept + able*, *laugh + able*, *pass + able*, *change + able*, *breathe + able*, *adapt + able*, and so on. The productivity of this rule is illustrated by the fact that we find *-able* affixed to new verbs such as *downloadable* and *faxable*.

The prefix *un-* derives same-class words with an opposite meaning: *unafraid*, *unfit*, *un-American*, and so on. Additionally, *un-* can be added to derived adjectives that have been formed by morphological rules, resulting in perfectly acceptable words such as *un + believe + able* or *un + pick + up + able*.

Yet *un-* is not fully productive. We find *happy* and *unhappy, cowardly* and *uncowardly*, but not *sad* and **unsad, brave* and **unbrave*, or *obvious* and **unobvious*. It appears that the "un-Rule" is most productive for adjectives that are derived from verbs, such as *unenlightened, unsimplified, uncharacterized, unauthorized, undistinguished*, and so on. It also appears that most acceptable *un-* words have polysyllabic bases, and while we have *unfit, uncool, unread*, and *unclean*, many of the unacceptable *-un* forms have monosyllabic stems such as **unbig, *ungreat, *unred, *unsad, *unsmall, *untall*.

The rule that adds an *-er* to verbs in English to produce a noun meaning "one who does" is a nearly productive morphological rule, giving us *examiner, examtaker, analyzer, lover, hunter*, and so forth, but fails full productivity owing to "unwords" like **chairer*, which is not "one who chairs." Other derivational morphemes fall farther short of productivity. Consider:

sincerity	from	*sincere*
warmth	from	*warm*
moisten	from	*moist*

The suffix *-ity* is found in many other words in English, like *chastity, scarcity*, and *curiosity*; and *-th* occurs in *health, wealth, depth, width*, and *growth*. We find *-en* in *sadden, ripen, redden, weaken*, and *deepen*. Still, the phrase "*The tragicity of Hamlet" sounds somewhat strange, as does "*I'm going to *heaten* the sauce." Someone may say *coolth*, but when "words" like *tragicity, heaten*, and *coolth* are used, it is usually either a slip of the tongue or an attempt at humor. Most adjectives will not accept any of these derivational suffixes. Even less productive to the point of rareness are such derivational morphemes as the diminutive suffixes in the words *pig + let* and *sap + ling*.

In the morphologically complex words that we have seen so far, we can generally predict the meaning based on the meaning of the morphemes that make up the word. *Unhappy* means "not happy" and *acceptable* means "fit to be accepted." However, one cannot always know the meaning of the words derived from free and derivational morphemes by knowing the morphemes themselves. The following *un-* forms have unpredictable meanings:

unloosen	"loosen, let loose"
unrip	"rip, undo by ripping"
undo	"reverse doing"
untread	"go back through in the same steps"
unearth	"dig up"
unfrock	"deprive (a cleric) of ecclesiastic rank"
unnerve	"fluster"

Morphologically complex words whose meanings are not predictable must be listed individually in our mental lexicons. However, the morphological rules must also be in the grammar, revealing the relation between words and providing the means for forming new words.

Exceptions and Suppletions

"Peanuts" copyright © United Feature Syndicate. Reprinted by permission.

The morphological process that forms plural from singular nouns does not apply to words like *child*, *man*, *foot*, and *mouse*. These words are exceptions to the English inflectional rule of plural formation. Similarly, verbs like *go*, *sing*, *bring*, *run*, and *know* are exceptions to the inflectional rule for producing past tense verbs in English.

When children are learning English, they first learn the regular rules, which they apply to all forms. Thus, we often hear them say *mans* and *goed*. Later in the acquisition process, they specifically learn irregular plurals like *men* and *mice*, and irregular past tense forms like *came* and *went*. These children's errors are actually evidence that the regular rules exist. This is discussed more fully in chapter 8.

Irregular, or **suppletive**, forms are treated separately in the grammar. That is, one cannot use the regular rules of inflectional morphology to add affixes to words that are exceptions like *child/children*, but must replace the uninflected form with another word. It is possible that for regular words, only the singular form need be specifically stored in the lexicon because we can use the inflectional rules to form plurals. But this can't be so with suppletive exceptions, and *children*, *mice*, and *feet* must be learned separately. The same is true for suppletive past tense forms and comparative forms. There are regular rules—suffixes *-ed* and *-er*—to handle most cases such as *walked* and *taller*, but words like *went* and *worse* need to be learned individually as meaning "goed" and "badder."

When a new word enters the language, the regular inflectional rules generally apply. The plural of *geek*, when it was a new word in English, was *geeks*, not **geeken*, although we are advised that some geeks wanted the plural of *fax* to be **faxen*, like *oxen*, when *fax* entered the language as a shortened form of *facsimile*. Never fear: its plural is *faxes*. The exception to this may be a word "borrowed" from a foreign language. For example, the plural of Latin *datum* has always been *data*, never *datums*, though nowadays *data*, the one-time plural, is treated by many as a singular word like *information*.

The past tense of the verb *hit*, as in the sentence "Yesterday you hit the ball," and the plural of the noun *sheep*, as in "The sheep are in the meadow," show that some morphemes seem to have no phonological shape at all. We know that *hit* in the above sentence is *hit + past* because of the time adverb *yesterday*, and we know that *sheep* is the phonetic form of *sheep + plural* because of the plural verb form *are*.

When a verb is derived from a noun, even if it is pronounced the same as an irregular verb, the regular rules apply to it. Thus *ring*, when used in the sense of encircle, is derived from the noun *ring*, and as a verb it is regular. We say *the police ringed the bank with armed men*, not **rang the bank with armed men*. In the jargon of baseball one says that the hitter *flied out* (hit a lofty ball that was caught), rather than **flew out*, because the verb came from the compound noun *fly ball*.

Indeed, when a noun is used in a compound in which its meaning is lost, such as *flatfoot*, meaning "cop," its plural follows the regular rule, so one says *two flatfoots* to refer to a pair of cops slangily, not **two flatfeet*. It's as if the noun is saying: "If you don't get your meaning from me, you don't get my special plural form."

Making compounds plural, however, is not always simply adding *-s* as in *girl-friends*. Thus for many speakers the plural of *mother-in-law* is *mothers-in-law*, whereas the possessive form is *mother-in-law's*; the plural of *court-martial* is *courts-martial* and the plural *of attorney general* is *attorneys general* in a legal setting, but for most of the rest of us it is *attorney generals*. If the rightmost word of a compound takes an irregular form, however, the entire compound generally follows suit, so the plural of *footman* is *footmen*, not **footmans* or **feetman* or **feetmen*.

Lexical Gaps

"Curiouser and curiouser!" cried Alice (she was so much surprised, that for the moment she quite forgot how to speak good English).

LEWIS CARROLL, *Alice's Adventures in Wonderland*, 1865

The redundancy of alternative forms such as *Chomskyan/Chomskyite*, all of which conform to the regular rules of word formation, may explain some of the **accidental gaps** (also called **lexical gaps**) in the lexicon. Accidental gaps are well-formed but nonexisting words. The actual words in a language constitute only a subset of the possible words. Speakers of a language may know tens of thousands of words. Dictionaries, as we noted, include hundreds of thousands of words, all of which are known by some speakers of the language. But no dictionary can list all **possible words**, because it is possible to add to the vocabulary of a language in many ways. (Some of these will be discussed here and some in chapter 11 on language change.) There are always gaps in the lexicon—words not present but that could be added. Some of the gaps are due to the fact that a permissible sound sequence has no meaning attached to it (like *blick*, or *slarm*, or *krobe*). Note that the sequence of sounds must be in keeping with the constraints of the language. **bnick* is not a "gap" because no word in English can begin with a *bn*. We will discuss such constraints in chapter 7.

Other gaps result when possible combinations of morphemes never come into use. Speakers can distinguish between impossible words such as **unsystem* and **needlessity*, and possible but nonexisting words such as *curiouser*, *linguisticism*, and *antiquify*. The ability to make this distinction is further evidence that the morphological component of our mental grammar consists of not just a lexicon—a list of existing words—but also of rules that enable us to create and understand new words, and to recognize possible and impossible words.

Other Morphological Processes

The various kinds of affixation that we have discussed are by far the most common morphological processes among the world's languages. But, as we continue to emphasize in this book, the human language capacity is enormously creative, and that creativity extends to ways other than affixation that words may be altered and created.

Back-Formations

[A girl] was delighted by her discovery that *eats* and *cats* were really *eat* + *-s* and *cat* + *-s*. She used her new suffix snipper to derive *mik* (mix), *upstair, downstair, clo* (clothes), *len* (lens), *brefek* (from *brefeks*, her word for breakfast), *trappy* (trapeze), even *Santa Claw*.

STEVEN PINKER, *Words and Rules: The Ingredients of Language,* 1999

Misconception can sometimes be creative, and nothing in this world both misconceives and creates like a child, as we shall see in chapter 8. A new word may enter the language because of an incorrect morphological analysis. For example, *peddle* was derived from *peddler* on the mistaken assumption that the *-er* was the agentive suffix. Such words are called **back-formations.** The verbs *hawk, stoke, swindle,* and *edit* all came into the language as back-formations—of *hawker, stoker, swindler,* and *editor. Pea* was derived from a singular word, *pease,* by speakers who thought *pease* was a plural.

Some word creation comes from deliberately miscast back-formations. The word *bikini* comes from the Bikini atoll of the Marshall Islands. Because the first syllable *bi-* is a morpheme meaning "two" in words like *bicycle,* some clever person called a topless bathing suit a *monokini.* Historically, a number of new words have entered the English lexicon in this way. Based on analogy with such pairs as *act/action, exempt/exemption,* and *revise/revision,* new words *resurrect, preempt,* and *televise* were formed from the existing words *resurrection, preemption,* and *television.*

Language purists sometimes rail against back-formations and cite *enthuse* and *liaise* (from *enthusiasm* and *liaison*) as examples of language corruption. However, language is not corrupt; it is adaptable and changeable. Don't be surprised to discover in your lifetime that *shevelled* and *chalant* have infiltrated the English language to mean "tidy" and "concerned," and if it happens do not cry "havoc"; all will be well.

Compounds

[T]he Houynhnms have no Word in their Language to express any thing that is evil, except what they borrow from the Deformities or ill Qualities of the Yahoos. Thus they denote the Folly of a Servant, an Omission of a Child, a Stone that cuts their feet, a Continuance of foul or unseasonable Weather, and the like, by adding to each the Epithet of Yahoo. For instance, Hnhm Yahoo, Whnaholm Yahoo, Ynlhmnawihlma Yahoo, and an ill contrived House, Ynholmhnmrohlnw Yahoo.

JONATHAN SWIFT, *Gulliver's Travels,* 1726

Two or more words may be joined to form new, **compound** words. English is very flexible in the kinds of combinations permitted, as the following table of compounds shows. Each entry in the table represents dozens of similar combinations.

	Adjective	Noun	Verb
Adjective	bittersweet	poorhouse	whitewash
Noun	headstrong	homework	spoonfeed
Verb	—	pickpocket	sleepwalk

Some compounds that have been introduced fairly recently into English are *Facebook, YouTube, power nap*, and *carjack*.

When the two words are in the same grammatical category, the compound will also be in this category: noun + noun = noun, as in *girlfriend, fighter-bomber, paper clip, elevator-operator, landlord, mailman*; adjective + adjective = adjective, as in *icy-cold, red-hot, worldly wise*. In English, the rightmost word in a compound is the **head** of the compound. The head is the part of a word or phrase that determines its broad meaning and grammatical category. Thus, when the two words fall into different categories, the class of the second or final word determines the grammatical category of the compound: noun + adjective = adjective, as in *headstrong*; verb + noun = noun, as in *pickpocket*. On the other hand, compounds formed with a preposition are in the category of the nonprepositional part of the compound, such as (to) *overtake* or (the) *sundown*. This is further evidence that prepositions form a closed-class category that does not readily admit new members.

Although two-word compounds are the most common in English, it would be difficult to state an upper limit: Consider *three-time loser, four-dimensional space-time, sergeant-at-arms, mother-of-pearl, man about town, master of ceremonies*, and *daughter-in-law*. Dr. Seuss uses the rules of compounding when he explains "when tweetle beetles battle with paddles in a puddle, they call it a tweetle beetle puddle paddle battle."[3]

Spelling does not tell us what sequence of words constitutes a compound; whether a compound is spelled with a space between the two words, with a hyphen, or with no separation at all depends on the idiosyncrasies of the particular compound, as shown, for example, in *blackbird, gold-tail*, and *smoke screen*.

Like derived words, compounds have internal structure. This is clear from the ambiguity of a compound like *top + hat + rack*, which can mean "a rack for top hats" corresponding to the structure in tree diagram (1), or "the highest hat rack," corresponding to the structure in (2).

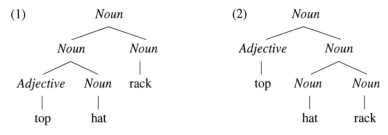

---

[3]From FOX IN SOCKS by Dr. Seuss, Trademark™ & copyright © by Dr. Seuss Enterprises, L.P., 1965, renewed 1993. Used by permission of Random House Children's Books, a division of Random House, Inc., and International Creative Management.

Meaning of Compounds

The meaning of a compound is not always the sum of the meanings of its parts; a *blackboard* may be green or white. Everyone who wears a red coat is not a *Redcoat* (slang for British soldier during the American Revolutionary War). The difference between the sentences "She has a red coat in her closet" and "She has a Redcoat in her closet" would have been highly significant in America in 1776.

Other compounds reveal other meaning relations between the parts, which are not entirely consistent because many compounds are idiomatic (idioms are discussed in chapter 5). A *boathouse* is a house for boats, but a *cathouse* is not a house for cats. (It is slang for a house of prostitution or whorehouse.) A *jumping bean* is a bean that jumps, a *falling star* is a star that falls, and a *magnifying glass* is a glass that magnifies; but a *looking glass* is not a glass that looks, nor is an *eating apple* an apple that eats, and *laughing gas* does not laugh. *Peanut oil* and *olive oil* are oils made from something, but what about *baby oil*? And is this a contradiction: "horse meat is dog meat"? Not at all, since the first is meat *from* horses and the other is meat *for* dogs.

In the examples so far, the meaning of each compound includes at least to some extent the meanings of the individual parts. However, many compounds nowadays do not seem to relate to the meanings of the individual parts at all. A *jack-in-a-box* is a tropical tree, and a *turncoat* is a traitor. A *highbrow* does not necessarily have a high brow, nor does a *bigwig* have a big wig, nor does an *egghead* have an egg-shaped head.

Like certain words with the prefix *un-*, the meaning of many compounds must be learned as if they were individual whole words. Some of the meanings may be figured out, but not all. If you had never heard the word *hunchback*, it might be possible to infer the meaning; but if you had never heard the word *flat-foot*, it is doubtful you would know it means "detective" or "policeman," even though the origin of the word, once you know the meaning, can be figured out.

The pronunciation of English compounds differs from the way we pronounce the sequence of two words that are not compounded. In an actual compound, the first word is usually stressed (pronounced somewhat louder and higher in pitch), and in a noncompound phrase the second word is stressed. Thus we stress *Red* in *Redcoat* but *coat* in *red coat*. (Stress, pitch, and other similar features are discussed in chapters 6 and 7.)

Universality of Compounding

Other languages have rules for conjoining words to form compounds, as seen by French *cure-dent*, "toothpick"; German *Panzerkraftwagen*, "armored car"; Russian *cetyrexetaznyi*, "four-storied"; and Spanish *tocadiscos*, "record player." In the Native American language Tohono O'odham, the word meaning "thing" is *haʔichu*, and it combines with *doakam*, "living creatures," to form the compound *haʔichu doakam*, "animal life."

In Twi, by combining the word meaning "son" or "child," *ɔba*, with the word meaning "chief," *ɔhene*, one derives the compound *ɔheneba*, meaning "prince." By adding the word "house," *ofi*, to *ɔhene*, the word meaning "palace," *ahemfi*, is derived. The other changes that occur in the Twi compounds are due to phonological and morphological rules in the language.

In Thai, the word "cat" is *mɛɛw*, the word for "watch" (in the sense of "to watch over") is *fâw*, and the word for "house" is *bâan*. The word for "watch cat" (like a watchdog) is the compound *mɛɛwfâwbâan*—literally, "catwatchhouse."

Compounding is a common and frequent process for enlarging the vocabulary of all languages.

"Pullet Surprises"

Our knowledge of the morphemes and morphological rules of our language is often revealed by the "errors" we make. We may guess the meaning of a word we do not know. Sometimes we guess wrong, but our wrong guesses are nevertheless "intelligent."

Amsel Greene collected errors made by her students in vocabulary-building classes and published them in a book called *Pullet Surprises*.[4] The title is taken from a sentence written by one of her high school students: "In 1957 Eugene O'Neill won a Pullet Surprise." What is most interesting about these errors is how much they reveal about the students' knowledge of English morphology. The creativity of these students is illustrated in the following examples:

Word	Student's Definition
deciduous	"able to make up one's mind"
longevity	"being very tall"
fortuitous	"well protected"
gubernatorial	"to do with peanuts"
bibliography	"holy geography"
adamant	"pertaining to original sin"
diatribe	"food for the whole clan"
polyglot	"more than one glot"
gullible	"to do with sea birds"
homogeneous	"devoted to home life"

The student who used the word *indefatigable* in the sentence

She tried many reducing diets, but remained indefatigable.

clearly shows morphological knowledge: *in* meaning "not" as in *ineffective*; *de* meaning "off" as in *decapitate*; *fat* as in "fat"; *able* as in *able*; and combined meaning, "not able to take the fat off." Our contribution to Greene's collection is *metronome*: "a city-dwelling diminutive troll."

Sign Language Morphology

Sign languages are rich in morphology. Like spoken languages, signs belong to grammatical categories. They have root and affix morphemes, free and bound morphemes, lexical content and grammatical morphemes, derivational and inflectional morphemes, and morphological rules for their combination to form

---

[4]Greene, A. 1969. *Pullet surprises*. Glenview, IL: Scott, Foresman.

| COMPARE | 'comparison' | MEASURE | 'the activity of measuring' |

FIGURE 3.2 | Derivationally related sign in ASL.

Copyright © 1987 Massachusetts Institute of Technology, by permission of The MIT Press.[5]

morphologically complex signs. The affixation is accomplished by preceding or following a particular gesture with another "affixing" gesture.

The suffix meaning "negation," roughly analogous to *-un* or *-non* or *-dis*, is accomplished as a rapid turning over of the hand(s) following the end of the root sign that is being negated. For example, "want" is signed with open palms facing upward; "don't want" follows that gesture with a turning of the palms to face downward. This "reversal of orientation" suffix may be applied, with necessary adjustments, to many root signs.

In sign language many morphological processes are not linear. Rather, the sign stem occurs nested within various movements and locations in signing space so that the gestures are simultaneous, an impossibility with spoken languages, as in the examples in Figure 3.2.

Figure 3.2 illustrates the derivational process in ASL that is equivalent to the formation of the nouns *comparison* and *measuring* from the verbs *compare* and *measure* in English. Everything about the root morpheme remains the same except for the movement of the hands.

Inflection of sign roots also occurs in ASL and all other sign languages, which characteristically modify the movement of the hands and the spatial contours of the area near the body in which the signs are articulated. For example, movement away from the signer's body toward the "listener" might inflect a verb as in "I see you," whereas movement away from the listener and toward the body would inflect the verb as in "you see me."

Morphological Analysis: Identifying Morphemes

Speakers of a language have knowledge of the internal structure of a word because their mental grammars include a mental lexicon of morphemes and the

---

[5]Poizner, Howard, Edward Klima, and Ursula Bellugi. "What the Hands Reveal about the Brain" figure: "Derivationally related signs in ASL." © 1987 Massachusetts Institute of Technology, by permission of The MIT Press.

morphological rules for their combination. Of course, mistakes are made while learning, but these are quickly remedied. (See chapter 8 for details of how children acquire language.)

Suppose you didn't know English and were a linguist from the planet Zorx wishing to analyze the language. How would you discover the morphemes of English? How would you determine whether a word in that language had one, two, or more morphemes?

The first thing to do would be to ask native speakers how they say various words. (It would help to have a Zorxese-English interpreter along; otherwise, copious gesturing is in order.) Assume you are talented in miming and manage to collect the following forms:

Adjective	Meaning
ugly	"very unattractive"
uglier	"more ugly"
ugliest	"most ugly"
pretty	"nice looking"
prettier	"more nice looking"
prettiest	"most nice looking"
tall	"large in height"
taller	"more tall"
tallest	"most tall"

To determine what the morphemes are in such a list, the first thing a field linguist would do is to see if some forms mean the same thing in different words, that is, to look for *recurring* forms. We find them: *ugly* occurs in *ugly, uglier*, and *ugliest*, all of which include the meaning "very unattractive." We also find that *-er* occurs in *prettier* and *taller*, adding the meaning "more" to the adjectives to which it is attached. Similarly, *-est* adds the meaning "most." Furthermore, by asking additional questions of our English speaker, we find that *-er* and *-est* do not occur in isolation with the meanings of "more" and "most." We can therefore conclude that the following morphemes occur in English:

ugly	root morpheme
pretty	root morpheme
tall	root morpheme
-er	bound morpheme "comparative"
-est	bound morpheme "superlative"

As we proceed we find other words that end with *-er* (e.g., *singer, lover, bomber, writer, teacher*) in which the *-er* ending does not mean "comparative" but, when attached to a verb, changes it to a noun who "verbs," (e.g., *sings, loves, bombs, writes, teaches*). So we conclude that this is a different morpheme, even though it is pronounced the same as the comparative. We go on and find words like *number, somber, butter, member*, and many others in which the *-er* has no separate meaning at all—a *somber* is not "one who sombs" and a *member* does not *memb*—and therefore these words must be monomorphemic.

Once you have practiced on the morphology of English, you might want to go on to describe another language. Paku was invented by the linguist Victoria Fromkin for a 1970s TV series called *Land of the Lost*, recently made into a major motion picture of the same name. This was the language used by the monkey people called Pakuni. Suppose you found yourself in this strange land and attempted to find out what the morphemes of Paku were. Again, you would collect your data from a native Paku speaker and proceed as the Zorxian did with English. Consider the following data from Paku:

me	"I"	meni	"we"
ye	"you (singular)"	yeni	"you (plural)"
we	"he"	weni	"they (masculine)"
wa	"she"	wani	"they (feminine)"
abuma	"girl"	abumani	"girls"
adusa	"boy"	adusani	"boys"
abu	"child"	abuni	"children"
Paku	"one Paku"	Pakuni	"more than one Paku"

By examining these words you find that the plural forms end in *-ni* and the singular forms do not. You therefore conclude that *-ni* is a separate morpheme meaning "plural" that is attached as a suffix to a noun.

Here is a more challenging example, but the principles are the same. Look for repetitions and near repetitions of the same word parts, taking your cues from the meanings given. These are words from Michoacan Aztec, an indigenous language of Mexico:

nokali	"my house"	mopelo	"your dog"
nokalimes	"my houses"	mopelomes	"your dogs"
mokali	"your house"	ikwahmili	"his cornfield"
ikali	"his house"	nokwahmili	"my cornfield"
nopelo	"my dog"	mokwahmili	"your cornfield"

We see there are three base meanings: *house*, *dog*, and *cornfield*. Starting with *house* we look for commonalities in all the forms that refer to "house." They all contain *kali* so that makes a good first guess. (We might, and you might, have reasonably guessed *kal*, but eventually we wouldn't know what to do with the *i* at the end of *nokali* and *mokali*.) With *kali* as "house" we may infer that *no* is a prefix meaning "my," and that is supported by *nopelo*, meaning "my dog." This being the case, we guess that *pelo* is "dog," and see where that leads us. If *pelo* is "dog" and *mopelo* is "your dog," then *mo* is probably the prefix for "your." Now that we think that the possessive pronouns are prefixes, we can look at *ikali* and deduce that *i* means "his." If we're right about the prefixes then we can separate out the word for "cornfield" as *kwahmili*, and at this point we're a-rockin' and a-rollin'. The only morpheme unaccounted for is "plural." We have two instances of plurality, *nokalimes* and *mopelomes*, but since we know *no*, *kali*, *mo*, and *pelo*, it is straightforward to identify the plural morpheme as the suffix *mes*.

In summary of our analysis, then:

kali	"house"
pelo	"dog"
kwahmili	"cornfield"
no-	"my"
mo-	"your"
i-	"his"
-mes	"plural"

By following the analytical principles just discussed, you should be able to solve some of the more complex morphological puzzles that appear in the exercises.

Summary

Knowing a language means knowing the **morphemes** of that language, which are the elemental units that constitute words. *Moralizers* is an English word composed of four morphemes: *moral + ize + er + s*. When you know a word or morpheme, you know both its **form** (sound or gesture) and its **meaning**; these are inseparable parts of the **linguistic sign**. The relationship between form and meaning is **arbitrary**. There is no inherent connection between them (i.e., the words and morphemes of any language must be learned).

Morphemes may be free or bound. **Free morphemes** stand alone like *girl* or *the*, and they come in two types: **open class**, containing the content words of the language, and **closed class**, containing function words such as *the* or *of*. **Bound morphemes** may be affixes or bound roots such as *-ceive*. Affixes may be **prefixes, suffixes, circumfixes**, and **infixes**. Affixes may be derivational or inflectional. **Derivational affixes** derive new words; **inflectional affixes**, such as the plural affix *-s*, make grammatical changes to words. Complex words contain a **root** around which **stems** are built by affixation. Rules of morphology determine what kind of affixation produces actual words such as *un + system + atic*, and what kind produces nonwords such as **un + system*.

Words have hierarchical structure evidenced by ambiguous words such as *unlockable*, which may be *un + lockable* "unable to be locked" or *unlock + able* "able to be unlocked."

Some morphological rules are **productive**, meaning they apply freely to the appropriate stem; for example, *re-* applies freely to verbal stems to give words like *redo, rewash*, and *repaint*. Other rules are more constrained, forming words like *young + ster* but not **smart + ster*. Inflectional morphology is extremely productive: the plural *-s* applies freely even to nonsense words. **Suppletive forms** escape inflectional morphology, so instead of **mans* we have *men*; instead of **bringed* we have *brought*.

There are many ways for new words to be created other than affixation. **Compounds** are formed by uniting two or more root words in a single word, such as *homework*. The **head** of the compound (the rightmost word) bears the basic meaning, so *homework* means a kind of work done at home, but often the meaning of compounds is not easily predictable and must be learned as individual lexical items, such as *laughing gas*. **Back-formations** are words created by misinterpreting an affix look-alike such as *er* as an actual affix, so the verb *burgle* was formed under the mistaken assumption that *burglar* was *burgle + er*.

The grammars of sign languages also include a morphological component consisting of a root, derivational and inflectional sign morphemes, and the rules for their combination.

Morphological analysis is the process of identifying form-meaning units in a language, taking into account small differences in pronunciation, so that *in-* and *im-* are seen to be the "same" prefix in English.

References for Further Reading

Anderson, S. R. 1992. *A-morphous morphology.* Cambridge, UK: Cambridge University Press.

Aronoff, M. 1976. *Word formation in generative grammar.* Cambridge, MA: MIT Press.

Bauer, L. 2003. *Introducing linguistic morphology,* 2nd edn. Washington, DC: Georgetown University Press.

Jensen, J. T. 1990. *Morphology: Word structure in generative grammar.* Amsterdam/Philadelphia: John Benjamins Publishing.

Katamba, F. 1993. *Morphology.* New York: Bedford/St. Martins.

Matthews, P. H. 1991. *Morphology: An introduction to the theory of word structure,* 2nd edn. Cambridge, UK: Cambridge University Press.

Stockwell, R., and D. Minkova. 2001. *English words: History and structure.* New York: Cambridge University Press.

Winchester, S. 2003. *The meaning of everything (The story of the Oxford English dictionary).* Oxford, UK: Oxford University Press.

_____. 1999. *The professor and the madman.* New York: HarperCollins.

Exercises

1. Here is how to estimate the number of words in your mental lexicon. Consult any standard dictionary.

   a. Count the number of entries on a typical page. They are usually bold-faced.

   b. Multiply the number of words per page by the number of pages in the dictionary.

   c. Pick four pages in the dictionary at random, say, pages 50, 75, 125, and 303. Count the number of words on these pages.

   d. How many of these words do you know?

   e. What percentage of the words on the four pages do you know?

   f. Multiply the words in the dictionary by the percentage you arrived at in (e). You know approximately that many English words.

2. Divide the following words by placing a + between their morphemes. (Some of the words may be monomorphemic and therefore indivisible.)

Example: replaces = re + place + s

a. retroactive
b. befriended
c. televise
d. margin
e. endearment
f. psychology
g. unpalatable
h. holiday
i. grandmother
j. morphemic
k. mistreatment
l. deactivation
m. saltpeter
n. airsickness

3. Match each expression under A with the one statement under B that characterizes it.

A		B	
a.	noisy crow	(1)	compound noun
b.	scarecrow	(2)	root morpheme plus derivational prefix
c.	the crow	(3)	phrase consisting of adjective plus noun
d.	crowlike	(4)	root morpheme plus inflectional affix
e.	crows	(5)	root morpheme plus derivational suffix
		(6)	grammatical morpheme followed by lexical morpheme

4. Write the one proper description from the list under B for the italicized part of each word in A.

A		B	
a.	terroriz*ed*	(1)	free root
b.	un*civil*ized	(2)	bound root
c.	terror*ize*	(3)	inflectional suffix
d.	*luke*warm	(4)	derivational suffix
e.	*im*possible	(5)	inflectional prefix
		(6)	derivational prefix
		(7)	inflectional infix
		(8)	derivational infix

5. **A.** Consider the following nouns in Zulu and proceed to look for the recurring forms.

umfazi	"married woman"	abafazi	"married women"
umfani	"boy"	abafani	"boys"
umzali	"parent"	abazali	"parents"
umfundisi	"teacher"	abafundisi	"teachers"
umbazi	"carver"	ababazi	"carvers"

umlimi	"farmer"	abalimi	"farmers"
umdlali	"player"	abadlali	"players"
umfundi	"reader"	abafundi	"readers"

  a. What is the morpheme meaning "singular" in Zulu?
  b. What is the morpheme meaning "plural" in Zulu?
  c. List the Zulu stems to which the singular and plural morphemes are attached, and give their meanings.

B. The following Zulu verbs are derived from noun stems by adding a verbal suffix.

| fundisa | "to teach" | funda | "to read" |
| lima | "to cultivate" | baza | "to carve" |

  d. Compare these words to the words in section A that are related in meaning, for example, *umfundisi* "teacher," *abafundisi* "teachers," *fundisa* "to teach." What is the derivational suffix that specifies the category verb?
  e. What is the nominal suffix (i.e., the suffix that forms nouns)?
  f. State the morphological noun formation rule in Zulu.
  g. What is the stem morpheme meaning "read"?
  h. What is the stem morpheme meaning "carve"?

6. Sweden has given the world the rock group ABBA, the automobile Volvo, and the great film director Ingmar Bergman. The Swedish language offers us a noun morphology that you can analyze with the knowledge gained reading this chapter. Consider these Swedish noun forms:

en lampa	"a lamp"	en bil	"a car"
en stol	"a chair"	en soffa	"a sofa"
en tidning	"a newspaper"	en katt	"a cat"
lampor	"lamps"	bilar	"cars"
stolar	"chairs"	soffor	"sofas"
tidningar	"newspapers"	kattar	"cats"
lampan	"the lamp"	bilen	"the car"
stolen	"the chair"	soffan	"the sofa"
tidningaren	"the newspaper"	katten	"the cat"
lamporna	"the lamps"	bilarna	"the cars"
stolarna	"the chairs"	sofforna	"the sofas"
tidningarna	"the newspapers"	kattarna	"the cats"

  a. What is the Swedish word for the indefinite article *a* (or *an*)?
  b. What are the two forms of the plural morpheme in these data? How can you tell which plural form applies?
  c. What are the two forms of the morpheme that make a singular word definite, that is, correspond to the English article *the*? How can you tell which form applies?
  d. What is the morpheme that makes a plural word definite?
  e. In what order do the various suffixes occur when there is more than one?

f. If *en flicka* is "a girl," what are the forms for "girls," "the girl," and "the girls"?

g. If *bussarna* is "the buses," what are the forms for "buses" and "the bus"?

7. Here are some nouns from the Philippine language Cebuano.

sibwano	"a Cebuano"	binisaja	"the Visayan language"
ilokano	"an Ilocano"	ininglis	"the English language"
tagalog	"a Tagalog person"	tinagalog	"the Tagalog language"
inglis	"an Englishman"	inilokano	"the Ilocano language"
bisaja	"a Visayan"	sinibwano	"the Cebuano language"

a. What is the exact rule for deriving language names from ethnic group names?

b. What type of affixation is represented here?

c. If *suwid* meant "a Swede" and *italo* meant "an Italian," what would be the words for the Swedish language and the Italian language?

d. If *finuranso* meant "the French language" and *inunagari* meant "the Hungarian language," what would be the words for a Frenchman and a Hungarian?

8. The following infinitive and past participle verb forms are found in Dutch.

Root	Infinitive	Past Participle	
wandel	wandelen	gewandeld	"walk"
duw	duwen	geduwd	"push"
stofzuig	stofzuigen	gestofzuigd	"vacuum-clean"

With reference to the morphological processes of prefixing, suffixing, infixing, and circumfixing discussed in this chapter and the specific morphemes involved:

a. State the morphological rule for forming an infinitive in Dutch.

b. State the morphological rule for forming the Dutch past participle form.

9. Below are some sentences in Swahili:

mtoto	amefika	"The child has arrived."
mtoto	anafika	"The child is arriving."
mtoto	atafika	"The child will arrive."
watoto	wamefika	"The children have arrived."
watoto	wanafika	"The children are arriving."
watoto	watafika	"The children will arrive."
mtu	amelala	"The person has slept."
mtu	analala	"The person is sleeping."
mtu	atalala	"The person will sleep."
watu	wamelala	"The persons have slept."
watu	wanalala	"The persons are sleeping."
watu	watalala	"The persons will sleep."
kisu	kimeanguka	"The knife has fallen."

kisu	kinaanguka	"The knife is falling."
kisu	kitaanguka	"The knife will fall."
visu	vimeanguka	"The knives have fallen."
visu	vinaanguka	"The knives are falling."
visu	vitaanguka	"The knives will fall."
kikapu	kimeanguka	"The basket has fallen."
kikapu	kinaanguka	"The basket is falling."
kikapu	kitaanguka	"The basket will fall."
vikapu	vimeanguka	"The baskets have fallen."
vikapu	vinaanguka	"The baskets are falling."
vikapu	vitaanguka	"The baskets will fall."

One of the characteristic features of Swahili (and Bantu languages in general) is the existence of noun classes. Specific singular and plural prefixes occur with the nouns in each class. These prefixes are also used for purposes of agreement between the subject noun and the verb. In the sentences given, two of these classes are included (there are many more in the language).

a. Identify all the morphemes you can detect, and give their meanings.

Example: -toto "child"
  m- noun prefix attached to singular nouns of Class I
  a- prefix attached to verbs when the subject is a singular noun of Class I

Be sure to look for the other noun and verb markers, including tense markers.

b. How is the verb constructed? That is, what kinds of morphemes are strung together and in what order?

c. How would you say in Swahili:
  (1) "The child is falling."
  (2) "The baskets have arrived."
  (3) "The person will fall."

10. We mentioned the morphological process of reduplication—the formation of new words through the repetition of part or all of a word—which occurs in many languages. The following examples from Samoan illustrate this kind of morphological rule.

manao	"he wishes"	mananao	"they wish"
matua	"he is old"	matutua	"they are old"
malosi	"he is strong"	malolosi	"they are strong"
punou	"he bends"	punonou	"they bend"
atamaki	"he is wise"	atamamaki	"they are wise"
savali	"he travels"	pepese	"they sing"
laga	"he weaves"		

a. What is the Samoan for:
  (1) "they weave"
  (2) "they travel"
  (3) "he sings"

b. Formulate a general statement (a morphological rule) that states how to form the plural verb form from the singular verb form.

11. Following are listed some words followed by incorrect (humorous?) definitions:

Word	Definition
stalemate	"husband or wife no longer interested"
effusive	"able to be merged"
tenet	"a group of ten singers"
dermatology	"a study of derms"
ingenious	"not very smart"
finesse	"a female fish"
amphibious	"able to lie on both sea and land"
deceptionist	"secretary who covers up for his boss"
mathemagician	"Bernie Madoff's accountant"
sexcedrin	"medicine for mate who says, 'sorry, I have a headache.'"
testostoroni	"hormonal supplement administered as pasta"
aesthetominophen	"medicine to make you look beautiful"
histalavista	"say goodbye to those allergies"
aquapella	"singing in the shower"
melancholy	"dog that guards the cantaloupe patch"

Give some possible reasons for the source of these silly "definitions." Illustrate your answers by reference to other words or morphemes. For example, *stalemate* comes from *stale* meaning "having lost freshness" and *mate* meaning "marriage partner." When mates appear to have lost their freshness, they are no longer as desirable as they once were.

12. a. Draw tree diagrams for the following words: *construal, disappearances, irreplaceability, misconceive, indecipherable, redarken.*

b. Draw two tree diagrams for *undarkenable* to reveal its two meanings: "able to be less dark" and "unable to be made dark."

13. There are many asymmetries in English in which a root morpheme combined with a prefix constitutes a word, but without the prefix is a nonword. A number of these are given in this chapter.

a. Following is a list of such nonword roots. Add a prefix to each root to form an existing English word.

Words	Nonwords
_____	*descript
_____	*cognito
_____	*beknownst
_____	*peccable
_____	*promptu
_____	*plussed

Words	Nonwords
_____	*domitable
_____	*nomer

    b. There are many more such multimorphemic words for which the root morphemes do not constitute words by themselves. Can you list five more?

14. We have seen that the meaning of compounds is often not revealed by the meaning of their composite words. Crossword puzzles and riddles often make use of this by providing the meaning of two parts of a compound and asking for the resulting word. For example, infielder = diminutive/cease. Read this as asking for a word that means "infielder" by combining a word that means "diminutive" with a word which means "cease." The answer is *shortstop*. See if you can figure out the following:

    a. sci-fi TV series = headliner/journey
    b. campaign = farm building/tempest
    c. at-home wear = tub of water/court attire
    d. kind of pen = formal dance/sharp end
    e. conservative = correct/part of an airplane

15. Consider the following dialogue between parent and schoolchild:

    PARENT: When will you be done with your eight-page book report, dear?
    CHILD: I haven't started it yet.
    PARENT: But it's due tomorrow, you should have begun weeks ago. Why do you always wait until the last minute?
    CHILD: I have more confidence in myself than you do.
    PARENT: Say what?
    CHILD: I mean, how long could it possibly take to read an eight-page book?

    The humor is based on the ambiguity of the compound *eight-page book report*. Draw two trees similar to those in the text for *top hat rack* to reveal the ambiguity.

16. One of the characteristics of Italian is that articles and adjectives have inflectional endings that mark agreement in gender (and number) with the noun they modify. Based on this information, answer the questions that follow the list of Italian phrases.

un uomo	"a man"
un uomo robusto	"a robust man"
un uomo robustissimo	"a very robust man"
una donna robusta	"a robust woman"
un vino rosso	"a red wine"
una faccia	"a face"
un vento secco	"a dry wind"

    a. What is the root morpheme meaning "robust"?
    b. What is the morpheme meaning "very"?

   c. What is the Italian for:
     (1) "a robust wine"
     (2) "a very red face"
     (3) "a very dry wine"

17. Following is a list of words from Turkish. In Turkish, articles and morphemes indicating location are affixed to the noun.

deniz	"an ocean"	evden	"from a house"
denize	"to an ocean"	evimden	"from my house"
denizin	"of an ocean"	denizimde	"in my ocean"
eve	"to a house"	elde	"in a hand"

   a. What is the Turkish morpheme meaning "to"?
   b. What kind of affixes in Turkish corresponds to English prepositions (e.g., prefixes, suffixes, infixes, free morphemes)?
   c. What would the Turkish word for "from an ocean" be?
   d. How many morphemes are there in the Turkish word *denizimde*?

18. The following are some verb forms in Chickasaw, a member of the Muskogean family of languages spoken in south-central Oklahoma.[6] Chickasaw is an endangered language. Currently, there are only about 100 speakers of Chickasaw, most of whom are over 70 years old.

sachaaha	"I am tall"
chaaha	"he/she is tall"
chichaaha	"you are tall"
hoochaaha	"they are tall"
satikahbi	"I am tired"
chitikahbitok	"you were tired"
chichchokwa	"you are cold"
hopobatok	"he was hungry"
hoohopobatok	"they were hungry"
sahopoba	"I am hungry"

   a. What is the root morpheme for the following verbs?
     (1) "to be tall"
     (2) "to be hungry"
   b. What is the morpheme meaning:
     (1) past tense
     (2) "I"
     (3) "you"
     (4) "he/she"
   c. If the Chickasaw root for "to be old" is *sipokni*, how would you say:
     (1) "You are old"
     (2) "He was old"
     (3) "They are old"

---

[6]The Chickasaw examples are provided by Pamela Munro.

19. The language Little-End Egglish, whose source is revealed in exercise 14, chapter 11, exhibits the following data:

a.	kul	"omelet"	zkulego	"my omelet"	zkulivo	"your omelet"
b.	vet	"yolk (of egg)"	zvetego	"my yolk"	zvetivo	"your yolk"
c.	rok	"egg"	zrokego	"my egg"	zrokivo	"your egg"
d.	ver	"egg shell"	zverego	"my egg shell"	zverivo	"your egg shell"
e.	gup	"soufflé"	zgupego	"my soufflé"	zgupivo	"your soufflé"

    i. Isolate the morphemes that indicate possession, first person singular, and second person (we don't know whether singular, plural, or both). Indicate whether the affixes are prefixes or suffixes.

    ii. Given that *vel* means egg white, how would a Little-End Egglisher say "my egg white"?

    iii. Given that *zpeivo* means "your hard-boiled egg," what is the word meaning "hard-boiled egg"?

    iv. If you knew that *zvetgogo* meant "our egg yolk," what would be likely to be the morpheme meaning "our"?

    v. If you knew that *borokego* meant "for my egg," what would be likely to be the morpheme bearing the benefactive meaning "for"?

20. **Research project:** Consider what are called "interfixes" such as -o- in English *jack-o-lantern*. They are said to be meaningless morphemes attached to two morphemes at once. What can you learn about that notion? Where do you think the -o- comes from? Are there languages other than English that have interfixes?

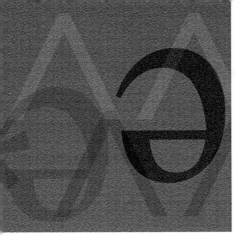

4

Syntax: The Sentence Patterns of Language

To grammar even kings bow.

J. B. MOLIÈRE, *Les Femmes Savantes, II*, 1672

It is an astonishing fact that any speaker of any human language can produce and understand an infinite number of sentences. We can show this quite easily through examples such as the following:

The kindhearted boy had many girlfriends.
The kindhearted, intelligent boy had many girlfriends.
The kindhearted, intelligent, handsome boy had many girlfriends.
.
.
.

John found a book in the library.
John found a book in the library in the stacks.
John found a book in the library in the stacks on the fourth floor.
.
.
.

The cat chased the mouse.
The cat chased the mouse that ate the cheese.
The cat chased the mouse that ate the cheese that came from the cow.
The cat chased the mouse that ate the cheese that came from the cow that grazed in the field.

In each case the speaker could continue creating sentences by adding another adjective, prepositional phrase, or relative clause. In principle, this could go on forever. All languages have mechanisms of this sort that make the number of sentences limitless. Given this fact, the sentences of a language cannot be stored in a dictionary format in our heads. Rather, sentences are composed of discrete units that are combined by rules. This system of rules explains how speakers can store infinite knowledge in a finite space—our brains.

The part of grammar that represents a speaker's knowledge of sentences and their structures is called **syntax**. The aim of this chapter is to show you what syntactic structures look like and to familiarize you with some of the rules that determine them. Most of the examples will be from the syntax of English, but the principles that account for syntactic structures are universal.

What the Syntax Rules Do

"Then you should say what you mean," the March Hare went on.

"I do," Alice hastily replied, "at least—I mean what I say—that's the same thing, you know."

"Not the same thing a bit!" said the Hatter. "You might just as well say that 'I see what I eat' is the same thing as 'I eat what I see'!"

"You might just as well say," added the March Hare, "that 'I like what I get' is the same thing as 'I get what I like'!"

"You might just as well say," added the Dormouse . . . "that 'I breathe when I sleep' is the same thing as 'I sleep when I breathe'!"

"It is the same thing with you," said the Hatter.

LEWIS CARROLL, *Alice's Adventures in Wonderland*, 1865

The **rules of syntax** combine words into phrases and phrases into sentences. Among other things, the rules specify the correct word order for a language. For example, English is a Subject–Verb–Object (SVO) language. The English sentence in (1) is grammatical because the words occur in the right order; the sentence in (2) is ungrammatical because the word order is incorrect for English. (Recall that the asterisk or star preceding a sentence is the linguistic convention for indicating that the sentence is ungrammatical or ill-formed according to the rules of the grammar.)

1. The President nominated a new Supreme Court justice.
2. *President the new Supreme justice Court a nominated.

A second important role of the syntax is to describe the relationship between the meaning of a particular group of words and the arrangement of those words. For example, Alice's companions show us that the word order of a sentence contributes crucially to its meaning. The sentences in (3) and (4) contain the same words, but the meanings are quite different, as the Mad Hatter points out.

3. I mean what I say.
4. I say what I mean.

The rules of the syntax also specify the **grammatical relations** of a sentence, such as **subject** and **direct object**. In other words, they provide the information about who is doing what to whom. This information is crucial to understanding the meaning of a sentence. For example, the grammatical relations in (5) and (6) are reversed, so the otherwise identical sentences have very different meanings.

5. Your dog chased my cat.
6. My cat chased your dog.

Syntactic rules also specify other constraints that sentences must adhere to. Consider, for example, the sentences in (7). As an exercise you can first read through them and place a star before those sentences that *you* consider to be ungrammatical.

7. (a) The boy found.
   (b) The boy found quickly.
   (c) The boy found in the house.
   (d) The boy found the ball.

We predict that you will find the sentence in (7d) grammatical and the ones in (7a–c) ungrammatical. This is because the syntax rules specify that a verb like *found* must be followed by something, and that something cannot be an expression like *quickly* or *in the house* but must be like *the ball*.

Similarly, we expect you will find the sentence in (8b) grammatical while the sentence in (8a) is not.

8. (a) Disa slept the baby.
   (b) Disa slept soundly.

The verb *sleep* patterns differently than *find* in that it may be followed solely by a word like *soundly* but not by other kinds of phrases such as *the baby*.

We also predict that you'll find that the sentences in (9a, d, e, f) are grammatical and that (9b, c) are not. The examples in (9) show that specific verbs, such as *believe*, *try*, and *want*, behave differently with respect to the patterns of words that may follow them.

9. (a) Zack believes Robert to be a gentleman.
   (b) Zack believes to be a gentleman.
   (c) Zack tries Robert to be a gentleman.
   (d) Zack tries to be a gentleman.
   (e) Zack wants to be a gentleman.
   (f) Zack wants Robert to be a gentleman.

The fact that all native speakers have the same judgments about the sentences in (7) to (9) tells us that grammatical judgments are neither idiosyncratic nor capricious, but are determined by rules that are shared by all speakers of a language.

In (10) we see that the phrase *ran up the hill* behaves differently from the phrase *ran up the bill*, even though the two phrases are superficially quite similar. For the expression *ran up the hill*, the rules of the syntax allow the word orders in (10a) and (10c), but not (10b). In *ran up the bill*, in contrast, the rules allow the order in (10d) and (10e), but not (10f).

10. (a) Jack and Jill ran up the hill.
    (b) Jack and Jill ran the hill up.
    (c) Up the hill ran Jack and Jill.
    (d) Jack and Jill ran up the bill.
    (e) Jack and Jill ran the bill up.
    (f) Up the bill ran Jack and Jill.

The pattern shown in (10) illustrates that sentences are not simply strings of words with no further organization. If they were, there would be no reason to expect *ran up the hill* to pattern differently from *ran up the bill*. These phrases act differently because they have different syntactic structures associated with them. In *ran up the hill*, the words *up the hill* form a unit, as follows:

He ran [up the hill]

The whole unit can be moved to the beginning of the sentence, as in (10c), but we cannot rearrange its subparts, as shown in (10b). On the other hand, in *ran up the bill*, the words *up the bill* do not form a natural unit, so they cannot be moved, and (10f) is ungrammatical.

Our syntactic knowledge crucially includes rules that tell us how words form groups in a sentence, or how they are *hierarchically* arranged with respect to one another. Consider the following sentence:

The captain ordered all old men and women off the sinking ship.

This phrase "old men and women" is ambiguous, referring either to old men and to women of any age or to old men and old women. The ambiguity arises because the words *old men and women* can be grouped in two ways. If the words are grouped as follows, *old* modifies only *men* and so the women can be any age.

[old men] and [women]

When we group them like this, the adjective *old* modifies both *men* and *women*.

[old [men and women]]

The rules of syntax allow both of these groupings, which is why the expression is ambiguous. The following hierarchical diagrams illustrate the same point:

In the first structure *old* and *men* are under the same node and hence old modifies *men*. In the second structure *old* shares a node with the entire conjunction *men and women*, and so modifies both.

This is similar to what we find in morphology for ambiguous words such as *unlockable*, which have two structures, corresponding to two meanings, as discussed in chapter 3.

Many sentences exhibit such ambiguities, often leading to humorous results. Consider the following two sentences, which appeared in classified ads:

For sale: an antique desk suitable for lady with thick legs and large drawers.
We will oil your sewing machine and adjust tension in your home for $10.00.

In the first ad, the humorous reading comes from the grouping [a desk] [for lady with thick legs and large drawers] as opposed to the intended [a desk for lady] [with thick legs and large drawers], where the legs and drawers belong to the desk. The second case is similar.

Because these ambiguities are a result of different structures, they are instances of **structural ambiguity**.

Contrast these sentences with:

This will make you smart.

The two interpretations of this sentence are due to the two meanings of smart—"clever" or "burning sensation." Such lexical or word-meaning ambiguities, as opposed to structural ambiguities, will be discussed in chapter 5.

Often a combination of differing structure and double word-meaning creates ambiguity (and humor) as in the cartoon:

Rhymes With Orange (105945) © Hilary B. Price. King Features Syndicate

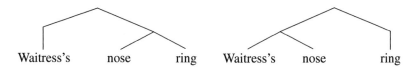

Syntactic rules reveal the grammatical relations among the words of a sentence as well as their order and hierarchical organization. They also explain how the grouping of words relates to its meaning, such as when a sentence or

phrase is ambiguous. In addition, the rules of the syntax permit speakers to produce and understand a limitless number of sentences never produced or heard before—*the creative aspect of linguistic knowledge*. A major goal of linguistics is to show clearly and explicitly how syntactic rules account for this knowledge. A theory of grammar must provide a complete characterization of what speakers implicitly know about their language.

What Grammaticality Is Not Based On

Colorless green ideas sleep furiously. This is a very interesting sentence, because it shows that syntax can be separated from semantics—that form can be separated from meaning. The sentence doesn't seem to mean anything coherent, but it sounds like an English sentence.

HOWARD LASNIK, *The Human Language: Part One,* 1995

Importantly, a person's ability to make grammaticality judgments does not depend on having heard the sentence before. You may never have heard or read the sentence

Enormous crickets in pink socks danced at the prom.

but your syntactic knowledge tells you that it is grammatical. As we showed at the beginning of this chapter, people are able to understand, produce, and make judgments about an infinite range of sentences, most of which they have never heard before. This ability illustrates that our knowledge of language is creative—not creative in the sense that we are all poets, which we are not, but creative in that none of us is limited to a fixed repertoire of expressions. Rather, we can exploit the resources of our language and grammar to produce and understand a limitless number of sentences embodying a limitless range of ideas and emotions.

We showed that the structure of a sentence contributes to its meaning. However, grammaticality and meaningfulness are not the same thing, as shown by the following sentences:

Colorless green ideas sleep furiously.
A verb crumpled the milk.

Although these sentences do not make much sense, they are syntactically well formed. They sound funny, but their funniness is different from what we find in the following strings of words:

*Furiously sleep ideas green colorless.
*Milk the crumpled verb a.

There are also sentences that we understand even though they are not well formed according to the rules of the syntax. For example, most English speakers could interpret

*The boy quickly in the house the ball found.

although they know that the word order is incorrect. Similarly, we could probably assign a meaning to sentence (8a) (Disa slept the baby) in the previous section. If asked to fix it up, we would probably come up with something like "Disa put the baby to sleep," but we also know that as it stands, (8a) is not a possible sentence of English. To be a sentence, words must conform to specific patterns determined by the syntactic rules of the language.

Some sentences are grammatical even though they are difficult to interpret because they include nonsense words, that is, words with no agreed-on meaning. This is illustrated by the following lines from the poem "Jabberwocky" by Lewis Carroll:

'Twas brillig, and the slithy toves
Did gyre and gimble in the wabe

These lines are grammatical in the linguistic sense that they obey the word order and other constraints of English. Such nonsense poetry is amusing precisely because the sentences comply with syntactic rules and sound like good English. Ungrammatical strings of nonsense words are not entertaining:

*Toves slithy the and brillig 'twas
wabe the in gimble and gyre did

Grammaticality also does not depend on the truth of sentences. If it did, lying would be impossible. Nor does it depend on whether real objects are being discussed or whether something is possible in the real world. Untrue sentences can be grammatical, sentences discussing unicorns can be grammatical, and sentences referring to pregnant fathers can be grammatical.

The syntactic rules that permit us to produce, understand, and make grammaticality judgments are unconscious rules. The grammar is a mental grammar, different from the prescriptive grammar rules that we are taught in school. We develop the mental rules of grammar long before we attend school, as we shall see in chapter 8.

Sentence Structure

I really do not know that anything has ever been more exciting than diagramming sentences.

GERTRUDE STEIN, "Poetry and Grammar," 1935

Suppose we wanted to write a template that described the structure of an English sentence, and more specifically, a template that gave the correct word order for English. We might come up with something like the following:

Det—N—V—Det—N

This template says that a determiner (an article) is followed by a noun, which is followed by a verb, and so on. It would describe English sentences such as the following:

The child found a puppy.
The professor wrote a book.
That runner won the race.

The implication of such a template would be that sentences are strings of words belonging to particular grammatical categories ("parts of speech") with no internal organization. We know, however, that such "flat" structures are incorrect. As noted earlier, sentences have a hierarchical organization; that is, the words are grouped into natural units. The words in the sentence

The child found a puppy.

may be grouped into [the child] and [found a puppy], corresponding to the subject and predicate of the sentence. A further division gives [the child] and then [[found] [a puppy]], and finally the individual words: [[the] [child]] [[found] [[a] [puppy]]]. It's sometimes easier to see the parts and subparts of the sentence in a **tree diagram**:

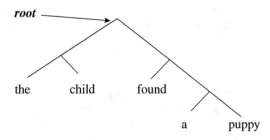

The "tree" is upside down with its "root" encompassing the entire sentence, "The child found a puppy," and its "leaves" being the individual words, *the*, *child*, *found*, *a*, *puppy*. The tree conveys the same information as the nested square brackets. The hierarchical organization of the tree reflects the groupings and subgroupings of the words of the sentence.

The tree diagram shows, among other things, that the phrase *found a puppy* divides naturally into two branches, one for the verb *found* and the other for the direct object *a puppy*. A different division, say, *found a* and *puppy*, is unnatural.

Constituents and Constituency Tests

Parts is parts.

WENDY'S COMMERCIAL, 2006

The natural groupings or parts of a sentence are called **constituents**. Various linguistic tests reveal the constituents of a sentence. The first test is the "stand alone" test. If a group of words can stand alone, they form a constituent. For example, the set of words that can be used to answer a question is a constituent. So in answer to the question "What did you find?" a speaker might answer *a puppy*, but not *found a. A puppy* can stand alone while *found a* cannot.

The second test is "replacement by a pronoun." Pronouns can substitute for natural groups. In answer to the question "Where did you find *a puppy*?" a speaker can say, "I found *him* in the park." Words such as *do* can also take the place of the entire predicate *found a puppy*, as in "John found a puppy and Bill *did* too." If a group of words can be replaced by a pronoun or a word like *do*, it forms a constituent.

A third test of constituency is the "move as a unit" test. If a group of words can be moved, they form a constituent. For example, if we compare the following sentences to the sentence "The child found a puppy," we see that certain elements have moved:

It was *a puppy* that *the child* found.
A puppy was found by *the child*.

In the first example, the constituent *a puppy* has moved from its position following *found*; in the second example, the positions of *a puppy* and *the child* have been changed. In all such rearrangements the constituents *a puppy* and *the child* remain intact. *Found a* does not remain intact, because it is not a constituent.

In the sentence "The child found a puppy," the natural groupings or constituents are the subject *the child*, the predicate *found a puppy*, and the direct object *a puppy*.

Some sentences have a prepositional phrase in the predicate. Consider

The puppy played in the garden.

We can use our tests to show that *in the garden* is also a constituent, as follows:

Where did the puppy play? *In the garden* (stand alone)
The puppy played *there*. (replacement by a pronoun-like word)
In the garden is where the puppy played. (move as a unit)
It was *in the garden* that the puppy played.

As before, our knowledge of the **constituent structure** of a sentence may be graphically represented by a tree diagram. The tree diagram for the sentence "The puppy played in the garden" is as follows:

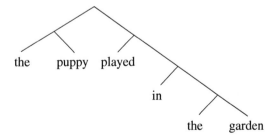

In addition to the syntactic tests just described, experimental evidence has shown that speakers do not represent sentences as strings of words but rather in terms of constituents. In these experiments, subjects listen to sentences that have clicking noises inserted into them at random points. In some cases the click occurs at a constituent boundary, and in other sentences the click is inserted in the middle of a constituent. The subjects are then asked to report where the click occurred. There were two important results: (1) Subjects noticed the click and recalled its location best when it occurred at a major constituent boundary (e.g., between the subject and predicate); and (2) clicks that occurred inside the constituent were reported to have occurred between constituents. In other words, subjects displaced the clicks and put them at constituent boundaries. These results show that speakers perceive sentences in chunks corresponding to grammatical constituents.

Every sentence in a language is associated with one or more constituent structures. If a sentence has more than one constituent structure, it is ambiguous, and each tree will correspond to one of the possible meanings. For example, the sentence "I bought an antique desk suitable for a lady with thick legs and large drawers" has two phrase structure trees associated with it. In one structure the phrase [a lady with thick legs and large drawers] forms a constituent. For example, it could stand alone in answer to the question "Who did you buy an antique desk for?" In its second meaning, the phrase *with thick legs and large drawers* modifies the phrase *a desk for a lady*, and thus the structure is [[a desk for a lady][with thick legs and large drawers]].

Syntactic Categories

" I MISS THE GOOD OLD DAYS WHEN ALL WE HAD TO WORRY ABOUT WAS NOUNS AND VERBS."

Each grouping in the tree diagrams of "The child found a puppy" is a member of a large family of similar expressions. For example, *the child* belongs to a family that includes *the police officer, your neighbor, this yellow cat, he, John,* and countless others. We can substitute any member of this family for the child without affecting the grammaticality of the sentence, although the meaning of course would change.

A police officer found a puppy.
Your neighbor found a puppy.
This yellow cat found a puppy.

A family of expressions that can substitute for one another without loss of grammaticality is called a **syntactic category**.

The child, a police officer, John, and so on belong to the syntactic category **noun phrase** (**NP**), one of several syntactic categories in English and every other language in the world. NPs may function as the subject or as an object in a sentence. NPs often contain a *determiner* (like *a* or *the*) and a noun, but they may also consist of a proper name, a pronoun, a noun without a determiner, or even a clause or a sentence. Even though a proper noun like *John* and pronouns such as *he* and *him* are single words, they are technically NPs, because they pattern like NPs in being able to fill a subject or object or other NP slots.

John found the puppy.
He found the puppy.
Boys love puppies.
The puppy loved him.
The puppy loved John.

NPs can be more complex as illustrated by the sentence:

The girl that Professor Snape loved married the man of her dreams.

The NP subject of this sentence is *the girl that Professor Snape loved,* and the NP object is *the man of her dreams.*

Syntactic categories are part of a speaker's knowledge of syntax. That is, speakers of English know that only items (a), (b), (e), (f), and (g) in the following list are NPs even if they have never heard the term *noun phrase* before.

1. (a) a bird
    (b) the red banjo
    (c) have a nice day
    (d) with a balloon
    (e) the woman who was laughing
    (f) it
    (g) John
    (h) went

You can test this claim by inserting each expression into three contexts: *Who found _____, _____ was seen by everyone,* and *What/who I heard was _____.* For example, **Who found <u>with a balloon</u>* is ungrammatical, as is **<u>Have a nice day</u> was seen by everyone,* as opposed to *Who found it?* or *John was seen by everyone.* Only NPs fit into these contexts because only NPs can function as subjects and objects.

There are other syntactic categories. The expression *found a puppy* is a **verb phrase (VP)**. A verb phrase always contains a **verb (V)**, and it may contain other categories, such as a noun phrase or **prepositional phrase (PP)**, which is a preposition followed by an NP, such as *in the park, on the roof, with a balloon*. In (2) the VPs are those phrases that can complete the sentence "The child _____ ."

2. (a) saw a clown
    (b) a bird
    (c) slept
    (d) smart
    (e) ate the cake
    (f) found the cake in the cupboard
    (g) realized that the earth was round

Inserting (a), (c), (e), (f), and (g) will produce grammatical sentences, whereas the insertion of (b) or (d) would result in an ungrammatical sentence. Thus, (a), (c), (e), (f), and (g) are verb phrases.

Lexical and Functional Categories

There are ten parts of speech, and they are all troublesome.

MARK TWAIN, "The Awful German Language," in *A Tramp Abroad*, 1880

Syntactic categories include both phrasal categories such as NP, VP, AdjP (adjective phrase), PP (prepositional phrase), and AdvP (adverbial phrase), as well as lexical categories such as noun (N), verb (V), preposition (P), adjective (Adj), and adverb (Adv). Each lexical category has a corresponding phrasal category. Following is a list of lexical categories with some examples of each type:

Lexical categories

Noun (N)	*puppy, boy, soup, happiness, fork, kiss, pillow, cake, cupboard*
Verb (V)	*find, run, sleep, throw, realize, see, try, want, believe*
Preposition (P)	*up, down, across, into, from, by, with*
Adjective (Adj)	*red, big, candid, hopeless, fair, idiotic, lucky*
Adverb (Adv)	*again, carefully, luckily, never, very, fairly*

Many of these categories may already be familiar to you. As mentioned earlier, some of them are traditionally referred to as *parts of speech*. Other categories may be less familiar, for example, the category **determiner (Det)**, which includes the articles *a* and *the*, as well as **demonstratives** such as *this, that, these*, and *those*, and "counting words" such as *each* and *every*. Another less familiar category is **auxiliary (Aux)**, which includes the verbs *have, had, be, was*, and *were*, and the **modals** *may, might, can, could, must, shall, should, will*, and *would*. Aux and Det are **functional categories**, so called because their members have a grammatical function rather than a descriptive meaning. For example, determiners specify whether a noun is indefinite or definite (*a boy* versus *the* *boy*), or the proximity of the person or object to the context (*this boy* versus *that boy*). Auxiliaries provide the verb with a time frame, whether ongoing (*John is dancing*), completed in the past (*John has danced*), or occurring in the future (*John will dance*). Auxiliaries may also express notions such as possibility (*John may dance*), necessity (*John must dance*), ability (*John can dance*), and so on.

Lexical categories typically have particular kinds of meanings associated with them. For example, verbs usually refer to actions, events, and states (*kick, marry, love*); adjectives to qualities or properties (*lucky, old*); common nouns to general entities (*dog, elephant, house*); and proper nouns to particular individuals (*Noam Chomsky*) or places (*Dodger Stadium*) or other things that people give names to, such as commercial products (*Coca-Cola, Viagra*). But the relationship between grammatical categories and meaning is more complex than these few examples suggest. For example, some nouns refer to events (*marriage* and *destruction*) and others to states (*happiness, loneliness*). We can use abstract nouns such as *honor* and *beauty*, rather than adjectives, to refer to properties and qualities. In the sentence "Seeing is believing," *seeing* and *believing* are nouns but are not entities. Prepositions are usually used to express relationships between two entities involving a location (e.g., *the boy is in the room, the cat is under the bed*), but this is not always the case; the prepositions *of, by, about,* and *with* are not locational. Because of the difficulties involved in specifying the precise meaning of lexical categories, we do not usually define categories in terms of their meanings, but rather on the basis of their syntactic distribution (where they occur in a sentence) and morphological characteristics. For example, we define a noun as a word that can occur with a determiner (*the boy*) and that can take a plural marker (*boys*), among other properties.

All languages have syntactic categories such as N, V, and NP. Speakers know the syntactic categories of their language, even if they do not know the technical terms. Our knowledge of the syntactic classes is revealed when we substitute equivalent phrases, as we just did in examples (1) and (2), and when we use the various syntactic tests that we have discussed.

Phrase Structure Trees and Rules

Who climbs the Grammar-Tree distinctly knows
Where Noun and Verb and Participle grows.

JOHN DRYDEN, "The Sixth Satyr of Juvenal," 1693

Now that you know something about constituent structure and grammatical categories, you are ready to learn how the sentences of a language are constructed. We will begin by building trees for simple sentences and then proceed to more complex structures. The trees that we will build here are more detailed than those we saw in the previous sections, because the branches of the tree will have category labels identifying each constituent. In this section we will also introduce the syntactic rules that **generate** (a technical term for describe or specify) the different kinds of structures.

The following tree diagram provides labels for each of the constituents of the sentence "The child found a puppy." These labels show that the entire sentence belongs to the syntactic category of S (because the S-node encompasses all the words). It also reveals that *the child* and *a puppy* belong to the category NP, that is, they are noun phrases, and that *found a puppy* belongs to the category VP or is a verb phrase, consisting of a verb and an NP. It also reveals the syntactic category of each of the words in the sentence.

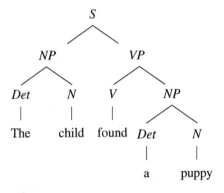

A tree diagram with syntactic category information is called a **phrase structure tree** or a **constituent structure tree**. This tree shows that a sentence is both a linear string of words and a hierarchical structure with phrases nested in phrases. Phrase structure trees (PS trees, for short) are explicit graphic representations of a speaker's knowledge of the structure of the sentences of his language.

PS trees represent three aspects of a speaker's syntactic knowledge:

1. The linear order of the words in the sentence
2. The identification of the syntactic categories of words and groups of words
3. The hierarchical structure of the syntactic categories (e.g., an S is composed of an NP followed by a VP, a VP is composed of a V that may be followed by an NP, and so on)

In chapter 3 we discussed the fact that the syntactic category of each word is listed in our mental dictionaries. We now see how this information is used by the syntax of the language. Words appear in trees under labels that correspond to their syntactic category. Nouns are under N, determiners under Det, verbs under V, and so on.

The larger syntactic categories, such as VP, consist of all the syntactic categories and words below that point, or **node**, in the tree. The VP in the PS tree above consists of syntactic category nodes V and NP and the words *found, a,* and *puppy.* Because *a puppy* can be traced up the tree to the node NP, this constituent is a noun phrase. Because *found* and *a puppy* can be traced up to the node VP, this constituent is a verb phrase. The PS tree reflects the speaker's intuitions about the natural groupings of words in a sentence. In discussing trees, every higher node is said to **dominate** all the categories beneath it. S dominates every node. A node is said to **immediately dominate** the categories one level below it. VP immediately dominates V and NP, the categories of which it is composed. Categories that are immediately dominated by the same node are **sisters**. V and NP are sisters in the phrase structure tree of "the child found a puppy."

A PS tree is a formal device for representing the speaker's knowledge of the structure of sentences in his language, as revealed by our linguistic intuitions. When we speak, we are not aware that we are producing sentences with such structures, but controlled experiments, such as the click experiments described earlier, show that we use them in speech production and comprehension. We will discuss these experiments further in chapter 9.

The information represented in a PS tree can also be represented by another formal device: phrase structure (PS) rules. PS rules capture the knowledge that speakers have about the possible structures of a language. Just as a speaker cannot have an infinite list of sentences in her head, so she cannot have an infinite set of PS trees in her head. Rather, a speaker's knowledge of the permissible and impermissible structures must exist as a finite set of rules that generate a tree for any sentence in the language. To express the structure given above, we need the following PS rules:

1. S   →   NP VP
2. NP   →   Det N
3. VP   →   V NP

Phrase structure rules specify the well-formed structures of a language precisely and concisely. They express the regularities of the language and make explicit a speaker's knowledge of the order of words and the grouping of words into syntactic categories. For example, in English an NP may contain a determiner followed by a noun. This is represented by rule 2. This rule conveys two facts:

A noun phrase can contain a determiner followed by a noun in that order.

A determiner followed by a noun is a noun phrase.

You can think of PS rules as templates that a tree must match to be grammatical. To the left of the arrow is the dominating category, in this case NP, and the categories that it immediately dominates—that comprise it—appear on the right side, in this case Det and N. The right side of the arrow also shows the linear order of these components. Thus, one subtree for the English NP looks like this:

Rule 1 says that a sentence (S) contains (immediately dominates) an NP and a VP in that order. Rule 3 says that a verb phrase consists of a verb (V) followed by an NP. These rules are general statements and do not refer to any specific VP, V, or NP. The subtrees represented by rules 1 and 3 are as follows:

A VP need not contain an NP object, however. It may include a verb alone, as in the following sentences:

The woman laughed.
The man danced.
The horse galloped.

These sentences have the structure:

Thus a tree must have a VP that immediately dominates V, as specified by rule 4, which is therefore added to the grammar:

4. VP → V

The following sentences contain prepositional phrases following the verb:

The puppy played in the garden.
The boat sailed up the river.
A girl laughed at the monkey.
The sheepdog rolled in the mud.

The PS tree for such sentences is

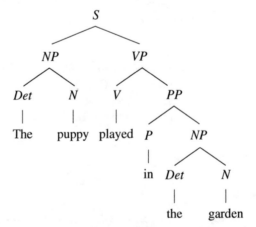

To permit structures of this type, we need two additional PS rules, as in 5 and 6.

5. VP → V PP
6. PP → P NP

Another option open to the VP is to contain or *embed* a sentence. For example, the sentence "The professor said that the student passed the exam" contains the sentence "the student passed the exam." Preceding the **embedded sentence** is the word *that,* which is a **complementizer (C).** C is a functional category, like Aux and Det. Here is the structure of such sentence types:

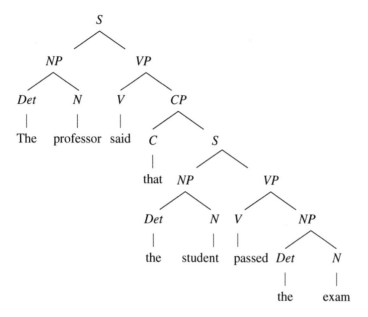

To allow such embedded sentences, we need to add these two new rules to our set of phrase structure rules.

7. VP → V CP
8. CP → C S

CP stands for complementizer phrase. Rule 8 says that CP contains a complementizer such as *that* followed by the embedded sentence. Other complementizers are *if* and *whether* in sentences like

I don't know <u>whether</u> I should talk about this.
The teacher asked <u>if</u> the students understood the syntax lesson.

that have structures similar to the one above.

Here are the PS rules we have discussed so far. A few other rules will be considered later.

1. S   →   NP VP
2. NP →   Det N
3. VP →   V NP
4. VP →   V
5. VP →   V PP
6. PP →   P NP
7. VP →   V CP
8. CP →   C S

Some Conventions for Building Phrase Structure Trees

Everyone who is master of the language he speaks . . . may form new . . . phrases, provided they coincide with the genius of the language.

JOHANN DAVID MICHAELIS, *Dissertation,* 1769

One can use the phrase structure rules as a guide for building trees that follow the structural constraints of the language. In so doing, certain conventions are followed. The S occurs at the top or "root" of the tree (it's upside down). Another convention specifies how the rules are applied: First, find the rule with S on the left side of the arrow, and put the categories on the right side below the S, as shown here:

Continue by matching any syntactic category at the bottom of the partially constructed tree to a category on the left side of a rule, then expand the tree with the categories on the right side. For example, we may expand the tree by applying the NP rule to produce:

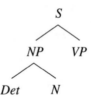

The categories at the bottom are Det, N, and VP, but only VP occurs to the left of an arrow in the set of rules and so needs to be expanded using one of the VP rules. Any one of the VP rules will work. The order in which the rules appear in the list of rules is irrelevant. (We could have begun by expanding the VP rather than the NP.) Suppose we use rule 5 next. Then the tree has grown to look like this:

Convention dictates that we continue in this way until none of the categories at the bottom of the tree appears on the left side of any rule (i.e., no phrasal categories may remain unexpanded). The PP must expand into a P and an NP (rule 6), and the NP into a Det and an N. We can use a rule as many times as it can apply. In this tree, we used the NP rule twice. After we have applied all the rules that can apply, the tree looks like this:

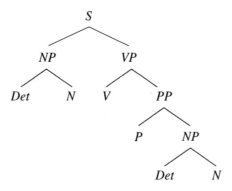

By following these conventions, we generate only trees specified by the PS rules, and hence only trees that conform to the syntax of the language. By implication, any tree not so specified will be ungrammatical, that is, not permitted by the syntax. At any point during the construction of a tree, any rule may be used as long as its left-side category occurs somewhere at the bottom of the tree. By choosing different VP rules, we could specify different structures corresponding to sentences such as:

The boys left. (VP $\rightarrow$ V)
The wind blew the kite. (VP $\rightarrow$ V NP)
The senator hopes that the bill passes. (VP $\rightarrow$ V CP)

Because the number of possible sentences in every language is infinite, there are also an infinite number of trees. However, all trees are built out of the finite set of substructures allowed by the grammar of the language, and these substructures are specified by the finite set of phrase structure rules.

The Infinity of Language: Recursive Rules

So, naturalists observe, a flea
Hath smaller fleas that on him prey;
And these have smaller still to bite 'em,
And so proceed ad infinitum.

JONATHAN SWIFT, "On Poetry, a Rhapsody," 1733

We noted at the beginning of the chapter that the number of sentences in a language is infinite and that languages have various means of creating longer and longer sentences, such as adding an adjective or a prepositional phrase. Even children know how to produce and understand very long sentences and know how to make them even longer, as illustrated by the children's rhyme about the house that Jack built.

This is the farmer sowing the corn,
that kept the cock that crowed in the morn,
that waked the priest all shaven and shorn,
that married the man all tattered and torn,
that kissed the maiden all forlorn,
that milked the cow with the crumpled horn,
that tossed the dog,

that worried the cat,
that killed the rat,
that ate the malt,
that lay in the house that Jack built.

The child begins the rhyme with *This is the house that Jack built*, continues by lengthening it to *This is the malt that lay in the house that Jack built*, and so on.

You can add any of the following to the beginning of the rhyme and still have a grammatical sentence:

I think that . . .
What is the name of the unicorn that noticed that . . .
Ask someone if . . .
Do you know whether . . .

Once we acknowledge the unboundedness of sentences, we need a formal device to capture that crucial aspect of speakers' syntactic knowledge. It is no longer possible to specify each legal structure; there are infinitely many.

To see how this works, let us first look at the case of multiple prepositional phrases such as [The girl walked [down the street] [over the hill] [through the woods] . . .]. VP substructures currently allow only one PP per sentence (VP → V PP—rule 5). We can rectify this problem by revising rule 5:

5. VP → VP PP

Rule 5 is different from the previous rules because it repeats its own category (VP) inside itself. This is an instance of a **recursive rule**. Recursive rules are of critical importance because they allow the grammar to generate an infinite set of sentences. Reapplying rule 5 shows how the syntax permits structures with multiple PPs, such as in the sentence "The girl walked down the street with a gun toward the bank."

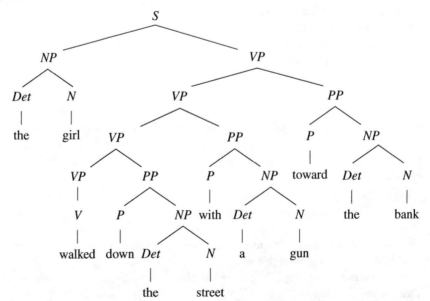

In this structure the VP rule 5 has applied three times and so there are three PPs: [down the street] [with a gun] [toward the bank]. It is easy to see that the rule could have applied four or more times, for example by adding a PP like *for no good purpose.*

NPs can also contain PPs recursively. An example of this is shown by the phrase *the man with the telescope in a box.*

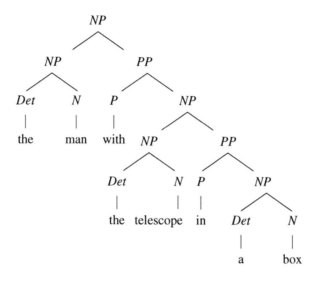

To show that speakers permit recursive NP structures of this sort, we need to include the following PS rule, which is like the recursive VP rule 5.

9. NP → NP PP

The PS rules define the allowable structures of the language, and in so doing make predictions about structures that we may not have considered when formulating each rule individually. These predictions can be tested, and if they are not validated, the rules must be reformulated because they must generate all and only the allowable structures. For example, rule 7 (VP → V CP) in combination with rules 8 (CP → C S) and 1 (S → NP VP) form a recursive set. (The recursiveness comes from the fact that S and VP occur on both the left and right side of the rules.) Those rules allow S to contain VP, which in turn contains CP, which in turn contains S, which in turn again contains VP, and so on, potentially without end. These rules, formulated for different purposes, correctly predict the limitlessness of language in which sentences are embedded inside larger sentences, such as *The children hope that the teacher knows that the principal said that the school closes for the day* as illustrated on the following page.

Recursive Adjectives and Possessives

"Very traditional. He's the noun. She's the adjective."

Now we consider the case of multiple adjectives, illustrated at the beginning of the chapter with sentences such as "The kindhearted, intelligent, handsome boy had many girlfriends." In English, adjectives occur before the noun. As a first approximation we might follow the system we have adopted thus far and introduce a recursive NP rule with a prenominal adjective:

NP → Adj NP

Repeated application of this rule would generate trees with multiple adjective positions, as desired.

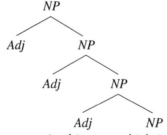

But there is something wrong in this tree, which is made apparent when we expand the lowest NP. The adjective can appear before the determiner, and this is not a possible word order in English NPs.

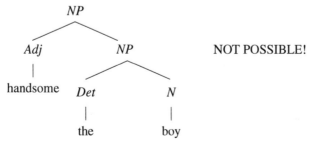

The problem is that although determiners and adjectives are both modifiers of the noun, they have a different status. First, an NP will never have more than one determiner in it, while it may contain many adjectives. Also, an adjective directly modifies the noun, while a determiner modifies the whole adjective(s) + noun complex. The expression "the big dog" refers to some specific dog that is big, and not just some dog of any size. In general, modification occurs between sisters. If the adjective modifies the noun, then it is sister to the noun. If the determiner modifies the adjective + noun complex, then the determiner is sister to this complex. We can represent these two sisterhood relations by introducing an additional level of structure between NP and N. We refer to this level as N-bar (written as N').

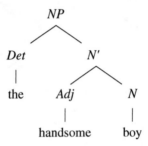

This structure provides the desired sisterhood relations. The adjective *handsome* is sister to the noun *boy*, which it therefore modifies, and the determiner is sister to the N' *handsome boy*. We must revise our NP rules to reflect this new structure, and add two rules for N'. Not all NPs have adjectives, of course. This is reflected in the second N' rule in which N' dominates only N.

NP → Det N' (revised version of NP → Det N)
N' → Adj N'
N' → N

Let us now see how these revised rules generate NPs with multiple (potentially infinitely many) adjectives.

Thus far all the NPs we have looked at are common nouns with a simple definite or indefinite determiner (e.g., the cat, a boy), but NPs can consist of a simple pronoun (e.g., he, she, we, they) or a proper name (e.g., Robert, California, Prozac). To reflect determiner-less NP structures, we will need the rule

NP → N'

But that's not all. We have possessive noun phrases such as *Melissa's garden*, *the girl's shoes*, and *the man with the telescope's hat*. In these structures the possessor NP (e.g., *Melissa's*, *the girl's*, etc.) functions as a determiner in that it further specifies its sister noun. The *'s* is the phonological realization of the abstract element *poss*. The structures are illustrated in each of the following trees.

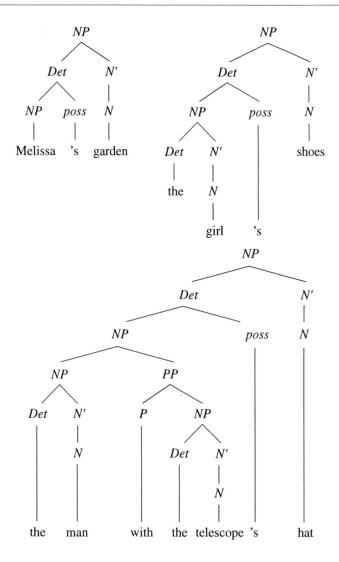

To accommodate the possessive structure we need an additional rule:

Det → NP poss

This rule forms a recursive set with the NP → Det N' rule. Together these rules allow an English speaker to have multiple possessives such as *The student's friend's cousin's book*.

The embedding of categories within categories is common to all languages. Our brain capacity is finite, able to store only a finite number of categories and rules for their combination. Yet this finite system places an infinite set of sentences at our disposal.

This linguistic property also illustrates the difference between competence and performance, discussed in chapter 1. All speakers of English (and other languages) have as part of their linguistic competence—their mental grammars—

the ability to embed phrases and sentences within each other ad infinitum. However, as the structures grow longer, they become increasingly more difficult to produce and understand. This could be due to short-term memory limitations, muscular fatigue, breathlessness, boredom, or any number of performance factors. (We will discuss performance factors more fully in chapter 9.) Nevertheless, these very long sentences would be well-formed according to the rules of the grammar.

Heads and Complements

"Mother Goose & Grimm" © Grimmy, Inc. Reprinted with permission of King Features Syndicate.

Phrase structure trees also show relationships among elements in a sentence. For example, the *subject* and *direct object* of the sentence can be structurally defined. The subject is the NP that is closest to, or immediately dominated by, the root S. The direct object is the NP that is closest to, or immediately dominated by, VP.

Another kind of relationship is that between the **head** of a phrase and its sisters. The head of a phrase is the word whose lexical category defines the type of phrase: the noun in a noun phrase, the verb in a verb phrase, and so on. Reviewing the PS rules in the previous section, we see that every VP contains a verb, which is its head. The VP may also contain other categories, such as an NP or CP. Those sister categories are **complements**; they complete the meaning of the phrase. Loosely speaking, the entire phrase refers to whatever the head verb refers to. For example, the VP *find a puppy* refers to an event of "finding." The NP object in the VP that completes its meaning is a complement. The underscored CP (complementizer phrase) in the sentence "I thought that the child found the puppy" is also a complement. (Please do not confuse the terms *complementizer* and *complement*.)

Every phrasal category, then, has a head of its same syntactic type. NPs are headed by nouns, PPs are headed by prepositions, CPs by complementizers, and so on; and every phrasal head can have a complement, which provides further information about the head. In the sentence "The death of Lincoln shocked the nation," the PP *of Lincoln* is the complement to the head noun *death*. Other examples of complements are illustrated in the following examples, with the head in italics and the complement underlined:

an *argument* <u>over jelly beans</u> (PP complement to noun)
his *belief* <u>that justice will prevail</u> (CP complement to noun)
happy <u>to be here</u> (infinitive complement to adjective)
about <u>the war in Iraq</u> (NP complement to preposition)
wrote <u>a long letter to his only sister</u> (NP—PP complement to verb)
tell <u>John that his mother is coming to dinner</u> (NP CP complements to verb)

Each of these examples is a phrase (NP, AdjP, PP, VP) that contains a head (N, Adj, P, V), followed by a complement of varying composition such as CP in the case of *belief*, or NP PP in the case of *wrote*, and so on. The head-complement relation is universal. All languages have phrases that are headed and that contain complements.

However, the order of the head and complement may differ in different languages. In English, for example, we see that the head comes first, followed by the complement. In Japanese, complements precede the head, as shown in the following examples:

Taro-ga	inu-o	mitsuketa	
Taro-subject marker	dog-object marker	found	(Taro found a dog)

Inu-ga	niwa-de	asonde	iru
dog-subject marker	garden-in	playing	is	(The dog is playing in the garden)

In the first sentence, the direct object complement *inu-o* "dog" precedes the head verb *mitsuketa* "found." In the second, the PP complement *niwa-de* "in the garden" also precedes the head verb phrase. English is a VO language, meaning that the verb ordinarily precedes its object. Japanese is an OV language, and this difference is also reflected in the head/complement word order.

Selection

Whether a verb takes a complement or not depends on the properties of the verb. For example, the verb *find* is a transitive verb. A transitive verb requires an NP complement (direct object), as in *The boy found the ball*, but not **The boy found*, or **The boy found in the house*. Some verbs like *eat* are optionally transitive. *John ate* and *John ate a sandwich* are both grammatical.

Verbs select different kinds of complements. For example, verbs like *put* and *give* take both an NP and a PP complement, but cannot occur with either alone:

Sam put the milk in the refrigerator.
*Sam put the milk.
Robert gave the film to his client.
*Robert gave to his client.

Sleep is an **intransitive verb**; it cannot take an NP complement.

Michael slept.
*Michael slept a fish.

Some verbs, such as *think*, select a sentence complement, as in "I think that Sam won the race." Other verbs, like *tell*, select an NP and a sentence, as in "I told Sam that Michael was on his bicycle"; yet other verbs like *feel* select either an AdjP or a sentence complement. (Complements are italicized.)

Paul felt *strong as an ox.*
He feels *that he can win.*

As we will discuss later, sentences that are complements must often be preceded by a complementizer *that.*

Other categories besides verbs also select their complements. For example, the noun *belief* selects either a PP or a CP, while the noun *sympathy* selects a PP, but not a CP, as shown by the following examples:

the belief *in freedom of speech*
the belief *that freedom of speech is a basic right*
their sympathy *for the victims*
*their sympathy that the victims are so poor

Adjectives can also have complements. For example, the adjectives *tired* and *proud* select PPs:

tired *of stale sandwiches*
proud *of her children*

With noun selection, the complement is often optional. Thus sentences like "He respected their belief," "We appreciated their sympathy," "Elimelech was tired," and "All the mothers were proud" are syntactically well-formed with a meaning that might be conveyed by an explicit complement understood from context. Verb selection is often not optional, however, so that *He put the milk* is ungrammatical even if it is clear from context where the milk was put.

The information about the complement types selected by particular verbs and other lexical items is called **C-selection** or **subcategorization,** and is included in the lexical entry of the item in our mental lexicon. (Here C stands for "categorial" and is not to be confused with the C that stands for "complementizer"—we apologize for the "clash" of symbols, but that's what it's like in the linguistic literature.)

Verbs also include in their lexical entry a specification of certain intrinsic semantic properties of their subjects and complements, just as they select for syntactic categories. This kind of selection is called **S-selection** (S for semantic). For example, the verb *murder* requires its subject and object to be human, while the verb *drink* requires its subject to be animate and its object liquid. Verbs such as *like, hate,* and so on select animate subjects. The following sentences violate S-selection and can only be used in a metaphorical sense. (We will use the symbol "!" to indicate a semantic anomaly.)

!The rock murdered the man.
!The beer drank the student.
!The tree liked the boy.

The famous sentence *Colorless green ideas sleep furiously,* discussed earlier in this chapter, is anomalous because (among other things) S-selection is violated (e.g., the verb *sleep* requires an animate subject). In chapter 5 we will discuss the semantic relationships between a verb and its subject and objects in far more detail.

The well-formedness of a phrase depends then on at least two factors: whether the phrase conforms to the structural constraints of the language as expressed in the PS rules, and whether it obeys the selectional requirements of the head, both syntactic (C-selection) and semantic (S-selection).

What Heads the Sentence

Might, could, would—they are contemptible auxiliaries.

GEORGE ELIOT (MARY ANN EVANS), *Middlemarch,* 1872

We said earlier that all phrases have heads. One category that we have not yet discussed in this regard is sentence (S). For uniformity's sake, we want all the categories to be headed, but what would the head of S be? To answer this question, let us consider sentences such as the following:

Sam will kick the soccer ball.
Sam has kicked the soccer ball.
Sam is kicking the soccer ball.
Sam may kick the soccer ball.

As noted earlier, words like *will, has, is,* and *may* are auxiliary verbs, belonging to the category Aux, which also includes modals such as *might, could, would, can,* and several others. They occur in structures such as the following one.

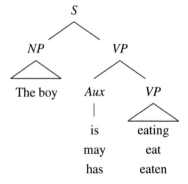

(From now on we will adopt the convention of using a triangle under a node when the content of a category is not crucial to the point under discussion.)

Auxiliary verbs specify a time frame for the event (or state) described by the verb, whether it will take place in the future, already took place in the past, or is taking place now. A modal such as *may* contains "possibility" as part of its meaning, and says it is possible that the event will occur at some future time. The category Aux is a natural category to head S. Just as the VP is about the situation described by the verb—*eat ice cream* is about "eating"—so a sentence is about a situation or state of affairs that occurs at some point in time.

The parallel with other categories extends further. In the previous PS tree, VP is the complement to Aux. The selectional relationship between Aux and VP is demonstrated by the fact that particular auxiliaries go with particular kinds of VPs. For example, the auxiliary *be* takes a progressive (-ing) form of the verb,

The boy **is** danc**ing.**

while the auxiliary *have* selects a past participle (-en) form of the verb,

The girl **has** eaten.

and the modals select the infinitival form of the verb (no affixes),

The child **must sleep**
The boy **may eat.**

To have a uniform notation, many linguists use the symbols **T** (= tense) and **TP** (= tense phrase) instead of Aux and S. Furthermore, just as the NP required the intermediate N-bar (N') category, the TP also has the intermediate T-bar (T') category, as in the phrase structure tree below.

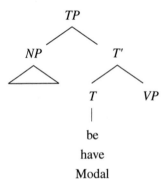

Indeed, many linguists assume that all XPs, where XP stands for any of NP, PP, VP, TP, AdjP, or CP, have three levels of structure. This is referred to as **X-bar theory.** The basic three-level X-bar schema is as follows:

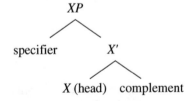

The first level is the XP itself. The second level consists of a **specifier,** which functions as a modifier (and which is generally an optional constituent), and an X' (i.e., "X-bar"). For example, an NP specifier is a determiner; a VP specifier is an adverb such as *never* or *often*; an AdjP specifier is a degree word such as *very* or *quite*. The third level is an expansion of X' and consists of a head X and a complement, which may itself be a phrasal category, thus giving rise to recursion. X-bar structure is thought to be universal, occurring in all the world's languages, though the order of the elements inside XP and X' may be reversed, as we saw in Japanese.

We will not use X-bar conventions in our description of syntax except on the few occasions where the notation provides an insight into the syntax of the language. For sentences we will generally use the more intuitive symbols S and Aux instead of TP and T, but you should think of Aux and S as having the same relationship to each other as V and VP, N and NP, and so on. To achieve this more straightforward approach, we will also ignore the T' category until it is needed later on in the description of the syntax of the main verb *be*.

Without the use of TP, T', and T, we need an additional PS rule to characterize structures containing Aux:

VP   →   Aux VP

Like the other recursive VP rules, this rule will allow multiple Aux positions.

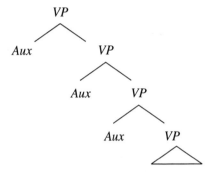

This is a desired consequence because English allows sentences with multiple auxiliaries such as:

The child may be sleeping.	(modal, be)
The dog has been barking all night.	(have, be)
The bird must have been flying home.	(modal, have, be)

The introduction of Aux into the system raises a question. Not all sentences seem to have auxiliaries. For example, the sentence "Sam kicked the soccer ball" has no modal, *have* or *be*. There is, however, a time reference for this sentence, namely, the past tense on the verb *kicked*. In sentences without auxiliaries, the tense of the sentence is its head. Instead of having a word under the category Aux (or T), there is a tense specification, *present* or *past*, as in the following tree:

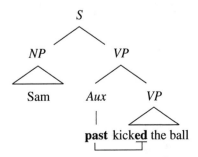

The inflection on the verb must match the tense in Aux. For example, if the tense of the sentence is *past*, then the verb must have an *-ed* affix (or must be an irregular past tense verb such as *ate*).

Thus, in English, and many other languages, the head of S may contain only an abstract tense specification and no actual word, as just illustrated. The actual morpheme, in this case *-ed* or an irregular past tense form such as *went*, is inserted into the tree after all the syntactic rules have applied. Most inflectional morphemes, which depend on elements of syntax, are represented in this way. Another example is the tense-bearing word *do* that is inserted into negative sentences such as *John did not go* and questions such as *Where did John go?* In these sentences *did* means "past tense." Later in this chapter we will see how *do*-insertion works.

In addition to specifying the time reference of the sentence, Aux specifies the agreement features of the subject. For example, if the subject is *we*, Aux contains the features first-person and plural; if the subject is *he* or *she*, Aux contains the features third-person and singular. So, another function of the syntactic rules is to use Aux as a "matchmaker" between the subject and the verb. When the subject and the verb bear the same features, Aux makes a match; when they have incompatible features, Aux cannot make a match and the sentence is ungrammatical. This matchmaker function of syntactic rules is more obvious in languages such as Italian, which have many different agreement morphemes, as discussed in chapter 3. Consider the Italian sentence for "I buy books."

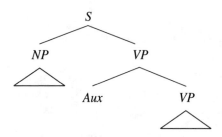

Io	Present	compro i libri
	first person	
*Io	Present	compri i libri
	second person	

The verb *compro*, "buy," in the first sentence bears the first-person singular morpheme, *-o*, which matches the agreement feature in Aux, which in turn matches the subject *Io*, "I." The sentence is therefore grammatical. In the second sentence, there is a mismatch between the first-person subject and the second-person features in Aux (and on the verb), and so the sentence is ungrammatical.

Structural Ambiguities

> The structure of every sentence is a lesson in logic.
>
> **JOHN STUART MILL,** Inaugural address at St. Andrews, 1867

As mentioned earlier, certain kinds of ambiguous sentences have more than one phrase structure tree, each corresponding to a different meaning. The sentence *The boy saw the man with the telescope* is structurally ambiguous. Its two meanings correspond to the following two phrase structure trees. (For simplicity we omit Aux in these structures and we return to the non-X-bar notation.)

1.

2.

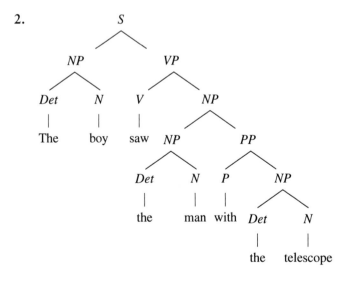

One meaning of this sentence is "the boy used a telescope to see the man." The first phrase structure tree represents this meaning. The key element is the position of the PP directly under the VP. Notice that although the PP is under VP, it is not a complement because phrasal categories don't take complements (only heads do), and because it is not selected by the verb. The verb *see* selects an NP. In this sentence, the PP has an adverbial function and modifies the verb.

In its other meaning, "the boy saw a man who had a telescope," the PP *with the telescope* occurs under the direct object NP, where it modifies the noun *man*. In this second meaning, the complement of the verb *see* is the entire NP—*the man with the telescope*.

The PP in the first structure is generated by the rule

VP   →   VP PP

In the second structure the PP is generated by the rule

NP   →   NP PP

Two interpretations are possible because the rules of syntax permit different structures for the same linear order of words.

Following is the set of PS rules that we have presented so far in the chapter. The rules have been renumbered.

1. S   →   NP VP
2. NP   →   Det N'
3. Det   →   NP poss
4. NP   →   N'
5. NP   →   NP PP
6. N'   →   Adj N'
7. N'   →   N
8. VP   →   V
9. VP   →   V NP
10. VP   →   V CP
11. VP   →   Aux VP
12. VP   →   VP PP
13. PP   →   P NP
14. CP   →   C S

This is not the complete set of PS rules for the language. Various structures in English cannot be generated with these rules, some of which we will talk about later. But even this mini phrase structure grammar generates an infinite set of possible sentences because the rules are recursive. These PS rules specify the word order for English (and other SVO languages, but not for Japanese, say, in which the object comes before the verb). Linear order aside, the hierarchical organization illustrated by these rules is largely true for all languages, as expressed by X-bar schema.

More Structures

"Shoe" © MacNelly. King Features Syndicate

Many English sentence types are not accounted for by the phrase structure rules given so far, including:

1. The dog completely destroyed the house.
2. The cat and the dog were friends.
3. The cat is coy.

The sentence in (1) contains the adverb (Adv) *completely*. Adverbs are modifiers that can specify how an event happens (*quickly, slowly, completely*) or when it happens (*yesterday, tomorrow, often*). As modifiers, adverbs are sisters to phrasal (XP) categories. In sentence (1) the adverb is a sister to VP, as illustrated in the following structure (we ignore Aux in this structure):

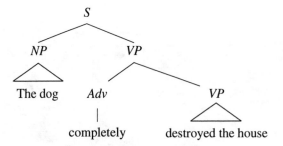

Temporal adverbs such as *yesterday, today, last week*, and manner adverbs such as *quietly, violently, suddenly, carefully*, also occur to the right of VP as follows:

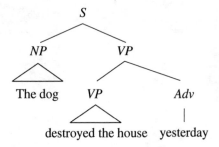

Adverbs also occur as sisters to S (which, recall, is also a phrasal category, TP).

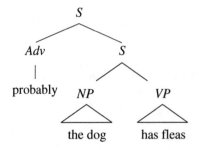

At this point you should be able to write the three PS rules that will account for the position of these adverbs.[1]

The "Shoe" cartoon's joke is based on the fact that *curse* may take an NP complement ("cursed *at* the day") and/or be modified by a temporal adverbial phrase (AdvP) ("cursed *on* the day"), leading to the structural ambiguity:

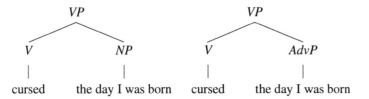

Interestingly, *I cursed the day I was born the day I was born,* with both the NP and AdvP modifying the verb, is grammatical and meaningful. (See exercise 23b.)

Sentence 2 contains a **coordinate structure** *The cat and the dog.* A coordinate structure results when two constituents of the same category (in this case, two NPs) are joined with a conjunction such as *and* or *or.* The coordinate NP has the following structure:

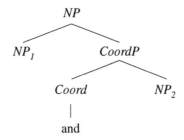

Though this may seem counterintuitive, in a coordinate structure the second member of the coordination (NP$_2$) forms a constituent with the conjunction *and.* We can show this by means of the "move as a unit" constituency test. In sentence (5) the words *and a CD* move together to the end of the sentence, whereas in (6) the constituent is broken, resulting in ungrammaticality.

4. Caley bought a book <u>and a CD</u> yesterday.
5. Caley bought a book yesterday <u>and a CD</u>.
6. *Caley bought a book and yesterday a CD.

Once again, we encourage you to write the two PS rules that generate this structure.[2]

---

[1] Answer: S → S AdvP   VP → Adv VP   VP → VP AdvP

[2] Answer: NP → NP CoordP, CoordP → Coord NP

You can also construct trees for other kinds of coordinate structures, such as VP or PP coordination, which follow the same pattern.

Michael writes poetry and surfs. (VP *and* VP)
Sam rode his bicycle to school and to the pool. (PP *and* PP)

Sentence (3) contains the main verb *be* followed by an adjective. The structure of main verb *be* sentences is best illustrated using T' notation. The main verb *be* acts like the modals and the auxiliaries *be* and *have*. For example, it is moved to the beginning of the sentence in questions (*Is the cat coy?*). For this reason we assume that the main verb *be* occurs under T and takes an XP complement. The XP may be AdjP, as shown in the tree structure for (3):

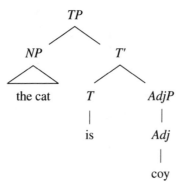

or an NP or PP as would occur in *The cat is a feline* or *The cat is in the tree.*

As before we will leave it as an exercise for you to construct the PS rules for these sentence types and the tree structures they generate.[3] (You might try drawing the tree structures; they should look very much like the one above.)

There are also embedded sentence types other than those that we have discussed, for example:

Hilary is waiting *for you to sing.* (Cf. You sing.)
The host wants *the president to leave early.* (Cf. The president leaves early.)
The host believes *the president to be punctual.* (Cf. The president is punctual.)

Although the detailed structure of these different embedded sentences is beyond the scope of this introduction, you should note that an embedded sentence may be an infinitive. An infinitive sentence does not have a tense. The embedded sentences *for you to sing, the president to leave early, and the president to be punctual* are infinitives. Such verbs as *want* and *believe,* among many others, can take infinitival complements. This information, like other selectional properties, belongs to the lexical entry of the selecting verb (the higher verb in the tree).

---

[3] Answer: TP → NP T', T' → T XP (where XP = AdjP, PP, NP)

Sentence Relatedness

I put the words down and push them a bit.

EVELYN WAUGH, quoted in *The New York Times,* April 11, 1966

Another aspect of our syntactic competence is the knowledge that certain sentences are related to one another, such as the following pair:

The boy is sleeping.   Is the boy sleeping?

These sentences describe the same situation. The sentence in the first column asserts that a particular situation exists, a boy-sleeping situation. Such sentences are called **declarative** sentences. The sentence in the second column asks whether such a boy-sleeping situation holds. Sentences of the second sort are called **yes-no questions**. The only actual difference in meaning between these sentences is that one asserts a situation and the other asks for confirmation of a situation. This element of meaning is indicated by the different word orders, which illustrates that two sentences may have a structural difference that corresponds *in a systematic way* to a meaning difference. The grammar of the language must account for this fact.

Transformational Rules

Method consists entirely in properly ordering and arranging the things to which we should pay attention.

RENÉ DESCARTES, *Oeuvres,* vol. X, c. 1637

Phrase structure rules account for much of our syntactic knowledge, but they do not account for the fact that certain sentence types in the language relate systematically to other sentence types. The standard way of describing these relationships is to say that the related sentences come from a common underlying structure. Yes-no questions are a case in point, and they bring us back to a discussion of auxiliaries. Auxiliaries are central to the formation of yes-no questions as well as certain other types of sentences in English. In yes-no questions, the auxiliary appears in the position preceding the subject. Here are a few more examples:

The boy is sleeping.   Is the boy sleeping?
The boy has slept.   Has the boy slept?
The boy can sleep.   Can the boy sleep?
The boy will sleep.   Will the boy sleep?

A way to capture the relationship between a declarative and a yes-no question is to allow the PS rules to generate a structure corresponding to the declarative sentence. Another formal device, called a **transformational rule,** then moves the auxiliary before the subject. The rule "Move Aux" is formulated as follows:

Move the highest Aux to adjoin to (the root) S.

That is, Move Aux applies to structures like:

to give structures like:

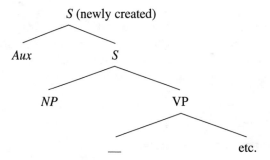

The "__" shows the position from which the Aux is moved. For example:

The boy is sleeping.   →   Is the boy __ sleeping?

The rule takes the basic (NP-Aux) structure generated by the phrase structure rules and derives a second tree (the dash represents the position from which a constituent has been moved). The Aux is attached to the tree by **adjunction.** Adjunction is an operation that copies an existing node (in this case S) and creates a new level to which the moved category (in this case Aux) is appended.

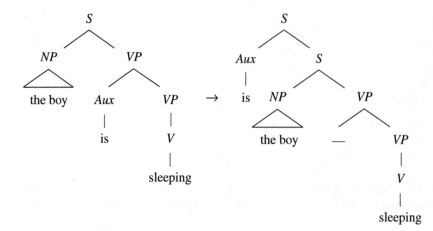

Yes-no questions are thus generated in two steps.

1. The phrase structure rules generate a basic structure.
2. Aux movement applies to produce the derived structure.

The basic structures of sentences, also called **deep structures** or **d-structures**, conform to the phrase structure rules. Variants on the basic sentence structures are derived via transformations. By generating questions in two steps, we are claiming that for speakers a relationship exists between a question and its corresponding statement. Intuitively, we know that such sentences are related. The transformational rule is a formal way of representing this knowledge.

The derived structures—the ones that follow the application of transformational rules—are called **surface structures** or **s-structures**. The phonological rules of the language—the ones that determine pronunciation—apply to s-structures. If no transformations apply, then d-structure and s-structure are the same. If transformations apply, then s-structure is the result after all transformations have had their effect. Many sentence types are accounted for by transformations, which can alter phrase structure trees by moving, adding, or deleting elements.

Other sentence pairs that are transformationally related are:

active-passive

The cat chased the mouse.   →   The mouse was chased by the cat.

there sentences

There was a man on the roof.   →   A man was on the roof.

PP preposing

The astronomer saw the quasar with the telescope.   →   With the telescope, the astronomer saw the quasar.

The Structural Dependency of Rules

"Peanuts" © United Feature Syndicate, Inc.

Transformations act on phrase structures without paying attention to the particular words that the structures contain. These rules are said to be **structure dependent**. The transformational rule of PP preposing moves any PP as long as it is immediately under the VP, as in *In the house, the puppy found the ball*; or *With the telescope, the boy saw the man*; and so on.

Evidence that transformations are structure dependent is provided by the fact that the sentence *With a telescope, the boy saw the man* is not ambiguous. It has only the meaning "the boy used a telescope to see the man," the meaning corresponding to the first phrase structure on page **149** in which the PP is immediately dominated by the VP. In the structure corresponding to the other meaning, "boy saw a man who had a telescope," the PP is in the NP as in the second tree on page **149**. The PP preposing transformation applies to the VP–PP structure and not to the NP–PP structure.

Another rule of English allows the complementizer *that* to be omitted when it precedes an embedded sentence but not a sentence that appears in subject position, as illustrated by these pairs:

I know that you know.   I know you know.
That you know bothers me.   *You know bothers me.

This is a further demonstration that rules are structure dependent.

Agreement rules are also structure dependent. In many languages, including English, the verb must agree with the subject. The verb is marked with an *-s* when the subject is third-person singular.

This guy seems kind of cute.
These guys seem kind of cute.

Now consider these sentences:

The *guy* we met at the party next door *seems* kind of cute.
The *guys* we met at the party next door *seem* kind of cute.

The verb *seem* must agree with the subject, *guy* or *guys*. Even though there are various words between the head noun and the verb, the verb always agrees with the head noun. Moreover, there is no limit to how many words may intervene, or whether they are singular or plural, as the following sentence illustrates:

The *guys* (*guy*) we met at the party next door that lasted until 3 A.M. and was finally broken up by the cops who were called by the neighbors *seem* (*seems*) kind of cute.

The phrase structure tree of such a sentence explains why this is so.

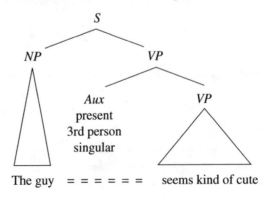

In the tree, "= = = = = =" represents the intervening structure, which may, in principle, be indefinitely long and complex. Speakers of English (and all other languages) know that agreement depends on sentence structure, not the linear order of words. Agreement is between the subject and the main verb, where the subject is structurally defined as the NP immediately dominated by S. The agreement relation is mediated by Aux, which contains the tense and agreement features that match up the subject and verb. As far as the rule of agreement is concerned, all other material can be ignored, although in actual performance, if the distance is too great, the speaker may forget what the head noun was.

The "Peanuts" cartoon also illustrates that agreement takes place between the head noun—the first occurrence of "refusal"—and the structurally highest verb in the sentence, which is the final occurrence of "do," despite the 14 intervening words.

A final illustration of structure dependency is found in the declarative-question pairs discussed previously. Consider the following sets of sentences:

The boy who is sleeping was dreaming.
Was the boy who is sleeping dreaming?
*Is the boy who sleeping was dreaming?

The boy who can sleep will dream.
Will the boy who can sleep dream?
*Can the boy who sleep will dream?

The ungrammatical sentences show that to form a question, the rule that moves Aux singles out the auxiliary dominated by the root S, and not simply the *first* auxiliary in the sentence. We can see this in the following simplified phrase structure trees. There are two auxiliaries, one in the subject relative clause and the other in the root clause. The rule affects the auxiliary in the higher main clause.

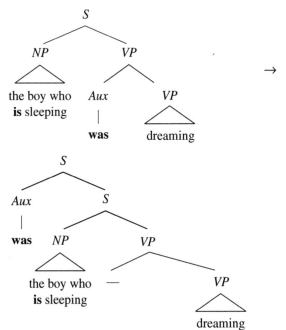

If the rule picked out the *first* Aux, we would have the ungrammatical sentence *Is the boy who__ sleeping was dreaming.* To derive the correct s-structures, transformations such as Move Aux must refer to phrase structure and not to the linear order of elements.

Structure dependency is a principle of Universal Grammar, and is found in all languages. For example, in languages that have subject-verb agreement, the dependency is between the verb and the head noun, and never some other noun such as the closest one, as shown in the following examples from Italian, German, Swahili, and English, respectively (the third-person singular agreement affix in the verb is in boldface and is governed by the boldfaced head noun, not the underlined noun, even though the latter is nearest the main verb):

La **madre** con tanti figli lavora molto.
Die **Mutter** mit den vielen Kindern arbeitet viel.
Mama anao watoto wengi anajitahidi.
The **mother** with many children works a lot.

Further Syntactic Dependencies

Sentences are organized according to two basic principles: constituent structure and syntactic dependencies. As we have discussed, constituent structure refers to the hierarchical organization of the subparts of a sentence, and transformational rules are sensitive to it. The second important property is the dependencies among elements in the sentence. In other words, the presence of a particular word or morpheme can be contingent on the presence of some other word or morpheme in a sentence. We have already seen at least two examples of syntactic dependencies. Selection is one kind of dependency. Whether there is a direct object in a sentence depends on whether the verb is transitive or intransitive. More generally, complements depend on the properties of the head of their phrase. Agreement is another kind of dependency. The features in Aux (and on the verb) must match the features of the subject.

Wh Questions

Whom are you? said he, for he had been to night school.

GEORGE ADE, "The Steel Box," in *Bang! Bang!,* 1928

The following *wh* questions illustrate another kind of dependency:

1. (a) What will Max chase?
   (b) Where has Pete put his bone?
   (c) Which dog do you think loves balls?

There are several points of interest in these sentences. First, the verb *chase* in sentence (a) is transitive, yet there is no direct object following it. There is a gap where the direct object should be. The verb *put* in sentence (b) selects a direct object and a prepositional phrase, yet there is no PP following *his bone*. Finally, the embedded verb *loves* in sentence (c) bears the third-person *-s* morpheme, yet there is no obvious subject to trigger this agreement. If we remove the *wh* phrases, the remaining sentences would be ungrammatical.

2. (a) *will Max chase ___?
    (b) *has Pete put his bone ___?
    (c) *do you think ___ loves balls?

The grammaticality of a sentence with a gap depends on there being a *wh* phrase at the beginning of the sentence. The sentences in (1) are grammatical because the *wh* phrase is acting like the object in (a), the prepositional phrase object in (b), and the embedded subject in (c).

We can explain the dependency between the *wh* phrase and the missing constituent if we assume that in each case the *wh* phrase originated in the position of the gap in a sentence with the corresponding declarative structure:

3. (a) Max will chase *what*?
    (b) Pete has put his bone *where*?
    (c) You think (that) *which dog* loves balls?

The *wh* phrase is then moved to the beginning of the sentence by a transformational rule: Move *wh*. Because embedded *wh* phrases (*I wonder <u>who Mary likes</u>*) are known to be complementizer phrases (CPs), we may deduce that main clause questions (*Who does Mary like?*) are also CPs, with the following structure (recall that C abbreviates "complementizer"):

The *wh* phrase moves to the empty C position at the left periphery of the sentence.

Thus, *wh* questions are generated in three steps:

1. The phrase structure rules generate the CP d-structure with the *wh* phrase occupying an NP position within the S: direct object in (3a); prepositional object in (3b); and subject in (3c).
2. Move Aux adjoins the auxiliary to S.
3. Move *wh* moves the *wh* phrase to C.

The following tree shows the d-structure of the sentence *What will Max chase?*

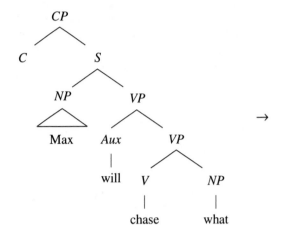

The s-structure representation of this sentence is:

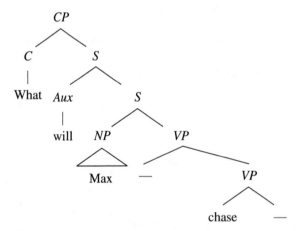

In question (1c), there is an auxiliary "do." Unlike the other auxiliaries (e.g., *can, have, be*), *do* is not part of the d-structure of the question. The d-structure of the question *Which dog did Michael feed?* is "Michael fed which dog?" Because Move Aux is structure dependent (like all rules), it ignores the content of the category. It will therefore move Aux even when Aux contains only a tense feature such as *past*. In this case, another rule called "*do* support," inserts *do* into the structure to carry the tense:

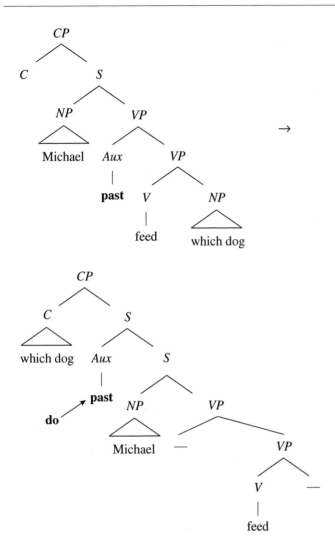

The first tree represents the d-structure to which the Aux and *wh* movement rules apply. The second tree shows the output of those transformations and the insertion of "do." "Do" combines with *past* to yield "did." Rules that convert inflectional features such as *past tense, third-person present tense*, and the possessive *poss* into their proper phonological forms are called **spell-out rules**.

Unlike the other rules we have seen, which operate inside a phrase or clause, Move *wh* can move the *wh* phrase outside of its own clause. There is no limit to the distance that a *wh* phrase can move, as illustrated by the following sentences. The dashes indicate the position from which the *wh* phrase has been moved.

Who did Helen say the senator wanted to hire ___?

Who did Helen say the senator wanted the congressional representative to try to hire ___?

Who did Helen say the senator wanted the congressional representative to try to convince the Speaker of the House to get the Vice President to hire ___?

"Long-distance" dependencies created by *wh* movement are a fundamental part of human language. They provide still further evidence that sentences are not simply strings of words but are supported by a rich scaffolding of phrase structure trees. These trees express the underlying structure of a sentence as well as its relation to other sentences in the language, and as always are reflective of a person's knowledge of syntax.

UG Principles and Parameters

Whenever the literary German dives into a sentence, that is the last you are going to see of him till he emerges on the other side of the Atlantic with his Verb in his mouth.

MARK TWAIN, *A Connecticut Yankee in King Arthur's Court,* 1889

In this chapter we have largely focused on English syntax, but many of the grammatical structures we have described for English also hold in other languages. This is because Universal Grammar (UG) provides the basic design for all human languages, and individual languages are simply variations on this basic design. Imagine a new housing development. All of the houses have the same floor plan, but the occupants have some choices to make. They can have carpet or hardwood floors, curtains or blinds; they can choose their kitchen cabinets and the countertops, the bathroom tiles, and so on. This is more or less how the syntax operates. Languages conform to a basic design, and then there are choice points or points of variation.

All languages have phrase structure rules that specify the allowable d-structures. In all languages, phrases consist of heads and complements, and sentences are headed by Aux (or T), which is specified for information such as tense, agreement, and modality. However, languages may have different word orders within the phrases and sentences. The word order differences between English and Japanese, discussed earlier, illustrate the interaction of general and language-specific properties. UG specifies the structure of a phrase. It must have a head and may take one or more complement types (the X-bar schema discussed earlier). However, each language defines for itself the relative order of these constituents: English is head initial, Japanese is head final. We call the points of variation **parameters**.

All languages seem to have movement rules. Move Aux is a version of a more general rule that exists in languages such as Dutch, in which the auxiliary moves, if there is one, as in (1), and otherwise the main verb moves, as in (2):

1. Zal Femke fietsen?
   will Femke bicycle ride   (Will Femke ride her bicycle?)
2. Leest Meindert veel boeken?
   reads Meindert many books   (Does Meindert read many books?)

In English, main verbs other than *be* do not move. Instead, English "do" spells out the stranded tense and agreement features. All languages have expressions for requesting information about *who, when, where, what,* and *how.* Even if the question words in other languages do not necessarily begin with "wh," we will refer to such questions as *wh* questions. In some languages, such as Japanese and Swahili, the *wh* phrase does not move. It remains in its original d-structure position. In Japanese the sentence is marked with a question morpheme, *no:*

Taro-ga   nani-o   mitsuketa-no?
Taro   what   found

Recall that Japanese word order is SOV, so the *wh* phrase nani ("what") is an object and occurs before the verb.

In Swahili the *wh* phrase—*nani* by pure coincidence—also stays in its base position:

Ulipatia   nani   Kitabu?
you gave   who   a book

However, in all languages with *wh* movement (i.e., movement of the question phrase), the question element moves to C (complementizer). The "landing site" of the moved phrase is determined by UG. Among the *wh* movement languages, there is some variation. In the Romance languages, such as Italian, the *wh* phrase moves as in English, but when the *wh* phrase questions the object of a preposition, the preposition must move together with the *wh* phrase. In English, by contrast, the preposition can be "stranded" (i.e., left behind in its original position):

A chi hai dato il libro?
To whom (did) you give the book?
*Chi hai dato il libro a?
Who(m) did you give the book to?

In some dialects of German, long-distance *wh* movement leaves a trail of *wh* phrases in the C position of the embedded sentence:

Mit   wem   Glaubst   Du   Mit   wem   Hans   spricht?
With   whom   think   you   with   whom   Hans   talks
(Whom do you think Hans talks to?)

Wen   willst   Du   Wen   Hans   anruft?
Whom   want   you   whom   Hans   call
(Whom do you want Hans to call?)

In Czech the question phrase "how much" can be moved, leaving behind the NP it modifies:

Jak   velké   Václav   koupil   auto?
How   big   Václav   bought car
(How big a car did Václav buy?)

Despite these variations, *wh* movement adheres to certain constraints. Although *wh* phrases such as *what, who,* and *which boy* can be inserted into any NP position, and are then free in principle to move to C, there are specific instances in which *wh* movement is blocked. For example, a *wh* phrase cannot move out of a relative clause like *the senator that wanted to hire who,* as in (1b). It also cannot move out of a clause beginning with *whether* or *if,* as in (2c) and (d). (Remember that the position from which the *wh* phrases have moved is indicated with ___.)

1. (a) Emily paid a visit to the senator that wants to hire who?
    (b) *Who did Emily pay a visit to the senator that wants to hire ___?

2. (a) Miss Marple asked Sherlock whether Poirot had solved the crime.
    (b) Who did Miss Marple ask ___ whether Poirot had solved the crime?
    (c) *Who did Miss Marple ask Sherlock whether ___ had solved the crime?
    (d) *What did Miss Marple ask Sherlock whether Poirot had solved ___?

The only difference between the grammatical (2b) and the ungrammatical (2c) and (d) is that in (2b) the *wh* phrase originates in the higher clause, whereas in (2c, d) the *wh* phrase comes from inside the *whether* clause. This illustrates that the constraint against movement depends on structure and not on the length of the sentence.

Some sentences can be very short and still not allow *wh* movement:

3. (a) Sam Spade insulted the fat man's henchman.
    (b) Who did Sam Spade insult?
    (c) Whose henchman did Sam Spade insult?
    (d) *Whose did Sam Spade insult henchman?

4. (a) John ate bologna and cheese.
    (b) John ate bologna with cheese.
    (c) *What did John eat bologna and?
    (d) What did John eat bologna with?

The sentences in (3) show that a *wh* phrase cannot be extracted from inside a possessive NP. In (3b) it is okay to question the whole direct object. In (3c) it is even okay to question a piece of the possessive NP, providing the entire *wh* phrase is moved, but (3d) shows that moving the *wh* word alone out of the possessive NP is illicit.

Sentence (4a) is a coordinate structure and has approximately the same meaning as (4b), which is not a coordinate structure. In (4c) moving a *wh* phrase out of the coordinate structure results in ungrammaticality, whereas in 4(d), moving the *wh* phrase out of the PP is fine. The ungrammaticality of 4(c), then, is related to its structure and not to its meaning.

The constraints on *wh* movement are not specific to English. Such constraints operate in all languages that have *wh* movement. Like the principle of structure dependency and the principles governing the organization of phrases, the constraints on *wh* movement are part of UG. These aspects of grammar need not be learned. They are part of the innate blueprint for language that the child brings to the task of acquiring a language. What children must learn are the language-specific aspects of grammar. Where there are parameters of variation, children must determine the correct choice for their language. The Japanese child must determine that the verb comes after the object in the VP, and the English-speaking child that the verb comes first. The Dutch-speaking child acquires a rule that moves the verb, while the English-speaking child must restrict his rule to auxiliaries. Italian, English, and Czech children learn that to form a question, the *wh* phrase moves, whereas Japanese and Swahili children determine that there is no movement. As far as we can tell, children fix these parameters very quickly. We will have more to say about how children set UG parameters in chapter 8.

Sign Language Syntax

All languages have rules of syntax similar in kind, if not in detail, to those of English, and sign languages are no exception. Signed languages have phrase structure rules that provide hierarchical structure and order constituents. A signer distinguishes *The dog chased the cat* from *The cat chased the dog* through the order of signing. The basic order of ASL is SVO. Unlike English, however, adjectives follow the head noun in ASL.

ASL has a category Aux, which expresses notions such as tense, agreement, modality, and so on. In Thai, to show that an action is continuous, the auxiliary verb *kamlang* is inserted before the verb. Thus *kin* means "eat" and *kamlang kin* means "is eating." In English a form of *be* is inserted and the main verb is changed to an *-ing* form. In ASL the sign for a verb such as *eat* may be articulated with a sweeping, repetitive movement to achieve the same effect. The sweeping, repetitive motion is a kind of auxiliary.

Many languages, including English, have a transformation that moves a direct object to the beginning of the sentence to draw particular attention to it, as in:

Many greyhounds, my wife has rescued.

The transformation is called **topicalization** because an object to which attention is drawn is generally the topic of the sentence or conversation. (The d-structure underlying this sentence is *My wife has rescued many greyhounds*.)

In ASL a similar reordering of signs accompanied by raising the eyebrows and tilting the head upward accomplishes the same effect. The head motion and facial expressions of a signer function as markers of the special word order, much as intonation does in English, or the attachment of prefixes or suffixes might in other languages.

There are constraints on topicalization similar to those on *wh* movement illustrated in a previous section. In English the following strings are ungrammatical:

*Henchman, Sam Spade insulted the fat man's.
*This film, John asked Mary whether she liked.
*Cheese, John ate bologna and for lunch.

Compare this with the grammatical:

The fat man's henchman, Sam Spade insulted.
This film, John asked Mary to see with her.
Bologna and cheese, John ate for lunch.

Sign languages exhibit similar constraints. The signed sequence *Henchman, Sam Spade insulted the fat man's* or the other starred examples are ungrammatical in ASL as in spoken languages.

ASL has *wh* phrases. The *wh* phrase in ASL may move or it may remain in its d-structure position as in Japanese and Swahili. The ASL equivalents of *Who did Bill see yesterday?* and *Bill saw who yesterday?* are both grammatical. As in topicalization, *wh* questions are accompanied by a nonmanual marker. For questions, this marker is a facial expression with furrowed brows and the head tilted back.

ASL and other sign languages show an interaction of universal and language-specific properties, just as spoken languages do. The rules of sign languages are structure dependent, and movement rules are constrained in various ways, as illustrated earlier. Other aspects are particular to sign languages, such as the facial gestures, which are an integral part of the grammar of sign languages but not of spoken languages. The fact that the principles and parameters of UG hold in both the spoken and manual modalities shows that the human brain is designed to acquire and use language, not simply speech.

Summary

Speakers of a language recognize the grammatical sentences of their language and know how the words in a sentence must be ordered and grouped to convey a certain meaning. All speakers are capable of producing and understanding an unlimited number of new sentences that have never before been spoken or heard. They also recognize ambiguities, know when different sentences mean the same thing, and correctly interpret the grammatical relations in a sentence, such as **subject** and **direct object**. This kind of knowledge comes from their knowledge of the **rules of syntax**.

Sentences have structure that can be represented by **phrase structure trees** containing **syntactic categories**. Phrase structure trees reflect the speaker's mental representation of sentences. Ambiguous sentences may have more than one phrase structure tree.

Phrase structure trees reveal the linear order of words and the constituency of each syntactic category. There are different kinds of syntactic categories: **Phrasal categories**, such as NP and VP, are composed of other syntactic categories; **lexical categories**, such as Noun and Verb, and **functional categories**, such as Det,

Aux, and C, are not decomposable and often correspond to individual words. The internal structure of the phrasal categories is universal. It consists of a **head** and its **complements**. The particular order of elements within the phrase is accounted for by the **phrase structure rules** of each language. NPs, VPs, and so on are headed by nouns, verbs, and the like. The sentence (S or TP) is headed by Aux (or T), which carries such information as tense, agreement, and modality.

A grammar is a formally stated, explicit description of the mental grammar or speaker's linguistic competence. Phrase structure rules characterize the basic phrase structure trees of the language, the **d-structures**.

Some PS rules allow the same syntactic category to appear repeatedly in a phrase structure tree, such as a sentence embedded in another sentence. These rules are **recursive** and reflect a speaker's ability to produce countless sentences.

The **lexicon** represents the knowledge that speakers have about the vocabulary of their language. This knowledge includes the syntactic category of words and what elements may occur together, expressed as **c-selection** or **subcategorization**. The lexicon also contains semantic information including the kinds of NPs that can function as semantically coherent subjects and objects, **s-selection**.

Transformational rules account for relationships between sentences such as declarative and interrogative pairs, including *wh* questions. Transformations can move constituents. Much of the meaning of a sentence is interpreted from its d-structure. The output of the transformational rules is the **s-structure** of a sentence, the structure to which the phonological rules of the language apply. Inflectional information such as tense, agreement, and possessive, among others, is represented as features in the phrase structure tree. After the rules of the syntax have applied, these features are sometimes spelled out as affixes such as *-ed* and *-'s* or as function words such as *do*.

The basic design of language is universal. Universal Grammar specifies that syntactic rules are **structure dependent** and that movement rules may not move phrases out of certain structures such as coordinate structures. These constraints exist in all languages—spoken and signed—and need not be learned. UG also contains parameters of variation, such as the order of heads and complements, and the variations on movement rules. A child acquiring a language must fix the parameters of UG for that language.

References for Further Reading

Baker, M. C. 2001. *The atoms of language: The mind's hidden rules of grammar*. New York: Basic Books.

Chomsky, N. 1995. *The minimalist program*. Cambridge, MA: MIT Press.

_____. 1972. *Language and mind*, rev. edn. New York: Harcourt Brace Jovanovich.

_____. 1965. *Aspects of the theory of syntax*. Cambridge, MA: MIT Press.

Jackendoff, R. S. 1994. *Patterns in the mind: Language and human nature*. New York: Basic Books.

Pinker, S. 1999. *Words and rules: The ingredients of language*. New York: HarperCollins.

Radford, A. 2009. *Analysing English sentences: A minimalist approach*. Cambridge, UK: Cambridge University Press.

_____. 2004. *English syntax: An introduction*. Cambridge, UK: Cambridge University Press.

Exercises

1. Besides distinguishing grammatical from ungrammatical sentences, the rules of syntax account for other kinds of linguistic knowledge, such as

   a. when a sentence is structurally ambiguous. (Cf. The boy saw the man with a telescope.)
   b. when two sentences with different structures mean the same thing. (Cf. The father wept silently and The father silently wept.)
   c. systematic relationships of form and meaning between two sentences, like declarative sentences and their corresponding interrogative form. (Cf. The boy can sleep and Can the boy sleep?)

   Draw on your linguistic knowledge of English to come up with an example illustrating each of these cases. (Use examples that are different from the ones in the chapter.) Explain why your example illustrates the point. If you know a language other than English, provide examples in that language, if possible.

2. Consider the following sentences:

   a. I hate war.
   b. You know that I hate war.
   c. He knows that you know that I hate war.
       A. Write another sentence that includes sentence (c).
       B. What does this set of sentences reveal about the nature of language?
       C. How is this characteristic of human language related to the difference between linguistic competence and performance? (*Hint:* Review these concepts in chapter 1.)

3. Paraphrase each of the following sentences in two ways to show that you understand the ambiguity involved:

   Example: Smoking grass can be nauseating.
       i. Putting grass in a pipe and smoking it can make you sick.
       ii. Fumes from smoldering grass can make you sick.

   a. Dick finally decided on the boat.
   b. The professor's appointment was shocking.
   c. The design has big squares and circles.
   d. That sheepdog is too hairy to eat.
   e. Could this be the invisible man's hair tonic?
   f. The governor is a dirty street fighter.
   g. I cannot recommend him too highly.
   h. Terry loves his wife and so do I.
   i. They said she would go yesterday.
   j. No smoking section available.

4. A. Consider the following baseball joke (knowledge of baseball required):

   Catcher to pitcher: "Watch out for this guy, he's a great fastball hitter." Pitcher to catcher: "No problem. There's no way I've got a great fastball."

Explain the humor either by paraphrasing, or even better, with a tree structure like the one we used early in the chapter for *old men and women* without the syntactic categories.

B. Do the same for the advertising executive's (honest?) claim that the new magazine "has between one and two billion readers."

5. Draw two phrase structure trees representing the two meanings of the sentence "The magician touched the child with the wand." Be sure you indicate which meaning goes with which tree.

6. Draw the subtrees for the italicized NPs in the following sentences:
   a. *Every child's mother* hopes he will be happy.
   b. *The big dog's bone* is buried in the garden.
   c. *Angry men in dark glasses* roamed the streets.
   d. *My aunt and uncle's trip* to Alaska was wonderful.
   e. **Challenge exercises:** *Whose dirty underwear* is this?
   f. *The boy's dog's bone* is in the pantry. (*Hint*: Use the rules NP → Det N', Det → NP poss, NP → N'.)

7. In all languages, sentences can occur within sentences. For example, in exercise 2, sentence (b) contains sentence (a), and sentence (c) contains sentence (b). Put another way, sentence (a) is embedded in sentence (b), and sentence (b) is embedded in sentence (c). Sometimes embedded sentences appear slightly changed from their normal form, but you should be able to recognize and underline the embedded sentences in the following examples. Underline in the non-English sentences, when given, not in the translations (the first one is done as an example):
   a. Yesterday I noticed <u>my accountant repairing the toilet</u>.
   b. Becky said that Jake would play the piano.
   c. I deplore the fact that bats have wings.
   d. That Guinevere loves Lorian is known to all my friends.
   e. Who promised the teacher that Maxine wouldn't be absent?
   f. It's ridiculous that he washes his own Rolls-Royce.
   g. The woman likes for the waiter to bring water when she sits down.
   h. The person who answers this question will win $100.
   i. The idea of Romeo marrying a 13-year-old is upsetting.
   j. I gave my hat to the nurse who helped me cut my hair.
   k. For your children to spend all your royalty payments on recreational drugs is a shame.
   l. Give this fork to the person I'm getting the pie for.
   m. khǎw chyâ waǎ khruu maa. (Thai)
      He believe that teacher come
      He believes that the teacher is coming.
   n. Je me demande quand il partira. (French)
      I me ask when he will leave
      I wonder when he'll leave.
   o. Jan zei dat Piet dit boek niet heeft gelezen. (Dutch)
      Jan said that Piet this book not has read
      Jan said that Piet has not read this book.

8. Following the patterns of the various tree examples in the text, draw phrase structure trees for the following sentences. (*Hint*: You may omit the N' level whenever N' dominates a single N, so that, for example, *the puppy* has the structure

a. The puppy found the child.
b. A frightened passenger landed the crippled airliner.
c. The house on the hill collapsed in the wind.
d. The ice melted.
e. The hot sun melted the ice.
f. A fast car with twin cams sped by the children on the grassy lane.
g. The old tree swayed in the wind.
h. **Challenge exercise:** The children put the toy in the box.
i. The reporter realized that the senator lied.
j. Broken ice melts in the sun.
k. My guitar gently weeps.
l. A stranger cleverly observed that a dangerous spy from the CIA lurks in the alley by the old tenement. (*Hint*: See footnote 1, page 153.)

9. Use the rules on page 150 to create five phrase structure trees of 6, 7, 8, 9, and 10 words. Use your mental lexicon to fill in the bottom of the tree.

10. We stated that the rules of syntax specify all and only the grammatical sentences of the language. Why is it important to say "only"? What would be wrong with a grammar that specified as grammatical sentences all of the truly grammatical ones plus a few that were not grammatical?

11. In this chapter we introduced X-bar theory, according to which each phrase has three levels of structure.

a. Draw the subtree corresponding to each phrasal category, NP, AdjP, VP, PP, as it would look according to X-bar notation.
b. **Challenge exercise:** What would the structure of CP be according to X-bar notation?
c. **Further challenge:** Give a sample phrase structure for each tree that fully exploits its entire structure—e.g., *the father of the bride* for the NP.

12. Using one or more of the constituency tests (i.e., stand alone, move as a unit, replacement by a pronoun) discussed in the chapter, determine which of the boldfaced portions in the sentences are constituents. Provide the grammatical category of the constituents.

a. Martha found **a lovely pillow** for the couch.
b. The **light in this room** is terrible.
c. I wonder **if Bonnie has finished packing her books.**

   d. Melissa slept **in her class.**
   e. **Pete and Max** are fighting over **the bone.**
   f. I gave a bone to Pete **and to Max** yesterday.
   g. I gave a bone to **Pete and** to Max yesterday.

13. The two sentences below contain a **verbal particle:**

    i.   He ran *up* the bill.
    ii. He ran the bill *up*.

    The verbal particle *up* and the verb *run* depend on each other for the unique idiosyncratic meaning of the phrasal verb *run up*. (*Running up a bill* involves neither running nor the location up.) We showed earlier that in such cases the particle and *object* do not form a constituent, hence they cannot move as a unit:

    iii. *Up the bill, John ran   (compare this to *Up the hill John ran*).

    a. Using adverbs such as *completely*, show that the particle forms a constituent with the *verb* in [*run up*] *the bill*, while in *run* [*up the hill*], the preposition and NP object form a constituent.
    b. Now consider the following data:

       i.   Michael ran up the hill and over the bridge.
       ii. *Michael ran up the bill and off his mouth.
       iii. Michael ran up the bill and ran off his mouth.

       Use the data to argue that expressions like *up the bill* and *off his mouth* are not constituents.

14. In terms of c-selection restrictions, explain why the following are ungrammatical:

    a. *The man located.
    b. *Jesus wept the apostles.
    c. *Robert is hopeful of his children.
    d. *Robert is fond that his children love animals.
    e. *The children laughed the man.

15. In the chapter, we looked at transitive verbs that select a single NP direct object like *chase*. English also has **ditransitive verbs**, ones that may be followed by two NPs, such as *give*:

    The emperor gave the vassal a castle.

    Think of three other ditransitive verbs in English and give example sentences.

16. For each verb, list the different types of complements it selects and provide an example of each type:

    a. want
    b. force
    c. try
    d. believe
    e. say

17. Tamil is a language spoken in India by upward of 70 million people. Others, but not you, may find that they talk "funny," as illustrated by word-for-word translations of PPs from Tamil to English:

    a. Tamil to English Meaning

       the bed on   "on the bed"
       the village from   "from the village"

       i. Based on these data, is Tamil a head initial or a head final language?
       ii. What would the phrase structure rule for PP look like in Tamil?

    b. Here are two more word-for-word glosses:

       she is a poet that think   "think that she is a poet"
       the cobra is deadly that know   "know that the cobra is deadly"

       i. Do these further data support or detract from your analysis in part (a)?
       ii. What would the pertinent VP and CP rules look like in Tamil, based on these data?

    c. Give a word-for-word translation from Tamil of *airplane on the runway* and *suppose that cobras spit*.
    d. **Challenge exercise:** Same as (c) for: *believe that she sits by the well*.

18. All *wh* phrases can move to the left periphery of the sentence.

    a. Invent three sentences beginning with *what, which,* and *where*, in which the *wh* word is not in its d-structure position in the sentence. Give both the s-structure and d-structure versions of your sentence. For example, using *when*: *When could Marcy catch a flight out of here?* from *Marcy could catch a flight out of here when?*
    b. Draw the phrase structure tree for one of these sentences using the phrase structure and movement rules provided in the chapter.
    c. **Challenge exercise:** How could you reformulate the movement rules used to derive a *wh* question such as *What has Mary done with her life?* using an X-bar CP structure (see question 11)?

19. There are many systematic, structure-dependent relationships among sentences similar to the one discussed in the chapter between declarative and interrogative sentences. Here is another example based on ditransitive verbs (see exercise 15):

    The boy wrote the senator a letter.
    The boy wrote a letter to the senator.
    A philanthropist gave the animal rights movement $1 million.
    A philanthropist gave $1 million to the animal rights movement.

    a. Describe the relationship between the first and second members of the pairs of sentences.
    b. State why a transformation deriving one of these structures from the other is plausible.

20. State at least three differences between English and the following languages, using just the sentence(s) given. Ignore lexical differences (i.e., the different vocabulary). Here is an example:

Thai: dèg   khon   níi   kamlang   kin.
       boy   *classifier* this   *progressive* eat
       "This boy is eating."

       mǎa   tua   nán   kin   khâaw.
       dog   *classifier* that   eat   rice
       "That dog ate rice."

Three differences are (1) Thai has "classifiers." They have no English equivalent. (2) The words (determiners, actually) "this" and "that" follow the noun in Thai, but precede the noun in English. (3) The "progressive" is expressed by a separate word in Thai. The verb does not change form. In English, the progressive is indicated by the presence of the verb *to be* and the adding of *-ing* to the verb.

   a. French

      cet   homme   intelligent   comprendra   la question.
      this   man   intelligent   will understand the question
      "This intelligent man will understand the question."

      ces   hommes   intelligents   comprendront   les questions.
      these men   intelligent   will understand the questions
      "These intelligent men will understand the questions."

   b. Japanese

      watashi ga   sakana   o   tabete   iru.
      I   *subject*   fish   *object*   eat (*ing*)   am
               marker   *marker*
      "I am eating fish."

   c. Swahili

      mtoto   alivunja   kikombe.
      m-   toto   a-   li-   vunja   ki-   kombe
      class   child   he   *past* break   *class*   cup
      marker   *marker*
      "The child broke the cup."

      watoto   wanavunja   vikombe.
      wa-   toto   wa- na-   vunja   vi-   kombe
      class   child   they *present* break   *class*   cup
      marker   *marker*
      "The children break the cups."

   d. Korean

      kɨ   sonyɔn-iee   wɨyu-lɨl   masi-ass-ta.
      kɨ   sonyɔn-   iee   wɨyu- lɨl   masi-   ass-   ta
      the   boy   *subject*   milk   *object*   drink   *past* *assertion*
                       marker   *marker*
      "The boy drank milk."

kɨ-nɨn	muɔs-ɨl		mɔk-ass-nɨnya.		
kɨ nɨn	muɔs-	ɨl	mɔk-	ass-	nɨnya
he *subject marker*	what	*object marker*	eat	*past*	*question*

"What did he eat?"

e. Tagalog

nakita	ni	Pedro-ng	puno	na	ang	bus.
nakita	ni	Pedro -ng	puno	na	ang	bus.
saw	*article*	Pedro that	full	already	*topic marker*	bus

"Pedro saw that the bus was already full."

21. Transformations may delete elements. For example, the s-structure of the ambiguous sentence "George wants the presidency more than Martha" may be derived from two possible d-structures:

   a. George wants the presidency more than he wants Martha.
   b. George wants the presidency more than Martha wants the presidency.

   A deletion transformation either deletes *he wants* from the structure of example (a), or *wants the presidency* from the structure of example (b). This is a case of **transformationally induced ambiguity**: two different d-structures with different semantic interpretations are transformed into a single s-structure.

   Explain the role of a deletion transformation similar to the ones just discussed in the following humorous dialogue between "two old married folks."

   HE: Do you still love me as much as you used to?
   SHE: As much as I used to what?

22. **Challenge exercise:** Compare the following French and English sentences:

French	English
Jean boit toujours du vin.	John always drinks some wine.
Jean drinks always some wine	*John drinks always some wine
(*Jean toujours boit du vin)	
Marie lit jamais le journal.	Mary never reads the newspaper.
Marie reads never the newspaper	*Mary reads never the newspaper.
(*Marie jamais lit le journal)	
Pierre lave souvent ses chiens.	Peter often washes his dogs.
Pierre washes often his dogs	*Peter washes often his dogs.
(*Pierre souvent lave ses chiens.)	

   a. Based on the above data, what would you hypothesize concerning the position of adverbs in French and English?
   b. Now suppose that UG specifies that in *all languages* adverbs of frequency (e.g., *always, never, often, sometimes*) immediately precede the VP, as in the following tree. What rule would you need to hypothesize to derive the correct surface word order for French? (*Hint:* Adverbs are not allowed to move.)

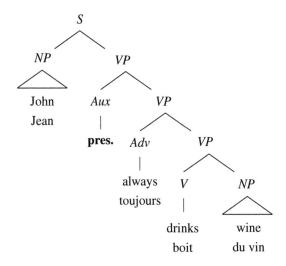

c. Do any verbs in English follow the same pattern as the French verbs?

23. a. Give the tree corresponding to the underlined portion of the sentence *The hole should have been being filled by the workcrew.*

b. Give the tree corresponding to the VP *cursed the day I was born the day I was born.*
    Which must come first, the AdvP or the NP? (You needn't worry about the internal structure of the AdvP or NP.)

24. Show that an embedded CP is a constituent by applying the constituency tests (stand alone, move as a unit, and replace with a pronoun). Consider the following sentences in formulating your answer, and provide further examples if you can. (The boldfaced words are the CP.)

Sam asked **if he could play soccer.**
I wonder **whether Michael walked the dog.**
Cher believes **that the students know the answer.**
It is a problem **that Sam broke his arm.**

25. Challenge exercise:

a. Give the d-structure tree for *Which dog does Michael think loves bones?* (*Hint*: The complementizer *that* must be present.)

b. Give the d-structure tree for *What does Michael think that his dog loves?*

c. Consider these data:

i. *Which dog does Michael think that loves bones?
ii. What does Michael think his dog loves?

In (ii) a complementizer deletion rule has deleted *that*. The rule is optional because the sentence is grammatical with or without *that*. In (i), however, the complementizer must be deleted to prevent the ungrammatical sentence from being generated. What factor governs the optionality of the rule?

26. Dutch and German are Germanic languages related to English, and as in English *wh* questions are formed by moving a *wh* phrase to sentence initial position.

   a. In what way are the rules of question formation in Dutch and German different from English? Base your answer on the following data:

German				Dutch			
i. Was	hat	Karl	gekauft?	Wat	heeft	Wim	gekocht?
what	has	Karl	bought	what	has	Wim	bought
"What has Karl bought?"				"What has Wim bought?"			
ii. Was	kauft	Karl?		Wat	koopt	Wim?	
What	buys	Karl		what	buys	Wim	
"What does Karl buy?"				"What does Wim buy?"			
iii. Kauft	Karl	das	Buch?	Koopt	Wim	het	boek?
buys	Karl	the	book	buys	Wim	the	book
"Does Karl buy the book?"				"Does Wim buy the book?"			

   b. **Challenge exercise:** Consider the following declarative sentences in Dutch and German:

iv. Karl	kaufte	das	Buch.	Wim	kocht	het	boek.
Karl	bought	the	book	Wim	bought	the	book
"Karl bought the book."				"Wim bought the book."			
v. Das	Buch	kaufte	Karl.	Het	boek	kocht	Wim.
The	book	bought	Karl	the	book	bought	Wim
"Karl bought the book."				"Wim bought the book."			

   vi. Das   Buch   kaufte   Karl   gestern.
       the   book   bought   Karl   yesterday
       "Karl bought the book yesterday."

       Het   boek   kocht   Wim   gisteren.
       the   book   bought   Wim   yesterday
       "Wim bought the book yesterday."

   vii. Gestern   kaufte   Karl   das   Buch
        Yesterday   bought   Karl   the   book
        "Yesterday Karl bought the book."

        Gisteren   kocht   Wim   het   boek.
        yesterday   bought   Wim   the   book
        "Yesterday Wim bought the book."

   What rules derive the different word order in declarative sentences? (*Hint*: There are two rules, one involving movement of the verb, and the other movement of an XP.)

   c. Are either of the rules in (b) familiar from the German/Dutch questions in (i)–(iii)?

3

The Psychology of Language

The field of psycholinguistics, or the psychology of language, is concerned with discovering the psychological processes that make it possible for humans to acquire and use language.

JEAN BERKO GLEASON AND NAN BERNSTEIN RATNER,
Psycholinguistics, 1993

8

Language Acquisition

[The acquisition of language] is doubtless the greatest intellectual feat any one of us is ever required to perform.

LEONARD BLOOMFIELD, *Language*, 1933

The capacity to learn language is deeply ingrained in us as a species, just as the capacity to walk, to grasp objects, to recognize faces. We don't find any serious differences in children growing up in congested urban slums, in isolated mountain villages, or in privileged suburban villas.

DAN SLOBIN, *The Human Language Series program 2*, 1994

Language is extremely complex. Yet very young children—before the age of five—already know most of the intricate system that is the grammar of a language. Before they can add 2 + 2, children are conjoining sentences, asking questions, using appropriate pronouns, negating sentences, forming relative clauses, and inflecting verbs and nouns and in general have the creative capacity to produce and understand a limitless number of sentences.

It is obvious that children do not learn a language simply by memorizing the sentences of the language. Rather, they acquire a system of grammatical rules of the sort we have discussed in the preceding chapters. No one teaches children the rules of the grammar. Their parents are no more aware of the phonological, morphological, syntactic, and semantic rules than are the children. Even if you remember your early years, do you remember anyone telling you to form a sentence by adding a verb phrase to a noun phrase, or to add [s] or [z] to form plurals? No one told you "This is a grammatical utterance and that is not." Yet somehow you were able, as all children are, to quickly and effortlessly extract the intricate system of rules from the language you heard around you and thereby "reinvent" the grammar of your parents. How the child accomplishes this phenomenal task is the subject of this chapter.

Mechanisms of Language Acquisition

There have been various proposals concerning the psychological mechanisms involved in acquiring a language. Early theories of language acquisition were heavily influenced by behaviorism, a school of psychology prevalent in the 1950s. As the name implies, behaviorism focused on people's behaviors, which are directly observable, rather than on the mental systems underlying these behaviors. Language was viewed as a kind of verbal behavior, and it was proposed that children learn language through imitation, reinforcement, analogy, and similar processes. B. F. Skinner, one of the founders of behaviorist psychology, proposed a model of language acquisition in his book *Verbal Behavior* (1957). Two years later, in a devastating reply to Skinner entitled *Review of Verbal Behavior* (1959), Noam Chomsky showed that language is a complex cognitive system that could not be acquired by behaviorist principles.

Do Children Learn through Imitation?

CHILD: My teacher holded the baby rabbits and we patted them.
ADULT: Did you say your teacher held the baby rabbits?
CHILD: Yes.
ADULT: What did you say she did?
CHILD: She holded the baby rabbits and we patted them.
ADULT: Did you say she held them tightly?
CHILD: No, she holded them loosely.

ANONYMOUS ADULT AND CHILD

At first glance the question of how children acquire language doesn't seem difficult to answer. Don't children just listen to what is said around them and imitate the speech they hear? Imitation is involved to some extent. An American child may hear *milk* and a Mexican child *leche* and each attempts to reproduce what is heard. But the early words and sentences that children produce show that they are not simply imitating adult speech. Many times the words are barely recognizable to an adult and the meanings are also not always like the adult's, as we will discuss below.

Children do not hear words like *holded* or *tooths* or sentences such as *Cat stand up table* or many of the other utterances they produce between the ages of two and three, such as the following:[1]

---

[1]Many of the examples of child language in this chapter are taken from CHILDES (Child Language Data Exchange System), a computerized database of the spontaneous speech of children acquiring English and many other languages. MacWhinney, B., and C. Snow. 1985. The child language data exchange system. *Journal of Child Language* 12:271–96.

a my pencil
two foot
what the boy hit?
other one pants
Mommy get it my ladder
cowboy did fighting me

Even when children are trying to imitate what they hear, they are unable to produce sentences outside of the rules of their developing grammar. The following are a child's attempt to imitate what the adult has said:

ADULT:	He's going out.	CHILD:	He go out.
ADULT:	That's an old-time train.	CHILD:	Old-time train.
ADULT:	Adam, say what I say.		
	Where can I put them?	CHILD:	Where I can put them?

Imitation also fails to account for the fact that children who are unable to speak for neurological or physiological reasons are able to learn the language spoken to them and understand it. When they overcome their speech impairment, they immediately use the language for speaking.

Do Children Learn through Correction and Reinforcement?

CHILD:	Nobody don't like me.
MOTHER:	No, say "Nobody likes me."
CHILD:	Nobody don't like me.
	(dialogue repeated eight times)
MOTHER:	Now, listen carefully; say "Nobody likes me."
CHILD:	Oh, nobody don't likes me.

ANONYMOUS MOTHER AND CHILD

Another proposal, in the behaviorist tradition, is that children learn to produce correct (grammatical) sentences because they are positively reinforced when they say something grammatical and negatively reinforced (corrected) when they say something ungrammatical. Roger Brown and his colleagues at Harvard University studied parent–child interactions. They report that correction seldom occurs, and when it does, it is usually for mispronunciations or incorrect reporting of facts and not for "bad grammar." They note, for example, that the ungrammatical sentence "Her curl my hair" was not corrected because the child's mother was in fact curling her hair. However, when the child uttered the grammatical sentence "Walt Disney comes on Tuesday," she was corrected because the television program was shown on Wednesday. Brown concludes that it is "truth value rather than syntactic well-formedness that chiefly governs explicit verbal reinforcement by parents—which renders mildly paradoxical the fact that the usual product of such a training schedule is an adult whose speech is highly grammatical but not notably truthful."

Adults will sometimes **recast** children's utterances into an adultlike form, as in the following examples:

Child	Mother
It fall.	It fell?
Where is them?	They're at home.
It doing dancing.	It's dancing, yes.

In these examples, the mother provides the correct model without actually correcting the child. Although recasts are potentially helpful to the child, they are not used in a consistent way. One study of forty mothers of children two to four years old showed that only about 25 percent of children's ungrammatical sentences are recast and that overall, grammatical sentences were recast as often as bad sentences. Parents tend to focus on the correctness of content more than on grammaticality. So parents allow many ungrammatical utterances to "slip by" and change many grammatical utterances. A child who relied on recasts to learn grammar would be mightily confused.

Even if adults did correct children's syntax more often than they do, it would still not explain how or what children learn from such adult responses, or how children discover and construct the correct rules. Children do not know what they are doing wrong and are unable to make corrections even when they are pointed out, as shown by the preceding example and the following one:

CHILD: Want other one spoon, Daddy.
FATHER: You mean, you want *the other spoon.*
CHILD: Yes, I want other one spoon, please, Daddy.
FATHER: Can you say "the other spoon"?
CHILD: Other . . . one . . . spoon.
FATHER: Say . . . "other."
CHILD: Other.
FATHER: Spoon.
CHILD: Spoon.
FATHER: Other . . . spoon.
CHILD: Other . . . spoon. Now give me other one spoon?

Such conversations between parents and children do not occur often; this conversation was between a linguist studying child language and his child. Mothers and fathers are usually delighted that their young children are talking and consider every utterance a gem. The "mistakes" children make are cute and repeated endlessly to anyone who will listen.

Do Children Learn Language through Analogy?

It has also been suggested that children put words together to form phrases and sentences by **analogy**, by hearing a sentence and using it as a model to form other sentences. But this is also problematic, as Lila Gleitman, an expert on developmental psycholinguistics, points out:

> [S]uppose the child has heard the sentence "I painted a red barn." So now, by analogy, the child can say "I painted a blue barn." That's exactly the

kind of theory that we want. You hear a sample and you extend it to all of the new cases by similarity. . . . In addition to "I painted a red barn" you might also hear the sentence "I painted a barn red." So it looks as if you take those last two words and switch their order. . . . So now you want to extend this to the case of seeing, because you want to look at barns instead of paint them. So you have heard, "I saw a red barn." Now you try (by analogy) a . . . new sentence—"I saw a barn red." Something's gone wrong. This is an analogy, but the analogy didn't work. It's not a sentence of English.[2]

This kind of problem arises constantly. Consider another example. The child hears the following pair of sentences:

The boy was sleeping.   Was the boy sleeping?

Based on pairs of sentences like this, he formulates a rule for forming questions: "Move the auxiliary to the position preceding the subject." He then acquires the more complex relative clause construction:

The boy who is sleeping is dreaming about a new car.

He now wants to form a question. What does he do? If he forms a question on analogy to the simple yes-no question, he will move the first auxiliary *is* as follows:

*Is the boy who sleeping is dreaming about a new car?

Studies of spontaneous speech, as well as experiments, show that children never make mistakes of this sort. As discussed in chapter 4, syntactic rules, such as the rule that moves the auxiliary, are sensitive to the structure of the sentence and not to the linear order of words. The available evidence shows that children know about the structure dependency of rules at a very early age.

In recent years, a computer model of language representation and acquisition called **connectionism** has been proposed that relies in part on behaviorist learning principles such as analogy and reinforcement. In the connectionist model, no grammatical rules are stored anywhere. Linguistic knowledge, such as knowledge of the past tense, is represented by a set of neuron-like connections between different phonological forms (e.g., between *play* and *played*, *dance* and *danced*, *drink* and *drank*). Repeated exposure to particular verb pairs in the input reinforces the connection between them, mimicking rule-like behavior. Based on similarities between words, the model can produce a past-tense form that it was not previously exposed to. On analogy to *dance-danced*, it will convert *prance* to *pranced*; on analogy to *drink-drank* it will convert *sink* to *sank*.

As a model of language acquisition, connectionism faces some serious challenges. The model assumes that the language of the child's environment has very specific properties. However, investigation of the input that children actually receive shows that it is not consistent with those assumptions. Another problem

---

[2]Gleitman, L. R., and E. Wanner. 1982. *Language acquisition: The state of the art.* Cambridge, UK: Cambridge University Press.

is that rules such as formation of past tense cannot be based on phonological form alone but must also be sensitive to information in the lexicon. For example, the past tense of a verb derived from a noun is always regular even if an irregular form exists. When a fly ball is caught in a baseball game, we say the batter *flied out*, not *flew out*. Similarly, when an irregular plural is part of a larger noun, it may be regularized. When we see several images of Walt Disney's famous rodent, we describe them as Mickey Mouses, not Mickey Mice.

Do Children Learn through Structured Input?

Yet another suggestion is that children are able to learn language because adults speak to them in a special "simplified" language sometimes called **motherese**, or **child-directed speech** (CDS) (or more informally, **baby talk**). This hypothesis places a lot of emphasis on the role of the environment in facilitating language acquisition.

In our culture adults do typically talk to young children in a special way. We tend to speak more slowly and more clearly, we may speak in a higher pitch and exaggerate our intonation, and sentences are generally grammatical. However, motherese is not syntactically simpler. It contains a range of sentence types, including syntactically complex sentences such as questions (*Do you want your juice now?*); embedded sentences (*Mommy thinks you should sleep now*); imperatives (*Pat the dog gently!*); and negatives with tag questions (*We don't want to hurt him, do we?*). And adults do not simplify their language by dropping inflections from verbs and nouns or by omitting function words such as determiners and auxiliaries, though children do this all the time. It is probably a good thing that motherese is not syntactically restricted. If it were, children might not have sufficient information to extract the rules of their language.

Although infants prefer to listen to motherese over normal adult speech, studies show that using motherese does not significantly affect the child's language development. In many cultures, adults do not use a special style of language with children, and there are even communities in which adults hardly talk to babies at all. Nevertheless, children around the world acquire language in much the same way, irrespective of these varying circumstances. Adults seem to be the followers rather than the leaders in this enterprise. The child does not develop linguistically because he is exposed to ever more adultlike language. Rather, the adult adjusts his language to the child's increasing linguistic sophistication. The exaggerated intonation and other properties of motherese may be useful for getting a child's attention and for reassuring the child, but it is not a driving force behind language development.

Analogy, imitation, and reinforcement cannot account for language development because they are based on the (implicit or explicit) assumption that what the child acquires is a set of sentences or forms rather than a set of grammatical rules. Theories that assume that acquisition depends on a specially structured input also place too much emphasis on the environment rather than on the grammar-making abilities of the child. These proposals do not explain the creativity that children show in acquiring language, why they go through stages, or why they make some kinds of "errors" but not others, for example, "Give me other one spoon" but not "Is the boy who sleeping is dreaming about a new car?"

Children Construct Grammars

We are designed to walk. . . . That we are taught to walk is impossible. And pretty much the same is true of language. Nobody is taught language. In fact you can't prevent the child from learning it.

NOAM CHOMSKY, *The Human Language Series* program 2, 1994

Language acquisition is a creative process. Children are not given explicit information about the rules, by either instruction or correction. They extract the rules of the grammar from the language they hear around them, and their linguistic environment does not need to be special in any way for them to do this. Observations of children acquiring different languages under different cultural and social circumstances reveal that the developmental stages are similar, possibly universal. Even deaf children of deaf signing parents go through stages in their signing development that parallel those of children acquiring spoken languages. These factors lead many linguists to believe that children are equipped with an innate template or blueprint for language—which we have referred to as Universal Grammar (UG)—and that this blueprint aids the child in the task of constructing a grammar for her language. This is referred to as the **innateness hypothesis**.

The Innateness Hypothesis

"WHAT'S THE BIG SURPRISE? ALL THE LATEST THEORIES OF LINGUISTICS SAY WE'RE BORN WITH THE INNATE CAPACITY FOR GENERATING SENTENCES."

The innateness hypothesis receives its strongest support from the observation that the grammar a person ends up with is vastly underdetermined by his linguistic experience. In other words, we end up knowing far more about language than is exemplified in the language we hear around us. This argument for the innateness of UG is called the **poverty of the stimulus**.

Although children hear many utterances, the language they hear is incomplete, noisy, and unstructured. We said earlier that child-directed speech is largely well formed, but children are also exposed to adult–adult interactions. These utterances include slips of the tongue, false starts, ungrammatical and incomplete sentences, and no consistent information as to which utterances are well formed and which are not. But most important is the fact that children come to know aspects of the grammar about which they receive *no* information. In this sense, the data they are exposed to is **impoverished**. It is less than what is necessary to account for the richness and complexity of the grammar they attain.

For example, we noted that the rules children construct are **structure dependent**. Children do not produce questions by moving the first auxiliary as in (1) below. Instead, they correctly invert the auxiliary of the main clause, as in (2). (We use ___ to mark the position from which a constituent moves.)

1. *Is the boy who ___ sleeping is dreaming of a new car?
2. Is the boy who is sleeping ___ dreaming of a new car?

To come up with a rule that moves the auxiliary of the main clause rather than the first auxiliary, the child must know something about the structure of the sentence. Children are not told about structure dependency. They are not told about constituent structure. Indeed, adults who have not studied linguistics do not explicitly know about structure dependency, constituent structure, and other abstract properties of grammar and so could not instruct their children even if they were so inclined. This knowledge is tacit or implicit. The input children get is a sequence of sounds, not a set of phrase structure trees. No amount of imitation, reinforcement, analogy, or structured input will lead the child to formulate a phrase structure tree, much less a principle of structure dependency. Yet, children do create phrase structures, and the rules they acquire are sensitive to this structure.

The child must also learn many aspects of grammar from her specific linguistic environment. English-speaking children learn that the subject comes first and that the verb precedes the object inside the VP, that is, that English is an SVO language. Japanese children acquire an SOV language. They learn that the object precedes the verb.

English-speaking children must learn that yes-no questions are formed by moving the auxiliary to the beginning of the sentence, as follows:

You will come home. → Will you ___ come home?

Japanese children learn that to form a yes-no question, the morpheme *-ka* is suffixed to a verb stem.

Tanaka ga sushi o tabete iru   "Tanaka is eating sushi."
Tanaka ga sushi o tabete iru**ka**   "Is Tanaka eating sushi?"

In Japanese questions, sentence constituents are not rearranged.

According to the innateness hypothesis, the child extracts from the linguistic environment those rules of grammar that are language specific, such as word order and movement rules. But he does not need to learn universal principles like structure dependency, or general principles of sentence formation such as the fact that heads of categories can take complements. All these principles are part of the innate blueprint for language that children use to construct the grammar of their language.

The innateness hypothesis provides an answer to *the logical problem of language acquisition* posed by Chomsky: What accounts for the ease, rapidity, and uniformity of language acquisition in the face of impoverished data? The answer is that children acquire a complex grammar quickly and easily without any particular help beyond exposure to the language because they do not start from scratch. UG provides them with a significant head start. It helps them to extract the rules of their language and to avoid many grammatical errors. Because the child constructs his grammar according to an innate blueprint, all children proceed through similar developmental stages, as we will discuss in the next section.

The innateness hypothesis also predicts that all languages will conform to the principles of UG. We are still far from understanding the full nature of the principles of UG. Research on more languages provides a way to test any principles that linguists propose. If we investigate a language in which a posited UG principle is absent, we will have to correct our theory and substitute other principles, as scientists must do in any field. But there is little doubt that human languages conform to abstract universal principles and that the human brain is specially equipped for acquisition of human language grammars.

Stages in Language Acquisition

... for I was no longer a speechless infant; but a speaking boy. This I remember; and have since observed how I learned to speak. It was not that my elders taught me words ... in any set method; but I ... did myself ... practice the sounds in my memory. ... And thus by constantly hearing words, as they occurred in various sentences ... I thereby gave utterance to my will.

ST. AUGUSTINE, *Confessions,* 398 C.E.

Children do not wake up one fine morning with a fully formed grammar in their heads. Relative to the complexity of the adult grammar that they eventually attain, the process of language acquisition is fast, but it is not instantaneous. From first words to virtual adult competence takes three to five years, during which time children pass through linguistic stages. They begin by babbling, they then acquire their first words, and in just a few months they begin to put words together into sentences.

Observations of children acquiring different languages reveal that the stages are similar, possibly universal. The earliest studies of child language acquisition come from diaries kept by parents. More recent studies include the use of tape recordings, videotapes, and controlled experiments. Linguists record the spontaneous utterances of children and purposefully elicit other utterances to study the child's production and comprehension. Researchers have also invented ingenious techniques for investigating the linguistic abilities of infants, who are not yet speaking.

Children's early utterances may not look exactly like adult sentences, but child language is not just a degenerate form of adult language. The words and sentences that the child produces at each stage of development conform to the set of grammatical rules he has developed to that point. Although child grammars and adult grammars differ in certain respects, they also share many formal properties. Like adults, children have grammatical categories such as NP and VP, rules for building phrase structures and for moving constituents, as well as phonological, morphological, and semantic rules, and they adhere to universal principles such as structure dependency.

From the perspective of the adult grammar, sentences such as *Nobody don't like me* and *Want other one spoon, Daddy* contain grammatical errors, but such "errors" often reflect the child's current stage of grammatical competence and therefore provide researchers with a window into their grammar.

The Perception and Production of Speech Sounds

An infant crying in the night:
An infant crying for the light:
And with no language but a cry.

ALFRED LORD TENNYSON, *In Memoriam A.H.H.*, 1849

The notion that a person is born with a mind like a blank slate is belied by a wealth of evidence that newborns are reactive to some subtle distinctions in their environment and not to others. That is, the mind appears to be attuned at birth to receive certain kinds of information. Infants will respond to visual depth and distance distinctions, to differences between rigid and flexible physical properties of objects, and to human faces rather than to other visual stimuli.

Infants also show a very early response to different properties of language. Experiments demonstrate that infants will increase their sucking rate—measured by ingeniously designed pacifiers—when stimuli (visual or auditory) presented to them are varied, but will decrease the sucking rate when the same stimuli are presented repeatedly. Early in acquisition when tested with a preferential listening technique, they will also turn their heads toward and listen longer to sounds, stress patterns, and words that are familiar to them. These instinctive responses can be used to measure a baby's ability to discriminate and recognize different linguistic stimuli.

A newborn will respond to phonetic contrasts found in human languages even when these differences are not phonemic in the language spoken in the baby's home. A baby hearing a human voice over a loudspeaker saying [pa] [pa] [pa] will slowly decrease her rate of sucking. If the sound changes to [ba] or even [pʰa], the sucking rate increases dramatically. Controlled experiments show that adults find it difficult to differentiate between the allophones of one phoneme, but for infants it comes naturally. Japanese infants can distinguish between [r] and [l] whereas their parents cannot; babies can hear the difference between aspirated and unaspirated stops even if students in an introductory linguistics course cannot. Babies can discriminate between sounds that are phonemic in other languages and nonexistent in the language of their parents. For example, in Hindi, there is a phonemic contrast between a retroflex "t" [ṭ] (made with the tongue curled back) and the alveolar [t]. To English-speaking adults, these may sound the same; to their infants, they do not.

Infants can perceive voicing contrasts such as [pa] versus [ba], contrasts in place of articulation such as [da] versus [ga], and contrasts in manner of articulation such as [ra] versus [la], or [ra] versus [wa], among many others. Babies will not react, however, to distinctions that never correspond to phonemic contrasts in any human language, such as sounds spoken more or less loudly or sounds that lie between two phonemes. Furthermore, a vowel that we perceive as [i], for example, is a different physical sound when produced by a male, female, or child, but babies ignore the nonlinguistic aspects of the speech signal just as adults do.

Infants appear to be born with the ability to perceive just those sounds that are phonemic in some language. It is therefore possible for children to learn any human language they are exposed to. During the first year of life, the infant's job is to uncover the sounds of the ambient language. From around six months, he begins to lose the ability to discriminate between sounds that are not phonemic in his own language. His linguistic environment molds the infant's initial perceptions. Japanese infants can no longer hear the difference between [r] and [l], which do not contrast in Japanese, whereas babies in English-speaking homes retain this perception. They have begun to learn the sounds of the language of their parents. Before that, they appear to know the sounds of human language in general.

Babbling

"Hi & Lois" © King Features Syndicate

The shaping by the linguistic environment that we see in perception also occurs in the speech the infant is producing. At around six months, the infant begins to babble. The sounds produced in this period include many sounds that do not occur in the language of the household. However, **babbling** is not linguistic chaos. The twelve most frequent consonants in the world's languages make up

95 percent of the consonants infants use in their babbling. There are linguistic constraints even during this very early stage. The early babbles consist mainly of repeated consonant-vowel sequences, like *mama*, *gaga*, and *dada*. Later babbles are more varied.

By the end of the first year the child's babbles come to include only those sounds and sound combinations that occur in the target language. Babbles begin to sound like words, although they may not have any specific meaning attached to them. At this point adults can distinguish the babbles of an English-babbling infant from those of an infant babbling in Cantonese or Arabic. During the first year of life, the infant's perceptions and productions are being fine-tuned to the surrounding language(s).

Deaf infants produce babbling sounds that are different from those of hearing children. Babbling is related to auditory input and is linguistic in nature. Studies of vocal babbling of hearing children and manual babbling of deaf children support the view that babbling is a linguistic ability related to the kind of language input the child receives. These studies show that four- to seven-month-old hearing infants exposed to spoken language produce a restricted set of phonetic forms. At the same age, deaf children exposed to sign language produce a restricted set of signs. In each case the forms are drawn from the set of possible sounds or possible gestures found in spoken and signed languages.

Babbling illustrates the readiness of the human mind to respond to linguistic input from a very early stage. During the babbling stage, the intonation contours produced by hearing infants begin to resemble the intonation contours of sentences spoken by adults. The different intonation contours are among the first linguistic contrasts that children perceive and produce. During this same period, the vocalizations produced by deaf babies are random and nonrepetitive. Similarly, the manual gestures produced by hearing babies differ greatly from those produced by deaf infants exposed to sign language. The hearing babies move their fingers and clench their fists randomly with little or no repetition of gestures. The deaf infants, however, use more than a dozen different hand motions repetitively, all of which are elements of American Sign Language or the sign languages used in deaf communities of other countries.

The generally accepted view is that humans are born with a predisposition to discover the units that serve to express linguistic meanings, and that at a genetically specified stage in neural development, the infant will begin to produce these units—sounds or gestures—depending on the language input the baby receives. This suggests that babbling is the earliest stage in language acquisition, in opposition to an earlier view that babbling was prelinguistic and merely neuromuscular in origin. The "babbling as language acquisition" hypothesis is supported by recent neurological studies that link babbling to the language centers of the left hemisphere, also providing further evidence that the brain specializes for language functions at a very early age, as discussed in chapter 2.

First Words

From this golden egg a man, Prajapati, was born. . . . A year having passed, he wanted to speak. He said "bhur" and the earth was created. He said "bhuvar" and the space of the air was created. He said "suvar" and the sky was created. That is why a child wants to speak after a year.... When Prajapati spoke for the first time, he uttered one or two syllables. That is why a child utters one or two syllables when he speaks for the first time.

HINDU MYTH

Some time after the age of one, the child begins to repeatedly use the same string of sounds to mean the same thing. At this stage children realize that sounds are related to meanings. They have produced their first true words. The age of the child when this occurs varies and has nothing to do with the child's intelligence. (It is reported that Einstein did not start to speak until he was three or four years old.)

The child's first utterances differ from adult language. The following words of one child, J. P., at the age of sixteen months, illustrate the point:

[ʔaʊ]	"not," "no," "don't"	[s:]	"aerosol spray"
[bʌʔ]/[mʌʔ]	"up"	[sʲuː]	"shoe"
[da]	"dog"	[haɪ]	"hi"
[iʔo]/[siʔo]	"Cheerios"	[sr]	"shirt," "sweater"
[sa]	"sock"	[sæː]/[əsæː]	"what's that?"/"hey, look!"
[aɪ]/[ʌɪ]	"light"	[ma]	"mommy"
[baʊ]/[daʊ]	"down"	[dæ]	"daddy"

Most children go through a stage in which their utterances consist of only one word. This is called the **holophrastic** or "whole phrase" stage because these one-word utterances seem to convey a more complex message. For example, when J. P. says "down" he may be making a request to be put down, or he may be commenting on a toy that has fallen down from the shelf. When he says "cheerios" he may simply be naming the box of cereal in front of him, or he may be asking for some Cheerios. This suggests that children have a more complex mental representation than their language allows them to express. Comprehension experiments confirm the hypothesis that children's productive abilities do not fully reflect their underlying grammatical competence.

It has been claimed that deaf babies develop their first signs earlier than hearing children speak their first words. This has led to the development of Baby Sign, a technique in which hearing parents learn and model for their babies various "signs," such as a sign for "milk," "hurt," and "mother." The idea is that the baby can communicate his needs manually even before he is able to articulate spoken words. Promoters of Baby Sign (and many parents) say that this leads to less frustration and less crying. The claim that signs appear earlier than words is controversial. Some linguists argue that what occurs earlier in both deaf and hearing babies are pre-linguistic gestures that lack the systematic meaning of true signs. Baby Sign may perhaps be exploiting this earlier manual dexterity, and not a precocious linguistic development. More research is needed.

Segmenting the Speech Stream

I scream, you scream, we all scream for ice cream.

TRANSCRIBED FROM VOCALS BY TOM STACKS, performing with Harry Reser's Six Jumping Jacks, January 14, 1928

The acquisition of first words is an amazing feat. How do infants discover where one word begins and another leaves off? Speech is a continuous stream broken only by breath pauses. Children are in the same fix that you might be in if you tuned in a foreign-language radio station. You wouldn't have the foggiest idea of what was being said or what the words were. Intonation breaks that do exist do not necessarily correspond to word, phrase, or sentence boundaries. The adult speaker with knowledge of the lexicon and grammar of a language imposes structure on the speech he hears, but a person without such knowledge cannot. How then do babies, who have not yet learned the lexicon or rules of grammar, extract the words from the speech they hear around them? The ability to segment the continuous speech stream into discrete units—words—is one of the remarkable feats of language acquisition.

Studies show that infants are remarkably good at extracting information from continuous speech. They seem to know what kind of cues to look for in the input that will help them to isolate words. One of the cues that English-speaking children attend to that helps them figure out word boundaries is stress.

As noted in chapter 7, every content word in English has a stressed syllable. (Function words such as *the, a, am, can,* etc. are ordinarily unstressed.) If the content word is monosyllabic, then that syllable is stressed as in *dóg* or *hám.* Bisyllabic content words can be **trochaic**, which means that stress is on the first syllable, as in *páper* or *dóctor,* or **iambic**, which means stress is on the second syllable, as in *giráffe* or *devíce.* The vast majority of English words have trochaic stress. In controlled experiments adult speakers are quicker to recognize words with trochaic stress than words with iambic stress. This can be explained if English-speaking adults follow a strategy of taking a stressed syllable to mark the onset of a new word.

But what about children? Could they avail themselves of the same strategy? Stress is very salient to infants, and they are quick to acquire the rhythmic structure of their language. Using the preferential listening technique mentioned earlier, researchers have shown that at just a few months old infants are able to discriminate native and non-native stress patterns. Before the end of the first year their babbling takes on the rhythmic pattern of the ambient language. At about nine months old, English-speaking children prefer to listen to bisyllabic words with initial rather than final stress. And most notably, studies show that infants acquiring English can indeed use stress cues to segment words in fluent speech. In a series of experiments, infants who were seven and a half months old listened to passages with repeated instances of a trochaic word such as *púppy,* and passages with iambic words such as *guitár.* They were then played lists of words, some of which had occurred in the previous passage and others that had not. Experimenters measured the length of time that they listened to the familiar versus unfamiliar words. The results showed that children listened significantly longer (indicated by turning their head in the direction of the loud-speaker) to words that they had heard in the passage, but only when the words had the trochaic pattern (*púppy*). For words with the iambic pattern (*guitár*), the children responded only to the stressed syllable (tár), though the monosyllabic word *tar* had not appeared in the passage. These results suggest that the infants—like adults—are taking the stressed syllable to mark the onset of a new word. Following such a strategy will sometimes lead to errors (for iambic words and unstressed function words), but it provides the child with a way of getting started. This is sometimes referred to as **prosodic bootstrapping**. Infants can use the stress pattern of the language as a start to word learning.

Infants are also sensitive to phonotactic constraints and to the distribution of allophones in the target language. For example, we noted in chapter 7 that in English aspiration typically occurs at the beginning of a stressed syllable—[pʰɪt] versus [spɪt]—and that certain combinations of sounds are more likely to occur at the end of a word rather than at the beginning, for example [rt]. Studies show that nine-month-olds can use this information to help segment speech into words in English.

Languages differ in their stress patterns as well as in their allophonic variation and phonotactics. Wouldn't the infant then need some way to first figure out what stress pattern he is dealing with, or what the allophones and possible sound combinations are, before he could use this information to extract the words of his language from fluent speech? This seems to be a classic chicken and egg problem—he has to know the language to learn the language. A way out of this conundrum is provided by the finding that infants may also rely on statistical properties of the input to segment words, such as the frequency with which particular sequences of sounds occur.

In one study, eight-month-old infants listened to two minutes of speech formed from four nonsense words, *pabiku, tutibu, golabu, babupu*. The words were produced by a speech synthesizer and strung together in three different orders, analogous to three different sentences, without any pauses or other phonetic cues to the word boundaries. Here is an example of what the children heard:

golabupabikututibubabupugolabubabupututibu. . . . .

After listening to the strings the infants were tested to see if they could distinguish the "words" of the language, for example *pabiku* (which, recall, they had never heard in isolation before), from sequences of syllables that spanned word boundaries, such as *bubabu* (also in the input). Despite the very brief exposure and the lack of boundary cues, the infants were able to distinguish the words from the nonwords. The authors of the study conclude that the children do this by tracking the frequency with which the different sequences of syllables occur: the sequences inside the words (e.g., pa-bi-ku) remain the same whatever order the words are presented in, but the sequences of syllables that cross word boundaries will change in the different presentations and hence these sequences will occur much less frequently. Though it is still unclear how much such statistical procedures can accomplish with real language input, which is vastly larger and more varied, this experiment and others like it suggest that babies are sensitive to statistical information as well as to linguistic structure to extract words from the input. It is possible that they first rely on statistical properties to isolate some words, and then, based on these words, they are able to detect the rhythmic, allophonic, and phonotactic properties of the language, and with this further knowledge they can do further segmentation. Studies that measure infants' reliance on statistics versus stress for segmenting words support this two stage model: younger infants (seven-and-a-half months old) respond to frequency while older infants (nine months old) attend to stress, allophonic, and phonotactic information.

The Development of Grammar

Children are biologically equipped to acquire all aspects of grammar. In this section we will look at development in each of the components of language, and we will illustrate the role that Universal Grammar and other factors play in this development.

The Acquisition of Phonology

"Baby Blues" © Baby Blues Partnership. Reprinted with permission of King Features Syndicate.

In terms of his phonology, J. P. is like most children at the one-word stage. The first words are generally monosyllabic with a CV (consonant-vowel) form. The vowel part may be a diphthong, depending on the language being acquired. The phonemic inventory is much smaller than is found in the adult language. It appears that children first acquire the small set of sounds common to all languages regardless of the ambient language(s), and in later stages acquire the less common sounds of their own language. For example, most languages have the sounds [p] and [s], but [θ] is a rare sound. J. P.'s sound system followed this pattern. His phonological inventory at an early stage included the consonants [b,m,d,k], which are frequently occurring sounds in the world's languages.

In general, the order of acquisition of classes of sounds begins with vowels and then goes by *manner* of articulation for consonants: nasals are acquired first, then glides, stops, liquids, fricatives, and affricates. Natural classes characterized by *place* of articulation features also appear in children's utterances according to a more or less ordered series: labials, velars, alveolars, and palatals. It is not surprising that *mama* is an early word for many children.

The distribution and frequency of sounds in a language can also influence the acquisition of certain segments. Sounds that are expected to be acquired late may appear earlier in children's language when they are frequently occurring. For example, the fricative [v] is a very late acquisition in English but it is an early phoneme in Estonian, Bulgarian, and Swedish, languages that have several [v]-initial words that are common in the vocabularies of young children.

If the first year is devoted to figuring out the sounds of the target language, the second year involves learning how these sounds are used in the phonology of the language, especially which contrasts are phonemic. When children first begin to contrast one pair of a set (e.g., when they learn that /p/ and /b/ are distinct phonemes due to a voicing difference), they also begin to distinguish between other similar pairs (e.g., /t/ and /d/, /s/ and /z/, and all the other voiceless–voiced phonemic pairs). As we would expect, the generalizations refer to natural classes of speech sounds.

Controlled experiments show that children at this stage can perceive or comprehend many more phonological contrasts than they can produce. The same child who says [wæbɪt] instead of "rabbit," and who does not seem to distinguish [w] and [r], will not make mistakes on a picture identification task in which she must point to either a ring or a wing. In addition, children sometimes produce two different sounds in a way that makes them indiscernible to adult observers. Acoustic analyses of children's utterances show that although a child's pronunciation of *wing* and *ring* may seem the same to the adult ear, they are physically different sounds. As a further example, a spectrographic analysis of *ephant*, "elephant," produced by a three-year-old child, clearly showed an [l] in the representation of the word, even though the adult experimenter could not hear it.

Many anecdotal reports also show the disparity between the child's production and perception at this stage. An example is the exchange between the linguist Neil Smith and his two-year-old son Amahl. At this age Amahl's pronunciation of "mouth" is [maʊs].

NS: What does [maʊs] mean?
A: Like a cat.
NS: Yes, what else?
A: Nothing else.
NS: It's part of your head.
A: (*fascinated*)
NS: (*touching A's mouth*) What's this?
A: [maʊs]

According to Smith, it took Amahl a few seconds to realize his word for "mouse" and his word for "mouth" were the same. It is not that Amahl and other children do not hear the correct adult pronunciation. They do, but they are unable in these early years to produce it themselves. Another linguist's child (yes, linguists love to experiment on their own children) pronounced the word *light* as *yight* [jaɪt] but would become very angry if someone said to him, "Oh, you want me to turn on the yight." "No no," he would reply, "not yight—yight!"

Therefore, even at this stage, it is not possible to determine the extent of the grammar of the child—in this case, the phonology—simply by observing speech production. It is sometimes necessary to use various experimental and instrumental techniques to tap the child's competence.

A child's first words show many substitutions of one feature for another or one phoneme for another. In the preceding examples, *mouth* [maʊθ] is pronounced *mouse* [maʊs], with the alveolar fricative [s] replacing the less common interdental fricative [θ]; *light* [laɪt] is pronounced *yight* [jaɪt], with the glide [j] replacing the liquid [l]; and *rabbit* is pronounced *wabbit*, with the glide [w] replacing the liquid [r]. Glides are acquired earlier than liquids, and hence substitute for them.

These substitutions are simplifications of the adult pronunciation. They make articulation easier until the child achieves greater articulatory control.

Children's early pronunciations are not haphazard, however. The phonological substitutions are rule governed. The following is an abridged lexicon for another child, Michael, between the ages of eighteen and twenty-one months:

[pun]	"spoon"	[maɪtl]	"Michael"
[peɪn]	"plane"	[daɪtər]	"diaper"
[tɪs]	"kiss"	[pati]	"Papi"
[tau]	"cow"	[mani]	"Mommy"
[tin]	"clean"	[bərt]	"Bert"
[polər]	"stroller"	[bərt]	"(Big) Bird"

Michael systematically substituted the alveolar stop [t] for the velar stop [k] as in his words for "cow," "clean," "kiss," and his own name. He also replaced labial [p] with [t] when it occurred in the middle of a word, as in his words for "Papi" and "diaper." He reduced consonant clusters in "spoon," "plane," and "stroller," and he devoiced final stops as in "Big Bird." In devoicing the final [d] in "bird," he created an ambiguous form [bərt] referring both to Bert and Big Bird. No wonder only parents understand their children's first words!

Michael's substitutions are typical of the phonological rules that operate in the very early stages of acquisition. Other common rules are reduplication— "bottle" becomes [baba], "water" becomes [wawa]; and the dropping of a final consonants—"bed" becomes [be], "cake" becomes [ke]. These two rules show that the child prefers a simple CV syllable.

Of the many phonological rules that children create, no child will necessarily use all rules. Early phonological rules generally reflect natural phonological processes that also occur in adult languages. For example, various adult languages have a rule of syllable-final consonant devoicing (German does—/bund/ is pronounced [bunt]—English doesn't). Children do not create bizarre or whimsical rules. Their rules conform to the possibilities made available by Universal Grammar.

The Acquisition of Word Meaning

Suddenly I felt a misty consciousness as of something forgotten—a thrill of returning thought; and somehow the mystery of language was revealed to me. . . . Everything had a name, and each name gave birth to a new thought.

HELEN KELLER, *The Story of My Life,* 1903

In addition to what it tells us about phonological regularities, the child's early vocabulary also provides insight into how children use words and construct word meaning. For J. P. the word *up* was originally used only to mean "Get me up!" when he was either on the floor or in his high chair, but later he used it to mean "Get up!" to his mother as well. J. P. used his word for *sock* not only for socks but also for other undergarments that are put on over the feet, such as undershorts. This illustrates how a child may extend the meaning of a word from a particular referent to encompass a larger class.

When J. P. began to use words, the object had to be physically present, but that requirement did not last very long. He first used "dog" only when pointing to a real dog, but later he used the word for pictures of dogs in various books. A new word that entered J. P.'s vocabulary at seventeen months was "uh-oh," which he would say after he had an accident like spilling juice, or when he deliberately poured his yogurt over the side of his high chair. His use of this word shows his developing use of language for social purposes. At this time he added two new words meaning "no," [doː] and [no], which he used when anyone attempted to take something from him that he wanted, or tried to make him do something he did not want to do. He used them either with the imperative meaning of "Don't do that!" or with the assertive meaning of "I don't want to do that." Even at this early stage, J. P. was using words to convey a variety of ideas and feelings, as well as his social awareness.

But how do children learn the meanings of words? Most people do not see this aspect of acquisition as posing a great problem. The intuitive view is that children look at an object, the mother says a word, and the child connects the sounds with the object. However, this is not as easy as it seems:

> A child who observes a cat sitting on a mat also observes . . . a mat supporting a cat, a mat under a cat, a floor supporting a mat and a cat, and so on. If the adult now says "The cat is on the mat" even while pointing to the cat on the mat, how is the child to choose among these interpretations of the situation?

Even if the mother simply says "cat," and the child accidentally associates the word with the animal on the mat, the child may interpret cat as "Cat," the name of a particular animal, or of an entire species. In other words, to learn a word for a class of objects such as "cat" or "dog," children have to figure out exactly what the word refers to. Upon hearing the word *dog* in the presence of a dog, how does the child know that "dog" can refer to any four-legged, hairy, barking creature? Should it include poodles, tiny Yorkshire terriers, bulldogs, and Great Danes, all of which look rather different from one another? What about cows, lambs, and other four-legged mammals? Why are they not "dogs"? The important and very difficult question is: What relevant features define the class of objects we call *dog*, and how does a child acquire knowledge of them? Even if a child succeeds in associating a word with an object, nobody provides explicit information about how to extend the use of that word to all the other objects to which that word refers.

It is not surprising, therefore, that children often **overextend** a word's meaning, as J. P. did with the word *sock*. A child may learn a word such as *papa* or *daddy*, which she first uses only for her own father, and then extend its meaning to apply to all men, just as she may use the word *dog* to mean any four-legged creature. After the child has acquired her first seventy-five to one hundred words, the overextended meanings start to narrow until they correspond to those of the other speakers of the language. How this occurs is still not entirely understood.

On the other hand, early language learning may involve **underextension**, in which a lexical item is used in an overly restrictive way. It is common for children to first apply a word like *bird* only to the family's pet canary without making a connection to birds in the tree outside, as if the word were a proper noun. And just as overextended meanings narrow in on the adult language, underextended meanings broaden their scope until they match the target language.

The mystery surrounding the acquisition of word meanings has intrigued philosophers and psychologists as well as linguists. We know that all children view the world in a similar fashion and apply the same general principles to help them determine a word's meaning. For example, overextensions are usually based on physical attributes such as size, shape, and texture. *Ball* may refer to all round things, *bunny* to all furry things, and so on. However, children will not make overextensions based on color. In experiments, children will group objects by shape and give them a name, but they will not assign a name to a group of red objects.

If an experimenter points to an object and uses a nonsense word like *blick*, saying *that's a blick*, the child will interpret the word to refer to the whole object, not one of its parts or attributes. Given the poverty of stimulus for word learning, principles like the "form over color principle" and the "whole object principle" help the child organize his experience in ways that facilitate word learning. Without such principles, it is doubtful that children could learn words as quickly as they do. Children learn approximately fourteen words a day for the first six years of their lives. That averages to about 5,000 words per year. How many students know 10,000 words of a foreign language after two years of study?

There is also experimental evidence that children can learn the meaning of one class of words—verbs—based on the syntactic environment in which they occur. If you were to hear a sentence such as *John blipped Mary the gloon*, you would not know exactly what John did, but you would likely understand that the sentence is describing a transfer of something from John to Mary. Similarly, if you heard *John gonked that Mary. . . .*, you would conclude that the verb *gonk* was a verb of communication like *say* or a mental verb like *think*. The complement types that a verb selects can provide clues to its meaning and thereby help the child. This learning of word meaning based on syntax is referred to as **syntactic bootstrapping**.

The Acquisition of Morphology

"Baby Blues" © Baby Blues Partnership. Reprinted with permission of King Features Syndicate.

The child's acquisition of morphology provides the clearest evidence of rule learning. Children's errors in morphology reveal that the child acquires the regular rules of the grammar and then overgeneralizes them. This **overgeneralization** occurs when children treat irregular verbs and nouns as if they were regular. We have probably all heard children say *bringed, goed, drawed,* and *runned,* or *foots, mouses, and sheeps.*

These mistakes tell us much about how children learn language because such forms could not arise through imitation; children use them in families in which the parents never speak "bad English." In fact, children generally go through three phases in the acquisition of an irregular form:

Phase 1	**Phase 2**	**Phase 3**
broke	breaked	broke
brought	bringed	brought

In phase 1 the child uses the correct term such as *brought* or *broke.* At this point the child's grammar does not relate the form *brought* to *bring,* or *broke* to *break.* The words are treated as separate lexical entries. Phase 2 is crucial. This is when the child constructs a rule for forming the past tense and attaches the regular past-tense morpheme to all verbs—*play, hug, help,* as well as *break* and *bring.* Children look for general patterns. What they do not know at phase 2 is that there are exceptions to the rule. Now their language is more regular than the adult language. During phase 3 the child learns that there are exceptions to the rule, and then once again uses *brought* and *broke,* with the difference being that these irregular forms will be related to the root forms.

The child's morphological rules emerge quite early. In a classic study, preschool children and children in the first, second, and third grades were shown a drawing of a nonsense animal like the funny creature shown in the following picture. Each "animal" was given a nonsense name. The experimenter would then say to the child, pointing to the picture, "This is a wug."

Then the experimenter would show the child a picture of two of the animals and say, "Now here is another one. There are two of them. There are two ___."

The child's task was to give the plural form, "wugs" [wʌgz]. Another little make-believe animal was called a "bik," and when the child was shown two biks, he or she again was to say the plural form [bɪks]. The children applied regular plural formation to words they had never heard, showing that they had acquired the plural rule. Their ability to add [z] when the animal's name ended with a voiced sound, and [s] when there was a final voiceless consonant, showed that the children were also using rules based on an understanding of natural classes of phonological segments, and not simply imitating words they had previously heard.

More recently, studies of children acquiring languages with richer inflectional morphologies than English reveal that they learn agreement at a very early age. For example, Italian verbs must be inflected for number and person to agree with the subject. This is similar to the English agreement rule "add *s* to the verb" for third-person, singular subjects—*He giggles a lot* but *We giggle a lot*— except that in Italian more verb forms must be acquired. Italian-speaking children between the ages of 1;10 (one year, ten months) and 2;4 correctly inflect the verb, as the following utterances of Italian children show:

Tu **leggi** il libro.	"You (second person singular) read the book."
Io **vado** fuori.	"I go (first person singular) outside."
Dorme miao dorme.	"Sleeps (third person singular) cat sleeps."
Leggiamo il libro.	"(We) read (first person plural) the book."

Children acquiring other richly inflected languages such as Spanish, German, Catalan, and Swahili quickly acquire agreement morphology. It is rare for them to make agreement errors, just as it is rare for an English-speaking child to say "I goes."

In these languages there is also gender and number agreement between the head noun and the article and adjectives inside the noun phrase. Children as young as two years old respect these agreement requirements when producing NPs, as shown by the following Italian examples:

E **mia** gonna.	"(It) is my (feminine singular) skirt."
Questo mio bimbo.	"This my (masculine singular) baby."
Guarda **la** mela piccolina.	"Look at the little (feminine singular) apple."
Guarda **il** topo piccolino.	"Look at the little (masculine singular) mouse."

Experimental studies with twenty-five-month-old French-speaking children also show that they use gender information on determiners to help identify the subsequent noun, for example, *le ballon* (the-masc. balloon) versus *la banane* (the-fem. banana).

Children also show knowledge of the derivational rules of their language and use these rules to create novel words. In English, for example, we can derive verbs from nouns. From the noun *microwave* we now have a verb *to microwave*; from the noun *e(lectronic) mail* we derived the verb *to e-mail*. Children acquire this derivational rule early and use it often because there are lots of gaps in their verb vocabulary.

Child Utterance	**Adult Translation**
You have to scale it.	"You have to weigh it."
I broomed it up.	"I swept it up."
He's keying the door.	"He's opening the door (with a key)."

These novel forms provide further evidence that language acquisition is a creative process and that children's utterances reflect their internal grammars, which include both derivational and inflectional rules.

The Acquisition of Syntax

When children are still in the holophrastic stage, adults listening to the one-word utterances often feel that the child is trying to convey a more complex message. Experimental techniques show that at that stage (and even earlier), children have knowledge of some syntactic rules. In these experiments the infant sits on his mother's lap and hears a sentence over a speaker while seeing two video displays depicting different actions, one of which corresponds to the sentence. Infants tend to look longer at the video that matches the sentence they hear. This methodology allows researchers to tap the linguistic knowledge of children who are using only single words or who are not talking at all. Results show that children as young as seventeen months can understand the difference between sentences such as "Ernie is tickling Bert" and "Bert is tickling Ernie." Because these sentences have all the same words, the child cannot be relying on the words alone to understand the meanings. He must also understand the word-order rules and how they determine the grammatical relations of subject and object. This same preferential looking technique has shown that eighteen-month-olds can distinguish between subject and object *wh* questions, such as *What is the apple hitting?* and *What hit the apple?* These results and many others strongly suggest that children's syntactic competence is ahead of their productive abilities, which is also how their phonology develops.

Around the time of their second birthday, children begin to put words together. At first these utterances appear to be strings of two of the child's earlier holophrastic utterances, each word with its own single-pitch contour. Soon, they begin to form actual two-word sentences with clear syntactic and semantic relations. The intonation contour of the two words extends over the whole utterance rather than being separated by a pause between the two words. The following utterances illustrate the kinds of patterns that are found in children's utterances at this stage:

allgone sock	hi Mommy
bye bye boat	allgone sticky
more wet	it ball
Katherine sock	dirty sock

These early utterances can express a variety of semantic and syntactic relations. For example, noun + noun sentences such as *Mommy sock* can express a subject + object relation in the situation when the mother is putting the sock on the child, or a possessive relation when the child is pointing to Mommy's sock. Two nouns can also be used to show a subject-locative relation, as in *sweater chair* to mean "The sweater is on the chair," or to show attribution as in *dirty sock*. Children often have a variety of modifiers such as *allgone*, *more*, and *bye bye*.

Because children mature at different rates and the age at which children start to produce words and put words together varies, chronological age is not a good measure of a child's language development. Instead, researchers use the child's **mean length of utterances** (MLU) to measure progress. MLU is the average length of the utterances the child is producing at a particular point. MLU can be measured in terms of morphemes, so words like *boys*, *danced*, and *crying* each have a value of two (morphemes). MLU can also be measured in term of words, which is a more revealing measure when comparing children acquiring languages with different morphological systems. Children with the same MLU are likely to have similar grammars even though they are different ages.

In their earliest multiword utterances, children are inconsistent in their use of function words (grammatical morphemes) such as *a* and *the*, subject pronouns, auxiliary verbs such as *can* and *is*, and verbal inflection. Many (though not all) utterances consist only of open-class or content words, while some or all of the function words, auxiliaries, and verbal inflection may be missing. During this stage children often sound as if they are sending an e-message or reading an old-fashioned telegram (containing only the required words for basic understanding), which is why such utterances are sometimes called "telegraphic speech," and we call this the **telegraphic stage** of the child's language development.

Cat stand up table.
What that?
He play little tune.
Andrew want that.
Cathy build house.
No sit there.
Ride truck.
Show Mommy that.

J. P.'s early sentences were similar (the words in parentheses are missing from J. P.'s sentences):

Age in Months

25	[danʔ ɪʔ tsɪʔ]	"Don't eat (the) chip."
	[bʷaʔ tat]	"Block (is on) top."
26	[mamis tu hæs]	"Mommy's two hands."
	[mo bʌs go]	"Where bus go?"
	[dædi go]	"(Where) Daddy go?"
27	[ʔaɪ gat tu dʲus]	"I got two (glasses of) juice."
	[do baɪʔ mi]	"Don't bite (kiss) me."
	[kʌder sʌni ber]	"Sonny color(ed a) bear."
28	[ʔaɪ gat pwe dɪs]	"I('m) play(ing with) this."
	[mamis tak mɛns]	"Mommy talk(ed to the) men."

It can take many months before children use all the grammatical morphemes and auxiliary verbs consistently. However, the child does not deliberately leave out function words as would an adult sending a twitter. The sentences reflect the child's linguistic capacity at that particular stage of language development.

There is a great deal of debate among linguists about how to characterize telegraphic speech: Do children omit function morphemes because of limitations in their ability to produce longer, more complex sentences, or do they omit these morphemes because their grammar permits such elements to be unexpressed? On the first account, telegraphic speech is due to performance limitations: Since there is an upper limit on the length of utterance a child can produce, and function morphemes are prosodically and semantically weak, they are omitted. On the second view, telegraphic speech is an early grammatical stage similar to languages like Italian or Spanish that allow subject pronouns to be dropped, as in *Hablo ingles* "(I) speak English," or Chinese, which lacks many types of determiners.

Although these sentences may lack certain morphemes, they nevertheless appear to have hierarchical constituent structures and syntactic rules similar to those in the adult grammar. For example, children almost never violate the word-order rules of their language. In languages with relatively fixed word order such as English and Japanese, children use the required order (SVO in English, SOV in Japanese) from the earliest stage. In languages with freer word order, like Turkish and Russian, grammatical relations such as subject and object are generally marked by inflectional morphology, such as case markers. Children acquiring these languages quickly learn the morphological case markers. For example, Russian- and German-speaking children mark subjects with nominative case and objects with accusative case with very few errors.

Telegraphic speech is also very good evidence against the hypothesis that children learn sentences by imitation. Adults—even when speaking motherese—do not drop function words when they talk to children.

The correct use of word order, case marking, and agreement rules shows that even though children may often omit function morphemes, they are aware of constituent structure and syntactic rules. Their utterances are not simply words randomly strung together. From a very early stage onward, children have a grasp of the principles of phrase and sentence formation and of the kinds of structure dependencies mentioned in chapter 4, as revealed by these constituent structure trees:

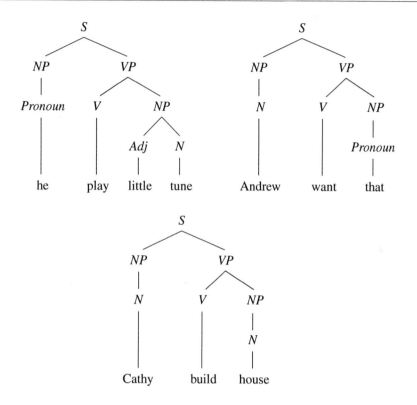

In order to apply morphological and syntactic rules the child must know what syntactic categories the words in his language belong to. But how exactly does the child come to know that *play* and *want* are verbs and *tune* and *house* are nouns? One suggestion is that children first use the meaning of the word to figure out its category. This is called **semantic bootstrapping**. The child may have rules such as "if a word refers to a physical object, it's a noun" or "if a word refers to an action, it's a verb," and so on. However, the rules that link certain meanings to specific categories are not foolproof. For example, the word *action* denotes an action but it is not a verb, *know* is not an action but is a verb, and *justice* is a noun though it is not a physical object. But the rules that drive semantic bootstrapping might be helpful for the kind of words children learn early on which tend to refer to objects and actions.

Word frames may also help the child to determine when words belong to the same category. Studies of the language used to children show that there are certain frames that occur frequently enough to be reliable for categorization, for example, "you __ it" and "the __ one." Most typically, verbs such as *see, do, did, win, fix, turned,* and *get* occur in the first frame, while adjectives like *red, big, wrong,* and *light* occur in the second. If a child knows that *see* is a verb, then he could also deduce that all the other words appearing in the same frame are also verbs. Like semantic bootstrapping, the distributional evidence is not foolproof. For example, "it __ the" can frame a verb, *it hit the ball*, but also a preposition, *I hit it across the street*. And also like semantic bootstrapping, this evidence may well be reliable enough to give the child a head start into the complex task of learning the syntactic categories of words.

The most frequent frames typically consist of function words, determiners such as *the* or *a* or pronouns like *it* or *one*. This suggests that children can learn from function morphemes in the input even though they omit these elements in their own speech. Indeed, comprehension studies show that children pay attention to function words. Two-year-olds respond more appropriately to grammatical commands such as *Find the bird* than to commands with an ungrammatically positioned function word as in *Find was bird*. Other studies suggest that function morphemes such as determiners help children in word segmentation and categorization.

Sometime between the ages of 2;6 and 3;6, a virtual language explosion occurs. At this point it is difficult to identify distinct stages because the child is undergoing so much development so rapidly. By the age of 3;0, most children are consistent in their use of function morphemes. Moreover, they have begun to produce and understand complex structures, including coordinated sentences and embedded sentences of various kinds, such as the following:

He was stuck and I got him out.
I want this doll because she's big.
I know what to do.
I like to play with something else.
I think she's sick.
Look at the train Ursula bought.
I gon' make it like a rocket to blast off with.
It's too early for us to eat.

Past the age of 3;6 children can generally form grammatical *wh* questions with the proper Aux inversion such as *What can I do tomorrow?* They can produce and understand relative clauses such as *This is the lion that chased the giraffe*, as well as other embedded clauses such as *I know that Mommy is home*. They can use reflexive pronouns correctly such as *I saw myself in the camera*. Somewhat beyond 4;0, depending on the individual, much of the adult grammar has been acquired.

The Acquisition of Pragmatics

"Baby Blues" © Baby Blues Partnership. Reprinted with permission of King Features Syndicate.

In addition to acquiring the rules of grammar, children must learn the appropriate use of language in context, or pragmatics. The cartoon is funny because of the inappropriateness of the interaction, showing that Zoe hasn't completely acquired the pragmatic "maxims of conversation" discussed in chapter 5.

Context is needed to determine the reference of pronouns. A sentence such as "Amazingly, he loves her anyway" is uninterpretable unless both speaker and hearer understand who the pronouns *he* and *her* refer to. If the sentence were preceded by "I saw John and Mary kissing in the park," then the referents of the pronouns would be clear. Children are not always sensitive to the needs of their interlocutors, and they may fail to establish the referents for pronouns. It is not unusual for a three- or four-year-old (or even older children) to use pronouns out of the blue, like the child who cries to her mother "He hit me" when mom has no idea who did the deed.

The speaker and listener form part of the context of an utterance. The meaning of *I* and *you* depends on who is talking and who is listening, which changes from situation to situation. Younger children (around age two) have difficulty with the "shifting reference" of these pronouns. A typical error that children make at this age is to refer to themselves as "you," for example, saying "You want to take a walk" when they mean "I want to take a walk."

Children also show a lack of pragmatic awareness in the way they sometimes use articles. Like pronouns, the interpretation of articles depends on context. The definite article *the*, as in "the boy," can be used felicitously only when it is clear to speaker and hearer what boy is being discussed. In a discourse the indefinite article *a/an* must be used for the first mention of a new referent, but the definite article (or pronoun) may be used in subsequent mentions, as illustrated following:

A boy walked into the class.
He was in the wrong room.
The teacher directed the boy to the right classroom.

Children do not always respect the pragmatic rules for articles. In experimental studies, three-year-olds may use the definite article for introducing a new referent. In other words, the child tends to assume that his listener knows who he is talking about without having established this in a linguistically appropriate way.

It may take a child several months or years to master those aspects of pragmatics that involve establishing the reference for function morphemes such as determiners and pronouns. Other aspects of pragmatics are acquired very early. Children in the holophrastic stage use their one-word utterances with different illocutionary force (see page 216). The utterance "up" spoken by J. P. at sixteen months might be a simple statement such as "The teddy is up on the shelf," or a request: "Pick me up."

The Development of Auxiliaries: A Case Study

We have seen in this chapter that language acquisition involves development in various components—the lexicon, phonology, morphology, and syntax, as well as pragmatics. These different modules interact in complex ways to chart an overall course of language development.

As an example, let us take the case of the English auxiliaries. As noted earlier, children in the telegraphic stage do not typically use auxiliaries such as *can, will,* or *do,* and they often omit *be* and *have* from their utterances. Several syntactic constructions in English depend on the presence of an auxiliary, the most central of which are questions and negative sentences. To negate a main verb requires an auxiliary verb (or *do* if there isn't one) as in the following examples:

I don't like this book.
I won't read this book.

An adult does not say "I not like this book."

Similarly, as discussed in chapter 4, English yes-no and *wh* questions are formed by moving an auxiliary to precede the subject, as in the following examples:

Can I leave now?
Do you love me?
Where should John put the book?

Although the two-year-old does not have productive control of auxiliaries, she is able to form negative sentences and questions. During the telegraphic stage, the child produces questions of the following sort:

Yes-No Questions
I ride train?
Mommy eggnog?
Have some?

These utterances have a rising intonation pattern typical of yes-no questions in English, but because there are no auxiliaries, there can be no auxiliary movement. In *wh* questions there is also no auxiliary, but there is generally a *wh* phrase that has moved to the beginning of the sentence. English-speaking children do not produce sentences such as "Cowboy doing what?" in which the *wh* phrase remains in its deep structure position.

The two-year-old has an insufficient lexicon. The lack of auxiliaries means that she cannot use a particular syntactic device associated with question formation in English—auxiliary movement. However, she has the pragmatic knowledge to make a request or ask for information, and she has the appropriate prosody, which depends on knowledge of phonology and the syntactic structure of the question. She also knows the grammatical rule that requires *wh* phrases to be in a fronted position. Many components of language must be in place to form an adultlike question.

In languages that do not require auxiliaries to form a question, children appear more adultlike. For example, in Dutch and Italian, the main verb moves. Because many main verbs are acquired before auxiliaries, Dutch and Italian children in the telegraphic stage produce questions that follow the adult rule:

Dutch

En wat doen ze daar?	and what do they there	"And what are they doing there?"
Wordt mama boos?	becomes mama angry	"Is mommy angry?"
Weet je n kerk?	know you a church	"Do you know a church?"

Italian

Cosa fanno questi bambini?	what do these children	"What are these babies doing?"
Chando vene a mama?	when comes the mommy	"When is Mommy coming?"
Vola cici?	flies birdie	"Is the birdie flying?"

The Dutch and Italian children show us there is nothing intrinsically difficult about syntactic movement rules. The delay that English-speaking children show in producing adultlike questions may simply be because auxiliaries are acquired later than main verbs and because English is idiosyncratic in forming questions by moving only auxiliaries.

The lack of auxiliaries during the telegraphic stage also affects the formation of negative sentences. During this stage the English-speaking child's negative sentences look like the following:

He no bite you.
Wayne not eating it.
Kathryn not go over there.
You no bring choo-choo train.
That no fish school.

Because of the absence of auxiliaries, these utterances do not look very adultlike. However, children at this stage understand the pragmatic force of negation. The child who says "No!" when asked to take a nap knows exactly what he means.

As children acquire the auxiliaries, they generally use them correctly; that is, the auxiliary usually appears before the subject in yes-no questions, but not always.

Yes-No Questions
Does the kitty stand up?
Can I have a piece of paper?
Will you help me?
We can go now?
***Wh* Questions**
Which way they should go?
What can we ride in?
What will we eat?

The introduction of auxiliaries into the child's grammar also affects negative sentences. We now find correctly negated auxiliaries, though *be* is still missing in many cases.

Paul can't have one.
Donna won't let go.
I don't want cover on it.
I am not a doctor.
It's not cold.
Paul not tired.
I not crying.

The child always places the negation in the correct position in relation to the auxiliary or *be*. Main verbs follow negation and *be* precedes negation. Children never produce errors such as "Mommy dances not" or "I not am going."

In languages such as French and German, which are like Italian and Dutch in having a rule that moves inflected verbs, the verb shows up before the negative marker. French and German children respect this rule, as follows. (In the German examples *nich* is the baby form of *nicht*.)

French

Veux pas lolo.	want not water	"I don't want water."
Marche pas.	walks not	"She doesn't walk."
Ça tourne pas.	that turns not	"That doesn't turn."

German

Macht nich aua.	makes not ouch	"It doesn't hurt."
Brauche nich lala.	need not pacifier	"I don't need a pacifier."
Schmeckt auch nich.	tastes also not	"It doesn't taste good either."

Though the stages of language development are universal, they are shaped by the grammar of the particular adult language the child is acquiring. During the telegraphic stage, German, French, Italian, and English-speaking children omit auxiliaries, but they form negative sentences and questions in different ways because the rules of question and negative formation are different in the respective adult languages. This tells us something essential about language acquisition: Children are sensitive to the rules of the adult language at the earliest stages of development. Just as their phonology is quickly fine-tuned to the ambient language(s), so is their syntactic system.

The ability of children to form complex rules and construct grammars of the languages around them in a relatively short time is phenomenal. That all children go through similar stages regardless of language shows that they are equipped with special abilities to know what generalizations to look for and what to ignore, and how to discover the regularities of language.

Setting Parameters

Children acquire some aspects of syntax very early, even while they are still in the telegraphic stage. Most of these early developments correspond to what we referred to as the parameters of UG in chapter 4. One such parameter determines whether the head of a phrase comes before or after its complements, for example, whether the order of the VP is verb-object (VO) as in English or OV as in Japanese. Children produce the correct word order of their language in their earliest multiword utterances, and they understand word order even when they are in the one-word stage of production. According to the parameter model of UG, the child does not actually have to formulate a word-order rule. Rather, he must choose between two already specified values: head first or head last. He determines the correct value based on the language he hears around him. The English-speaking child can quickly figure out that the head comes before its complements; a Japanese-speaking child can equally well determine that his language is head final.

Other parameters of UG involve the verb movement rules. In some languages the verb can move out of the VP to higher positions in the phrase structure tree. We saw this in the Dutch and Italian questions discussed in the last section. In other languages, such as English, verbs do not move (only auxiliaries do). The verb movement parameters provide the child with an option: my language does/does not allow verb movement. As we saw, Dutch- and Italian-speaking children quickly set the verb movement parameters to the "does allow" value, and so they form questions by moving the verb. English-speaking children never make the mistake of moving the verb, even when they don't yet have auxiliaries. In both cases, the children have set the parameter at the correct value for their language. Even after English-speaking children acquire the auxiliaries and the Aux movement rule, they never overgeneralize this movement to include verbs. This supports the hypothesis that the parameter is set early in development and cannot be undone. In this case as well, the child does not have to formulate a rule of verb movement; he does not have to learn when the verb moves and where it moves to. This is all given by UG. He simply has to decide whether verb movement is possible in his language.

The parameters of UG limit the grammatical options to a small well-defined set—is my language head first or head last, does my language have verb movement, and so on. Parameters greatly reduce the acquisition burden on the child and contribute to explaining the ease and rapidity of language acquisition.

The Acquisition of Signed Languages

Deaf children who are born to deaf signing parents are naturally exposed to sign language just as hearing children are naturally exposed to spoken language. Given the universal aspects of sign and spoken languages, it is not surprising that language development in these deaf children parallels the stages of spoken language acquisition. Deaf children babble, they then progress to single signs similar to the single words in the holophrastic stage, and finally they begin to combine signs. There is also a telegraphic stage in which the function signs may be omitted. Use of function signs becomes consistent at around the same age for deaf children as function words in spoken languages. The ages at which signing children go through each of these stages are comparable to the ages of children acquiring a spoken language.

Both spoken and signed language acquisition adhere to a set of universal principles, overlaid by language-particular components. We saw earlier that English-speaking children easily acquire *wh* movement, which is governed by universal principles, but they show some delay in their use of Aux movement, which is specific to English. In *wh* questions in ASL, the *wh* word can move or it can be left in its original position. Both of the following sentences are grammatical:

```
_____whq
```
WHO BILL SEE YESTERDAY?

```
_____ whq
```
BILL SAW WHO YESTERDAY?

(*Note*: We follow the convention of writing the glosses for signs in uppercase letters.)

There is no Aux movement in ASL, but a question is accompanied by a facial expression with furrowed brows and the head tilted back. This is represented by the "whq" above the ASL glosses. This *non-manual marker* is part of the grammar of ASL. It is like the rising intonation we use when we ask questions in English and other spoken languages.

In the acquisition of *wh* questions in ASL, signing children easily learned the rules associated with the *wh* phrase. The children sometimes move the *wh* phrase and sometimes leave it in place, as adult signers do. But they often omit the non-manual marker, an omission that is not grammatical in the adult language.

Sometimes the parallels between the acquisition of signed and spoken languages are striking. For example, some of the grammatical morphemes in ASL are semantically transparent or **iconic**, that is, they look like what they mean; for example, the sign for the pronoun "I" involves the speaker pointing to his chest. The sign for the pronoun "you" is a point to the chest of the addressee. As noted earlier, at around age two, children acquiring spoken languages often reverse the pronouns "I" and "you." Interestingly, at this same age signing children make this same error. They will point to themselves when they mean "you" and point to the addressee when they mean "I." Children acquiring ASL make this error despite the transparency or iconicity of these particular signs, because signing children (like signing adults) treat these pronouns as linguistic symbols and not simply as pointing gestures. As part of the language, the shifting reference of these pronouns presents the same problem for signing children that it does for speaking children.

Hearing children of deaf parents acquire both sign language and spoken language when exposed to both. Studies show that Canadian bilingual children who acquire Langues des Signes Quebecoise (LSQ), or Quebec Sign Language, develop the two languages exactly as bilingual children acquiring two spoken languages. The LSQ–French bilinguals reached linguistic milestones in each of their languages in parallel with Canadian children acquiring French and English. They produced their first words, as well as their first word combinations, at the same time in each language. In reaching these milestones, neither group showed any delay compared to monolingual children.

Deaf children of hearing parents who are not exposed to sign language from birth suffer a great handicap in acquiring language. It may be many years before these children are able to use a spoken language or before they encounter a conventional sign language. Yet the instinct to acquire language is so strong in humans that these deaf children begin to develop their own manual gestures to express their thoughts and desires. A study of six such children revealed that they not only developed individual signs but joined pairs and formed sentences with definite syntactic order and systematic constraints. Although these "home signs," as they are called, are not fully developed languages like ASL or LSQ, they have a linguistic complexity and systematicity that could not have come from the input, because there was no input. Cases such as these demonstrate not only the strong drive that humans have to communicate through language, but also the innate basis of language structure.

Knowing More Than One Language

He that understands grammar in one language, understands it in another as far as the essential properties of Grammar are concerned. The fact that he can't speak, nor comprehend, another language is due to the diversity of words and their various forms, but these are the accidental properties of grammar.

ROGER BACON (1214–1294)

People can acquire a second language under many different circumstances. You may have learned a second language when you began middle school, or high school, or college. Moving to a new country often means acquiring a new language. Other people live in communities or homes in which more than one language is spoken and may acquire two (or more) languages simultaneously. The term **second language acquisition, or L2 acquisition,** generally refers to the acquisition of a second language by someone (adult or child) who has already acquired a first language. This is also referred to as **sequential bilingualism.** **Bilingual language acquisition** refers to the (more or less) simultaneous acquisition of two languages beginning in infancy (or before the age of three years), also referred to as **simultaneous bilingualism.**

Childhood Bilingualism

© 2009 Tundra Comics

Approximately half of the people in the world are native speakers of more than one language. This means that as children they had regular and continued exposure to those languages. In many parts of the world, especially in Africa and Asia, bilingualism (even multilingualism) is the norm. In contrast, many Western countries (though by no means all of them) view themselves as monolingual, even though they may be home to speakers of many languages. In the United States and many European countries, bilingualism is often viewed as a transitory phenomenon associated with immigration.

Bilingualism is an intriguing topic. People wonder how it's possible for a child to acquire two (or more) languages at the same time. There are many questions, such as: Doesn't the child confuse the two languages? Does bilingual language development take longer than monolingual development? Are bilingual children brighter, or does acquiring two languages negatively affect the child's cognitive development in some way? How much exposure to each language is necessary for a child to become bilingual?

Much of the early research into bilingualism focused on the fact that bilingual children sometimes mix the two languages in the same sentences, as the following examples from French-English bilingual children illustrate. In the first example, a French word appears in an otherwise English sentence. In the other two examples, all of the words are English but the syntax is French.

His nose is perdu.	"His nose is lost."
A house pink	"A pink house"
That's to me.	"That's mine."

In early studies of bilingualism, this kind of language mixing was viewed negatively. It was taken as an indication that the child was confused or having difficulty with the two languages. In fact, many parents, sometimes on the advice of educators or psychologists, would stop raising their children bilingually when faced with this issue. However, it now seems clear that some amount of language mixing is a normal part of the early bilingual acquisition process and not necessarily an indication of any language problem.

Theories of Bilingual Development

These mixed utterances raise an interesting question about the grammars of bilingual children. Does the bilingual child start out with only one grammar that is eventually differentiated, or does she construct a separate grammar for each language right from the start? The **unitary system hypothesis** says that the child initially constructs only one lexicon and one grammar. The presence of mixed utterances such as the ones just given is often taken as support for this hypothesis. In addition, at the early stages, bilingual children often have words for particular objects in only one language. For example, a Spanish-English bilingual child may know the Spanish word for milk, *leche*, but not the English word, or she may have the word *water* but not *agua*. This kind of complementarity has also been taken as support for the idea that the child has only one lexicon.

However, careful examination of the vocabularies of bilingual children reveals that although they may not have exactly the same words in both languages, there is enough overlap to make the single lexicon idea implausible. The reason children may not have the same set of words in both languages is that they use their two languages in different circumstances and acquire the vocabulary appropriate to each situation. For example, the bilingual English-Spanish child may hear only Spanish during mealtime, and so he will first learn the Spanish words for foods. Also, bilingual children have smaller vocabularies in each of their languages than the monolingual child has in her one language. This makes sense because a child can only learn so many words a day, and the bilingual child has two lexicons to build. For these reasons the bilingual child may have more lexical gaps than the monolingual child at a comparable stage of development, and those gaps may be different for each language.

The **separate systems hypothesis** says that the bilingual child builds a distinct lexicon and grammar for each language. To test the separate systems hypothesis, it is necessary to look at how the child acquires those pieces of grammar that are different in his two languages. For example, if both languages have SVO word order, this would not be a good place to test this hypothesis. Several studies have shown that where the two languages diverge, children acquire the different rules of each language. Spanish-English and French-German bilingual children have been shown to use the word orders appropriate to each language, as well as the correct agreement morphemes for each language. Other studies have found that children set up two distinct sets of phonemes and phonological rules for their languages.

The separate systems hypothesis also receives support from the study of the LSQ-French bilinguals discussed earlier. These children have semantically equivalent words in the two languages, just as bilinguals acquiring two spoken languages do. In addition, these children, like all bilingual children, were able to adjust their language choice to the language of their addressees, showing that they differentiated the two languages. Like most bilingual children, the LSQ-French bilinguals produced mixed utterances that had words from both languages. What is especially interesting is that these children showed simultaneous language mixing. They would produce an LSQ sign and a French word at the same time, something that is only possible if one language is spoken and the other signed. However, this finding has implications for bilingual language acquisition in general. It shows that the language mixing of bilingual children is not caused by confusion, but is rather the result of two grammars operating simultaneously.

If bilingual children have two grammars and two lexicons, what explains the mixed utterances? Various explanations have been offered. One suggestion is that children mix because they have lexical gaps; if the French-English bilingual child does not know the English word *lost*, she will use the word she does know, *perdu*—the "any port in a storm" strategy. Another possibility is that the mixing in child language is similar to **codeswitching** used by many adult bilinguals (discussed in chapter 10). In specific social situations, bilingual adults may switch back and forth between their two languages in the same sentence, for example, "I put the forks en las mesas" (I put the forks on the tables). Codeswitching reflects the grammars of both languages working simultaneously; it is not "bad grammar" or "broken English." Adult bilinguals codeswitch only when speaking to other bilingual speakers. It has been suggested that the mixed utterances of bilingual children are a form of codeswitching. In support of this proposal, various studies have shown that bilingual children as young as two make contextually appropriate language choices: In speaking to monolinguals the children use one language, and in speaking to bilinguals they mix the two languages.

Two Monolinguals in One Head

Although we must study many bilingual children to reach any firm conclusions, the evidence accumulated so far seems to support the idea that children construct multiple grammars from the outset. Moreover, it seems that bilingual children develop their grammars along the same lines as monolingual children. They go through a babbling stage, a holophrastic stage, a telegraphic stage, and so on. During the telegraphic stage they show the same characteristics in each of their languages as the monolingual children. For example, monolingual English-speaking children omit verb endings in sentences such as "Eve play there" and "Andrew want that," and German-speaking children use infinitives as in "S[ch]okolade holen" (chocolate get-infinitive). Spanish- and Italian-speaking monolinguals never omit verbal inflection or use infinitives in this way. Remarkably, two-year-old German-Italian bilinguals use infinitives when speaking German but not when they speak Italian. Young Spanish-English bilingual children drop the English verb endings but not the Spanish ones, and German-English bilinguals omit verbal inflection in English and use the infinitive in German. Results such as these have led some researchers to suggest that from a grammar-making point of view, the bilingual child is like "two monolinguals in one head."

The Role of Input

One issue that concerns researchers studying bilingualism, as well as parents of bilingual children, is the relationship between language input and proficiency. What role does input play in helping the child to separate the two languages? One input condition that is thought to promote bilingual development is *une personne–une langue* (one person, one language)—as in, Mom speaks only language A to the child and Dad speaks only language B. The idea is that keeping the two languages separate in the input will make it easier for the child to acquire each without influence from the other. Whether this method influences bilingual development in some important way has not been established. In practice this "ideal" input situation may be difficult to attain. It may also be unnecessary. We saw earlier that babies are attuned to various phonological properties of the input language such as prosody and phonotactics. Various studies suggest that this sensitivity provides a sufficient basis for the bilingual child to keep the two languages separate.

Another question is, how much input does a child need in each language to become "native" in both? The answer is not straightforward. It seems intuitively clear that if a child hears twelve hours of English a day and only two hours of Spanish, he will probably develop English much more quickly and completely than Spanish. In fact, under these conditions he may never achieve the kind of grammatical competence in Spanish that we associate with the normal monolingual Spanish speaker. In reality, bilingual children are raised in a variety of circumstances. Some may have more or less equal exposure to the two languages; some may hear one language more than the other but still have sufficient input in the two languages to become "native" in both; some may ultimately have one language that is dominant to a lesser or greater degree. Researchers simply do not know how much language exposure is necessary in the two languages to produce a balanced bilingual. For practical purposes, the rule of thumb is that the child should receive roughly equal amounts of input in the two languages to achieve native proficiency in both.

Cognitive Effects of Bilingualism

Bilingual Hebrew-English-speaking child: "I speak Hebrew and English."
Monolingual English-speaking child: "What's English?"
SOURCE UNKNOWN

Another issue is the effect of bilingualism on intellectual or cognitive development. Does being bilingual make you more or less intelligent, more or less creative, and so on? Historically, research into this question has been fraught with methodological problems and has often been heavily influenced by the prevailing political and social climate. Many early studies (before the 1960s) showed that bilingual children did worse than monolingual children on IQ and other cognitive and educational tests. The results of more recent research indicate that bilingual children outperform monolinguals in certain kinds of problem solving. Also, bilingual children seem to have better **metalinguistic awareness**, which refers to a speaker's conscious awareness *about* language rather than *of* language. This is illustrated in the epigraph to this section. Moreover, bilingual children have an earlier understanding of the arbitrary relationship between an object and its name. Finally, they have sufficient metalinguistic awareness to speak the contextually appropriate language, as noted earlier.

Whether children enjoy some cognitive or educational benefit from being bilingual seems to depend in part on extralinguistic factors such as the social and economic position of the child's group or community, the educational situation, and the relative "prestige" of the two languages. Studies that show the most positive effects (e.g., better school performance) generally involve children reared in societies where both languages are valued and whose parents were interested and supportive of their bilingual development.

Second Language Acquisition

In contrast to the bilinguals just discussed, many people are introduced to a second language (L2) after they have achieved native competence in a first language (L1). If you have had the experience of trying to master a second language as an adult, no doubt you found it to be a challenge quite unlike your first language experience.

Is L2 Acquisition the Same as L1 Acquisition?

With some exceptions, adults do not simply pick up a second language. It usually requires conscious attention, if not intense study and memorization, to become proficient in a second language. Again, with the exception of some remarkable individuals, adult second-language learners (L2ers) do not often achieve native-like grammatical competence in the L2, especially with respect to pronunciation. They generally have an accent, and they may make syntactic or morphological errors that are unlike the errors of children acquiring their first language

(L1ers). For example, L2ers often make word order errors, especially early in their development, as well as morphological errors in grammatical gender and case. L2 errors may **fossilize** so that no amount of teaching or correction can undo them.

Unlike L1 acquisition, which is uniformly successful across children and languages, adults vary considerably in their ability to acquire an L2 completely. Some people are very talented language learners. Others are hopeless. Most people fall somewhere in the middle. Success may depend on a range of factors, including age, talent, motivation, and whether you are in the country where the language is spoken or sitting in a classroom five mornings a week with no further contact with native speakers. For all these reasons, many people, including many linguists who study L2 acquisition, believe that second language acquisition is something different from first language acquisition. This hypothesis is referred to as the **fundamental difference hypothesis** of L2 acquisition.

In certain important respects, however, L2 acquisition is like L1 acquisition. Like L1ers, L2ers do not acquire their second language overnight; they go through stages. Like L1ers, L2ers construct grammars. These grammars reflect their competence in the L2 at each stage, and so their language at any particular point, though not native-like, is rule-governed and not haphazard. The intermediate grammars that L2ers create on their way to the target have been called **interlanguage grammars**.

Consider word order in the interlanguage grammars of Romance (e.g., Italian, Spanish, and Portuguese) speakers acquiring German as a second language. The word order of the Romance languages is Subject-(Auxiliary)-Verb-Object (like English). German has two basic word orders depending on the presence of an auxiliary. Sentences with auxiliaries have Subject-Auxiliary-Object-Verb, as in (1). Sentences without auxiliaries have Subject-Verb-Object, as in (2). (Note that as with the child data above, these L2 sentences may contain various "errors" in addition to the word order facts we are considering.)

1. Hans hat ein Buch gekauft.   "Hans has a book bought."
2. Hans kauft ein Buch.   "Hans is buying a book."

Studies show that Romance speakers acquire German word order in pieces. During the first stage they use German words but the S-Aux-V-O word order of their native language, as follows:

Stage 1:   Mein Vater hat gekauft ein Buch.
        "My father has bought a book."

At the second stage, they acquired the VP word order Object-Verb.

Stage 2:   Vor Personalrat auch meine helfen.
        in the personnel office [a colleague] me helped
        "A colleague in the personnel office helped me."

At the third stage they acquired the rule that places the verb or (auxiliary) in second position.

Stage 3: Jetzt kann sie mir eine Frage machen.
          now can she me a question ask
          "Now she can ask me a question."
          I kenne nich die Welt.
          I know not the world.
          "I don't know the world."

These stages differ from those of children acquiring German as a first language. For example, German children know early on that the language has SOV word order.

Like L1ers, L2ers also attempt to uncover the grammar of the target language, but with varying success, and they often do not reach the target. Proponents of the *fundamental difference hypothesis* believe that L2ers construct grammars according to different principles than those used in L1 acquisition, principles that are not specifically designed for language acquisition, but for the problem-solving skills used for tasks like playing chess or learning math. According to this view, L2ers lack access to the specifically linguistic principles of UG that L1ers have to help them.

Opposing this view, others have argued that adults are superior to children in solving all sorts of nonlinguistic problems. If they were using these problem-solving skills to learn their L2, shouldn't they be uniformly more successful than they are? Also, linguistic savants such as Christopher, discussed in chapter 2, argue against the view that L2 acquisition involves only nonlinguistic cognitive abilities. Christopher's IQ and problem-solving skills are minimal at best, yet he has become proficient in several languages.

Many L2 acquisition researchers do not believe that L2 acquisition is fundamentally different from L1 acquisition. They point to various studies that show that interlanguage grammars do not generally violate principles of UG, which makes the process seem more similar to L1 acquisition. In the German L2 examples above, the interlanguage rules may be wrong for German, or wrong for Romance, but they are not impossible rules. These researchers also note that although L2ers may fall short of L1ers in terms of their final grammar, they appear to acquire rules in the same way as L1ers.

Native Language Influence in L2 Acquisition

One respect in which L1 acquisition and L2 acquisition are clearly different is that adult L2ers already have a fully developed grammar of their first language. As discussed in chapter 1, linguistic competence is unconscious knowledge. We cannot suppress our ability to use the rules of our language. We cannot decide not to understand English. Similarly, L2ers—especially at the beginning stages of acquiring their L2—seem to rely on their L1 grammar to some extent. This is shown by the kinds of errors L2ers make, which often involve the **transfer** of grammatical rules from their L1. This is most obvious in phonology. L2ers generally speak with an accent because they may transfer the phonemes, phonological rules, or syllable structures of their first language to their second language. We see this in the Japanese speaker, who does not distinguish between *write* [raɪt] and *light* [laɪt] because the r/l distinction is not phonemic in Japanese; in the French speaker, who says "ze cat in ze hat" because French does not have [ð];

in the German speaker, who devoices final consonants, saying [hæf] for *have*; and in the Spanish speaker, who inserts a schwa before initial consonant clusters, as in [əskul] for *school* and [əsnab] for *snob*.

Similarly, English speakers may have difficulty with unfamiliar sounds in other languages. For example, in Italian long (or double) consonants are phonemic. Italian has minimal pairs such as the following:

ano	"anus"	anno	"year"
pala	"shovel"	palla	"ball"
dita	"fingers"	ditta	"company"

English-speaking L2 learners of Italian have difficulty in hearing and producing the contrast between long and short consonants. This can lead to very embarrassing situations, for example on New Year's Eve, when instead of wishing people *buon anno* (good year), you wish them *buon ano*.

Native language influence is also found in the syntax and morphology. Sometimes this influence shows up as a wholesale transfer of a particular piece of grammar. For example, a Spanish speaker acquiring English might drop subjects in nonimperative sentences because this is possible in Spanish, as illustrated by the following examples:

Hey, is not funny.
In here have the mouth.
Live in Colombia.

Or speakers may begin with the word order of their native language, as we saw in the Romance-German interlanguage examples.

Native language influence may show up in more subtle ways. For example, people whose L1 is German acquire English yes-no questions faster than Japanese speakers do. This is because German has a verb movement rule for forming yes-no questions that is very close to the English Aux movement rule, while in Japanese there is no syntactic movement in question formation.

The Creative Component of L2 Acquisition

It would be an oversimplification to think that L2 acquisition involves only the transfer of L1 properties to the L2 interlanguage. There is a strong creative component to L2 acquisition. Many language-particular parts of the L1 grammar do not transfer. Items that a speaker considers irregular, infrequent, or semantically difficult are not likely to transfer to the L2. For example, speakers will not typically transfer L1 idioms such as *He hit the roof* meaning "He got angry." They are more likely to transfer structures in which the semantic relations are transparent. For example, a structure such as (1) will transfer more readily than (2).

1. It is awkward to carry this suitcase.
2. This suitcase is awkward to carry.

In (1) the NP "this suitcase" is in its logical direct object position, while in (2) it has been moved to the subject position away from the verb that selects it.

Many of the "errors" that L2ers do make are not derived from their L1. For example, in one study Turkish speakers at a particular stage in their development of German used S-V-Adv (Subject-Verb-Adverb) word order in embedded clauses (the *wenn* clause in the following example) in their German interlanguage, even though both their native language and the target language have S-Adv-V order:

Wenn	ich	geh	zuruck	ich	arbeit elektriker	in der Türkei.
if	I	go	back,	I	work (as an) electrician	in Turkey

(Cf. *Wenn ich zuruck geh ich arbeit elektriker*, which is grammatically correct German.)

The embedded S-V-Adv order is most likely an overgeneralization of the verb-second requirement in German main clauses. As we noted earlier, overgeneralization is a clear indication that a rule has been acquired.

Why certain L1 rules transfer to the interlanguage grammar and others don't is not well understood. It is clear, however, that although construction of the L2 grammar is influenced by the L1 grammar, developmental principles—possibly universal—also operate in L2 acquisition. This is best illustrated by the fact that speakers with different L1s go through similar L2 stages. For example, Turkish, Serbo-Croatian, Italian, Greek, and Spanish speakers acquiring German as an L2 all drop articles to some extent. Because some of these L1s have articles, this cannot be caused by transfer but must involve some more general property of language acquisition.

Is There a Critical Period for L2 Acquisition?

I don't know how you manage, Sir, amongst all the foreigners; you never know what they are saying. When the poor things first come here they gabble away like geese, although the children can soon speak well enough.

MARGARET ATWOOD, *Alias Grace*, 1996

Age is a significant factor in L2 acquisition. The younger a person is when exposed to a second language, the more likely she is to achieve native-like competence.

In an important study of the effects of age on ultimate attainment in L2 acquisition, Jacqueline Johnson and Elissa Newport tested several groups of Chinese and Korean speakers who had acquired English as a second language. The subjects, all of whom had been in the United States for at least five years, were tested on their knowledge of specific aspects of English morphology and syntax. They were asked to judge the grammaticality of sentences such as:

The little boy is speak to a policeman.
The farmer bought two pig.
A bat flewed into our attic last night.

Johnson and Newport found that the test results depended heavily on the age at which the person had arrived in the United States. The people who arrived as children (between the age of three and eight) did as well on the test as American native speakers. Those who arrived between the ages of eight and fifteen did not perform like native speakers. Moreover, every year seemed to make a difference for this group. The person who arrived at age nine did better than the one who arrived at age ten; those who arrived at age eleven did better than those who arrived at age twelve, and so on. The group that arrived between the ages of seventeen and thirty-one had the lowest scores.

Does this mean that there is a critical period for L2 acquisition, an age beyond which it is *impossible* to acquire the grammar of a new language? Most researchers would hesitate to make such a strong claim. Although age is an important factor in achieving native-like L2 competence, it is certainly possible to acquire a second language as an adult. Many teenage and adult L2 learners become proficient, and a few highly talented ones even manage to pass for native speakers. Also, the Newport and Johnson studies looked at the end state of L2 acquisition, after their subjects had been in an English-speaking environment for many years. It is possible that the ultimate attainment of adult L2ers falls short of native competence, but that the process of L2 acquisition is not fundamentally different from L1 acquisition.

It is more appropriate to say that L2 acquisition abilities gradually decline with age and that there are "sensitive periods" for the native-like mastery of certain aspects of the L2. The sensitive period for phonology is the shortest. To achieve native-like pronunciation of an L2 generally requires exposure during childhood. Other aspects of language, such as syntax, may have a larger window.

Recent research with learners of their "heritage language" (the ancestral language not learned as a child, such as Gaelic in Ireland) provides additional support for the notion of sensitive periods in L2 acquisition. This finding is based on studies into the acquisition of Spanish by college students who had overheard the language as children (and sometimes knew a few words), but who did not otherwise speak or understand Spanish. The *overhearers* were compared to people who had no exposure to Spanish before the age of fourteen. All of the students were native speakers of English studying their heritage language as a second language. These results showed that the overhearers acquired a more native-like accent than the other students did. However, the overhearers did not show any advantage in acquiring the grammatical morphemes of Spanish. Early exposure may leave an imprint that facilitates the late acquisition of certain aspects of language.

Recent research on the neurological effects of acquiring a second language shows that left hemisphere cortical density is increased in bilinguals relative to monolinguals and that this increase is more pronounced in early versus late second-language learners. The study also shows a positive relationship between brain density and second-language proficiency. The researchers conclude that the structure of the human brain is altered by the experience of acquiring a second language.

Summary

When children acquire a language, they acquire the grammar of that language—the phonological, morphological, syntactic, and semantic rules. They also acquire the pragmatic rules of the language as well as a lexicon. Children are not taught language. Rather, they extract the rules (and much of the lexicon) from the language around them.

Several learning mechanisms have been suggested to explain the acquisition process. Imitations of adult speech, reinforcement, and analogy have all been proposed. None of these possible learning mechanisms account for the fact that children creatively form new sentences according to the rules of their language, or for the fact that children make certain kinds of errors but not others. Empirical studies of the motherese hypothesis show that grammar development does not depend on structured input. **Connectionist models** of acquisition also depend on the child having specially structured input.

The ease and rapidity of children's language acquisition and the uniformity of the stages of development for all children and all languages, despite the **poverty of the stimulus** they receive, suggest that the language faculty is innate and that the infant comes to the complex task already endowed with a Universal Grammar. UG is not a grammar like the grammar of English or Arabic, but represents the principles to which all human languages conform. Language acquisition is a creative process. Children create grammars based on the linguistic input and are guided by UG.

Language development proceeds in stages, which are universal. During the first year of life, children develop the sounds of their language. They begin by producing and perceiving many sounds that do not exist in their language input, the **babbling stage**. Gradually, their productions and perceptions are fine-tuned to the environment. Children's late babbling has all the phonological characteristics of the input language. Deaf children who are exposed at birth to sign languages also produce manual babbling, showing that babbling is a universal first stage in language acquisition that is dependent on the linguistic input received.

At the end of the first year, children utter their first words. During the second year, they learn many more words and they develop much of the phonological system of the language. Children's first utterances are one-word "sentences" (the **holophrastic** stage).

Many experimental studies show that children are sensitive to various linguistic properties such as stress and phonotactic constraints, and to statistical regularities of the input that enable them to segment the fluent speech that they hear into words. One method of segmenting speech is **prosodic bootstrapping**. Other bootstrapping methods can help the child to learn verb meaning based on syntactic context (**syntactic bootstrapping**), or syntactic categories based on word meaning (**semantic bootstrapping**) and distributional evidence such as word frames.

After a few months, the child puts two or more words together. These early sentences are not random combinations of words—the words have definite patterns and express both syntactic and semantic relationships. During the telegraphic stage, the child produces longer sentences that often lack function or grammatical morphemes. The child's early grammar still lacks many of the rules of the adult grammar, but is not qualitatively different from it. Children at this stage have correct word order and rules for agreement and case, which show their knowledge of structure.

Children make specific kinds of errors while acquiring their language. For example, they will **overgeneralize** morphology by saying *bringed* or *mans*. This shows that they are acquiring rules of their particular language. Children never make errors that violate principles of Universal Grammar.

In acquiring the lexicon of the language children may **overextend** word meaning by using *dog* to mean any four-legged creature. As well, they may **underextend** word meaning and use dog only to denote the family pet and no other dogs, as if it were a proper noun. Despite these categorization "errors," children's word learning, like their grammatical development, is guided by general principles.

Deaf children exposed to **sign language** show the same stages of language acquisition as hearing children exposed to spoken languages. That all children go through similar stages regardless of language shows that they are equipped with special abilities to know what generalizations to look for and what to ignore, and how to discover the regularities of language, irrespective of the modality in which their language is expressed.

Children may acquire more than one language at a time. **Bilingual** children seem to go through the same stages as monolingual children except that they develop two grammars and two lexicons simultaneously. This is true for children acquiring two spoken languages as well as for children acquiring a spoken language and a sign language. Whether the child will be equally proficient in the two languages depends on the input he or she receives and the social conditions under which the languages are acquired.

In **second language acquisition**, L2 learners construct grammars of the target language—called **interlanguage grammars**—that go through stages, like the grammars of first-language learners. Influence from the speaker's first language makes L2 acquisition appear different from L1 acquisition. Adults often do not achieve native-like competence in their L2, especially in pronunciation. The difficulties encountered in attempting to learn languages after puberty may be because there are sensitive periods for L2 acquisition. Some theories of second language acquisition suggest that the same principles operate that account for first language acquisition. A second view suggests that the acquisition of a second language in adulthood involves general learning mechanisms rather than the specifically linguistic principles used by the child.

The universality of the language acquisition process, the stages of development, and the relatively short period in which the child constructs a complex grammatical system without overt teaching suggest that the human species is innately endowed with special language acquisition abilities and that language is biologically and genetically part of the human neurological system.

All normal children learn whatever language or languages they are exposed to, from Afrikaans to Zuni. This ability is not dependent on race, social class, geography, or even intelligence (within a normal range). This ability is uniquely human.

References for Further Reading

Brown, R. 1973. *A first language: The early stages*. Cambridge, MA: Harvard University Press.

Clark, E. 2002. *First language acquisition*. New York: Cambridge University Press.

Guasti, M. T. 2002. *Language acquisition: The growth of grammar*. Cambridge, MA: MIT Press.

Hakuta, K. 1986. *Mirror of language: The debate on bilingualism.* New York: Basic Books.

Ingram, D. 1989. *First language acquisition: Method, description and explanation.* New York: Cambridge University Press.

Jakobson, R. 1971. *Studies on child language and aphasia.* The Hague: Mouton.

Klima, E. S., and U. Bellugi. 1979. *The signs of language.* Cambridge, MA: Harvard University Press.

O'Grady, W. 2005. *How children learn language.* Cambridge, UK: Cambridge University Press.

White, L. 2003. *Second language acquisition and Universal Grammar.* Cambridge, UK: Cambridge University Press.

Exercises

1. *Baby talk* is a term used to label the word forms that many adults use when speaking to children. Examples in English are *choo-choo* for "train" and *bow-wow* for "dog." Baby talk seems to exist in every language and culture. At least two things seem to be universal about baby talk: The words that have baby-talk forms fall into certain semantic categories (e.g., food and animals), and the words are phonetically simpler than the adult forms (e.g., "tummy" /tʌmi/ for "stomach" /stʌmɪk/). List all the baby-talk words you can think of in your native language; then (1) separate them into semantic categories, and (2) try to state general rules for the kinds of phonological reductions or simplifications that occur.

2. In this chapter we discussed the way children acquire rules of question formation. The following examples of children's early questions are from a stage that is later than those discussed in the chapter. Formulate a generalization to describe this stage.

Can I go?	Can I can't go?
Why do you have one tooth?	Why you don't have a tongue?
What do frogs eat?	What do you don't like?
Do you like chips?	Do you don't like bananas?

3. Find a child between two and four years old and play with the child for about thirty minutes. Keep a list of all words and/or "sentences" that are used inappropriately. Describe what the child's meanings for these words probably are. Describe the syntactic or morphological errors (including omissions). If the child is producing multiword sentences, write a grammar that could account for the data you have collected.

4. Roger Brown and his coworkers at Harvard University studied the language development of three children, referred to in the literature as Adam, Eve, and Sarah. The following are samples of their utterances during the "two-word stage."

see boy	push it
see sock	move it
pretty boat	mommy sleep

pretty fan   bye bye melon
more taxi   bye bye hot
more melon

A. Assume that these utterances are grammatical sentences in the children's grammars.

(1) Write a minigrammar that would account for these sentences.

Example: One rule might be: VP → V N

(2) Draw phrase structure trees for each utterance.

Example:

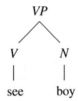

B. One observation made by Brown was that many of the sentences and phrases produced by the children were ungrammatical from the point of view of the adult grammar. The research group concluded, based on utterances such as those below, that a rule in the children's grammar for a noun phrase was:

NP → M N (where M = any modifier)

A coat	My stool	Poor man
A celery	That knee	Little top
A Becky	More coffee	Dirty knee
A hands	More nut	That Adam
My mummy	Two tinker-toy	Big boot

(3) Mark with an asterisk any of the above NPs that are ungrammatical in the adult grammar of English.

(4) State the "violation" for each starred item.

For example, if one of the utterances were *Lotsa book*, you might say: "The modifier *lotsa* must be followed by a plural noun."

5. In the holophrastic (one-word) stage of child language acquisition, the child's phonological system differs in systematic ways from that in the adult grammar. The inventory of sounds and the phonemic contrasts are smaller, and there are greater constraints on phonotactic rules. (See chapter 7 for a discussion of these aspects of phonology.)

A. For each of the following words produced by a child, state what the substitution is, and any other differences that result.

Example:

spook   [pʰuk] Substitution: initial cluster [sp] reduced to single consonant; /p/ becomes aspirated, showing that child has acquired aspiration rule.

(1) don't   [dot]
(2) skip   [kʰɪp]
(3) shoe   [su]
(4) that   [dæt]
(5) play   [pʰe]
(6) thump   [dʌp]
(7) bath   [bæt]
(8) chop   [tʰap]
(9) kitty   [kɪdi]
(10) light   [waɪt]
(11) dolly   [daʊi]
(12) grow   [go]

B. State general rules that account for the children's deviations from the adult pronunciations.

6. Children learn demonstrative words such as *this, that, these, those*; temporal terms such as *now, then, tomorrow*; and spatial terms such as *here, there, right,* and *behind* relatively late. What do all these words have in common? (*Hint:* See the pragmatics section of chapter 5.) Why might that factor delay their acquisition?

7. We saw in this chapter how children overgeneralize rules such as the plural rule, producing forms such as *mans* or *mouses*. What might a child learning English use instead of the adult words given?

   a. children
   b. went
   c. better
   d. best
   e. brought
   f. sang
   g. geese
   h. worst
   i. knives
   j. worse

8. The following words are from the lexicons of two children ages one year six months (1;6) and two (2;0) years old. Compare the pronunciation of the words to adult pronunciation.

   Child 1 (1;6)

soap	[doup]	bib	[bɛ]
feet	[bit]	slide	[daɪ]
sock	[kak]	dog	[da]
goose	[gos]	cheese	[tʃis]
dish	[dɪtʃ]	shoes	[dus]

   Child 2 (2;0)

light	[waɪt]	bead	[biː]
sock	[sʌk]	pig	[pɛk]
geese	[gis]	cheese	[tis]
fish	[fɪs]	biz	[bɪs]
sheep	[ʃip]	bib	[bɪp]

   a. What happens to final consonants in the language of these two children? Formulate the rule(s) in words. Do all final consonants behave the same way? If not, which consonants undergo the rule(s)? Is this a natural class?

b. On the basis of these data, do any pairs of words allow you to identify any of the phonemes in the grammars of these children? What are they? Explain how you were able to determine your answer.

9. Make up a "wug test" to test a child's knowledge of the following morphemes:

comparative	-er	(as in *bigger*)
superlative	-est	(as in *biggest*)
progressive	-ing	(as in *I am dancing*)
agentive	-er	(as in *writer*)

10. Children frequently produce sentences such as the following:

Don't giggle me.
I danced the clown.
Yawny Baby—you can push her mouth open to drink her.
Who deaded my kitty cat?
Are you gonna nice yourself?

a. How would you characterize the difference between the grammar or lexicon of children who produce such sentences and adult English?

b. Can you think of similar, but well-formed, examples in adult English?

11. Many Arabic speakers tend to insert a vowel in their pronunciation of English words. The first column has examples from L2ers whose L1 is Egyptian Arabic and the second column from L2ers who speak Iraqi Arabic (consider [tʃ] to be a single consonant):

L1 = Egyptian Arabic		**L1 = Iraqi Arabic**	
[bilastik]	plastic	[ifloːr]	floor
[θiriː]	three	[ibleːn]	plane
[tiransilet]	translate	[tʃilidren]	children
[silaɪd]	slide	[iθriː]	three
[firɛd]	Fred	[istadi]	study
[tʃildiren]	children	[ifrɛd]	Fred

a. What vowel do the Egyptian Arabic speakers insert and where?

b. What vowel do the Iraqi Arabic speakers insert and where?

c. Based on the position of the italicized epenthetic vowel in "I wrote to him," can you guess which list, A or B, belongs to Egyptian Arabic and which belongs to Iraqi Arabic?

Arabic A		**Arabic B**	
kitabta	"I wrote him"	katabtu	"I wrote him"
kitabla	"He wrote to him"	katablu	"He wrote to him"
kitabɪtla	"I wrote to him"	katabtɪlu	"I wrote to him"

12. Following is a list of utterances recorded from Sammy at age two-and-a-half:

a. Mikey not see him.
b. Where ball go?
c. Look Mommy, doggie.
d. Big doggie.
e. He no bite ya.
f. He eats mud.
g. Kitty hiding.
h. Grampie wear glasses.
i. He funny.
j. He loves hamburgers.
k. Daddy ride bike.
l. That's mines.
m. That my toy.
n. Him sleeping.
o. Want more milk.
p. Read moon book.
q. Me want that.
r. Teddy up.
s. Daddy 'puter.
t. 'Puter broke.
u. Cookies and milk!!!
v. Me Superman.
w. Mommy's angry.
x. Allgone kitty.
y. Here my batball.

A. What stage of language development is Sammy in?
B. Calculate the number of morphemes in each of Sammy's utterances.
C. What is Sammy's MLU in morphemes? In words?
D. **Challenge question:** Deciding the morpheme count for several of Sammy's words requires some thought. For each of the following, determine whether it should count as one or two morphemes and why.

allgone
batball
glasses
cookies

13. The following sentences were uttered by children in the telegraphic stage (the second column contains a word-by-word gloss, and the last column is a translation of the sentence that includes elements that the child omitted):

	Child's utterance	Gloss	Translation
Swedish	Se, blomster har	look flowers have	"Look, (I) have flowers."
English	Tickles me		"It tickles me."
French	Mange du pain	eat some bread	"S/he eats some bread."
German	S[ch]okolade holen	chocolate get	"I/we get chocolate."

| Dutch | Earst kleine boekje lezen | first little book read | "First, I/we read a little book." |

In each of the children's sentences, the subject is missing, although this is not grammatical in the respective adult languages (in contrast to languages such as Spanish and Italian in which it is grammatical to omit the subject).

a. Develop two hypotheses as to why the child might omit sentence subjects during this stage. For example, one hypothesis might be "children are limited in the length of sentences they can produce, so they drop subjects."

b. Evaluate the different hypotheses. For example, an objection to the hypothesis given in (a) might be "If length is the relevant factor, why do children consistently drop subjects but not objects?"

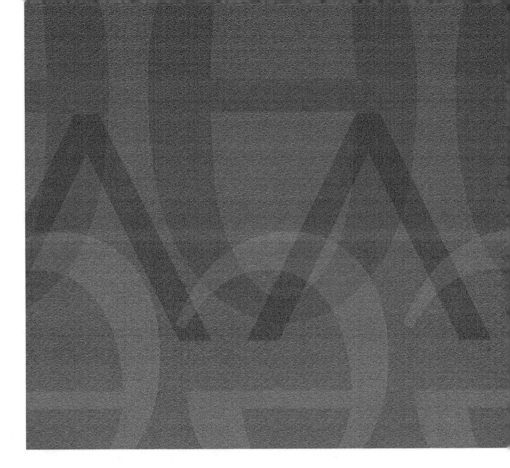

4

Language and Society

Language is not an abstract construction of the learned, or of dictionary-makers, but is something arising out of the work, needs, ties, joys, affections, tastes, of long generations of humanity, and has its bases broad and low, close to the ground.

WALT WHITMAN, *"Slang in America,"* 1885

10

Language in Society

Language is a city to the building of which every human being brought a stone.

RALPH WALDO EMERSON, *Letters and Social Aims*, 1876

Dialects

A language is a dialect that has an army and a navy.

MAX WEINREICH (1894–1969)

All speakers of English can talk to each other and pretty much understand each other. Yet, no two of us speak exactly alike. Some differences are the result of age, sex, social situation, and where and when the language was learned. These differences are reflected in word choices, the pronunciation of words, and grammatical rules. The language of an individual speaker with its unique characteristics is referred to as the speaker's **idiolect**. English may then be said to consist of anywhere from 450 million to 850 million idiolects, or the number of speakers of English (which seems to be growing every day and is difficult to estimate).

Like individuals, different groups of people who speak the same language speak it differently. Bostonians, New Yorkers, Texans, blacks in Chicago, whites in Denver, and Hispanics in Albuquerque all exhibit variation in the way they speak English. When there are systematic differences in the way groups speak a language, we say that each group speaks a **dialect** of that language. Dialects are *mutually intelligible* forms of a language that *differ in systematic ways*. *Every* speaker, whether rich or poor, regardless of region or racial origin, speaks at least one dialect, just as each individual speaks an idiolect. A dialect is *not* an inferior or degraded form of a language, and logically could not be so because a language is a collection of dialects.

It is not always easy to decide whether the differences between two speech communities reflect two dialects or two languages. Sometimes this rule-of-thumb definition is used: When dialects become mutually *un*intelligible—when the speakers of one dialect group can no longer understand the speakers of another dialect group—these dialects become different languages.

However, this rule of thumb does not always jibe with how languages are officially recognized, which is determined by political and social considerations. For example, Danes speaking Danish and Norwegians speaking Norwegian and Swedes speaking Swedish can converse with each other. Nevertheless, Danish and Norwegian and Swedish are considered separate languages because they are spoken in separate countries and because there are regular differences in their grammars. Similarly, Hindi and Urdu are mutually intelligible "languages" spoken in Pakistan and India, although the differences between them are not much greater than those between the English spoken in America and the English spoken in Australia.

The recent history of Serbo-Croatian, the language of the former nation of Yugoslavia, illustrates the factors that can determine if a particular way of speaking is considered to be a dialect or a language. From a linguistic point of view, Serbo-Croatian is a single Slavic language: Even though Croats use Roman script (like English) while Serbs use Cyrillic script (like Russian), in speech the varieties are mutually intelligible, differing slightly in vocabulary just as the British and American English dialects do. But from a sociopolitical point of view, following the breakup of Yugoslavia in the 1990s, the Serbo-Croatian language "broke up" as well. After years of conflict, the two now-independent nations declare that they speak not just different dialects but different languages.

On the other hand, linguistically distinct languages in China, such as Mandarin and Cantonese, although mutually unintelligible when spoken, are nevertheless referred to as dialects of Chinese in the media and elsewhere because they have a common writing system that can be read by all speakers (because it's ideographic—see chapter 12), and because they are spoken in a single country.

It is also not easy to draw a distinction between dialects and languages on strictly linguistic grounds. Dialects and languages reflect the underlying grammars and lexicons of their speakers. It would be completely arbitrary to say, for example, that grammars that differ from one another by, say, twenty rules represent different languages whereas grammars that differ by less than twenty rules are dialects. Why not ten rules or thirty rules? In reality, what one finds is that there is no sudden major break between dialects. Rather, dialects merge into each other, forming a **dialect continuum**. Imagine, for example, a traveler journeying from Vienna to Amsterdam by bicycle. She would notice small changes in the German spoken as she bicycled from village to village, and the people in adjacent villages would have no trouble communicating with one another. Yet by the time our traveler reached Dutch-speaking Amsterdam, she would realize that the accumulated differences made the German of Vienna and the Dutch of Amsterdam nearly mutually unintelligible.

Because neither mutual intelligibility, nor degree of grammatical difference, nor the existence of political or social boundaries is decisive, it is not possible to precisely define the difference between a language and a dialect. We shall, however, use the rule-of-thumb definition and refer to dialects of one language as mutually intelligible linguistic systems, with systematic differences among them.

As we will discuss in the next chapter, languages change continually but these changes occur gradually. They may originate in one geographic region or in one social group and spread slowly to others, and often over the life spans of several generations of speakers. Dialect diversity develops when the changes that occur in one region or group do not spread. When speakers are in regular contact with one another, linguistic properties spread and are acquired by children. However, when some communication barrier separates groups of speakers—be it a physical barrier such as an ocean or a mountain range, or social barriers of a political, racial, class, educational, or religious kind—linguistic changes do not spread so readily, and the differences between groups are reinforced and grow in number.

Dialect leveling is movement toward greater uniformity and less variation among dialects. Though one might expect dialect leveling to occur as a result of the ease of travel and mass media, this is not generally the case. Dialect variation in the United Kingdom is maintained although only a few major dialects are spoken on national radio and television. There may actually be an increase in dialects in urban areas, where different groups attempt to maintain their distinctness and group identity.

Regional Dialects

Phonetics ... the science of speech. That's my profession. ... (I) can spot an Irishman or a Yorkshireman by his brogue. I can place any man within six miles. I can place him within two miles in London. Sometimes within two streets.

GEORGE BERNARD SHAW, *Pygmalion,* 1912

The educated Southerner has no use for an r except at the beginning of a word.

MARK TWAIN, *Life on the Mississippi,* 1883

When various linguistic differences accumulate in a particular geographic region (e.g., the city of Boston or the southern area of the United States), the language spoken has its own character. Each version of the language is referred to as a **regional dialect.** The hypothetical journey from Vienna to Amsterdam discussed previously crossed regional dialects. In the United States, most dialectal differences are based on geographic region.

The origins of many regional dialects of American English can be traced to the people who settled in North America in the seventeenth and eighteenth centuries. Because they came from different parts of England, these early settlers already spoke different dialects of English, and these differences were carried to the original thirteen American colonies. By the time of the American Revolution, there were three major dialect areas in the British colonies: the Northern dialect spoken in New England and around the Hudson River; the Midland dialect spoken in Pennsylvania; and the Southern dialect. These dialects differed from one another and from the English spoken in England in systematic ways. Some of the changes that occurred in British English spread to the colonies; others did not.

How dialects develop is illustrated by the pronunciation of words with an *r* in different parts of United States. As early as the eighteenth century, the British in southern England were dropping their *r*'s before consonants and at the ends of words. Words such as *farm, farther,* and *father* were pronounced as [faːm], [faːðə], and [faːðə], respectively. By the end of the eighteenth century, *r*-drop was a general rule among the early settlers in New England and the southern Atlantic seaboard. Close commercial ties were maintained between the New England colonies and London, and Southerners sent their children to England to be educated, which reinforced the *r*-drop rule. The *r*-less dialect still spoken today in Boston, New York, and Savannah maintains this characteristic. Later settlers, however, came from northern England, where the *r* had been retained; as the frontier moved westward, so did the *r*. Pioneers from all three dialect areas spread westward. The mingling of their dialects leveled many of their dialect differences, which is why the English used in large sections of the Midwest and the West is similar.

Regional phonological or phonetic distinctions are often referred to as different **accents**. A person is said to have a Boston or Brooklyn or Midwestern accent, a Southern drawl, an Irish brogue, and so on. Thus, *accent* refers to the characteristics of speech that convey information about the speaker's dialect, which may reveal in what country or in what part of the country the speaker grew up, or to which sociolinguistic group the speaker belongs. People in the United States often refer to someone as having a British accent or an Australian accent; in Britain they refer to an American accent.

The term *accent* is also used to refer to the speech of non-native speakers, who have learned a language as a second language. For example, a native French speaker's English is described as having a French accent. In this sense, *accent* refers to phonological differences caused by one's native language. Unlike regional dialect accents, such foreign accents do not reflect differences in the speech of the community where the language was learned.

Regional dialects may differ not only in their pronunciation but also in their lexical choices and grammatical rules. A comedian once remarked that "the Mason-Dixon line is the dividing line between *you-all* and *youse-guys*." In the following sections we discuss the different linguistic levels at which dialects may vary.

Phonological Differences

I have noticed in traveling about the country a good many differences in the pronunciation of common words. . . . Now what I want to know is whether there is any right or wrong about this matter. . . . If one way is right, why don't we all pronounce that way and compel the other fellow to do the same? If there isn't any right or wrong, why do some persons make so much fuss about it?

LETTER QUOTED IN "THE STANDARD AMERICAN," in J. V. Williamson and V. M. Burke, eds., *A Various Language,* 1971

A comparison of the *r*-drop and other dialects illustrates the many phonological differences among dialects of American English. These variations created difficulties for us in writing chapter 6 (phonetics), where we wished to illustrate the different sounds of English by using key words in which the sounds occur. As mentioned, some people pronounce *caught* [kɔt] with the vowel [ɔ] and *cot* [kat] with [a], whereas others pronounce them both [kat]. Some pronounce *Mary,* *merry,* and *marry* the same; others pronounce the three words differently as [meri], [mɛri], and [mæri]; and still others pronounce two of them the same. In the southern area of the country, *creek* is pronounced with a tense [i] as [krik], and in the north Midlands, it is pronounced with a lax [ɪ] as [krɪk]. Many speakers of American English pronounce *pin* and *pen* identically, whereas others pronounce the first [pĩn] and the second [pẽn].

The pronunciation of British English (or many dialects of it) differs in systematic ways from pronunciations in many dialects of American English. In a survey of hundreds of American and British speakers conducted via the Internet, 48 percent of the Americans pronounced the mid consonants in *luxury* as voiceless [lʌkʃəri], whereas 96 percent of the British pronounced them as voiced [lʌgʒəri]. Sixty-four percent of the Americans pronounced the first vowel in *data* as [e] and 35 percent as [æ], as opposed to 92 percent of the British pronouncing it with an [e] and only 2 percent with [æ]. The most consistent difference occurred in the placement of primary stress, with most Americans putting stress on the first syllable and most British on the second or third in polysyllabic words like *cigarette, applicable, formidable,* and *laboratory.*

The United Kingdom also has many regional dialects. The British vowels described in the phonetics chapter are used by speakers of the dialect called RP for "received pronunciation" because it is "received" (accepted) in the court of the monarch. In this dialect, *h* is pronounced at the beginning of both *head* and *herb,* whereas in most American English dialects *h* is not pronounced in *herb.* In some British English dialects the *h* is regularly dropped from most words in which it is pronounced in American, such as *house,* pronounced [aus], and *hero,* pronounced [iro]. As is true of the origin of certain American dialects, many of the regional dialects of British English, such as the West Country dialect, the East Anglia dialect, and the Yorkshire dialect, are not deviations from the "standard" dialect spoken in London, but are direct descendants of earlier varieties that existed alongside London English as far back as the eleventh century.

English is the most widely spoken language in the world (as a first or second language). It is the national language of several countries, including the United States, large parts of Canada, the British Isles, Australia, and New Zealand. For many years it was the official language in countries that were once colonies of Britain, including India, Nigeria, Ghana, Kenya, and the other "anglophone" countries of Africa. There are many other phonological differences in the various dialects of English used around the globe.

Lexical Differences

"Liberty Meadows" copyright © 1998. By permission of Frank Cho and Creators Syndicate, Inc.

Regional dialects may differ in the words people use for the same object, as well as in phonology. Hans Kurath, an eminent dialectologist, in his paper "What Do You Call It?" asked:

> Do you call it a *pail* or a *bucket*? Do you draw water from a *faucet* or from a *spigot*? Do you pull down the *blinds*, the *shades*, or the *curtains* when it gets dark? Do you *wheel* the baby, or do you *ride* it or *roll* it? In a *baby carriage*, a *buggy*, a *coach*, or a *cab*?

People take a *lift* to the *first floor* (our *second floor*) in England, but an *elevator* in the United States; they fill up with *petrol* (not *gas*) in London; in Britain a *public school* is "private" (you have to pay), and if a student showed up there wearing *pants* ("underpants") instead of *trousers* ("pants"), he would be sent home to get dressed.

If you ask for a *tonic* in Boston, you will get a drink called *soda* or *soda-pop* in Los Angeles; and a *freeway* in Los Angeles is a *thruway* in New York, a *parkway* in New Jersey, a *motorway* in England, and an *expressway* or *turnpike* in other dialect areas.

Dialect Atlases

Linguist Hans Kurath published **dialect maps** and **dialect atlases** of a region on which dialect differences are geographically plotted (see Figure 10.1). The dialectologists who created the map noted the places where speakers use one word or another word for the same item. For example, the area where the term *Dutch cheese* is used is not contiguous; there is a small pocket mostly in West Virginia where speakers use that term for what other speakers call *smearcase* (from the Dutch word *smeerkaas*, a compound made from the verb *smeren* "to spread" and *kaas* "cheese").

In similar maps, areas were differentiated based on the variation in pronunciation of the same word, such as [krik] and [krɪk] for *creek*. The concentrations defined by different word usages and varying pronunciations, among other linguistic differences, form **dialect areas**.

A line drawn on the map to separate the areas is called an **isogloss**. When you cross an isogloss, you are passing from one dialect area to another. Sometimes several isoglosses coincide, often at a political boundary or at a natural barrier such as a river or mountain range. Linguists call these groupings a *bundle* of isoglosses. Such a bundle can define a regional dialect.

DARE is the acronym for the *Dictionary of American Regional English*, whose chief editor was the distinguished American dialectologist Frederick G. Cassidy (1907–2000). This work represents decades of research and scholarship by Cassidy and other American dialectologists and is a major resource for those interested in American English dialects. Its first four volumes, covering *A* through *Sk*, are published; volume 5, covering *Sk* through *Z*, is due to be published in 2011. Its purpose is described on its Web site as follows:

> The *Dictionary of American Regional English (DARE)* is a reference tool unlike any other. Its aim is not to prescribe how Americans should speak, or even to describe the language we use generally, the "standard" language. Instead, it seeks to document the varieties of English that are **not** found everywhere in the United States—those words, pronunciations, and phrases that vary from one region to another, that we learn at home rather than at school, or that are part of our oral rather than our written culture. Although American English is remarkably homogeneous considering the tremendous size of the country, there are still many thousands of differences that characterize the various dialect regions of the United States. It is these differences that *DARE* records.

While Professor Cassidy did not live to see the completion of DARE, he took his life's work with him to the grave, where on his tombstone is inscribed "On to Z!"

Syntactic Differences

Dialects can also be distinguished by systematic syntactic differences. In most American dialects, sentences may be conjoined as follows:

FIGURE 10.1 │ A dialect map showing the isoglosses separating the use of different words that refer to the same cheese.

Kurath, Hans. *A Word Geography of the Eastern United States*. Ann Arbor, MI: University of Michigan Press, copyright © 1949. Reprinted with permission of University of Michigan Press.

1. John will eat and Mary will eat. → John and Mary will eat.

In the Ozark dialect of southern Missouri, the following conjoining is also possible:

2. John will eat and Mary will eat. → John will eat and Mary.

In (1) the VP *will eat* in the first conjunct is deleted, while in (2) the VP in the second conjunct is deleted. Most dialects of English allow deletion of only the first conjunct and in those dialects *John will eat and Mary* is ungrammatical. The Ozark dialect differs in allowing the second VP to delete.

Speakers of some American dialects say *Have them come early!* where others would say *Have them **to** come early!* Many speakers of the latter dialect also exhibit "double modals," and expressions like *He **might could** do it* or *You **might should** go home* are grammatical. While Aux recursion (see chapter 4) is permitted in all English dialects, most dialects constrain verb phrases to contain no more than one modal verb.

Some of the dialects that permit double modals (e.g., Appalachian English) also exhibit double objects (e.g., *I caught me a fish*); and *a*-prefixing with progressives, *He came a-runnin'*. Several distinguishing syntactic characteristics contribute to a *bundle* of syntactic isoglosses that separate these regional dialects.

In some American English dialects, the pronoun *I* occurs when *me* would be used in other dialects. This difference is a syntactically conditioned morphological difference.

Dialect 1	**Dialect 2**
between you and I	between you and me
Won't he let you and I swim?	Won't he let you and me swim?
*Won't he let I swim?	

The use of *I* in these structures is only permitted in a conjoined NP, as the starred (ungrammatical) sentence shows. *Won't he let me swim?*, however, is grammatical in both dialects. Dialect 1 is growing, and these forms are becoming Standard English, spoken by TV announcers, political leaders, and university professors, although language purists still frown on this usage.

In British English the pronoun *it* in the sentence *I could have done it* can be deleted. British speakers say *I could have done*, which is not in accordance with the syntactic rules of American English. American English, however, permits the deletion of *done it*, and Americans say *I could have*, which does not accord with the British syntactic rules.

Despite such differences, we are still able to understand speakers of other English dialects. Although regional dialects differ in pronunciation, vocabulary, and syntactic rules, the differences are minor when compared with the totality of the grammar. Dialects typically share most rules and vocabulary, which explains why the dialects of a language are mutually intelligible.

Social Dialects

The limits of my language mean the limits of my world.

LUDWIG WITTGENSTEIN, *Tractatus Logico-Philosophicus,* 1922

"For Better or for Worse" copyright © 2005 Lynn Johnston Productions. Dist. by Universal Press Syndicate. Reprinted with permission. All rights reserved.

In many respects, social boundaries and class differences are as confining as the physical barriers that often define regional dialects. It is therefore not surprising that different dialects of a language evolve within social groups.

The social boundaries that give rise to dialect variation are numerous. They may be based on socioeconomic status, religious, ethnic or racial differences, country of origin, and even gender. Middle-class American and British speakers are often distinguishable from working-class speakers; in Baghdad the Christian, Muslim, and Jewish groups all speak different varieties of Arabic; in India people often use different dialects of a standard regional language such as Hindi, Gujarati, or Bengali depending on the social *caste* they belong to; in America, many speakers of African descent speak a different dialect than those of European, Asian, or Hispanic descent; and, as we shall see, women and men each have their own distinguishing speech characteristics.

Dialect differences that seem to come about because of social factors are called **social dialects,** as opposed to *regional dialects,* which are spawned by geographical factors. However, there are regional aspects to social dialects and, clearly, social aspects to regional dialects, so the distinction is not entirely cut and dried.

The "Standard"

We don't talk fancy grammar and eat anchovy toast. But to live under the kitchen doesn't say we aren't educated.

MARY NORTON, *The Borrowers,* 1952

Even though every language is a composite of dialects, many people talk and think about a language as if it were a well-defined fixed system with various dialects diverging from this norm. This is false, although it is a falsehood that is widespread. One writer of books on language accused the editors of *Webster's Third New International Dictionary*, published in 1961, of confusing "to the point of obliteration the older distinction between standard, substandard, colloquial, vulgar, and slang," attributing to them the view that "good and bad, right and wrong, correct and incorrect no longer exist." In the next section we argue that such criticisms are ill founded.

Language Purists

A woman who utters such depressing and disgusting sounds has no right to be anywhere—no right to live. Remember that you are a human being with a soul and the divine gift of articulate speech: that your native language is the language of Shakespeare and Milton and the Bible; and don't sit there crooning like a bilious pigeon.

GEORGE BERNARD SHAW, *Pygmalion,* 1912

Prescriptive grammarians, or language purists, usually consider the dialect used by political leaders and national newscasters as the correct form of the language. (See chapter 1 for a discussion of prescriptive grammars.) This is the dialect taught in "English" or "grammar" classes in school, and it is closer to the written form of the language than many other dialects, which also lends it an air of superiority.

Otto Jespersen, the great Danish linguist, ridiculed the view that a particular dialect is better than any other when he wrote: "We set up as the best language that which is found in the best writers, and count as the best writers those that best write the language. We are therefore no further advanced than before."

The dominant, or **prestige**, dialect is often called the standard dialect. **Standard American English (SAE)** is a dialect of English that many Americans *nearly* speak; divergences from this "norm" are labeled "Philadelphia dialect," "Chicago dialect," "African American English," and so on.

SAE is an idealization. Nobody speaks this dialect; and if somebody did, we would not know it, because SAE is not defined precisely (like most dialects, none of which are easy to clarify). Teachers and linguists held a conference in the 1990s that attempted to come up with a precise definition of SAE. This meeting did not succeed in satisfying everyone's view of SAE. SAE was once represented by the language used by national news broadcasters, but today many of them speak a regional dialect or a style of English that is not universally accepted as "standard." For example, the British Broadcasting Corporation (BBC) once used mostly speakers of RP English, but today speakers of Irish, Welsh, Scottish, and other regional dialects of English are commonly heard on BBC programs. The BBC describes its English as "the speech of educated professionals."

A standard dialect (or prestige dialect) of a particular language may have social functions. Its use in a group may bind people together or provide a common written form for multidialectal speakers. If it is the dialect of the wealthy, influential, and powerful members of society, this may have important implications for the entire society. All speakers who aspire to become successful may be required to speak that dialect even if it isn't their own.

In 1954 the British scholar Alan Ross published *Linguistic Class-Indicators in Present-Day English,* in which he compared the speech habits of the English upper class, whom he labeled "U," with the speech habits of "non-U" speakers. Ross concluded that although the upper class had words and pronunciations peculiar to it, the main characteristic of U speech is the avoidance of non-U speech; and the main characteristic of non-U speech is, ironically, the effort to sound U. "They've a lovely home," for example, is pure non-U, because it is an attempt to be refined. Non-U speakers say "wealthy" and "ever so"; U speakers say "rich" and "very." Non-U speakers "recall"; U-speakers simply "remember."

Non-U speech habits often include **hypercorrections**, deviations from the norm *thought* to be "proper English," such as pronouncing *often* with a [t], or saying *between you and I*, while U speakers, who are generally more secure about their dialect, say [ɔfən] and *between you and me*. Ironically, in some cases non-U speech is so pervasive it eventually becomes part of the prestige dialect, as we are seeing today with *often* and *between you and I/me*.

No dialect, however, is more expressive, less corrupt, more logical, more complex, or more regular than any other dialect or language. They are simply different. More precisely, dialects represent different set of rules or lexical items represented in the minds of its speakers. Any judgments, therefore, as to the superiority or inferiority of a particular dialect or language are social judgments, which have no linguistic or scientific basis.

To illustrate the arbitrariness of "standard usage," consider the English *r*-drop rule discussed earlier. Britain's prestigious RP accent omits the *r* in words such as "car," "far," and "barn." Thus an *r*-less pronunciation is thought to be better than the less prestigious rural dialects that maintain the *r*. However, *r*-drop in the northeast United States is generally considered substandard, and the more prestigious dialects preserve the *r*, though this was not true in the past when *r*-drop was considered more prestigious. This shows that there is nothing inherently better or worse about one pronunciation over another, but simply that one variant is perceived of as better or worse depending on a variety of social factors.

Banned Languages

Language purists wish to prevent language or dialect differentiation because of their false belief that some languages are better than others, or that change leads to corruption. Languages and dialects have also been banned as a means of political control. Russian was the only legal language permitted by the Russian tsars, who banned the use of Ukrainian, Lithuanian, Georgian, Armenian, Azeri, and all the other languages spoken by national groups under the rule of Russia.

Cajun English and French were once banned in southern Louisiana by practice if not by law. Even as recently as August 8, 2006, Mary Tutwiler writes in a blog entitled "The French Connection," "Many local French speakers were so traumatized by the experience of being punished for speaking their mother tongue in school that they suppress their linguistic knowledge in public."

For many years, American Indian languages were banned in federal and state schools on reservations. Speaking Faroese was formerly forbidden in the Faroe Islands. A proscription against speaking Korean was imposed by the Japanese during their occupation of Korea between 1910 and 1945. Throughout history many languages and dialects have been banned to various degrees.

In France, a notion of the "standard" (the dialect spoken in Paris) as the only correct form of the language is promoted by the French Academy, an official panel of "scholars" who determine what usage constitutes the "official French language." Some years ago, the Academy enacted a law forbidding the use of "Franglais," which are words of English origin like *le parking*, *le weekend*, and *le hotdog*. The French, of course, continue to use them, and because such words are notorious, they are widely used in advertising, where being noticed is more important than being correct. Only in government documents can these proscriptions be enforced.

In the past (and to some extent in the present), a French citizen from the provinces who wished to succeed in French society nearly always had to learn the prestigious Parisian French dialect. Then, several decades ago, members of regional autonomy movements demanded the right to use their own languages in their schools and for official business. In the section of France known as l'Occitanie, the popular singers sing in Langue d'oc, a Romance language of the region, both as a protest against the official language policy and as part of the cultural revival movement.

In many places in the world (including the United States), the use of sign languages of the deaf was once banned. Children in schools for the deaf were often punished if they used any gestures at all. The aim of these schools was to teach deaf children to read lips and to communicate through sound. This view prevented early exposure to language. It was mistakenly thought that children, if exposed to sign, would not learn to read lips or produce sounds. Individuals who become deaf after learning a spoken language are often able to use their knowledge to learn to read lips and continue to speak. This is, however, very difficult if one has never heard speech sounds. Furthermore, even the best lip readers can comprehend only about one-third of the sounds of spoken language. Imagine trying to decide whether *lid* or *led* was said by reading the speaker's lips. Mute the sound on a TV set and see what percentage of a news broadcast you can understand, even if recorded and played back in slow motion, and even if you know the subject matter.

In recent years in the United States, a movement has arisen to establish English as an official language by amending the Constitution. An "Official English" initiative was passed by the electorate in California in 1986; in Colorado, Florida, and Arizona in 1988; and in Alabama in 1990. Such measures have also been adopted by seventeen state legislatures. This kind of linguistic chauvinism is opposed by civil rights minority-group advocates, who point out that such a measure could be used to prevent large numbers of non-English-speaking citizens from participating in civil activities such as voting, and from receiving the benefits of a public education, for which they pay through taxes. Fortunately, as of this writing, the movement appears to have lost momentum.

African American English

The language, only the language.... It is the thing that black people love so much—the saying of words, holding them on the tongue, experimenting with them, playing with them. It's a love, a passion. Its function is like a preacher's: to make you stand up out of your seat, make you lose yourself and hear yourself. The worst of all possible things that could happen would be to lose that language.

TONI MORRISON, interviewed in *The New Republic,* March 21, 1981

Most regional dialects of the United States are largely free from stigma. Some regional dialects, like the *r*-less NewYorkese, are the victims of so-called humor, and speakers of one dialect may ridicule the "drawl" of southerners or the "nasal twang" of Texans (even though not all speakers of southern dialects drawl, nor do all Texans twang).

There is, however, a *social* dialect of North American English that has been a victim of prejudicial ignorance. This dialect, **African American English (AAE)**,[1] is spoken by a large population of Americans of African descent. The distinguishing features of this English dialect persist for social, educational, and economic reasons. The historical discrimination against African Americans has created the social boundaries that permit this dialect to thrive. In addition, particularly in recent years, many blacks have embraced their dialect as a means of positive group identification. AAE is generally used in casual and informal situations, and is much more common among working class people. African Americans from middle class backgrounds and with higher levels of education are now more likely to be speakers of SAE. U.S. President Barack Obama and First Lady Michelle Obama are cases in point.

Since the onset of the civil rights movement in the 1960s, AAE has been the focus of national attention. Some critics attempt to equate its use with inferior genetic intelligence and cultural deprivation, justifying these incorrect notions by stating that AAE is a "deficient, illogical, and incomplete" language. Such epithets cannot be applied to any language, and they are as unscientific in reference to AAE as to Russian, Chinese, or Standard American English. The cultural-deprivation myth is as false as the idea that some dialects or languages are inferior. A person may be "deprived" of one cultural background, but be rich in another.

Some people, white and black, think they can identify the race of a person by speech alone, believing that different races inherently speak differently. This belief is patently false. A black child raised in Britain will speak the British dialect of the household. A white child raised in an environment where AAE is spoken will speak AAE. Children construct grammars based on the language they hear.

AAE is discussed here more extensively than other American dialects because it provides an informative illustration of the morphological and syntactic regularities of a dialect of a major language, and the systematic differences from the so-called standard dialects of that language. A vast body of research shows that there are the same kinds of linguistic differences between AAE and SAE as occur between many of the world's major dialects.

Phonological Differences between African American English and SAE

Because AAE is not a single, monolithic dialect, but rather refers to a collection of tightly related dialects, not everything discussed in this section applies to all speakers of AAE.

r-Deletion

Like several dialects of both British and American English, AAE includes a rule of *r-deletion* that deletes /r/ everywhere except before a vowel. Pairs of words like *guard* and *god*, *nor* and *gnaw*, *sore* and *saw*, *poor* and *Poe*, *fort* and *fought*,

---

[1]AAE is actually a group of closely related dialects also variously called African American Vernacular English (AAVE), Black English (BE), Inner City English (ICE), and Ebonics.

and *court* and *caught* are pronounced identically in AAE because of this phonological rule. There is also an *l-deletion* rule for some speakers of AAE, creating identically pronounced pairs like *toll* and *toe*, *all* and *awe*, *help* and *hep*.

A *consonant cluster reduction* rule in AAE simplifies consonant clusters, particularly at the ends of words and when one of the two consonants is an alveolar (/t/, /d/, /s/, /z/). The application of this rule may delete the past-tense morpheme so that *meant* and *mend* are both pronounced as *men*, and *past* and *passed* (*pass + ed*) may both be pronounced like *pass*. When speakers of this dialect say *I pass the test yesterday*, they are not showing an ignorance of past and present-tense forms of the verb, but are pronouncing the past tense according to this rule in their grammar.

The deletion rule is optional; it does not always apply, and studies have shown that it is more likely to apply when the final [t] or [d] does not represent the past-tense morpheme, as in nouns like *paste* [pest] as opposed to verbs like *chased* [tʃest], where the final past tense [t] will not always be deleted. This has also been observed with final [s] or [z], which will be retained more often by speakers of AAE in words like *seats* /sit + s/, where the /s/ represents plural, than in words like *Keats* /kits/, where it is more likely to be deleted to yield the surface form [kit].

Consonant cluster reduction is not unique to AAE. It exists optionally for many speakers of other dialects including SAE. For example, in SAE the medial [d] in *didn't* is often deleted, producing [dɪ̃nt]. Furthermore, nasals are commonly deleted before final voiceless stops, to result in [hɪ̃t] versus [hɪ̃nt].

Neutralization of [ɪ] and [ɛ] before Nasal Consonants

AAE shares with many regional dialects a lack of distinction between /ɪ/ and /ɛ/ before nasal consonants, producing identical pronunciations of *pin* and *pen*, *bin* and *Ben*, *tin* and *ten*, and so on. The vowel sound in these words is roughly between the [ɪ] of *pit* and the [ɛ] of *pet*.

Diphthong Reduction

AAE has a rule that reduces the diphthong /ɔɪ/ (particularly before /l/) to the simple vowel [ɔ] without the glide, so that *boil* and *boy* are pronounced [bɔ].

$$/ɔɪ/ \rightarrow /ɔ/$$

This rule is common throughout the regional dialects of the South irrespective of race and social class.

Loss of Interdental Fricatives

A regular feature is the change of a /θ/ to /f/ and /ð/ to /v/ so that *Ruth* is pronounced [ruf] and *brother* is pronounced [brʌvər]. This [θ]-[f] correspondence also holds in some dialects of British English, where /θ/ is not even a phoneme in the language. *Think* is regularly [fɪ̃nk] in Cockney English.

Initial /ð/ in such words as *this*, *that*, *these*, and *those* are pronounced as [d]. This is again not unique to AAE, but a common characteristic of certain regional, nonethnic dialects of English, many found in the state of New Jersey as well as in New York City and Boston.

Another regular feature found in many varieties of AAE (and non-AAE) is the substitution of a glottal stop for an alveolar stop at the end of non-word-final syllables; thus the name *Rodman* is pronounced [raʔmə̃n], but the word *rod* is pronounced [rad]. In fact, we observed in chapter 6 on phonetics that the glottal stop [ʔ] is a common allophone of /t/ in many dialects of English.

All of these differences are rule-governed and similar to the kinds of phonological variations that are found in languages all over the world, including Standard English.

Syntactic Differences between AAE and SAE

And of his port as meeke as is a mayde
He nevere yet no vileynye ne sayde

GEOFFREY CHAUCER, Prologue to *The Canterbury Tales,* 14th century

Syntactic differences also exist between dialects. They have often been used to illustrate the illogic of AAE, and yet these differences are evidence that AAE is as syntactically complex and as logical as SAE.

Multiple Negatives
Constructions with multiple negatives akin to AAE *He don't know nothing* are commonly found in languages of the world, including French, Italian, and the English of Chaucer, as illustrated in the epigraph from *The Canterbury Tales.* The multiple negatives of AAE are governed by rules of syntax and are not illogical.

Deletion of the Verb "Be"
In most cases, if in Standard English the verb can be contracted, in African American English sentences it is deleted; where it can't be contracted in SAE, it can't be deleted in AAE, as shown in the following sentences:

SAE	AAE
He is nice/He's nice.	He nice.
They are mine/They're mine.	They mine.
I am going to do it/I'm gonna do it.	I gonna do it.
He is/he's as nice as he says he is.	He as nice as he say he is.
*He's as nice as he says he's	*He as nice as he say he
How beautiful you are.	How beautiful you are.
*How beautiful you're	*How beautiful you
Here I am.	Here I am.
*Here I'm	*Here I

These examples show that syntactic reduction rules operate in both dialects although they show small systematic differences.

Habitual "Be"
In SAE, the sentence *John is happy* can be interpreted to mean *John is happy now* or *John is generally happy.* One can make the distinction clear in SAE only by lexical means, that is, the addition of words. One would have to say *John is generally happy* or *John is a happy person* to disambiguate the meaning from *John is presently happy.*

In AAE, this distinction is made syntactically; an uninflected form of *be* is used if the speaker is referring to *habitual* state.

John be happy.	"John is always happy."
John happy.	"John is happy now."
*John be happy at the moment.	
He be late.	"He is habitually late."
He late.	"He is late this time."
*He be late this time.	
Do you be tired?	"Are you generally tired?"
You tired?	"Are you tired now?"
*Do you be tired today?	

The ungrammatical sentences are caused by a conflict of the habitual meaning with the momentary meaning conveyed by *at the moment*, *this time*, and *today*. The syntactic distinction between habitual and nonhabitual aspect also occurs in SAE, but with verbs other than *be*. In SAE eventive verbs such as *eat* and *dance*, when marked with the present-tense *-s* morpheme, have only a habitual meaning and cannot refer to an ongoing situation, in contrast to stative verbs such as *think* or *love*, as exemplified by the following sentences:

John dances every Saturday night.
*John dances now.
John loves Mary now and forever.

"There" Replacement

Some AAE dialects replace SAE *there* with *it's* in positive sentences, and *don't* or *ain't* in negative sentences.

It's a fly messing with me.	"There's a fly messing with me."
Ain't no one going to help you.	
Don't no one going to help you.	"There's no one going to help you."

Combined with multiple negatives, consonant cluster simplification, and complement deletion, speakers produce highly condemned, but clear, logically sound sentences like *Ain't no hard worker never get no good payin' job*: "There isn't a hard worker who never gets a good paying job."

Latino (Hispanic) English

A major group of American English dialects is spoken by native Spanish speakers or their descendants. For more than a century large numbers of immigrants from Spanish-speaking countries of South and Central America and the Caribbean islands have been enriching the United States with their language and culture. Among these groups are native speakers of Spanish who have learned or are learning English as a second language. There are also those born in Spanish-speaking homes whose native language is English, some of whom are monolingual, and others who speak Spanish as a second language.

One cannot speak of a homogeneous Latino dialect. In addition to the differences between bilingual and monolingual speakers, the dialects spoken by Puerto Rican, Cuban, Guatemalan, and El Salvadoran immigrants or their children are somewhat different from one another and also from those spoken by many Mexican Americans in the Southwest and California, called Chicano English (ChE).

Although ChE is not homogeneous, we can still recognize it as a distinct dialect of American English with systematic differences from other dialects of English.

Chicano English (ChE)

Chicano English is acquired as a first language by many children, making it the native language of hundreds of thousands, if not millions, of Americans. It is not English with a Spanish accent but, like African American English, a mutually intelligible dialect that differs systematically from SAE. Many of the differences, however, depend on the social context of the speaker. (This is also true of AAE and most "minority" dialects.) Linguistic differences of this sort that vary with the social situation of the speaker are termed **sociolinguistic variables**. For example, the use of nonstandard forms like double negation is often associated with pride of ethnicity, which is part of the social context. Many Chicano speakers (and speakers of AAE) are **bidialectal**; they can use either ChE (or AAE) or SAE, depending on the social situation.

Phonological Variables of ChE

Phonological differences between ChE and SAE reveal the influence of Spanish on ChE. For example, as discussed in chapters 6 and 7, English has eleven vowel phonemes (not counting the diphthongs): /i, ɪ, e, ɛ, æ, u, ʊ, o, ɔ, a, ʌ/. Spanish, however, has only five: /i, e, u, o, a/. Chicano speakers whose native language is Spanish may substitute the Spanish vowel system for the English. When this is done, several homonyms result that have distinct pronunciations in SAE. Thus *ship* and *sheep* are both pronounced like *sheep*; *rid* is pronounced like *read*, and so on. Chicano speakers whose native language is English may *choose to speak the ChE dialect* despite having knowledge of the full set of American English vowels.

Other differences involve consonants. The affricate /tʃ/ and the fricative /ʃ/ are interchanged, so that *shook* is pronounced as if spelled with a *ch* and *check* as if spelled with an *sh*. Also, some consonants are devoiced; for example, /z/ is pronounced [s] in words like *easy* [isi] and *guys* [gaɪs]. Another difference is the substitution of /t/ for /θ/, and /d/ for /ð/ word initially, so *thin* is pronounced like *tin* or *teen* and *they* is pronounced *day*.

ChE has word-final consonant cluster reduction. *War* and *ward* are both pronounced like *war*; *star* and *start* like *star*. This process may also delete past-tense suffixes (*poked* is pronounced like *poke*) and third-person singular agreement suffixes (*He loves her* becomes *he love her*). Word-final alveolar-cluster reduction (e.g., pronouncing *fast* as if it were spelled *fass*) has become widespread among all dialects of English, including SAE. Although this process is often singled out for speakers of ChE and AAE, it is actually no longer dialect specific.

Prosodic aspects of speech in ChE such as vowel length and intonation patterns may also differ from SAE and give ChE a distinctive flavor. The Spanish sequential constraint, which does not permit a word to begin with an /s/ cluster, is sometimes carried over to ChE in speakers who acquire English after early childhood. Thus *scare* may be pronounced as if it were spelled *escare*, and *school* as if it were spelled *eschool*.

Syntactic Variables in ChE

There are also regular syntactic differences between ChE and SAE. In Spanish, a negative sentence uses a negative morpheme before the verb even if another negative appears; thus negative concord (the multiple negatives mentioned earlier) is a regular rule of ChE syntax:

SAE	**ChE**
I don't have any money.	I don have no money.
I don't want anything.	I no want nothin.

Lexical differences also occur, such as the use of *borrow* in ChE for *lend* in SAE (*Borrow me a pencil*), or *barely* in ChE for *just* in SAE (*The new Prius had barely come out when I bought one*), as well as many other often subtle differences.

Genderlects

© 2006 Berkeley Breathed

Dialects are defined in terms of groups of speakers, and speakers are most readily grouped by geography. Thus, regional dialects are the most apparent and generally are what people mean when they use the word *dialect*. Social groups are more amorphous, and social dialects correspondingly less well delineated and, until recently, less well studied. Surprisingly, the most obvious division of humankind into groups—women and men—has not engendered (if you'll pardon the expression) much dialectal attention until relatively recently.

In 1973, the linguist Robin Lakoff wrote the first article specifically concerned with women and language to be published in a major linguistics journal.[2] Lakoff identified a number of features that occurred more frequently in women's speech than in men's. For example, women "hedge" their speech more often than men do, with expressions like *I suppose, I would imagine, This is probably wrong, sort of, but . . .* , and so on. Women also use tag questions more frequently to qualify their statements (*He's not a very good actor, is he?*), as well as words of politeness (e.g., *please, thank you*) and intensifying adjectives such as *really* and *so* (*It's a really good film, It's so nice of you*). Lakoff claimed that the use of these devices was due to uncertainty and a lack of confidence on the part of women.

Since Lakoff's study, an increasing number of scholars have been conducting research on language, gender, and sexism, investigating the differences between male and female speech and their underlying causes. Many sociolinguists studying gender differences in speech now believe that women use hedges and other, similar devices not because they lack confidence but in order to express friendliness and solidarity, a sharing of attitudes and values, with their listeners.

There is a widespread belief that when men and women converse, women talk more and also that they tend to interrupt more than men in conversation. This is a frequent theme in sitcoms and the subject of jokes and sayings in various cultures, such as the English proverb "Women's tongues are like lambs' tails—they are never still," or the Chinese proverb "The tongue is the word of a woman and she never lets it become rusty." However, serious studies of mixed-sex conversations show that in a number of different contexts men dominate the talking, particularly in non-private conversation such as television interviews, business meetings, and conference discussion where talking can increase one's status.

This dominance of males in mixed speech situations seems to develop at an early age. It occurs in classroom situations in which boys dominate talk time with the teachers. One study found that boys were eight times more likely to call out answers than girls. There is also evidence that teachers encourage this dominant behavior, reprimanding girls more often than boys when they call out.

It has also been observed that women are more conservative in their speech style. For example, they are less likely to use vernacular forms such as the reduction of *-ing* to *-in'* or *him* to *'im* as in *I was walkin' down the street when I saw 'im*. Some dialects of British English drop word initial "h" in casual speech as in *'arf an hour* (half an hour), *'enry* (Henry), *'appy* (happy). This *h*-less pronunciation happens more frequently in the speech of men than women. The tendency for women to speak more "properly" than men has been confirmed in many studies and appears to develop at an early age. Children as young as six show this pattern, with girls avoiding the vernacular forms used more commonly by boys from the same background.

Lakoff observed this effect in her early study and proposed that women spoke more "proper" English than men because of an insecurity caused by sexism in

---

[2]Lakoff, R. 1973. Language and woman's place. *Language in Society* 2:45–80.

society. This explanation is generally supported by other linguists who have elaborated on this general idea. Among the more specific reasons that have been suggested are that women use more standard language to gain access to senior-level jobs that are often less available to them, that society tends to expect "better" behavior in general from women than men, that people who find themselves in subordinate roles (as women do in many societies) must be more polite, and that men prefer to use more vernacular forms because it helps to identify them as tough and strong. The linguist Janet Holmes has also suggested that most sociolinguistic experiments are conducted by middle-class, well-educated academics and it is possible that the women who are interviewed "accommodate" to the interviewer, changing their speech to be more like the interviewer's or simply in response to the more formal nature of the interview situation. Men, on the other hand, may be less responsive to these perceived pressures.

The linguist Deborah Tannen calls the different variants of English used by men and women "genderlects" (a blend of *gender* and *dialect*). Variations in the language of men and women occur in many, if not all, languages. In Japanese, women may choose to speak a distinct female dialect, although they know the standard dialect used by both men and women. The Japanese language has many *honorific* words—words intended to convey politeness, respect, humility, and lesser social status in addition to their regular meaning. As noted earlier, women tend to use polite forms more often than men. Japanese has formal and informal verbal inflections (see exercise 17, chapter 7), and again, women use the formal forms more frequently. There are also different words in Japanese used in males and female speech, for example,

	Women's Word	Men's Word
stomach	onaka	hara
delicious	oishii	umai
I/me	watashi	boku

and phrases such as:

	Women's Word	Men's Word
eat a meal	gohan-o taberu	meshi-o kuu
be hungry	onaka-ga suita	hara-ga hetta
	stomach become empty	stomach decrease

One effect of the different genderlects of Japanese shows up in the training of guide and helper dogs. The animals learn their commands in English because the sex of the owner is not known in advance, and it is easier for an impaired person to use English commands than it is for trainers to train the dog in both language styles.

The differences discussed thus far have more to do with language use—lexical choices and conversational style—than with grammatical rules. There are, however, cases in which the language spoken by men and women differ in their grammars. In the Muskogean language Koasati, spoken in Louisiana, words that end in an /s/ when spoken by men, end in /l/ or /n/ when used by women; for example, the word meaning "lift it" is *lakawhol* for women and *lakawhos* for men. Similarly, in Bengali women often use an [l] at the beginning of words where men use an [n].

In Yana, women's words are sometimes shorter than men's because of a suffix that men use. For example, the women's form for "deer" is *ba*, the men's *ba-na*, for "person" we find *yaa* versus *yaa-na*, and so on. Early explorers reported that the men and women of the Carib Indians used different dialects. The historical reason for this is that long ago a group of Carib-speaking men invaded an area inhabited by Arawak-speaking people and killed all the men. The women who remained then continued to use Arawak while their new husbands spoke Carib.

In Chiquitano, a Bolivian language, the grammar of male language includes a noun-class gender distinction, with names for males and supernatural beings morphologically marked in one way, and nouns referring to females marked in another. In Thai, utterances may end with "politeness particles," *kʰrap* for men and *kʰa* for women (tones omitted). Thai also has different pronouns and fixed expressions like *please* and *thank you* that give each genderlect a distinctive character.

One obvious phonetic characteristic of female speech is its relatively higher pitch, caused mainly by shorter vocal tracts. Nevertheless, studies have shown that the difference in pitch between male and female voices is generally greater than could be accounted for by physiology alone, suggesting that some social factors may be at work, possibly beginning during language acquisition.

Margaret Thatcher, the former prime minister of England, is a well-known example of a woman altering her vocal pitch, in this case for political reasons. Thatcher's regular speaking voice was quite high and a little shrill. She was counseled by her advisors to lower her voice and to speak more slowly and monotonously in order to sound more like an authoritative man. This artificial speaking style became a strong characteristic of her public addresses.

Sociolinguistic Analysis

Speakers from different socioeconomic classes often display systematic speech differences, even when region and ethnicity are not factors. These social-class dialects differ from other dialects in that their sociolinguistic variables are often statistical in nature. With regional and social dialects, a differing factor is either present or absent (for the most part), so regional groups who say *faucet* say it pretty much all the time, as do the regional groups who say *spigot*. Speakers of AAE dialects will say *she pretty* meaning "she is pretty" with great regularity, other factors being equal. But social-class dialects differentiate themselves in a more quantitative way; for example, one class of speakers may apply a certain rule 80 percent of the time to distinguish it from another that applies the same rule 40 percent of the time.

The linguist William Labov carried out a sociolinguistic analysis in New York City that focused on the rule of *r*-dropping that we discussed earlier, and its use by upper-, middle-, and lower-class speakers.[3] In this classic study, a model for subsequent sociolinguistic analyses, Labov first identified three department stores that catered primarily to the three classes: Saks Fifth Avenue, Macy's, and S. Klein—upper, middle, and lower, respectively. To elicit data, he would go to the three stores and ask questions that he knew would evoke the words *fourth* and

---

[3]Labov, W. 1966. *The social stratification of English in New York City*. Washington, DC: Center for Applied Linguistics.

floor. People who applied the *r*-dropping rule would pronounce these words [fɔθ] and [flɔ], whereas ones who did not apply the rule would say [fɔrθ] and [flɔr].

The methodology behind much of Labov's research is important to note. Labov interacted with all manner of people in their own environment where they were comfortable, although he took care when analyzing the data to take into account ethnic and gender differences. In gathering data he was careful to elicit naturally spoken language through his casual, unassuming manner. Finally, he would evoke the same answer twice by pretending not to hear or understand, and in that way was able to collect both informal, casual utterances, and utterances spoken (the second time) with more care.

In Saks, a high-end department store, 62 percent of respondents pronounced the *r* at least some of the time; in Macy's, a less expensive store, it was 52 percent, and in Klein's, a lower-end retailer, a mere 21 percent. The *r*-dropping rule, then, is socially "stratified," to use Labov's terminology, with the lower socio-class dialects applying the rule most often. What makes Labov's work so distinctive is his methodology and his discovery that the differences among dialects can be usefully defined on a quantitative basis of rule applications rather than the strict presence or absence of a rule. He also showed that social context and the sociolinguistic variables that it governs play an important role in language change (discussed in chapter 11).

Languages in Contact

"Bizarro" copyright © 1994 by Dan Piraro. Reprinted with permission of King Features Syndicate. All rights reserved.

Even a dog we do know is better company than a man whose language we know not.

ST. AUGUSTINE, *City of God,* 5th century

Human beings are great travelers and traders and colonizers. The mythical tales of nearly all cultures tell of the trials and tribulations of travel and exploration, such as those of Odysseus (Ulysses) in Homer's *Odyssey*. Surely one of the tribulations of ranging outward from your home is that sooner or later you will encounter people who do not speak your language, nor you theirs. In some parts of the world, for example in bilingual communities, you may not have to travel very far at all to find the language disconnect, and in other parts you may have to cross an ocean. Because this situation is so common in human history and society, several solutions for bridging this communication gap have arisen.

Lingua Francas

Language is a steed that carries one into a far country.

ARAB PROVERB

Many areas of the world are populated by people who speak diverse languages. In such areas, where groups desire social or commercial communication, one language is often used by common agreement. Such a language is called a **lingua franca**.

In medieval times, a trade language based largely on the languages that became modern Italian and Provençal came into use in the Mediterranean ports. That language was called Lingua Franca, "Frankish language." The term *lingua franca* was generalized to other languages similarly used. Thus, any language can be a lingua franca.

English has been called "the lingua franca of the whole world" and is standardly used at international business meetings and academic conferences. French, at one time, was "the lingua franca of diplomacy." Russian serves as the lingua franca in the countries of the former Soviet Union, where many different local languages are spoken. Latin was a lingua franca of the Roman Empire and of western Christendom for a millennium, just as Greek served eastern Christendom as its lingua franca. Yiddish has long served as a lingua franca among Jewish people, permitting Jews of different nationalities to communicate with one another.

More frequently, lingua francas serve as trade languages. East Africa is populated by hundreds of villages, each speaking its own language, but most Africans of this area learn at least some Swahili as a second language, and this lingua franca is used and understood in nearly every marketplace. A similar situation exists in Nigeria, where Hausa is the lingua franca.

Hindi and Urdu are the lingua francas of India and Pakistan. The linguistic situation of this area of the world is so complex that there are often regional lingua francas—usually a local language surrounding a commercial center. Thus the Dravidian language Kannada is a lingua franca for the area surrounding the southwestern Indian city of Mysore. A similar situation existed in Imperial China.

In modern China, 94 percent of the people speak Han languages, which can be divided into eight major language groups that for the most part are mutually unintelligible. Within each language group there are hundreds of dialects. In addition to the Han languages, there are more than fifty "national minority" languages, including the five principal ones: Mongolian, Uighur, Tibetan, Zhuang, and Korean.

The situation is complex, and therefore the government inaugurated an extensive language reform policy to establish as a lingua franca the Beijing dialect of Mandarin, with elements of grammar from northern Chinese dialects, and enriched with the vocabulary of modern colloquial Chinese. They called this dialect "Putonghua," meaning "common speech." The native languages and dialects are not considered inferior. Rather, the approach is to spread the "common speech" so that all may communicate with one another in this lingua franca.

Certain lingua francas arise naturally; others are instituted by government policy and intervention. In many parts of the world, however, people still cannot speak with their neighbors only a few miles away.

Contact Languages: Pidgins and Creoles

I include "pidgin-English" . . . even though I am referred to in that splendid language as "Fella bilong Mrs. Queen."

PRINCE PHILIP, husband of Queen Elizabeth II

A lingua franca is typically a language with a broad base of native speakers, likely to be used and learned by persons with different native languages (usually in the same language family). Often in history, however, speakers of mutually unintelligible languages have been brought into contact under specific socioeconomic and political conditions and have developed a language to communicate with one another that is not native to anyone. Such a language is called a **pidgin**.

Many pidgins developed during the seventeenth, eighteenth, and nineteenth centuries, in trade colonies along the coasts of China, Africa, and the New World. These pidgins arose through contact between speakers of colonial European languages such as English, French, Portuguese, and Dutch, and the indigenous, non-European languages. Some pidgins arose among extended groups of slaves and slave owners in the United States and the Caribbean in the nineteenth century. Other cases include Hawaiian Pidgin English, which was established on the pineapple plantations of Hawaii among immigrant workers from Japan, China, Portugal, and the Philippines; Chinook Jargon, which evolved among the Indian tribes of the Pacific Northwest as a lingua franca among the tribes themselves as well as between the tribes and European traders; and various pidgins that arose during the Korean and Vietnam Wars for use between foreign soldiers and local civilians.

In all these cases the contact is too specialized and the cultures too widely separated for the native language of any one group to function effectively as a lingua franca. Instead, the two or more groups use their native languages as a basis for developing a rudimentary lingua franca with reduced grammatical structures and small lexicons. Also in these situations, it is generally the case that one linguistic group is in a more powerful position, economically or otherwise, such as the relationship of plantation owner to worker or slave owners to slaves. Most of the lexical items of the pidgin come from the language of the dominant group. This language is called **superstrate** or **lexifier language**. For example, English (the language of the plantation owners) is the superstrate language for Hawaiian Pidgin English, Swahili for the various forms of Pidgin Swahili spoken in East and Central Africa, and Bazaar Malay for pidgins spoken in Malaysia, Singapore, and Indonesia. The other language or languages also contribute to the lexicon and grammar, but in a less obvious way. These are called **substrate languages**. Japanese, Chinese, Tagalog, and Portuguese were the substrate languages of Hawaiian Pidgin English and all contributed to its grammar. Chinook Jargon had features both from indigenous languages of the area such as Chinook and Nootka, as well as French and English.

Many linguists believe that pidgins form part of a linguistic "life cycle." In the very early stage of development the pidgin has no native speakers and is strictly a contact language. Its use is reserved for specialized functions, such as trading or work-oriented tasks, and its speakers speak their (respective) native languages in all other social contexts. In this early stage the pidgin has little in the way of clear grammatical rules and few (usually specialized) words. Later, however, if the language continues to exist and be necessary, a much more regular and complex form of pidgin evolves, what is sometimes called a "stabilized pidgin," and this allows it to be used more effectively in a variety of situations. Further development leads to the creation of a **creole**, which most linguists believe has all the grammatical complexity of ordinary languages. **Pidginization** (the creation of a pidgin) thus involves a *simplification* of languages and a reduction in the number of domains of use. **Creolization**, in contrast, involves the linguistic *expansion* in the lexicon and grammar of existing pidgins, and an increase in the contexts of use. We discuss creoles and creolization further in the next section.

Although pidgins are in some sense rudimentary, they are not devoid of rules. The phonology is rule-governed, as in any human language. The inventory of phonemes is generally small; for example, whereas Standard English has fourteen distinct vowel sounds, pidgins commonly have only five to seven, and each phoneme may have many allophonic pronunciations. In one English-based pidgin, for example, [s], [ʃ], and [tʃ] are all possible pronunciations of the phoneme /s/; [masin], [maʃin], and [matʃin] all mean "machine." Sounds that occur in both the superstrate and substrate languages will generally be maintained, but if a sound occurs in the superstrate but not in the substrates, it will tend to be eliminated. For example, the English sounds [ð] and [θ] as in "this" and "thing" are quite uncommon across languages. Many speakers of English pidgins convert these "th" sounds to more common ones, pronouncing "this thing" as dis ting.

Typically, pidgins lack grammatical words such as auxiliary verbs, prepositions, and articles, and inflectional morphology including tense and case endings, as in

He bad man.   "He is a bad man."
I no go bazaar.   "I'm not going to the market."

Affixal morphology is largely absence. For example, some English pidgins have the word *sus* from the English "shoes," but *sus* does not include a plural morpheme as it is used to refer to both a single shoe as well as multiple shoes. Note that this has happened in the development of English, too. Originally, the ending *-en* in *chicken* was a plural marker (as in *oxen*) referring to more than one chick, but it has lost that function and the plural of *chicken* is now *chickens*.

Verbs and nouns usually have a single shape and are not altered to mark tense, number, gender, or case. The set of pronouns is often simpler in pidgins. In Kamtok, an English-based pidgin spoken in Cameroon, the pronoun system does not show gender or all the case differences that exist in Standard English (SE).

Kamtok			**SE**		
a	mi	ma	I	me	my
yu	yu	yu	you	you	your
i	i/am	i	he	him	his
i	i/am	i	she	her	her
wi	wi	wi	we	us	our
wuna	wuna	wuna	you	you	your
dem	dem/am	dem	they	them	their

Pidgins also may have fewer prepositions than the languages on which they are based. In Kamtok, for example, fɔ means "to," "at," "in," "for," and "from," as shown in the following examples:

Gif di buk fɔ mi.	"Give the book to me."
I dei fɔ fam.	"She is at the farm."
Dɛm dei fɔ chɔs.	"They are in the church."
Du dis wan fɔ mi, a bɛg.	"Do this for me, please."
Di mɔni dei fɔ tebul.	"The money is on the table."
You fit muf tɛn frank fɔ ma kwa.	"You can take ten francs from my bag."

Other morphological processes are more productive in pidgins. Reduplication is common, often to indicate emphasis. For example, in Komtok, *big* means "big" and *big-big* means "enormous"; *luk* means "look" and *luk-luk* means "stare at." Compounding is also productive and serves to increase the otherwise small lexicons. The reference to Prince Philip in the epigraph at the beginning of this section is an example (*fella bilong* [meaning "husband"] *Mrs. Queen*), as are the following:

big ai	greedy
drai ai	brave
gras bilong fes	beard
gras antap long ai	eyebrow
gras bilong head	hair
han bilong pisin	wing (of a bird)

Most words in pidgin languages also function as if they belong to several syntactic categories. For example, the Kamtok word *bad* can function as an adjective, noun, or adverb:

Adjective	tu bad pikin	two bad children
Noun	We no laik dis kain bad.	We don't like this kind of badness.
Adverb	A liakam bad.	I liked it very much.

In terms of syntax, early pidgins have a simple clausal structure, lacking embedded sentences and other complex complements. And word order may be variable so that speakers from different linguistic backgrounds can adopt the order of their native language and still be understood. For example, Japanese is an SOV (verb last) language, and a Japanese speaker of an English-based pidgin may put the verb last, as in *The poor people all potato eat*. On the other hand, a Filipino speaker of Tagalog, a VSO language, may put the verb first, as in *Work hard these people*. Word order becomes more rigid in stabilized pidgins and creoles, which are more like other languages with respect to the range of clause types.

Pidgin has come to have negative connotations, perhaps because many pidgins were associated with European colonial empires. The *Encyclopedia Britannica* once described pidgins as "an unruly bastard jargon, filled with nursery imbecilities, vulgarisms and corruptions." It no longer uses such a definition. In recent times there is greater recognition that pidgins reflect human creative linguistic ability and show many of the same design properties as other languages.

Pidgins also serve a useful function. For example, it is possible to learn an English-based pidgin well enough in six months to begin many kinds of semiprofessional training. Learning English for the same purpose might take ten times as long. In areas with many mutually unintelligible languages, a pidgin can play a vital role in unifying people of different cultures and ethnicities.

In general, pidgins are short-lived, perhaps spanning several human generations, though a few have lasted much longer. Pidgins may die out because the speakers all come to share a common language. This was the fate of Chinook Jargon, whose speakers all learned English. Also, because pidgins are often disdained, there is social pressure for speakers to learn a "standard" language, usually the one on which the pidgin is based. For example, through massive education, English replaced a pidgin spoken on New Zealand by the Maoris. Though it failed to succumb to years of government interdiction, Chinese Pidgin English could not resist the onslaught of English that fueled its demise by the close of the nineteenth century. Finally, and ironically, the death of a pidgin language may come about because of its success in uniting diverse communities; the pidgin proves so useful and becomes so widespread that successive generations in the communities in which it is spoken adopt it as their native tongue, elaborating its lexicon and grammar to become a creole.

Creoles and Creolization

Padi dɛm; kɔntri; una ɔl we de na Rom.
Mɛk una ɔl kak una yes. A kam bɛr Siza,
a nɔ kam prez am.

WILLIAM SHAKESPEARE, *Julius Caesar*, translated to Krio by Thomas Decker

> Creoles are particularly interesting because they represent an extreme of language change, but it is the mechanisms of language change, which are ubiquitous in the history of every language and every language family, that have made creoles what they are.
>
> **IAN ROBERTS,** "Verb Movement and Markedness," in Michel DeGraff, ed., *Language Creation and Language Change*, 1999

A creole is defined as a language that has evolved in a contact situation to become the native language of a generation of speakers. The traditional view is that creoles are the creation of children who, exposed to an impoverished and unstable pidgin, develop a far richer and more complex language that shares the fundamental characteristics of a "regular" human language and allows speakers to use the language in all domains of daily life.

In contrast to pidgins, creoles may have inflectional morphology for tense, plurality, and so on. For example, in creoles spoken in the South Pacific the affix *-im* is added to transitive verbs, but when the verb has no object the *-im* ending does not occur:

Man i pairip**im** masket.
man be fired-him musket
"The man fired the musket."

Masket i pairip.
"The gun was fired."

The same affix *-im* is used derivationally to convert adjectives into verbs like English *-en* in "redden":

bik	big	bikim	to make something big
daun	down	daunim	to lower something down
nogut	no good	nogutim	to spoil, damage

Creoles typically develop more complex pronoun systems. For example, in the creoles of the South Pacific there are two forms of the pronoun "we," inclusive we referring to speaker and listener, and exclusive we referring to the speaker and other people but not the listener. The Portuguese-based Cape Verdean Creole has three classes of pronouns: strong, weak, and clitic (meaning affixed to another word, like the possessive *'s* of English), as illustrated in the following table.

	Emphatic (Strong) Forms	Free (Weak) Forms	Subject Clitics	Object Clitics
1sg	ami	mi	N-	-m
2sg (informal)	abo	bo	bu-	-bu/-u
2sg (formal, masc.)	anho	nho	nhu-	
2sg (formal, fem.)	anha	nha		
3sg	ael	el	e-	-l
1pl	anos	nos	nu-	-nu
2pl	anhos	nhos		
3pl	aes	es	-s	

The compounds of pidgins often reduce in creoles; for example, *wara bilong skin* (water belong skin) meaning "sweat" becomes *skinwara*. The compound *baimbai* (by and by), used to indicate future time, becomes a tense inflection *ba* in the creole. Thus, the sentence *baimbai yu go* ("you will go") becomes *yu bago*. The phrasal structure of creoles is also vastly enriched, including embedded and relative clauses, among many other features of "regular" languages.

How are children able to construct a creole based on the rudimentary input of the pidgin? One answer is that they used their innate linguistic capacities to rapidly transform the pidgin into a full-fledged language. This would account for the many grammatical properties that creoles have in common, for example, SVO word order and tense and aspect distinctions.

It should be noted that defining pidgins and creoles in terms of whether they are native (creoles) versus non-native second languages (pidgins) is not without problems. There are languages such as Tok Pisin, widely spoken in New Guinea, which are first languages to many speakers, but also used as a second contact language by other speakers. Some linguists have also rejected the idea that creoles derive from pidgins, claiming that the geographic areas and social conditions under which they develop are different.

Moreover, the view that children are the creators of creoles is not universally accepted. Various linguists believe that creoles are the result of imperfect second language learning of the lexifier or dominant language by adults and the "transfer" of grammatical properties from their native non-European languages. This hypothesis would account for some of the characteristics that creoles share with L2 "interlanguages" (see chapter 8), for example, invariant verb forms, lack of determiners, and the use of adverbs rather than verbs and auxiliaries to express tense and modality.

Although some linguists believe that creoles are simpler systems than "regular" languages, most researchers who have closely examined the grammatical properties of various creoles argue that they are not structurally different from non-creole languages and that the only exceptional property of creoles is the sociohistorical conditions under which they evolve.

Creoles often arose on slave plantations where Africans of many different tribes spoke mutually incomprehensible African languages. Haitian Creole, based on French, developed in this way, as did the "English" spoken in parts of Jamaica. Gullah is an English-based creole spoken by the descendants of African slaves on islands off the coast of Georgia and South Carolina. Louisiana Creole, related to Haitian Creole, is spoken by large numbers of blacks and whites in Louisiana. Krio, the language spoken by as many as a million Sierra Leoneans, and illustrated in the epigraph to this section, developed at least in part from an English-based pidgin.

One of the theories concerning the origins of African American English is that it derives from an earlier English-based creole that developed when Africans slaves had no common language other than the English spoken by their colonial masters. Proponents of this hypothesis point out that many of the unique features of AAE are traceable to influences of the West African languages spoken by the slaves. Also, several of the features of AAE, such as aspect marking (distinct from that which occurs in Standard English), are typical of creole languages. The alternative view is that AAE formed directly from

English without any pidgin/creole stage. It is apparent that AAE is closer to Southern dialects of American English than to other dialects. It is possible that the African slaves learned the English of white Southerners as a second language. It is also possible that many of the distinguishing features of Southern dialects were acquired from AAE during the many decades in which a large number of Southern white children were raised by black women and played with black children.

Tok Pisin, originally a pidgin, was gradually creolized throughout the twentieth century. It evolved from Melanesian Pidgin English, once a widely spoken lingua franca of Papua New Guinea used by English-speaking traders and the native population. Because New Guinea is so linguistically diverse—more than eight hundred different languages were once spoken throughout the island—the pidgin came to be used as a lingua franca among the indigenous population as well.

Tok Pisin has its own writing system, its own literature, and its own newspapers and radio programs; it has even been used to address a United Nations meeting. Papers in (not *on*!) Tok Pisin have been presented at linguistics conferences in Papua New Guinea, and it is commonly used for debates in the parliament of the country. Today, Tok Pisin is one of the three recognized national languages of The Independent State of Papua New Guinea, alongside English and Kiri Motu, another creole.

Sign languages may also be pidgins. In Nicaragua in the 1980s, adult deaf people came together and constructed a crude system of "home" signs and gestures in order to communicate. It had the characteristics of a pidgin in that different people used it differently and the grammatical rules were few and varied. However, when young deaf children joined the community, an amazing event took place. The crude sign language of the adults was tremendously enhanced by the children learning it, so much so that it emerged as a rich and complex sign language called Idioma de Signos Nicaragüense (ISN), or Nicaraguan Sign Language. ISN provides an impressive demonstration of the development of a grammatically complex language from impoverished input and the power of human linguistic creativity.

The study of pidgins and creoles has contributed a great deal to our understanding of the nature of human language and the processes involved in language creation and language change, and of the sociohistorical conditions under which these instances of language contact occurred.

Bilingualism

He who has two languages has two souls.

ANONYMOUS

The term **bilingualism** refers to the ability to speak two (or more) languages, either by an individual speakers, **individual bilingualism**, or within a society, **societal bilingualism**. In chapter 8 we discussed how bilingual children may simultaneously acquire their two languages, and how second languages are acquired by children and adults. There are various degrees of individual bilingualism. Some people have native-like control of two languages, whereas others make regular use of two languages with a high degree of proficiency but lack the linguistic competence of a native or near native speaker in one or the other language. Also, some bilinguals may have oral competence but not read or write one or more of their languages.

The situations under which people become bilingual may vary. Some people grow up in a household in which more than one language is spoken; others move to a new country where they acquire the local language, usually from people outside the home. Still others learn second languages in school. In communities with rich linguistic diversity, contact between speakers of different languages may also lead to bilingualism.

Bilingualism (or multilingualism) also refers to the situation in nations in which two (or more) languages are spoken and recognized as official or national languages. Societal bilingualism exists in many countries, including Canada, where English and French are both official languages, and Switzerland, where French, German, Italian, and Romansch all have official status.

Interestingly, research shows that there are fewer bilingual individuals in bilingual countries than in so-called "unilingual" countries. This makes sense when you consider that in unilingual countries such as the United States, Italy, and France, people who do not speak the dominant language must learn some amount of it to function. Also, the main concern of multilingual states has been the maintenance and use of two or more languages, rather than the promotion of individual bilingualism among its citizens.

The United States is broadly perceived as a monolingual English-speaking society even though there is no reference to a national language in the Constitution. However, there are numerous bilingual communities with long histories throughout the country. According to the 2000 U.S. Census, about 18 percent of those age five and over, or 47 million people, speak a language other than English at home. Sixty percent of these, about 25 million people (8 percent of the U.S. population), profess to being bilingual in English and Spanish with varying degrees of English proficiency. Between 1990 and 2000 the number of Spanish speakers in the United States increased by about 60 percent, and the number of speakers other than Spanish by about 50 percent. It should be noted that not all Latinos are bilingual; as many as 20 percent may be monolingual English speakers. Recent studies also show that the shift to monolingual English is growing rapidly and that knowledge of Spanish is being lost faster in the twenty-first century than was seen with speakers of Dutch, Italian, German, and Polish in the first half of the twentieth century.

Codeswitching

Codeswitching is a speech style unique to bilinguals, in which fluent speakers switch languages between or within sentences, as illustrated by the following sentence:.

Sometimes I'll start a sentence in English and termino en español.
Sometimes I'll start a sentence in English and finish it in Spanish.

Codeswitching is a universal language-contact phenomenon that reflects the grammars of both languages working simultaneously. Bilingual Spanish-English speakers may switch between English and Spanish as in the above example, whereas Quebecois in Canada switch between French and English:

I mean, c'est un idiot, ce mec-là.
I mean he's an idiot, that guy.

The following examples are from German-English, Korean-English, and Mandarin-English bilinguals:

Johan hat mir gesagt that you were going to leave.
Johan told me you were going to leave.

Chigum ton-uls ops-nunde, I can't buy it.
As I don't have money now, I can't buy it.

Women zuotian qu kan de movie was really amazing.
The movie we went to see yesterday was really amazing.

Codeswitching occurs wherever groups of bilinguals speak the same two languages. Furthermore, codeswitching occurs in specific social situations, enriching the repertoire of the speakers.

A common misconception is that codeswitching is indicative of a language disability of some kind, for example, that bilinguals use codeswitching as a coping strategy for incomplete mastery of both languages, or that they are speaking "broken" English. These characterizations are completely inaccurate. Recent studies of the social and linguistic properties of codeswitching indicate that it is a marker of bilingual identity, and has its own internal grammatical structure. For example, bilinguals will commonly codeswitch between a subject and a verb as in:

Mis amigos finished first.   My friends finished first.

but would judge ungrammatical a switch between a subject pronoun and a verb as in:

*Ellos finished first.   They finished first.

Codeswitchers also follow the word order rules of the languages. For example, in a Spanish noun phrase, the adjective usually follows the noun, as opposed to the English NP in which it precedes, as shown by the following:

English: My mom fixes **green tamales**.   Adj N
Spanish: Mi mamá hace **tamales verdes**.   N Adj

A speaker might codeswitch as follows:

My mom fixes **tamales verdes**.
or   Mi mamá hace **green tamales**.

but would not accept or produce such utterances as

                    *My mom fixes **verdes tamales**.

or   *Mi mamá hace **tamales green**.

because the word order within the NPs violates the rules of the language.

Codeswitching is to be distinguished from (bilingual) **borrowing**, which occurs when a word or short expression from one language occurs embedded among the words of a second language and adapts to the regular phonology, morphology, and syntax of the second language. In codeswitching, in contrast, the two languages that are interwoven preserve their own phonological and other grammatical properties. Borrowing can be easily distinguished from codeswitching by the pronunciation of an element. Sentence (1) involves borrowing, and (2) codeswitching.

(1) I love biscottis [bɪskaɾiz] with my coffee.
(2) I love biscotti [bɪskoːti] with my coffee.

In sentence (1) *biscotti* takes on an (American) English pronunciation and plural *-s* morphology, while in (2) it preserves the Italian pronunciation and plural morpheme *-i* (plural for *biscotto* "cookie").

What needs to be emphasized is that people who codeswitch have knowledge not of one but of two (or more) languages, and that codeswitching, like linguistic knowledge in general, is highly structured and rule-governed.

Language and Education

Outside of a dog, a book is a man's best friend; inside of a dog, it's too dark to read.
GROUCHO MARX (1890–1977)

The study of language has important implications in various educational arenas. An understanding of the structure, acquisition, and use of language is essential to the teaching of foreign and second languages, as well as to reading instruction. It can also promote a fuller understanding of language variation and use in the classroom and inform the often heated debates surrounding issues such as how to teach reading to children, bilingual education, and Ebonics.

Second-Language Teaching Methods

Many approaches to second or foreign language teaching have been developed over the years. Though these methods can differ significantly from one another, many experts believe that there is no single best method for teaching a second language. All methods have something to offer, and virtually any method can succeed with a gifted teacher who is a native or near-native speaker, motivated students, and appropriate teaching materials. All methods are most effective when they fit a given educational setting and when they are understood and embraced by the teacher.

Second-language teaching methods fall into two broad categories: the *synthetic approach* and the *analytic approach*. As the name implies, the synthetic approach stresses the teaching of the grammatical, lexical, phonological, and functional units of the language step by step. This is a bottom-up method. The task of the learner is to put together—or synthesize—the discrete elements that make up the language. The more traditional language teaching methods, which stress grammar instruction, fall into this category.

An extreme example of the synthetic approach is the **grammar translation** method favored up until the mid-1960s, in which students learned lists of vocabulary, verb paradigms, and grammatical rules. Learners translated passages from the target language into their native language. The teacher typically conducted class in the students' native language, focusing on the grammatical parsing of texts, and there was little or no contextualization of the language being taught. Reading passages were carefully constructed to contain only vocabulary and structures to which learners had already been exposed, and errors in translation were corrected on the spot. Learners were tested on their mastery of rules, verb paradigms, and vocabulary. The students did not use the target language very much except in reading translated passages aloud.

Analytic approaches are more top-down. The goal is not to explicitly teach the component parts or rules of the target language. Rather, the instructor selects topics, texts, or tasks that are relevant to the needs and interests of the learner, whose job then is to discover the constituent parts of the language. This approach assumes that adults can extract the rules of the language from unstructured input, more or less like a child does when acquiring his first language.

Currently, one of the most widely practiced analytic approaches is *content-based instruction*, in which the focus is on making the language meaningful and on getting the student to communicate in the target language. Learners are encouraged to discuss issues and express opinions on various topics of interest to them in the target language. Topics for discussion might include "Online Romance" or "Taking Responsibility for Our Environment." Grammar rules are taught on an as-needed basis, and fluency takes precedence over grammatical accuracy. Classroom texts (both written and aural) are generally taken from sources that were not created specifically for language learners, on the assumption that these will be more interesting and relevant to the student. Assessment is based on the learner's comprehension of the target language.

Not all second-language teaching methods fall clearly into one or the other category. The synthetic and analytic approaches should be viewed as the opposite ends of a continuum along which various second-language methods may fall. Also, teachers practicing a given method may not strictly follow all the principles of the method. Actual classroom practices tend to be more eclectic, with teachers using techniques that work well for them and to which they are accustomed—even if these techniques are not in complete accordance with the method they are practicing.

Teaching Reading

"Baby Blues" © Baby Blues Partnership. Reprinted with permission of King Features Syndicate.

In chapter 8 we discussed how young children acquire their native language. We noted that language development (whether of a spoken or sign language) is a biologically driven process with a substantial innate component. Parents do not teach their children the grammatical rules of their language. Indeed, they are not even aware of the rules themselves. Rather, the young child is naturally predisposed to uncover these rules from the language he hears around him. The way we learn to read and write, however, is quite different from the way we acquire the spoken/signed language.

First, and most obviously, children learn to talk (or sign) at a very young age, while reading typically begins when the child is school-age (around five or six years old in most cases, although some children are not reading-ready until even later). A second important difference is that across cultures and languages, all children acquire a spoken/signed language while many children never learn to read or write. This may be because they are born into cultures for which there is no written form of their language. It is also unfortunately the case that even some children born into literate societies do not learn to read, either because they suffer from a specific reading disability—**dyslexia**—or because they have not been properly taught. It is important to recognize, however, that even illiterate children and adults have a mental grammar of their language and are able to speak/sign and understand perfectly well.

The most important respect in which spoken/signed language development differs from learning to read is that reading requires specific instruction and conscious effort, whereas language acquisition does not. Which kind of instruction works best for teaching reading has been a topic of considerable debate for many decades. Three main approaches have been tried.

The first—the *whole-word approach*—teaches children to recognize a vocabulary of some fifty to one hundred words by rote learning, often by seeing the words used repeatedly in a story, for example, *Run, Spot, Run* from the Dick and Jane series well-known to people who learned to read in the 1950s. Other words are acquired gradually. This approach does not teach children to "sound out" words according to the individual sounds that make up the words. Rather, it treats the written language as though it were a logographic system, such as Chinese, in which a single written character corresponds to a whole word or word root. In other words, the whole-word approach fails to take advantage of the fact that English (and the writing systems of most literate societies) is based on an alphabet, in which the symbols correspond to the individual sounds (roughly phonemes) of the language. This is ironic because alphabetic writing systems are the easiest to learn and are maximally efficient for transcribing any human language.

A second approach—*phonics*—emphasizes the correspondence between letters and the sounds associated with them. Phonics instruction begins by teaching children the letters of the alphabet and then encourages them to sound out words based on their knowledge of the sound-letter correspondences. So, if you have learned to read the word *gave* (understanding that the *e* is silent), then it is easy to read *save* and *pave*.

However, English and many other languages do not show a perfect correspondence between sounds and letters. For example, the rule for *gave*, *save*, and *pave* does not extend to *have*. The existence of many such exceptions has encouraged some schools to adopt a third approach to reading, the *whole-language approach* (also called "literature-based" or "guided reading"), which was most popular in the 1990s. The key principle is that phonics should not be taught directly. Rather, the child is supposed to make the connections between sounds and letters herself based on exposure to text. For example, she would be encouraged to figure out an unfamiliar word based on the context of the sentence or by looking for clues in the story line or the pictures rather than by sounding it out, as illustrated in the cartoon.

The philosophy behind the whole-language approach is that learning to read, like learning to speak, is a natural act that children can basically do on their own—an assumption that, as we noted earlier, is questionable at best. With the whole-language approach, the main job of the teacher is to make the reading experience an enjoyable one. To this end, children are presented with engaging books and are encouraged to write stories of their own as a way of instilling a love of reading and words.

Despite the intuitive appeal of the whole-language approach—after all, who would deny the educational value of good literature and creative expression in learning?—research has clearly shown that understanding the relationship between letters and sounds is critically important in reading. One of the assumptions of the whole-language approach is that skilled adult readers do not sound out words when reading, so proponents question the value of focusing on sounding out in reading instruction. However, research shows that the opposite is true: skilled adult readers *do* sound out words mentally, and they do so very rapidly. Another study compared groups of college students who were taught to read unfamiliar symbols such as Arabic letters, one group by a phonics approach and the other with a whole-word approach. Those trained with phonics could read many more new words. Similar results have been obtained through computer modeling of how children learn to read. Classroom studies have also compared phonics with whole-word or whole-language approaches and have shown that phonics instruction produces better results for beginning readers.

The advantage of phonics is not contradicted by studies showing that deaf children who have fully acquired a sign language have difficulty learning to read. This is understandable because the alphabetic principle requires an understanding of sound-symbol regularities, which deaf children do not have. It seems reasonable, then, that hearing children should not be deprived of the advantage they would have if their unconscious knowledge of phonemes is made conscious.

At this point, the consensus among psychologists and linguists who do research on reading—and a view shared by many teachers—is that reading instruction must be grounded in a firm understanding of the connections between letters and sounds, and that whole-language activities that make reading fun and meaningful for children should be used to supplement phonics instruction. Based on such research, the federal government now promotes the inclusion of phonics in reading programs across the United States.

Bilingual Education

As discussed earlier, there are many bilingual communities in the United States and members of these communities typically have varying levels of English proficiency. People who have recently arrived in the United States may have virtually no knowledge of English, other individuals may have only limited knowledge, and others may be fully bilingual. Native language development is untutored and happens before children begin school, but many children find themselves in classroom situations in which their native language is not the language of instruction. There has been a great deal of debate among researchers, teachers, parents, and the general public over the best methods for teaching English to school-age children as well as over the value of maintaining and promoting their native language abilities.

There are several kinds of bilingual programs in American schools for immigrant children. In **Transitional Bilingual Education (TBE)** programs, students receive instruction in both English and their native language, and the native language support is gradually phased out over two or three years. In **Bilingual Maintenance (BM)** programs, students remain in bilingual classes for their entire educational experience. Another program, **Dual Language Immersion**, enrolls English-speaking children and students who are native in another language in roughly equal numbers. The goal here is for all the students to become bilingual. This kind of program serves as a BM program for non-English speakers and a foreign language immersion program for the English-speaking children.

Many studies have shown that immigrant children benefit from instruction in their native language. Bilingual classes allow the children to first acquire in their native language school-related vocabulary, speech styles, and other aspects of language that are specific to a school environment while they are learning English. It also allows them to learn content material and keep up with other children during the time it takes them to master English. Recent studies that compared the effectiveness of different types of programs have found that children enrolled in bilingual programs outperformed children in English-only programs, and that children enrolled in BM programs did better than TBE students.

Despite the benefits that a bilingual education affords immigrant students, these programs have been under increasing attack since the 1970s. In the past few years measures against bilingual education have been passed in several states, including California, Arizona, and Massachusetts. These measures mandate that immigrant students "be taught English by being taught in English" in an English-only approach known as Sheltered English Immersion (SEI). Proponents claim that one year of SEI is sufficient for children, especially young children, to learn English well enough to be transferred to a mainstream classroom. Research does not bear out these claims, however. Studies show that only a small minority of children, around 3 percent to 4 percent of children in SEI programs and 13 percent to 14 percent in bilingual programs, acquire English within a year. A considerable body of research shows that for the vast majority of children it takes from two to five years to develop oral proficiency in English and four to seven years to develop proficiency in academic English.

There are several possible causes for the chasm between research results and public policy regarding bilingual education. Bilingual programs can be poorly implemented and so not achieve the desired results. There may also be a public perception that it is too costly to implement bilingual programs. It is likely that some of the backlash against bilingual education is due to anti-immigrant sentiment, but there are also many well-intentioned people who mistakenly believe that bilingualism is a handicap and that children will be more successful academically and socially if they are quickly and totally immersed in the more prestigious majority language.

"Ebonics"

Children who speak a dialect of English that differs from the language of instruction—usually close to Standard English—may also be disadvantaged in a school setting. Literacy instruction is generally based on SAE. It has been argued that the phonological and grammatical differences between African American English (AAE)—termed "Ebonics" in the popular press—and SAE make it harder for AAE-speaking children to learn to read and write.

One approach to this problem has been to discourage children from speaking AAE and to correct each departure from SAE that the children produce. SAE is presented as the "correct" way to speak and AAE as substandard or incorrect. This approach has been criticized as being psychologically damaging to the child as well as impractical. Attempts to consciously correct children's nonstandard dialect speech are routinely met with failure. Moreover, one's language/dialect expresses group identity and solidarity with friends and family. A child may take a rejection of his language as a rejection of him and his culture.

A more positive approach to teaching literacy to speakers of nonstandard dialects is to encourage **bidialectalism**. This approach teaches children to take pride in their language, encouraging them to use it in informal circumstances, with family and friends, while also teaching them a second dialect—SAE—that is necessary for reading, writing, and classroom discussion. As a point of comparison, in many countries, including Switzerland, Germany, and Italy, children grow up speaking a nonstandard dialect at home but learn the standard language once they enter school. This underscores that bidialectalism that combines a home dialect and a school/national language is entirely feasible. Educational programs that respect the home language may better facilitate the acquisition of a standard dialect. Ideally, the bidialectal method would also include class discussion of the phonological and grammatical differences between the two dialects, which would require that teachers understand the linguistic properties of AAE, as well as some linguistics in general.

Language in Use

One of the themes of this book is that you have a lot of linguistic knowledge that you may not be aware of, but that can be made explicit through the rules of phonology, morphology, syntax, and semantics. You also have a deep social knowledge of your language. You know the appropriate way to talk to your parents, your friends, your clergy, and your teachers. You know about "politically correct" (PC) language, to say "mail *carrier*," "fire*fighter*," and "police *officer*," and not to say "nigger," "wop," and "bitch." In short, you know how to *use* your language appropriately, even if you sometimes choose not to. This section discusses some of the many ways in which the use of language varies in society.

Styles

Most speakers of a language speak one way with friends, another on a job interview or presenting a report in class, another talking to small children, another with their parents, and so on. These "situation dialects" are called **styles**, or **registers**.

Nearly everybody has at least an informal and a formal style. In an informal style, the rules of contraction are used more often, the syntactic rules of negation and agreement may be altered, and many words are used that do not occur in the formal style.

Informal styles, although permitting certain abbreviations and deletions not permitted in formal speech, are also rule-governed. For example, questions are often shortened with the subject *you* and the auxiliary verb deleted. One can ask *Running the marathon?* or *You running the marathon?* instead of the more formal *Are you running the marathon?* but you cannot shorten the question to **Are running the marathon?* Informal talk is not anarchy. It is rule-governed, but the rules of deletion, contraction, and word choice are different from those of the formal language.

It is common for speakers to have competence in several styles, ranging between the two extremes of formal and informal. The use of styles is often a means of identification with a particular group (e.g., family, gang, church, team), or a means of excluding groups believed to be hostile or undesirable (cops, teachers, parents).

Many cultures have rules of social behavior that govern style. Some Indo-European languages distinguish between "you (familiar)" and "you (polite)." German *du* and French *tu* are to be used only with "intimates"; *Sie* and *vous* are more formal and used with nonintimates. Thai has three words meaning "eat" depending on the social status of who is speaking with whom.

Social situations affect the details of language usage, but the core grammar remains intact, with a few superficial variations that lend a particular flavor to the speech.

Slang

Slang is a language that rolls up its sleeves, spits on its hands, and goes to work.

CARL SANDBURG, quoted in "Minstrel of America: Carl Sandburg," *New York Times*, February 13, 1959

One mark of an informal style is the frequent occurrence of **slang**. Slang is something that nearly everyone uses and recognizes, but nobody can define precisely. It is more metaphorical, playful, elliptical, vivid, and shorter-lived than ordinary language.

The use of slang has introduced many new words into the language by recombining old words into new meanings. *Spaced out*, *right on*, *hang-up*, and *rip-off* have all gained a degree of acceptance. Slang also introduces entirely new words such as *barf*, *flub*, and *dis*. Finally, slang often consists of ascribing entirely new meanings to old words. *Rave* has broadened its meaning to "an all-night dance party," where *ecstasy* (slang for a kind of drug) is taken to provoke wakefulness; *crib* refers to one's home and *posse* to one's cohorts. *Grass* and *pot* widened their meaning to "marijuana"; *pig* and *fuzz* are derogatory terms for "police officer"; *rap*, *cool*, *dig*, *stoned*, *bread*, *split*, and *suck* have all extended their semantic domains.

The words we have cited may sound slangy because they have not gained total acceptability. Words such as *dwindle*, *freshman*, *glib*, and *mob* are former slang words that in time overcame their "unsavory" origin. It is not always easy to know where to draw the line between slang words and regular words. The borderland between slang and formal language is ill-defined and is more of a continuum than a strict boundary.

There are scads (another slang word) of sources of slang. It comes from the underworld: *crack*, *payola*, *to hang paper*. It comes from college campuses: *crash*, *wicked*, *peace*. It even comes from the White House: *pencil* (writer), *still* (photographer), *football* (black box of security secrets).

Slang is universal. It is found in all languages and all time periods. It varies from region to region, and from past to present. Slang meets a variety of social needs and rather than a corruption of the language, it is yet further evidence of the creativity of the human language user.

Jargon and Argot

Practically every conceivable science, profession, trade, and occupation uses specific slang terms called **jargon**, or **argot**. Linguistic jargon, some of which is used in this book, consists of terms such as *phoneme, morpheme, case, lexicon, phrase structure rule*, and so on. Part of the reason for specialized terminology is for clarity of communication, but part is also for speakers to identify themselves with persons with whom they share interests.

Because the jargon used by different professional and social groups is so extensive (and so obscure in meaning), court reporters in the Los Angeles Criminal Courts Building have a library that includes books on medical terms, guns, trade names, and computer jargon, as well as street slang.

The computer age not only ushered in a technological revolution, it also introduced a slew of jargon, called, slangily, "computerese," used by computer "hackers" and others. So vast is this specialized vocabulary that *Webster's New World Computer Dictionary* has four hundred pages and contains thousands of computer terms as entries. A few such words that are familiar to most people are *modem* (from *modulator-demodulator*), *bit* (from *binary digit*), and *byte* (eight *bits*). Acronyms and alphabetic abbreviations abound in computer jargon. *ROM* (read-only memory), *RAM* (random-access memory), *CPU* (central processing unit), and *DVD* (digital video disk) are a small fraction of what's out there.

Some jargon may over time pass into the standard language. Jargon, like all types of slang, spreads from a narrow group that originally embraced it until it is used and understood by a large segment of the population.

Taboo or Not Taboo?

Sex is a four-letter word.

BUMPER STICKER SLOGAN

"There are some words I will not tolerate in this house—and 'awesome' is one of them."

An item in a newspaper once included the following paragraph:

> "This is not a Sunday school, but it is a school of law," the judge said in warning the defendants he would not tolerate the "use of expletives during jury selection." "I'm not going to have my fellow citizens and prospective jurors subjected to filthy language," the judge added.

How can language be filthy? In fact, how can it be clean? The filth or beauty of language must be in the ear of the listener, or in the collective ear of society. The writer Paul Theroux points this out:

> A foreign swear-word is practically inoffensive except to the person who has learned it early in life and knows its social limits.

Nothing about a particular string of sounds makes it intrinsically clean or dirty, ugly or beautiful. If you say that you pricked your finger when sewing, no one would raise an eyebrow, but if you refer to your professor as a prick, the judge quoted previously would undoubtedly censure this "dirty" word.

You know the obscene words of your language, and you know the social situations in which they are desirable, acceptable, forbidden, and downright dangerous to utter. This is true of all speakers of all languages. All societies have their taboo words. (*Taboo* is a Tongan word meaning "forbidden.") People everywhere seem to have a need for undeleted expletives to express their emotions or attitudes.

Forbidden acts or words reflect the particular customs and views of the society. Among the Zuni Indians, it is improper to use the word *takka*, meaning "frogs," during a religious ceremony. In the world of Harry Potter, the evil Voldemort is not to be named, but is referred to as "You-Know-Who." In some religions believers are forbidden to "take the Lord's name in vain," and this prohibition often extends to other religious jargon. Thus the taboo words *hell* and *damn* are changed to *heck* and *darn*, though the results are sometimes not euphonious. Imagine the last two lines of Act II, Scene 1, of *Macbeth* if they were "cleaned up":

> Hear it not, Duncan; for it is a knell
> That summons thee to heaven, or to heck

Words relating to sex, sex organs, and natural bodily functions make up a large part of the set of taboo words of many cultures. Often, two or more words or expressions can have the same linguistic meaning, with one acceptable and the other taboo. In English, words borrowed from Latin sound "scientific" and therefore appear to be technical and "clean," whereas native Anglo-Saxon counterparts are taboo. Such pairs of words are illustrated as follows:

Anglo-Saxon Taboo Words	Latinate Acceptable Words
cunt	vagina
cock	penis
prick	penis
tits	mammaries
shit	feces, defecate

There is no grammatical reason why the word *vagina* [vədʒāɪnə] is "clean" whereas *cunt* [kʌ̃nt] is "dirty," or why *balls* is taboo but *testicles* acceptable. Although there is no grammatical basis for such preferences, there certainly are sociolinguistic reasons to embrace or eschew such usages, just as there are sociolinguistic reasons for speaking formally, respectfully, disrespectfully, informally, jargon riddled, and so on.

Euphemisms

Banish the use of the four-letter words
Whose meaning is never obscure.
The Anglos, the Saxons, those bawdy old birds
Were vulgar, obscene, and impure.
But cherish the use of the weaseling phrase
That never quite says what it means;
You'd better be known for your hypocrite ways
Than vulgar, impure, and obscene.

**FOLK SONG ATTRIBUTED TO WARTIME ROYAL AIR FORCE
OF GREAT BRITAIN**

The existence of taboo words and ideas motivates the creation of **euphemisms**. A euphemism is a word or phrase that replaces a taboo word or serves to avoid frightening or unpleasant subjects. In many societies, because death is feared, there are many euphemisms related to this subject. People are less apt to *die* and more apt to *pass on* or *pass away*. Those who take care of your loved ones who have passed away are more likely to be *funeral directors* than *morticians* or *undertakers*. And then there's *feminine protection* . . .

The use of euphemisms is not new. It is reported that the Greek historian Plutarch in the first century C.E. wrote that "the ancient Athenians . . . used to cover up the ugliness of things with auspicious and kindly terms, giving them polite and endearing names. Thus they called harlots *companions*, taxes *contributions*, and prison a *chamber*."

Just as surely as all languages and societies have taboo words, they have euphemisms. The aforementioned taboo word *takka*, meaning "frogs," is replaced during a Zuni religious ceremony by a complex compound word that literally translates as "several-are-sitting-in-a-shallow-basin-where-they-are-in-liquid." The euphemisms for bodily excretions and sexual activity are legion, and lists of them may be found in online dictionaries of slang. There you will find such gems for urination as *siphon the python* and *point Percy at the porcelain*, and for intercourse *shag*, *hide the ferret* (*salami*, *sausage*), and *toss a little leg*, among a gazillion others.

These euphemisms, as well as the difference between the accepted Latinate "genteel" terms and the "dirty" Anglo-Saxon terms, show that a word or phrase has not only a linguistic **denotative meaning** but also a **connotative meaning** that reflects attitudes, emotions, value judgments, and so on. In learning a language, children learn which words are taboo, and these taboo words differ from one child to another, depending on the value system accepted in the family or group in which the child grows up.

Racial and National Epithets

The use of epithets for people of different religions, nationalities, or races tells us something about the speakers. Words like *kike* (for Jew), *wop* (for Italian), *nigger* or *coon* (for African American), *slant* (for Asian), *towelhead* (for Middle Eastern Arab), and so forth reflect racist and chauvinist views of society.

Even words that sound like epithets are perhaps to be avoided (see exercise 13). An administrator in Washington, D.C. described a fund he administers as "niggardly," meaning stingy. He resigned his position under fire for using a word "so close to a degrading word."

Language, however, is creative, malleable, and ever changing. The epithets used by a majority to demean a minority may be reclaimed as terms of bonding and friendship among members of the minority. Thus, for some—we emphasize *some*—African Americans, the word *nigger* is used to show affection. Similarly, the ordinarily degrading word *queer* is used among *some* gay persons as a term of endearment, as is *cripple* or *crip* among *some* individuals who share a disability.

Language and Sexism

doctor, n. . . . a man of great learning.

THE AMERICAN COLLEGE DICTIONARY, 1947

A businessman is aggressive; a businesswoman is pushy. A businessman is good on details; she's picky. . . . He follows through; she doesn't know when to quit. He stands firm; she's hard. . . . He isn't afraid to say what is on his mind; she's mouthy. He exercises authority diligently; she's power mad. He's closemouthed; she's secretive. He climbed the ladder of success; she slept her way to the top.

FROM "HOW TO TELL A BUSINESSMAN FROM A BUSINESSWOMAN," *The Balloon,* Graduate School of Management, UCLA, 1976

The discussion of obscenities, blasphemies, taboo words, and euphemisms showed that words of a language are not intrinsically good or bad, but reflect individual or societal values. This is also seen where a woman may be referred to as a *castrating female, ballsy women's libber,* or *courageous feminist advocate,* depending on who is talking.

Early dictionaries often gave clues to the social attitudes of that time. In some twentieth-century dictionaries, examples used to illustrate the meaning of words include "manly courage" and "masculine charm," as opposed to "womanish tears" and "feminine wiles." Contemporary dictionaries are far more enlightened and try to be scrupulous in avoiding sexist language.

Until recently, most people who heard "My cousin is a professor (or a doctor, or the chancellor of the university, or a steelworker)" would assume that the cousin is a man; if they heard "My cousin is a nurse (or elementary school teacher, or clerk-typist, or house worker)," they would conclude that the cousin is a woman. This is changing because society is changing and people of either sex commonly hold jobs once held primarily by one sex.

Despite flashes of enlightenment, words for women abound with abusive or sexual overtones: *dish, piece, piece of ass, piece of tail, bunny, chick, pussy, bitch, doll, slut, cow*—to name just a few. Far fewer such sexual terms exist for men, and those that do, such as *boy toy, stud muffin, hunk,* or *jock,* are not pejorative in the same way.

It's clear that language reflects sexism. It reflects any societal attitude, positive or negative; languages are infinitely flexible and expressive. But is language itself amoral and neutral? Or is there something about language, or a particular language, that abets sexism? Before we attempt to answer that question, let's look more deeply into the subject, using English as the illustrative language.

Marked and Unmarked Forms

If the English language had been properly organized . . . then there would be a word which meant both "he" and "she," and I could write, "If John or Mary comes, heesh will want to play tennis," which would save a lot of trouble.

A. A. MILNE, *The Christopher Robin Birthday Book,* 1930

In chapter 5 we saw that with gradable antonyms such as *high/low,* one is marked (*low*) and the other unmarked. Ordinarily, the unmarked member of the pair is the one used in questions (*How high is the building?*), measurements (*The building is twenty stories high*), and so on.

Similar to this is an asymmetry between male and female terms in many languages where there are male/female pairs of words. The male form is generally unmarked and the female term is created by adding a bound morpheme. We have many such examples in English:

Male	Female
heir	heiress
major	majorette
hero	heroine
Robert	Roberta
equestrian	equestrienne
aviator	aviatrix

When referring in general to the profession of acting, or flying, or riding horseback, the unmarked terms *actor, aviator,* and *equestrian* are used. The marked terms are used to emphasize the female gender.

Moreover, the unmarked third person pronoun in English is male (*he, him, his*). *Everybody had better pay his fee next time* allows for the client to be male or female, but *Everybody had better pay her fee next time* presupposes a female client. While there has been some attempt to neutralize the pronoun by using *they,* as in *Every teenager loves their first car,* most teachers find this objectionable and it is unlikely to become common practice. Other attempts to find a suitable genderless third person pronoun have produced such attempts as *e, hesh, po, tey, co, jhe, ve, xe, he'er, thon, na,* none of which speakers have the least inclination to adopt, and it appears likely that *he* and *she* are going to be with us for a while.

Since the advent of the feminist movement, many of the marked female forms have been replaced by the male forms, which are used to refer to either sex. Thus women, as well as men, are authors, actors, poets, heroes, and heirs. Women, however, remain countesses, duchesses, and princesses, if they are among this small group of female aristocrats.

The Sapir-Whorf hypothesis, discussed in chapter 1, proposes that the way a language encodes—puts into words—different categories like male and female subtly affects the way speakers of the language think about those categories. Thus, it may be argued that because English speakers are often urged to choose *he* as the unmarked pronoun (*Everyone should respect himself*), and to choose *she* only when the referent is overtly female, they tend to think of the male sex as predominant. Likewise, the fact that nouns require special affixes to make them feminine forces people to think in terms of male and female, with the female somehow more derivative because of affixing. The different titles, Mr., Mrs., Miss, and Ms., also emphasize the male/female distinction. Finally, the preponderance of words denigrating females in English and many other languages may create a climate that is more tolerant of sexist behavior.

Nevertheless, although people can undoubtedly be sexist and even cultures can be sexist, can language be sexist? That is, can we be molded by our language to be something we may not want to be? Or does language merely facilitate any natural inclinations we may have? Is it simply a reflection of societal values? These questions are disputed today by linguists, anthropologists, psychologists, and philosophers, and no definitive answer has yet emerged.

Secret Languages and Language Games

Throughout the world and throughout history, people have invented secret languages and language games. They have used these special languages as a means of identifying with their group and/or to prevent outsiders from knowing what is being said. One such case is *Nushu*, the women's secret writing of Chinese, which originated in the third century as a means for women to communicate with one another in the sexually repressive societies of imperial China (see exercise 17, chapter 12). American slaves developed an elaborate code that could not be understood by the slave owners. References to "the promised land" or the "flight of the Israelites from Egypt" sung in spirituals were codes for the North and the Underground Railroad.

Language games such as Pig Latin[4] and Ubbi Dubbi (see exercise 7) are used for amusement by children and adults. They exist in all the world's languages and take a wide variety of forms. In some, a suffix is added to each word; in others a syllable is inserted after each vowel. There are rhyming games and games in which phonemes are reversed. A game in Brazil substitutes an /i/ for all the vowels.

The Walbiri, natives of central Australia, play a language game in which the meanings of words are distorted. In this play language, all nouns, verbs, pronouns, and adjectives are replaced by a semantically contrastive word. Thus, the sentence *Those men are small* means *This woman is big*.

---

[4]*Dog* is pronounced *og-day*, *parrot* as *arrot-pay*, and *elephant* as *elephant-may*, etc., but see exercise 6.

These language games provide evidence for the phonemes, words, morphemes, semantic features, and so on that are posited by linguists for descriptive grammars. They also illustrate the boundless creativity of human language and human speakers.

Summary

Every person has a unique way of speaking, called an **idiolect**. The language used by a group of speakers is a **dialect**. The dialects of a language are the mutually intelligible forms of that language that differ in systematic ways from each other. Dialects develop because languages change, and the changes that occur in one group or area may differ from those that occur in another. **Regional dialects** and **social dialects** develop for this reason. Some differences in U.S. regional dialects may be traced to the dialects spoken by colonial settlers from England. Those from southern England spoke one dialect and those from the north spoke another. In addition, the colonists who maintained close contact with England reflected the changes occurring in British English, while earlier forms were preserved among Americans who spread westward and broke communication with the Atlantic coast. The study of regional dialects has produced **dialect atlases**, with **dialect maps** showing the areas where specific dialect characteristics occur in the speech of the region. A boundary line called an **isogloss** delineates each area.

Social dialects arise when groups are isolated socially, such as Americans of African descent in the United States, many of whom speak dialects collectively called African American (Vernacular) English, which are distinct from the dialects spoken by non-Africans.

Dialect differences include phonological or pronunciation differences (often called **accents**), vocabulary distinctions, and syntactic rule differences. The grammar differences among dialects are not as great as the similarities, thus permitting speakers of different dialects to communicate.

In many countries, one dialect or dialect group is viewed as the **standard**, such as **Standard American English (SAE)**. Although this particular dialect is not linguistically superior, some language purists consider it the only correct form of the language. Such a view has led to the idea that some nonstandard dialects are deficient, as is erroneously suggested regarding **African American English** (sometimes referred to as **Ebonics**), a collection of dialects used by some African Americans. A study of African American English shows it to be as logical, complete, rule-governed, and expressive as any other dialect. This is also true of the dialects spoken by Latino Americans whose native language or those of their parents is Spanish. There are bilingual and monolingual Latino speakers of English. One Latino dialect spoken in the Southwest, referred to as **Chicano English (ChE)**, shows systematic phonological and syntactic differences from SAE that stem from the influence of Spanish. Other differences are shared with many nonstandard ethnic and nonethnic dialects. **Codeswitching** is shifting between languages within a single sentence or discourse by a bilingual speaker. It reflects both grammars working simultaneously and does not represent a form of "broken" English or Spanish or whatever language.

Attempts to legislate the use of a particular dialect or language have been made throughout history and exist today, even extending to banning the use of languages other than the preferred one.

In areas where many languages are spoken, one language may become a **lingua franca** to ease communication among people. In other cases, where traders, missionaries, or travelers need to communicate with people who speak a language unknown to them, a **pidgin** may develop. A pidgin is a simplified system with properties of both the **superstrate (lexifier)** and **substrate** languages. When a pidgin is widely used, and constitutes the primary linguistic input to children, it is *creolized*. The grammars of **creole** languages are similar to those of other languages, and languages of creole origin now exist in many parts of the world and include sign languages of the deaf.

The study of language has important implications for education especially as regards reading instruction, and the teaching of second language learners, language-minority students, and speakers of nonstandard dialects. Several second-language teaching methods have been proposed for adult second language learners. Some of them focus more on the grammatical aspects of the target language, and others focus more on getting students to communicate in the target language, with less regard for grammatical accuracy.

Writing and reading, unlike speaking and understanding, must be deliberately taught. Three methods of teaching reading have been used in the United States: *whole-word*, *whole-language*, and *phonics*. In the whole-word and whole-language approaches, children are taught to recognize entire words without regard to individual letters and sounds. The phonics approach emphasizes the spelling-sound correspondences of the language, and thus draws on the child's innate phonological knowledge.

Immigrant children must acquire English (or whatever the majority language is in a particular country). Younger students must at the same time acquire literacy skills (reading and writing), and students of all ages must learn content material such as math, science, and so on. This is a formidable task. **Bilingual education** programs are designed to help achieve these multiple aims by teaching children literacy and content material in their native language while they are acquiring English. Research has shown that immigrant children benefit from instruction in their native language, but many people oppose these programs.

Children who speak a nonstandard dialect of English that differs from the language of instruction may also be at a disadvantage in a school setting, especially in learning reading and writing. There have been contentious debates over the use of Ebonics in the classroom as a method for helping speakers of AAE learn Standard English.

Besides regional and social dialects, speakers may use different **styles**, or **registers**, depending on the context. **Slang** is not often used in formal situations or writing but is widely used in speech; **argot** and **jargon** refer to the unique vocabulary used by particular groups of people to facilitate communication, provide a means of bonding, and exclude outsiders.

In all societies, certain acts or behaviors are frowned on, forbidden, or considered **taboo**. The words or expressions referring to these taboo acts are then also avoided or considered "dirty." Language cannot be obscene or clean; attitudes toward specific words or linguistic expressions reflect the views of a culture or society toward the behaviors and actions of the language users. At times, slang words may be taboo where scientific or standard terms with the same meaning are acceptable in "polite society." Taboo words and acts give rise to **euphemisms,** which are words or phrases that replace the expressions to be avoided. Thus, *powder room* is a euphemism for *toilet,* which started as a euphemism for *lavatory,* which is now more acceptable than its replacement.

Just as the use of some words may indicate society's views toward sex, natural bodily functions, or religious beliefs, some words may also indicate racist, chauvinist, or sexist attitudes. Language is not intrinsically racist or sexist but reflects the views of various sectors of a society. However, the availability of offensive terms, and particular grammatical peculiarities such as the lack of a genderless third-person singular pronoun, may perpetuate and reinforce biased views and be demeaning and insulting to those addressed. Thus culture influences language, and, arguably, language may have an influence on the culture in which it is spoken.

The invention or construction of secret languages and language games like Pig Latin attest to human creativity with language and the unconscious knowledge that speakers have of the phonological, morphological, and semantic rules of their language.

References for Further Reading

Carver, C. M. 1987. *American regional dialects: A word geography.* Ann Arbor, MI: University of Michigan Press.

Cassidy, F. G. (chief ed.). 1985, 1991, 1996, 2002. *Dictionary of American regional English,* Volumes 1, 2, 3, 4. Cambridge, MA: Harvard University Press.

Chambers, J., and P. Trudgill. 1998. *Dialectology,* 2nd edn. Cambridge, UK: Cambridge University Press.

Finegan, E., and J. Rickford (eds.). 2004. *Language in the USA.* Cambridge, UK: Cambridge University Press.

Holm, J. 2000. *An introduction to pidgins and creoles.* Cambridge, UK: Cambridge University Press.

Labov, W. 1972. *Sociolinguistic patterns.* Philadelphia: University of Pennsylvania Press.

_____. 1969. The logic of nonstandard English. *Georgetown University 20th Annual Round Table, Monograph Series on Languages and Linguistics,* No. 22.

_____. 1966. *The social stratification of English in New York City.* Washington, DC: Center for Applied Linguistics.

Lakoff, R. 1990. *Talking power: The politics of language.* New York: Basic Books.

Roberts, I. 1999. Verb movement and markedness. In Michel DeGraff (ed.), *Language creation and language change, creolization, diachrony and development.* Cambridge, MA: MIT Press, 287–327.

Tannen, D. 1994. *Gender and discourse.* New York: Oxford University Press.

_____. 1990. *You just don't understand: Women and men in conversation.* New York: Ballantine.

Trudgill, P. 2001. *Sociolinguistics: An introduction to language and society,* 4th edn. London: Penguin Books.

Wolfram, W., and N. Schilling-Estes. 1998. *American English dialects and variation.* London: Blackwell Publishers.

Exercises

1. Each pair of words is pronounced as shown phonetically in at least one American English dialect. Write in phonetic transcription your pronunciation of each word that you pronounce differently.

a.	horse	[hɔrs]	hoarse	[hors]
b.	morning	[mɔrnĭŋ]	mourning	[mornĭŋ]
c.	for	[fɔr]	four	[for]
d.	ice	[ʌɪs]	eyes	[aɪz]
e.	knife	[nʌɪf]	knives	[naɪvz]
f.	mute	[mjut]	nude	[njud]
g.	din	[dĭn]	den	[dɛ̃n]
h.	hog	[hɔg]	hot	[hat]
i.	marry	[mæri]	Mary	[meri]
j.	merry	[mɛri]	marry	[mæri]
k.	rot	[rat]	wrought	[rɔt]
l.	lease	[lis]	grease (v.)	[griz]
m.	what	[ʌat]	watt	[wat]
n.	ant	[æ̃nt]	aunt	[ã̃nt]
o.	creek	[kʰrɪk]	creak	[kʰrik]

2. **A.** Below is a passage from the Gospel according to St. Mark in Cameroon English Pidgin. See how much you can understand before consulting the English translation given below. State some of the similarities and differences between CEP and SAE.

   a. Di fos tok fo di gud nuus fo Jesus Christ God yi Pikin.

   b. I bi sem as i di tok fo di buk fo Isaiah, God yi nchinda (Prophet), "Lukam, mi a di sen man nchinda fo bifo yoa fes weh yi go fix yoa rud fan."

   c. Di vos fo som man di krai fo bush: "Fix di ples weh Papa God di go, mek yi rud tret."

   Translation:

   a. The beginning of the gospel of Jesus Christ, the Son of God.

   b. As it is written in the book of Isaiah the prophet, "Behold, I send my messenger before thy face, which shall prepare thy way before thee."

   c. The voice of one crying in the wilderness, "Prepare ye the way of the Lord, make his paths straight."

   B. Here are some words from Tok Pisin. What are the English words from which they are derived? The answer is shown for the first entry.

Tok Pisin	Gloss	Answer
taim bilong kol	winter	time belong cold
pinga bilong fut	toe	
hamas krismas yu gat?	how old are you?	
kukim long paia	barbecue	

sapos	if
haus moni	bank
kamup	arrive
tasol	only
olgeta	all
solwara	sea
haus sik	hospital
handet yia	century

3. In the period from 1890 to 1904, *Slang and Its Analogues*, by J. S. Farmer and W. E. Henley, was published in seven volumes. The following entries are included in this dictionary. For each item (1) state whether the word or phrase still exists; (2) if not, state what the modern slang term would be; and (3) if the word remains but its meaning has changed, provide the modern meaning.

all out: completely, as in "All out the best." (The expression goes back to as early as 1300.)

to have apartments to let: be an idiot; one who is empty-headed.

been there: in "Oh, yes, I've been there." (Applied to a man who is shrewd and who has had many experiences.)

belly-button: the navel.

berkeleys: a woman's breasts.

bitch: most offensive appellation that can be given to a woman, even more provoking than that of *whore*.

once in a blue moon: seldom.

boss: master; one who directs.

bread: employment. (1785—"out of bread" = "out of work.")

claim: to steal.

cut dirt: to escape.

dog cheap: of little worth. (Used in 1616 by Dekker: "Three things there are dog-cheap, learning, poorman's sweat, and oathes.")

funeral: as in "It's not my funeral." "It's no business of mine."

to get over: to seduce, to fascinate.

groovy: settled in habit; limited in mind.

grub: food.

head: toilet (nautical use only).

hook: to marry.

hump: to spoil.

hush money: money paid for silence; blackmail.

itch: to be sexually excited.

jam: a sweetheart or a mistress.

leg bags: stockings.

to lie low: to keep quiet; to bide one's time.

to lift a leg on: to have sexual intercourse.

looby: a fool.

malady of France: syphilis. (Used by Shakespeare in 1599.)

nix: nothing.

noddle: the head.

old: money. (1900—"Perhaps it's somebody you owe a bit of the old to, Jack.")

to pill: talk platitudes.

pipe layer: a political intriguer; a schemer.

poky: cramped, stuffy, stupid.

pot: a quart; a large sum; a prize; a urinal; to excel.

puny: a freshman.

puss-gentleman: an effeminate.

4. Suppose someone asked you to help compile items for a new dictionary of slang. List ten slang words, and provide a short definition for each.

5. Below are some words used in British English for which different words are usually used in American English. See if you can match the British and American equivalents.

	British	American
a.	clothes peg	candy
b.	braces	truck
c.	lift	line
d.	pram	main street
e.	waistcoat	crackers
f.	shop assistant	suspenders
g.	sweets	wrench
h.	boot (of car)	flashlight
i.	bobby	potato chips
j.	spanner	vacation
k.	biscuits	baby buggy
l.	queue	elevator
m.	torch	can
n.	underground	cop
o.	high street	wake up
p.	crisps	trunk
q.	lorry	vest
r.	holiday	subway
s.	tin	clothes pin
t.	knock up	clerk

6. Pig Latin is a common language game of English; but even Pig Latin has dialects, forms of the "language game" with different rules.

   A. Consider the following data from three dialects of Pig Latin, each with its own rule applied to words beginning with vowels:

	Dialect 1	Dialect 2	Dialect 3
"eat"	[itme]	[ithe]	[ite]
"arc"	[arkme]	[arkhe]	[arke]
"expose"	[ɛkspozme]	[ɛkspozhe]	[ɛkspoze]

   i. State the rule that accounts for the Pig Latin forms in each dialect.

ii. How would you say *honest*, *admire*, and *illegal* in each dialect? Give the phonetic transcription of the Pig Latin forms.

B. In one dialect of Pig Latin, the word "strike" is pronounced [aɪkstre], and in another dialect it is pronounced [traɪkse]. In the first dialect "slot" is pronounced [atsle] and in the second dialect, it is pronounced [latse].

   i. State the rules for each of these dialects that account for these different Pig Latin forms of the same words.

   ii. Give the phonetic transcriptions for *spot*, *crisis*, and *scratch* in both dialects.

7. Below are some sentences representing different English language games. Write each sentence in its undistorted form; state the language-game rule.

   a. /aɪ-o tʊk-o maɪ-o dag-o aʊt-o saɪd-o/
   b. /hirli ɪzli əli mɔrli kamliplʲlilikelitədli gemli/
   c. Mary-shmary can-shman talk-shmalk in-shmin rhyme-shmyme.
   d. Betpeterer latepate thanpan nevpeverer.
   e. thop-e fop-oot bop-all stop-a dop-i op-um blop-ew dop-own/ðapə fapʊt bapɔl stape dapi apəm blapu dapaʊn/
   f. /kʌbæn jʌbu spʌbik ðʌbɪs kʌbaɪnd ʌbəv ʌbɪŋglʌbɪʃ/ (This sentence is in "Ubby Dubby" from a children's television program popular in the 1970s.)

8. Below are sentences that might be spoken between two friends chatting informally. For each, state what the nonabbreviated full sentence in SAE would be. In addition, state in your own words (or formally if you wish) the rule or rules that derived the informal sentences from the formal ones.

   a. Where've ya been today?
   b. Watcha gonna do for fun?
   c. Him go to church?
   d. There's four books there.
   e. Who ya wanna go with?

9. Compile a list of argot (or jargon) terms from some profession or trade (e.g., lawyer, musician, doctor, longshoreman). Give a definition for each term in nonjargon terms.

10. "Translate" the first paragraph of any well-known document or speech—such as the Declaration of Independence, the Gettysburg Address, or the Preamble to the U.S. Constitution—into informal, colloquial language.

11. Cockney rhyming slang, which arose in the East End of London in the nineteenth century, is a language game played by creating a rhyme as a substitute for a specific word. Thus, for *table* the rhymed slang may be *Cain and Abel*; *missus* is *cows and kisses*; *stairs* are *apples and pears*; *head* is *loaf of bread*, and so on. Column A contains some Cockney rhyming slang expressions. Match these to the items in Column B to which they refer.

	A	**B**
a.	drip dry	balls (testicles)
b.	in the mood	bread
c.	insects and ants	ale
d.	orchestra stalls	cry
e.	Oxford scholar	food
f.	strike me dead	dollar
g.	ship in full sail	pants

Now construct your own version of Cockney rhyming slang for the following words:

h. chair
i. house
j. coat
k. eggs
l. pencil

12. Column A lists euphemisms for words in Column B. Match each item in A with its appropriate B word.

	A	**B**
a.	Montezuma's revenge	condom
b.	joy stick	genocide
c.	friggin'	fire
d.	ethnic cleansing	diarrhea
e.	French letter (old)	masturbate
f.	diddle oneself	kill
g.	holy of holies	urinate
h.	spend a penny (British)	penis
i.	ladies' cloak room	die
j.	knock off (from 1919)	waging war
k.	vertically challenged	vagina
l.	hand in one's dinner pail	women's toilet
m.	sanitation engineer	short
n.	downsize	fuckin'
o.	peace keeping	garbage collector

13. Defend or criticize the following statement in a short essay:

    A person who uses the word *niggardly* in a public hearing should be censured for being insensitive and using a word that resembles a degrading, racist word.

14. The words *waitron* and *waitperson* are currently fighting it out to see which, if either, will replace *waitress* as a gender-neutral term. Using dictionaries, the Internet, and whatever other resources you can think of, predict the winner or the failure of both candidates. Give reasons for your answers. If you count hits on Google, analyze the sources to support your conclusions.

15. Search for Tok Pisin on the Internet. You will quickly find Web sites where it is possible to hear Tok Pisin spoken. Listen to a passage several times. How much of it can you understand without looking at the text or the translation? Then follow along with the text (generally provided) until you can hear the individual words. Now try a new passage. Does your comprehension improve? How much practice do you think you would need before you could understand roughly half of what is being said the first time you heard it?

16. A language game that is so popular it has appeared in the *Washington Post* is to take a word or (well-known) expression and alter it by adding, subtracting, or changing one letter, and supplying a new (clever) definition. Read the following examples, try to figure out the expression from which they are derived, and then try to produce ten on your own. (*Hint*: Lots of Latin.)

Cogito eggo sum	I think, therefore I am a waffle.
Foreploy	A misrepresentation about yourself for the purpose of getting laid
Veni, vipi, vici	I came, I am important, I conquered.
Giraffiti	Dirty words sprayed very, very high
Ignoranus	A person who is both stupid and an asshole
Rigor Morris	The cat is dead (maybe for older students)
Felix navidad	Our cat has a boat.
Veni, vidi, vice	I came, I saw, I sold my sister.
Glibido	All talk, no action
Haste cuisine	Fast French food
L'état, c'est moo	I'm bossy around here.
Intaxication	The euphoria that accompanies a tax refund
Ex post fucto	Lost in the mail

17. In his original, highly influential novel *1984*, George Orwell introduces Newspeak, a government-enforced language designed to keep the masses subjugated. He writes:

> Its vocabulary was so constructed as to give exact and often very subtle expression to every meaning that a Party member could properly wish to express, while excluding all other meanings and also the possibility of arriving at them by indirect methods. This was done partly by the invention of new words, but chiefly by eliminating undesirable words and by stripping such words as remained of unorthodox meanings, and so far as possible of all secondary meanings whatever. To give a single example, the word *free* still existed in Newspeak, but it could only be used in such statements as "This dog is free from lice" or "This field is free from weeds." It could not be used in its old sense of "politically free" or "intellectually free," since political and intellectual freedom no longer existed even as concepts, and were therefore of necessity nameless.

Critique Newspeak. Will it achieve its goal? Why or why not? (*Hint*: You may want to review concepts such as language creativity and arbitrariness as discussed in the first few pages of chapter 1.)

18. In *1984* Orwell proposed that if a concept does not exist, it is nameless. In the passage quoted below, he suggests that if a crime were nameless, it would be unimaginable, hence impossible to commit:

    > A person growing up with Newspeak as his sole language would no more know that . . . *free* had once meant "intellectually free," than, for instance, a person who had never heard of chess would be aware of the secondary meanings attaching to *queen* and *rook* and *checkmate*. There would be many crimes and errors which it would be beyond his power to commit, simply because they were nameless and therefore unimaginable.

    Critique this notion.

19. One aspect of different English genderlects is lexical choice. For example, women say *darling* and *lovely* more frequently than men; men use sports metaphors such as *home run* and *slam dunk* more than women. Think of other lexical usages that appear to be asymmetric between the sexes.

20. **Research project:** Throughout history many regimes have banned languages. Write a report in which you mention several such regimes, the languages they banned, and possible reasons for banning them (e.g., you might have discovered that the Basque language was banned in Spain under the regime of Francisco Franco (1936–1975) owing in part to the separatist desires of the Basque people and because the Basques opposed his dictatorship).

21. Abbreviated English (AE) is a register of written English used in newspaper headlines and elsewhere. Some examples follow:

    CLINTON IN BULGARIA THIS WEEK
    OLD MAN FINDS RARE COIN
    BUSH HIRES WIFE AS SECRETARY
    POPE DIES IN VATICAN

    AE does not involve an arbitrary omission of parts of the sentence but is regulated by grammatical rules.

    A. Translate each of these headlines into Standard American English (SAE).
    B. What features or rules distinguish AE from SAE?
    C. Are there other contexts (besides headlines) in which we find AE? If so, provide examples.
    Challenge exercises:
    D. What is the time reference of the above headlines (e.g., present, recent past, remote past, future)?
    E. Is there a difference in possible tense interpretations when the predicate is eventive (e.g., *dies*) than when it is stative (e.g., *in Bulgaria*)? (You may have to review these terms in chapter 5.)

22. Watch several hours of daytime soap operas on television. Write down any euphemisms you think you hear, and what taboo subject they conceal. And

yes, if anybody rags on you for wasting your life on daytime TV, show them this homework assignment.

23. You overhear somebody say, "That's not a language, it's a dialect." Compose a brief retort.

24. Recommend three ways in which society can act to preserve linguistic diversity. Be realistic and concrete. For example, "Encourage children of endangered languages to learn the language" is *not* a good answer, being neither sufficiently realistic (why should they want to?), nor sufficiently concrete (what is meant by "encourage"?).

25. Research the history and controversy surrounding the use of "Ebonics" in the classroom. The Internet is a good place to start. Consider both sides of the argument and discuss whether you think this is a good idea and why or why not.

11

Language Change: The Syllables of Time

> No language as depending on arbitrary use and custom can ever be permanently the same, but will always be in a mutable and fluctuating state; and what is deem'd polite and elegant in one age, may be accounted uncouth and barbarous in another.
>
> **BENJAMIN MARTIN** (1704–1782)

All living languages change with time. It is fortunate that they do so rather slowly compared to the human life span. It would be inconvenient to have to relearn our native language every twenty years. Stargazers find a similar situation. Because of the movement of individual stars, the constellations are continuously changing their shape. Fifty thousand years from now we would hardly recognize Orion or the Big Dipper, but from season to season the changes are imperceptible. Linguistic change is also slow, in human—if not astronomical—terms. As years pass we hardly notice any change. Yet if we were to turn on a radio and miraculously receive a broadcast in our "native language" from the year 3000, we would probably think we had tuned into a foreign language station. Many language changes are revealed in written records. We know a great deal of the history of English because it has been a written language for about 1,000 years. Old English, spoken in England around the end of the first millennium, is scarcely recognizable as English. (Of course, our linguistic ancestors did not call their language Old English!) A speaker of Modern English would find the language unintelligible. There are college courses in which Old English is studied as a foreign language.

A line from *Beowulf* illustrates why Old English must be translated:[1]

---

[1]The letter þ is called *thorn* and is pronounced [θ] in this example.

Wolde guman findan þone þe him on sweofote sare geteode.
"He wanted to find the man who harmed him while he slept."

Approximately five hundred years after *Beowulf*, Chaucer wrote *The Canter-bury Tales* in what is now called Middle English, spoken from around 1100 to 1500. It is more easily understood by present-day readers, as seen by reading the opening of the *Tales*:

Whan that Aprille with his shoures soote
The droght of March hath perced to the roote . . .
"When April with its sweet showers
The drought of March has pierced to the root . . ."

Two hundred years after Chaucer, in a language that is considered an earlier form of Modern English, Shakespeare's *Hamlet* says:

A man may fish with the worm that hath eat of a king, and eat of the fish that hath fed of that worm.

The stages of English are Old English (449–1100 C.E.), Middle English (1100–1500), and Modern English (1500–present). This division is somewhat arbitrary, being marked by important dates in English history, such as the Norman Conquest of 1066, the results of which profoundly influenced the English language.

The branch of linguistics that deals with how languages change, what kinds of changes occur, and why they occurred is called **historical and comparative linguistics**. It is "historical" because it deals with the history of particular languages; it is "comparative" because it deals with relations among languages.

Changes in a language are changes in the grammars and the lexicon of people who speak the language and are perpetuated as new generations of children acquire the altered language and make further changes. All parts of the grammar are subject to change over the course of time—the phonological, morphological, syntactic, and semantic components may be affected. Although most of the examples in this chapter are from English, the histories of all languages show similar effects. This is true of sign languages as well as spoken languages. Like all living languages, American Sign Language continues to change. Not only have new signs entered the language over the past two hundred years, but also the forms of the signs have changed in ways similar to spoken languages.

The Regularity of Sound Change

That's not a regular rule: you invented it just now.

LEWIS CARROLL, *Alice's Adventures in Wonderland*, 1865

The southern United States represents a major dialect area of American English. For example, words pronounced with the diphthong [aɪ] in non-Southern English will usually be pronounced with the monophthong [aː] in the South. Local radio and TV announcers at the 1996 Olympics in Atlanta called athletes to the [haː]

"high" jump, and local natives invited visitors to try Georgia's famous pecan [pɑː] "pie." The [aɪ]-[ɑː] correspondence of these two dialects is an example of a **regular sound correspondence**. When [aɪ] occurs in a word in non-Southern dialects, [ɑː] occurs in the Southern dialect, and *this is true for all such words*.

The different pronunciations of *I*, *my*, *high*, *pie*, and so on did not always exist in English. In this chapter we will discuss how such dialect differences arose and why the sound differences are usually regular and not confined to just a few words. We will also consider changes that occur in other parts of the grammar and in the lexicon.

Sound Correspondences

In Middle English a *mouse* [maʊs] was called a *mūs* [muːs], and this *mūs* may have lived in someone's *hūs* [huːs], as *house* [haʊs] was pronounced at that time. In general, Middle English speakers pronounced [uː] where we now pronounce [aʊ]. This is a regular correspondence like the one between [aɪ] and [ɑː]. Thus *out* [aʊt] was pronounced [uːt], *south* [saʊθ] was pronounced [suːθ], and so on. Many such regular correspondences show the relation of older and newer forms of English.

The regular sound correspondences we observe between older and modern forms of a language are the result of phonological changes that affect certain sounds, or classes of sounds, rather than individual words. Centuries ago English underwent a phonological change called a **sound shift** in which [uː] became [aʊ].

Phonological changes can also account for dialect differences. At an earlier stage of American English a sound shift of [aɪ] to [ɑː] took place among certain speakers in the southern region of the United States. The change did not spread beyond the South because the region was somewhat isolated. Many dialect differences in pronunciation result from sound shifts whose spread is limited.

Regional dialect differences may also arise when innovative changes occur everywhere but in a particular region. The regional dialect may be conservative relative to other dialects. The pronunciation of *it* as *hit*, found in the Appalachian region of the United States, was standard in older forms of English. The dropping of the [h] was the innovation.

Ancestral Protolanguages

Many modern languages developed from regional dialects that became widely spoken and highly differentiated, finally becoming separate languages. The Romance languages—French, Spanish, and so on—were once dialects of Latin spoken in the Roman Empire. There is nothing degenerate about regional pronunciations. They are the result of natural sound changes that occur wherever human language is spoken.

In a sense, the Romance languages are the offspring of Latin, their metaphorical parent. Because of their common ancestry, the Romance languages are **genetically related**. Early forms of English and German, too, were once dialects of a common ancestor called **Proto-Germanic**. A **protolanguage** is the ancestral language from which related languages have developed. Both Latin and Proto-Germanic were descendants of an older language called **Indo-European** or

Proto-Indo-European. Thus, Germanic languages such as English and German are genetically related to the Romance languages such as French and Spanish. All these national languages were once regional dialects.

How do we know that the Germanic and Romance languages have a common ancestor? One clue is the large number of sound correspondences. If you have studied a Romance language such as French or Spanish, you may have noticed that where an English word begins with *f*, the corresponding word in a Romance language often begins with *p*, as shown in the following examples:

English /f/	French /p/	Spanish /p/
Father	Père	Padre
Fish	Poisson	Pescado

This /f/-/p/ correspondence is another example of a regular sound correspondence. There are many such correspondences between the Germanic and Romance languages, and their prevalence cannot be explained by chance. What then accounts for them? A reasonable guess is that a common ancestor language used a *p* in words for *fish*, *father*, and so on. We posit a /p/ rather than an /f/ because more languages show a /p/ in these words. At some point speakers of this language separated into two groups that lost contact with each other. In one of the groups a sound change of *p → f* took place. The language spoken by this group eventually became the ancestor of the Germanic languages. This ancient sound change left its trace in the *f-p* sound correspondence that we observe today, as illustrated in the diagram.

Phonological Change

> Etymologists . . . for whom vowels did not matter and who cared not a jot for consonants.
> **VOLTAIRE** (1694–1778)

Regular sound correspondences illustrate changes in the phonological system of a language. In earlier chapters we discussed speakers' knowledge of phonology, including knowledge of the phonemes and phonological rules of the language. Either of these aspects of the phonology is subject to change.

The velar fricative /x/ is no longer part of the phonemic inventory of most Modern English dialects. Night used to be pronounced [nɪxt] and drought was pronounced [druxt]. This phonological change—the loss of /x/—took place between the times of Chaucer and Shakespeare. All words that were once pronounced with an /x/ no longer include this sound. In some cases it disappeared altogether, as in *night* and *light*. In other cases the /x/ became a /k/, as in *elk* (Old

English *eolh* [ɛɔlx]). In yet other cases it disappeared to be replaced by a vowel, as in *hollow* (Old English *holh* [hɔlx]). Dialects of Modern English spoken in Scotland have retained the /x/ sound in some words, such as *loch* [lɔx] meaning "lake."

These examples show that changes in the inventory of sounds in a language can occur through the loss of phonemes. The inventory can also change through the addition of phonemes. Old English did not have the phoneme /ʒ/ of *leisure* [liʒər]. Through a process of palatalization—a change in place of articulation to the palatal region—certain occurrences of /z/ were pronounced [ʒ]. Eventually the [ʒ] sound became a phoneme in its own right, reinforced by the fact that it occurs in French words familiar to many English speakers such as *azure* [æʒər].

An allophone of a phoneme may, through sound change, become a separate phoneme, thus adding to the phonemic inventory. Old English lacked a /v/ phoneme. The phoneme /f/, however, had the allophone [v] when it occurred between vowels. Thus *ofer* /ofer/ meaning "over" was pronounced [ɔvər]. Old English also had a long consonant phoneme /f:/ that contrasted with /f/ between vowels. The name *Offa* /ɔf:a/ was pronounced [ɔf:a]. A sound change occurred in which the pronunciation of /f:/ was simplified to [f]. Now /f:/ was pronounced [f] between vowels so it contrasted with [v]. This made it possible for English to have minimal pairs involving [f] and [v] such as *feel* and *veal*. Speakers therefore perceived the two sounds as separate phonemes, in effect creating a new phoneme /v/.

Similar changes occur in the history of all languages. Neither /tʃ/ nor /ʃ/ were phonemes of Latin, but /tʃ/ is a phoneme of modern Italian and /ʃ/ a phoneme of modern French, both of which descended from Latin. In American Sign Language many signs that were originally formed at the waist or chest level are now produced at a higher level near the neck or upper chest, a reflection of changes in the "phonology."

Phonological Rules

An interaction of phonological rules may result in changes in the lexicon. The nouns *house* and *bath* were once differentiated from the verbs *house* and *bathe* by the fact that the verbs ended with a short vowel sound. Furthermore, the same rule that realized /f/ as [v] between vowels also realized /s/ and /θ/ as the allophones [z] and [ð] between vowels. This general rule added voicing to intervocalic fricatives. Thus the /s/ in the verb *house* was pronounced [z], and the /θ/ in the verb *bathe* was pronounced [ð].

Later, a rule was added to the grammar of English deleting unstressed short vowels at the end of words (even though the final vowel still appears in the written words). A contrast between the voiced and voiceless fricatives resulted, and the new phonemes /z/ and /ð/ were added to the phonemic inventory. The verbs *house* [haʊz] and *bathe* [beð] were now represented in the mental lexicon with final voiced consonants.

Eventually, both the unstressed vowel deletion rule and the intervocalic-voicing rule were lost from the grammar of English. The set of phonological rules can change both by addition and loss of rules.

Changes in phonological rules can, and often do, result in dialect differences. In the previous chapter we discussed the addition of an *r*-dropping rule in English (/r/ is not pronounced unless followed by a vowel) that did not spread throughout the language. Today, we see the effect of that rule in the *r*-less pronunciation of British English and of American English dialects spoken in the northeastern and the southern United States.

From the standpoint of the language as a whole, phonological changes occur gradually over the course of many generations of speakers, although any given speaker's grammar may or may not reflect the change. The changes are not planned any more than we are presently planning what changes will take place in English by the year 2300. In a single generation changes are evident only through dialect differences.

The Great Vowel Shift

Between 1400 and 1600 a major change took place in English that resulted in new phonemic representations of words and morphemes. This phonological restructuring is known as the **Great Vowel Shift**. The seven long, or tense, vowels of Middle English underwent the following change:

Shift		Example		
Middle English	**Modern English**	**Middle English**	**Modern English**	
[iː] →	[aɪ]	[miːs] →	[maɪs]	mice
[uː] →	[aʊ]	[muːs] →	[maʊs]	mouse
[eː] →	[iː]	[geːs] →	[giːs]	geese
[oː] →	[uː]	[goːs] →	[guːs]	goose
[ɛː] →	[eː]	[brɛːken] →	[breːk]	break
[ɔː] →	[oː]	[brɔːken] →	[broːk]	broke
[aː] →	[eː]	[naːmə] →	[neːm]	name

By diagramming the Great Vowel Shift on a vowel chart (Figure 11.1), we can see that the high vowels [iː] and [uː] became the diphthongs [aɪ] and [aʊ], while

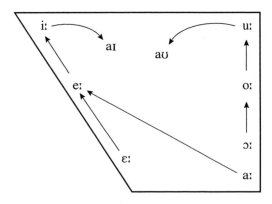

FIGURE 11.1 | The Great Vowel Shift.

TABLE 11.1 | Effect of Vowel Shift on Modern English

Middle English Vowel	Shifted Vowel	Short Vowel	Word with Shifted Vowel	Word with Short Vowel
ī	aɪ	ɪ	divine	divinity
ū	aʊ	ʌ	abound	abundant
ē	i	ɛ	serene	serenity
ō	u	a	fool	folly
ā	e	æ	sane	sanity

the long vowels underwent an increase in tongue height, as if to fill in the space vacated by the high vowels. In addition, [a:] was fronted to become [e:].

These changes are among the most dramatic examples of regular sound shift. The phonemic representation of many thousands of words changed. Today, some reflection of this vowel shift is seen in the alternating forms of morphemes in English: *please—pleasant*; *serene—serenity*; *sane—sanity*; *crime—criminal*; *sign—signal*; and so on. Before the Great Vowel Shift, the vowels in each pair were pronounced the same. Then the vowels in the second word of each pair were shortened by the **Early Middle English Vowel Shortening** rule. As a result, the Great Vowel Shift, which occurred later and applied only to long vowels, affected only the first word in each pair. This is why the vowels in the morphologically related words are pronounced differently today, as shown in Table 11.1.

The Great Vowel Shift is a primary source of many spelling inconsistencies of English because our spelling system still reflects the way words were pronounced before it occurred. In general, the written language is more conservative, that is, slower to change, than the spoken language.

Morphological Change

And is he well content his son should find
No nourishment to feed his growing mind,
But conjugated verbs and nouns declin'd?
WILLIAM COWPER, "Tirocinium," 1785

Like phonological rules, rules of morphology may be lost, added, or changed. We can observe some of these changes by comparing older and newer forms of the language or by looking at different dialects.

Extensive changes in morphology have occurred in the history of the Indo-European languages. Latin had **case endings**, suffixes on the noun based on its thematic role or its grammatical relationship to the verb. These are no longer found in the Romance languages. (See chapter 5 for a more extensive discussion of thematic roles; the terms used by historical linguists are somewhat different than those used by modern semanticists.) The following is a **declension**, or list of cases, for the Latin noun *lupus*, "wolf":

Noun	Noun Stem		Case Ending	Case	Example
lupus	lup	+	us	nominative	The *wolf* runs.
lupī	lup	+	ī	genitive	A sheep in *wolf's* clothing.
lupō	lup	+	ō	dative	Give food to *the wolf.*
lupum	lup	+	um	accusative	I love *the wolf.*
lupō	lup	+	ō	ablative	She walked with *the wolf.*
lupe	lup	+	e	vocative	*Wolf,* come here!

In *Alice's Adventures in Wonderland*, Lewis Carroll has Alice give us a brief lesson in grammatical case. Alice has become very small and is swimming around in a pool of her own tears with a mouse that she wishes to befriend:

> "Would it be of any use, now," thought Alice, "to speak to this mouse? Everything is so out-of-the-way down here, that I should think very likely it can talk: at any rate, there's no harm in trying." So she began: "O Mouse, do you know the way out of this pool? I am very tired of swimming about here, O Mouse!" (Alice thought this must be the right way of speaking to a mouse: she had never done such a thing before, but she remembered having seen in her brother's Latin Grammar, "A mouse-of a mouse-to a mouse-a mouse-O mouse!")

Alice gives the English corresponding to the nominative, genitive, dative, accusative, and vocative cases, which existed in Latin and in Old English but not in Modern English, where word order and prepositions convey the same information.

Ancient Greek and Sanskrit also had extensive case systems expressed through noun suffixing, as did Old English, as illustrated by the following noun forms:

Case	OE Singular		OE Plural	
nominative	stān	"stone"	stānas	"stones"
genitive	stānes	"stone's"	stāna	"stones'"
dative	stāne	"stone"	stānum	"stones"
accusative	stān	"stone"	stānas	"stones"

Lithuanian and Russian retain much of the early Indo-European case system, but it is all but obliterated in most modern Indo-European languages. In English, phonological changes over the centuries resulted in the loss of many case endings.

English retains the genitive case, which is written with an apostrophe *s*, as in *Robert's dog*, but that's all that remains as far as nouns are concerned. Pronouns retain a few more case distinctions: *he/she* are nominative, *him/her* accusative and dative, and *his/hers* genitive.

English has replaced its depleted case system with an equally expressive system of prepositions. For example, what would be the dative case is often indicated by the preposition *to*, the genitive case by the preposition *of*, and the accusative case by no preposition together with the word order V—NP in d-structure.

English and most of the Indo-European languages have undergone extensive morphological changes over the past 1,000 years, many of them induced by changes that took place in the phonological rules of the language.

Syntactic Change

Understanding changes in grammar is a key component in understanding changes in language.

DAVID LIGHTFOOT, *The Development of Language,* 1999

When we see a word-for-word translation of older forms of English, we are most struck by the differences in word order. Consider again the opening lines of *The Canterbury Tales,* this time translated word-for-word:

Whan that Aprille with his shoures soote
"When that April with its showers sweet"
The droght of March hath perced to the roote . . .
"The drought of March has pierced to the root . . ."

In modern English, adjectives generally precede the nouns they modify, thus we would say *sweet showers* in place of *showers sweet.* Moreover, direct objects now generally follow their verb, so *has pierced the drought of March to the root* would be a modern rendering of the second line.

However, there are some exceptions to the Adj-Noun order in Modern English; examples such as the following:

a man alone	*an alone man	a lone man
no man alive	*no alive man	no live man
a lion asleep	*an asleep lion	a sleeping lion
the passengers aboard	*the aboard passengers	the boarded passengers

The adjectives that must occur following the noun all begin with *a-.* According to the UCLA linguist Ed Keenan, these *a-* adjectives originated as prepositional phrases in Old English:

on + weg → away   on + slep → asleep   on + life → alive

The preposition *on* weakened to a prefix *a-* in these cases, but the original position of the PP, which followed the Noun in OE (and also in Modern English), was preserved. In some cases, the PP still exists alongside the derived adjective, for example, *on board/aboard* and *on fire/afire.*

These exceptions aside, it is safe to say that syntactic change in English and other languages is most evident in the changes of permitted word orders.

Syntactic change in English is a good illustration of the interrelationship of the various modules of the grammar. Changes in syntax were often influenced by changes in morphology, and these in turn by changes in the phonology of the language.

When the rich system of case-endings of Old English became simplified in part because of phonological changes, speakers of English were forced to rely more heavily on word order to convey the function of noun phrases. A sentence such as

sē	man	þone	kyning	sloh
the (nominative)	man	the (accusative)	king	slew

was understood to mean "the man slew the king" because of the case markings (given in parentheses). There would have been no confusion on the listeners' part as to who did what to whom. Also, in earlier stages of English the verb had a richer system of subject-verb agreement. For example, the verb *to sing* had the following forms: *singe* (I sing), *singest* (you sing), *singeth* (he sings), and *singen* (we, plural you, they sing). It was therefore also possible in many cases to identify the subject on the basis of verb inflection. In Modern English the only marker of agreement is the third person singular *-s* in *He sings*.

Thus, in Modern English *the man the king slew* is only grammatical as a relative clause meaning "the man that the king slew," with the subject and object of *slew* reversed. To convey the meaning "the man slew the king," Modern English speakers must rely on word order—subject-verb-object—or other syntactic devices such as the ones that generate sentences like *It was the king that the man slew*.

The change in English word order reflects a change in the rules of grammar. In Old English the VP was head final, as indicated by the following PS rule:

VP → NP V

The Old English phrase structure was like the phrase structure of Dutch and German, closely related languages. The English VP (but not German and Dutch) underwent a change in parameter setting and became head initial as follows:

VP → V NP

As a result Modern English has SVO word order whereas Old English (and modern Dutch and German) have a basic SOV word order. However, Modern English still has remnants of the original SOV word order in "old-fashioned" kinds of expressions such as *I thee wed*. In short, as morphological distinctions vanished over the centuries, word order became stricter.

As discussed in chapter 4, in today's English we form questions by moving an auxiliary verb, if there is one, before the NP subject:

Can the girl kiss the boy?
Will the girl kiss the boy?
Has the girl kissed the boy yet?
Was the girl kissing the boy when you arrived?

However, if an auxiliary verb is absent, modern English requires the word *do* to spell out the tense of the sentence:

Does the girl kiss the boy often?
*Kisses the girl the boy often?

Older forms of English had a more general rule that moved the first verbal element, which meant that if no auxiliary occurred in the sentence, then the main verb moved. The question

Kisses the girl the boy often?

was grammatical in English through the time of Shakespeare. This more general verb movement rule still exists in languages like Dutch and German. In English the rule of question formation changed, so that now only auxiliary verbs move and if no auxiliary verb is present, a *do* fills its role. This rule change was motivated in part by the fact that in Old English, *the girl* and *the boy* would have been marked for case, so there was no possibility of misunderstanding who was kissing whom. In effect, the sentence would be:

Kisses the (nominative) girl the (accusative) boy often?

Modern English, with its rudimentary case system, defines grammatical relations structurally: the direct object is the NP that is sister to the verb. If the main verb were to move, this sisterhood configuration would be violated. The introduction of *do* allows the verb to remain in its base position, and the sentence thus retains the SVO word order that most plainly indicates the subject and object of the sentence. Another syntactic change in English affected the rules of comparative and superlative constructions. Today we form the comparative by adding *-er* to the adjective or by inserting *more* before it; the superlative is formed by adding *-est* or by inserting *most*. In Malory's *Tales of King Arthur*, written in 1470, double comparatives and double superlatives occur, which today are ungrammatical: *more gladder, more lower, moost royallest, moost shamefullest.*

Both Old English and Middle English permitted *split genitives*, that is, possessive constructs in which the words that describe the possessor occur on both sides of the head noun:

Inwæres   broþur   ond   Healfdenes (Old English)
Inwær's   brother   and   Healfden's
"Inwær's and Healfden's brother"

The Wife's tale of Bath (Middle English)
"The Wife of Bath's tale"

Modern English does not allow such structures, but it does permit rather complex genitive expressions to precede the head noun:

The man with the two small children's hat
The girl whose sister I'm dating's roommate
When does you guys's party begin? (Cf. When does your (pl.) party begin?)

When we study a language solely from written records, which is necessarily the case with languages such as Old or Middle English, we see only sentences that are grammatical unless ungrammatical sentences are used deliberately, perhaps as lines for a buffoon character in a play. Without native speakers to query, we can only infer what was ungrammatical. Such inference leads us to believe that expressions like *the Queen of England's crown* were ungrammatical in earlier periods of English. The title *The Wife's Tale of Bath* (rather than *The Wife of Bath's Tale*) in *The Canterbury Tales* supports this inference.

Once again it was the loss of case endings that resulted in this syntactic change. As the case system weakened, there was insufficient noun morphology to carry the semantic burden of expressing possession. Over the centuries the use of *'s* replaced the defunct genitive case, and in so doing generalized to syntactic units larger than merely the noun. The word order allowed in possessive constructs became more fixed and split genitives are now ungrammatical.

The big picture is that the loss of information that accompanies morphological simplification can be compensated for by more rigid rules of word order. Such syntactic changes may take centuries to be completed, and there are often intermediate stages.

Modern Brazilian Portuguese (BP) may illustrate one such intermediate stage of language change. Until the middle of the nineteenth century, speakers of BP didn't need to explicitly mention a subject pronoun because that information came from the person and number agreement on the verb, as illustrated for the verb *cozinhar* meaning "to cook."

cozinh<u>o</u>	I cook	cozinh<u>amos</u>	we cook
cozinh<u>as</u>	you cook		
cozinh<u>a</u>	he/she cooks	cozinh<u>am</u>	they/you (pl.) cook

At that time speakers dropped subjects in about 80 percent of their sentences, as in the second sentence of the following example:

A	Clara	sabe	fazer	tudo	muito	bem.
the	Clara	knows how	to do	everything	very	well

Cozinha		que	é	uma	maravilha.
cooks (3rd per.)		that	is	a	marvel

"Clara knows how to do everything well. She cooks wonderfully."

By the end of the twentieth century, subject-drop was reduced to 20 percent and the agreement endings were also reduced. In certain dialects only a two-way distinction is maintained: first-person singular is marked with *-o*, as in *cozinho*, and all other grammatical persons are marked with *-a*. While sentences without subjects are still grammatical in European Portuguese (spoken in Portugal), they are ungrammatical for most speakers of Modern BP, which requires the expression of an overt subject, for example *ela* "she" as follows:

A Clara sabe fazer tudo muito bem. Ela cozinha que é uma maravilha.

Many of the other Romance languages, including Italian, Spanish, Catalan, and European Portuguese, are still null-subject languages and maintain a rich verb morphology as illustrated for Italian in chapter 3. In the future null subjects may become ungrammatical for all speakers in BP. If so, BP will follow the route of another Romance language, French, which evolved from a richly inflected null-subject language in the thirteenth century to a language that now requires subject pronouns and that in its spoken form also has a very impoverished verb morphology.

Just as the loss of Old English noun and verb morphology resulted in stricter word order in Modern English, so the loss of agreement morphology in Brazilian Portuguese, and earlier in French, gave rise to a syntactic change from a null-subject grammar to one that requires subjects. In this respect Brazilian Portuguese is diverging from the other Romance languages, as French did in earlier times.

Lexical Change

Changes in the lexicon also occur, among which are changes in the lexical categories of words (i.e., their "parts of speech"), addition of new words, the "borrowing" of words from another language, the loss of words, and the shift in the meaning of words over time.

Change in Category

"Get Fuzzy" © Darby Conley/Dist. by United Feature Syndicate, Inc.

The words *food* and *verb* are ordinarily used as nouns, but Bucky the cat refuses to be so restricted and "wordifies" them into verbs. If we speakers of English adopt Bucky's usage, then *food* and *verb* will become verbs in addition to nouns. Recently, a radio announcer said that Congress was "to-ing and fro-ing" on a certain issue, to mean "wavering." This strange compound verb is derived from the adverb *to and fro*. In British English, *hoover* is a verb meaning "to vacuum up," derived from the proper noun *Hoover*, the name of a vacuum cleaner manufacturer. American police *Mirandize* arrested persons, meaning to read them their rights according to the Miranda rule. The judicial ruling was made in 1966, so we have a complete history of how a proper name became a verb. More recently the noun *text* has been "verbed" and means "to communicate by text message," and even more recent is the hijacking of the verb *twitter* as the name of a social networking and micro-blogging service.

Addition of New Words

And to bring in a new word by the head and shoulders, they leave out the old one.

MONTAIGNE (1533–1592)

One of the most obvious ways a language changes is through the addition of new words. Unlike grammatical change, which may take generations to notice, new words are readily apparent. Societies often require new words to describe changes in technology, sports, entertainment, and so on. Languages are accommodating and inventive in meeting these needs.

In chapter 3 we discussed some ways in which new words are born, such as through derivational processes, back-formations, and compounding. There are other ways that words may enter the vocabulary of a language, thus adding to the inventory of lexical items. These include out-and-out word coinage, deriving words from names, blending words to form new words, shortening old words to form new ones, forming acronyms, and borrowing words from other languages.

Word Coinage

Words may be created outright to fit some purpose. The advertising industry has added many words to English, such *as Kodak, nylon, Orlon,* and *Dacron.* Specific brand names such as *Xerox, Band-Aid, Kleenex, Jell-O, Brillo,* and *Vaseline* are now sometimes used as the generic name for different brands of these types of products. Some of these words were actually created from existing words (e.g., *Kleenex* from the word *clean* and *Jell-O* from *gel*).

The sciences have given us a raft of newly coined words over the ages. Words like *asteroid, neutron, genome, krypton, brontosaurus,* and *vaccine* were created to describe the objects or processes arising from scientific investigation.

A word so new that its spelling is still in doubt is *dot-com,* also seen in magazines as *.com, dot.com,* and even *dot com* without the hyphen. It means "a company whose primary business centers on the Internet." *Bling* (or *bling-bling*), meaning "gaudy jewelry," was a possible but nonexistent word like *blick* until a few years ago, and unless you have a recently published dictionary or use an online dictionary, you won't find an entry for *bling*. (Indeed, the word processor on which we are typing your book tells us that *bling* is a misspelling by underlining it in red.) Also new to this millennium are *Bollywood,* "the film industry of India," and *sudoku,* a "certain kind of puzzle." Sometimes words originally coined for one purpose, such as the company name *Google,* are put to work to serve a related purpose, such as *google,* meaning "to search on the Internet."

Greek roots borrowed into English have also provided a means for coining new words. *Thermos* "hot" plus *metron* "measure" gave us *thermometer.* From *akros* "topmost" and *phobia* "fear," we get *acrophobia,* "dread of heights." To avoid going out on Friday the thirteenth, you may say that you have *triskaidekaphobia,* a profound fear of the number 13. An ingenious cartoonist, Robert Osborn, has "invented" some phobias, to each of which he gives an appropriate name:[2]

logizomechanophobia	"fear of reckoning machines" from Greek *logizomai* "to reckon or compute" + *mekhane* "device" + *phobia*
ellipsosyllabophobia	"fear of words with a missing syllable" from Greek *elleipsis* "a falling short" + *syllabē* "syllable" + *phobia*
pornophobia	"fear of prostitutes" from Greek *porne* "harlot" + *phobia*

[2]From *An Osborn Festival of Phobias* by Robert Osborn and Eve Wengler. Copyright © 1971 Robert Osborn. Text copyright © 1971 Eve Wengler. Used by permission of Liveright Publishing Corporation.

Without a doubt the phobic TV detective Adrian Monk has, had, or will have all of these phobias in one episode or another.

Latin, like Greek, has also provided prefixes and suffixes that are used productively with both native and nonnative roots. The prefix *ex-* comes from Latin:

ex-husband   ex-wife   ex-sister-in-law   ex-teacher

The suffix *-able/-ible* is also Latin and can be attached to almost any English verb:

writable   readable   answerable   movable   learnable

Even new bound morphemes may enter the language. The prefix *e-*, as in *e-commerce*, *e-mail*, and *e-trade*, meaning "electronic," is barely two decades old, and most interestingly has given rise to the prefix *s-* as in *s-mail* to contrast with *e-mail*. The suffix *-gate*, meaning "scandal," which was derived from the Watergate scandal of the 1970s, may now be suffixed to a word to convey that meaning. Thus *Irangate* means a scandal involving Iran, and *Dianagate*, a British usage, refers to a scandal involving wiretapped conversations of the late Princess of Wales, Diana. A change currently under way is the use of *-peat* to mean "win a championship so many years in succession," as in *threepeat* and *fourpeat*, which we have observed in the newspaper.

Also so new that it hasn't made the dictionaries are words that take *-zilla* as a bound suffix with the meaning "huge or extreme," as in *shopzilla*, *bridezilla*, and the British band *Dogzilla*, with its source being the world-famous Japanese movie monster *Godzilla*. The bound prefix *uber-* of German origin meaning "the best" or "the most" allows myriad new words to be formed by "supersizing" old ones, as in *linguistics is uber-cool*, or *the jokes in this book are uber-lame*.

Words from Names

Eponyms are words that are coined from proper names and are another of the many creative ways that the vocabulary of a language expands. Here are some examples:

sandwich	Named for the fourth Earl of Sandwich, who put his food between two slices of bread so that he could eat while he gambled.
robot	After the mechanical creatures in the Czech writer Karel Capek's play *R.U.R.*, the initials standing for "Rossum's Universal Robots."
gargantuan	Named for Gargantua, the creature with a huge appetite created by Rabelais.
jumbo	After an elephant brought to the United States by P. T. Barnum. ("Jumbo olives" need not be as big as an elephant, however.)

We admit to ignorance of the Susan, an unknown servant from whom the compound *lazy susan* is derived; or the Betty or Charlotte or Chuck from whom we got *brown betty, charlotte russe,* or *chuck wagon.* We can point out, however, that *denim* was named for the material used for overalls and carpeting, which originally was imported *de Nîmes* ("from Nîmes") in France, and *argyle* from the kind of socks worn by the chiefs of Argyll of the Campbell clan in Scotland.

The word *paparazzo,* "a freelance photographer who doggedly pursues celebrities," was a little-known word until the death of Princess Diana in 1997, who was hounded by paparazzi (plural) before her fatal automobile accident. This eponym comes from the news photographer character Signor Paparazzo in the motion picture *La Dolce Vita.*

Blends

Blends are similar to compounds in that they are produced by combining two words, but parts of the words that are combined are deleted. *Smog,* from *smoke + fog; brunch,* from *breakfast* and *lunch; motel,* from *motor + hotel; infomercial,* from *info + commercial;* and *urinalysis,* from *urine + analysis* are examples of blends that have attained full lexical status in English. *Podcast* (*podcasting, podcaster*) is a relatively new word meaning "Internet audio broadcast" and recently joined the English language as a blend of *iPod* and *broadcast.* Lewis Carroll's *chortle,* from *chuckle + snort,* has achieved limited acceptance in English. Carroll is famous for both coining and blending words. In *Through the Looking-Glass,* he describes the "meanings" of the made-up words in "Jabberwocky" as follows:

> . . . "Brillig" means four o' clock in the afternoon—the time when you
> begin broiling things for dinner . . . "Slithy" means "lithe and slimy" . . .
> You see it's like a portmanteau—there are two meanings packed up into
> one word. . . . "Toves" are something like badgers—they're something
> like lizards—and they're something like corkscrews . . . also they make
> their nests under sun-dials—also they live on cheese. . . . To "gyre" is
> to go round and round like a gyroscope. To "gimble" is to make holes
> like a gimlet. And "the wabe" is the grass-plot round a sun-dial . . .
> It's called "wabe" . . . because it goes a long way before it and a long
> way behind it. . . . "Mimsy" is "flimsy and miserable" (there's another
> portmanteau . . . for you).

Carroll's "portmanteaus" are what we have called blends, and such words can become part of the regular lexicon.

Blending is even done by children. The blend *crocogator* from crocodile + alligator is attributed to three-year-old Elijah Peregrine. Grandmothers are not to be left out, and a Jewish one of African descent that we know came up with *shugeleh,* "darling," which we think is a blend of *sugar + bubeleh,* and which we confess we don't know how to spell. (*Bubeleh* is a Yiddish term of endearment.) And we recently heard the expression *the* [jʊd] (compare *the 'hood*), which we do not know how to spell (*the yud, the yood?*), and was applied to a neighborhood with many speakers of Yiddish, perhaps a blend of *Yiddish* and *neighborhood.* Finally, the social network Twitter has given us the new blend *twitterific.*

Reduced Words

Speakers tend to abbreviate words in various ways to shorten the messages they convey. We used to find this in telegrams and telexes. Now it is seen dramatically in the creativity used on messages typed into cell phones in text messaging and similar communication technologies. However, we will concern ourselves with *spoken* language and observe three reduction phenomena: *clipping, acronyms,* and *alphabetic abbreviations.*

Clipping is the abbreviation of longer words into shorter ones, such as *fax* for *facsimile,* the British word *telly* for *television, prof* for *professor, piano* for *pianoforte,* and *gym* for *gymnasium.* Once considered slang, these words have now become lexicalized, that is, full words in their own right. These are only a few examples of such clipped forms that are now used as whole words. Other examples are *ad, bike, math, gas, phone, bus,* and *van* (from *advertisement, bicycle, mathematics, gasoline, telephone, omnibus,* and *caravan*). More recently, *dis* and *rad* (from *disrespect* and *radical*) have entered the language, and *dis* has come to be used as a verb meaning "to show disrespect."

Acronyms are words derived from the initials of several words. Such words are pronounced as the spelling indicates: *NASA* [næsə] from *National Aeronautics* and *Space Administration, UNESCO* [yunɛsko] from *United Nations Educational, Scientific,* and *Cultural Organization,* and *UNICEF* [yunisɛf] from *United Nations International Children's Emergency Fund. Radar* from "*ra*dio *detecting and ranging,*" *laser* from "*l*ight *a*mplification by *s*timulated *e*mission of *r*adiation," *scuba* from "*s*elf-*c*ontained *u*nderwater *b*reathing *a*pparatus," and *RAM* from "*r*andom *a*ccess *m*emory" show the creative efforts of word coiners, as does *snafu,* which was coined by soldiers in World War II and is rendered in polite circles as "*s*ituation *n*ormal, *a*ll *f*ouled *u*p." Recently coined additions are *AIDS* (1980s), from the initials of *a*cquired *i*mmune *d*eficiency *s*yndrome, and *SARS* (2000s), from *s*evere *a*cute *r*espiratory *s*yndrome.

When the string of letters is not easily pronounced as a word, the "acronym" is produced by sounding out each letter, as in *NFL* [ɛnɛfɛl] for *National Football League, UCLA* [yusiele] for *University of California, Los Angeles,* and *MRI* [ɛ̃maraɪ] for *magnetic resonance imaging.* These special kinds of acronyms are sometimes called **alphabetic abbreviations.**

Acronyms and alphabetic abbreviations are being added to the vocabulary daily with the proliferation of computers and widespread use of the Internet, including *blog* (we*b* *log*), *jpeg* (*j*oint *p*hotographics *e*xpert *g*roup), *GUI,* pronounced "gooey," for *graphical user interface, PDA* (*personal digital assistant*), and *MP3* for *MPEG layer 3,* where *MPEG* itself is the acronym for *m*oving *p*icture *e*xperts *group.*

Unbelievable though it may seem, acronyms in use somewhere in the English-speaking world number into the tens of thousands if not hundreds of thousands, a dramatic nod to the creativity and changeability of human language.

Borrowings or Loan Words

Neither a borrower, nor a lender be.

WILLIAM SHAKESPEARE, *Hamlet,* c. 1600

Languages pay little attention to Polonius's admonition quoted above, and many are avid borrowers and lenders. **Borrowing** words from other languages is an important source of new words, which are called **loan words**. Borrowing occurs when one language adds a word or morpheme from another language to its own lexicon. This often happens in situations of language contact, when speakers of different languages regularly interact with one another, and especially where there are many bilingual or multilingual speakers.

The pronunciation of loan words is often (but not always) altered to fit the phonological rules of the borrowing language. For example, English borrowed *ensemble* [āsābəl] from French but pronounce it [ānsāmbəl], with [n] and [m] inserted, because English doesn't ordinarily have syllables centered on nasal vowels alone. Other borrowed words such as the composer's name *Bach* will often be pronounced as the original German [bax], with a final velar fricative, even though such a pronunciation does not conform to the rules of English.

Larger units than words may be borrowed. French provides us with *ménage à trois* [mẽnaʒ a tʀa], where [ʀ] is a uvular trill, meaning a "three-way romance," and which is pronounced in the French way by those who know French, but is also anglicized in various ways such as [mẽnadʒ a twa].

When an expression is borrowed and then translated into the borrowing language, such as *worldview* from German *Weltanschauung*, it is called a **loan translation**. *It goes without saying* from French *il va sans dire* is a loan translation from French. On the other hand, Spanish speakers eat *perros calientes*, a loan translation of *hot dogs* with an adjustment reversing the order of the adjective and noun, as required by the rules of Spanish syntax.

The lexicons of most languages can be divided into native words and loan words. A native word is one whose history or **etymology** can be traced back to the earliest known stages of the language.

A language may borrow a word directly or indirectly. A direct borrowing means that the borrowed item is a native word in the language from which it is borrowed. For example, *feast* was borrowed directly from French, along with a host of terms as a result of the Norman conquest. By contrast, the word *algebra* was borrowed from Spanish, which in turn had borrowed it from Arabic. Thus *algebra* was indirectly borrowed from Arabic, with Spanish as an intermediary. Some languages are heavy borrowers. Albanian has borrowed so heavily that few native words are retained. On the other hand, most Native American languages borrowed little from their neighbors.

English has borrowed extensively. Of the 20,000 or so words in common use, about three-fifths are borrowed. But of the 500 most frequently used words, only two-sevenths are borrowed, and because these words are used repeatedly in sentences—they are mostly function words—the actual frequency of appearance of native words is about 80 percent. The frequently used function words *and*, *be*, *have*, *it*, *of*, *the*, *to*, *will*, *you*, *on*, *that*, and *is* are all native to English.

Language may borrow not only words and phrases but other linguistic units as well. We saw earlier how English in effect borrowed the phonemes /v/ and /ʒ/ from French. The bound morpheme suffixes *ible/able* were also borrowed from French, arriving in English by hitchhiking on French words such as *incredible* but soon attaching themselves to native words such as *drinkable*.

History through Loan Words

A morsel of genuine history is a thing so rare as to be always valuable.

THOMAS JEFFERSON, in a letter to John Adams, 1817

We may trace the history of the English-speaking peoples by studying the kinds of loan words in their language, their source, and when they were borrowed. Until the Norman Conquest in 1066, the Angles, the Saxons, and the Jutes inhabited England. They were of Germanic origin when they came to Britain in the fifth century to eventually become the English. Originally, they spoke Germanic dialects, from which Old English developed. These dialects contained some Latin borrowings but few foreign elements beyond that. These Germanic tribes had displaced the earlier Celtic inhabitants, whose influence on Old English was confined to a few Celtic place names. (The modern languages Welsh, Irish, and Scots Gaelic are descended from the Celtic dialects.)

The Normans spoke French, and for three centuries after the Conquest, French was used for all affairs of state and for most commercial, social, and cultural matters. The West Saxon literary language was abandoned, but regional varieties of English continued to be used in homes, churches, and the marketplace. This was a situation of language contact between French, the culturally dominant language at the time, and English. During these three centuries, vast numbers of French words entered English, of which the following are representative:

government	crown	prince	estate	parliament
nation	jury	judge	crime	sue
attorney	saint	miracle	charity	court
lechery	virgin	value	pray	mercy
religion	chapel	royal	money	society

Until the Normans came, when an Englishman slaughtered an ox for food, he ate *ox*. If it was a pig, he ate *pig*. If it was a sheep, he ate *sheep*. However, "ox" served at the Norman tables was *beef* (*boeuf*), "pig" was *pork* (*porc*), and "sheep" was *mutton* (*mouton*). These words were borrowed from French into English, as were the food-preparation words *boil*, *fry*, *stew*, and *roast*. Over the years French foods have given English a flood of borrowed words for menu preparers:

aspic	bisque	bouillon	brie	brioche
canapé	caviar	consommé	coq au vin	coupe
crêpe	croissant	croquette	crouton	escargot
fondue	mousse	pâté	quiche	ragout

English borrowed many "learned" words from foreign sources during the Renaissance. In 1475 William Caxton introduced the printing press in England. By 1640, 55,000 books had been printed in English. The authors of these books used many Greek and Latin words, which consequently entered the language.

From Greek came *drama, comedy, tragedy, scene, botany, physics, zoology,* and *atomic.* Latin loan words in English are numerous. They include:

bonus   scientific   exit   alumnus   quorum   describe

During the ninth and tenth centuries, Scandinavian raiders, who eventually settled in the British Isles, left their traces in the English language. The pronouns *they, their,* and *them* are loan words from Old Norse, the predecessor of modern Danish, Norwegian, and Swedish. This period is the only time that English ever borrowed pronouns.

Bin, flannel, clan, slogan, and *whisky* are all words of Celtic origin, borrowed at various times from Welsh, Scots Gaelic, or Irish. Dutch was a source of borrowed words, too, many of which are related to shipping: *buoy, freight, leak, pump, yacht.* From German came *quartz, cobalt,* and—as we might guess—*sauerkraut.* From Italian, many musical terms, including words describing opera houses, have been borrowed: *opera, piano, virtuoso, balcony,* and *mezzanine.* Italian also gave us *influenza,* which was derived from the Italian word for "influence" because the Italians were convinced that the disease was *influenced* by the stars.

Many scientific words were borrowed indirectly from Arabic, because early Arab scholarship in these fields was quite advanced. *Alcohol, algebra, cipher,* and *zero* are a small sample. Spanish has loaned us (directly) *barbecue, cockroach,* and *ranch,* as well as *California,* literally "hot furnace." In America, the English-speaking colonists borrowed from Native American languages, another situation of language contact, but in which English is the culturally dominant language. Native American languages provided us with *hickory, chipmunk, opossum,* and *squash,* to mention only a few. Nearly half the names of U.S. states are borrowed from one American Indian language or another.

English has borrowed from Yiddish. Many non-Jews as well as non-Yiddish-speaking Jews use Yiddish words. There was once even a bumper sticker proclaiming: "Marcel Proust is a yenta." *Yenta* is a Yiddish word meaning "gossipy woman." *Lox,* meaning "smoked salmon," and *bagel,* "a doughnut dipped in cement," now belong to English, as well as Yiddish expressions like *chutzpah, schmaltz, schlemiel, schmuck, schmo, schlep,* and *kibitz.*

English is a lender of many words to other languages, especially in the areas of technology, sports, and entertainment. Words and expressions such as *jazz, whisky, blue jeans, rock music, supermarket, baseball, picnic,* and *computer* have been borrowed from English into languages as diverse as Twi, Hungarian, Russian, and Japanese.

Loss of Words

Pease porridge hot
Pease porridge cold
Pease porridge in the pot nine days old
NURSERY RHYME

Languages can also lose words, although the departure of an old word is never as striking as the arrival of a new one. When a new word comes into vogue, its unusual presence draws attention, but a word is lost through inattention—nobody thinks of it, nobody uses it, and it fades away.

A reading of Shakespeare's works shows that English has lost many words, such as these taken from *Romeo and Juliet*: *beseem*, "to be suitable," *mammet*, "a doll or puppet," *wot*, "to know," *gyve*, "a fetter," *fain*, "gladly," and *wherefore*, "why," as in Juliet's plaintive cry: "O Romeo, Romeo! wherefore art thou Romeo," in which she is questioning why he is so named, not his current whereabouts.

More recently, there are expressions used by your grandparents that have already been lost. For example, *two bits*, meaning "twenty-five cents," is no longer used; nor is *lickety-split*, meaning "very fast." And even words used by your parents (and us) sound dated, for example, *groovy* ("excellent"), *davenport* ("sofa"), and *grass* and *Mary Jane*, both referring to "marijuana." The word *stile*, meaning "steps crossing a fence or gate," is no longer widely understood. Other similar words for describing rural objects are fading out of the language as a result of urbanization. *Pease*, from which *pea* is a back-formation, is gone, and *porridge*, meaning "boiled cereal grain," is falling out of usage, although it is sustained by a discussion of its ideal serving temperature in the children's story *Goldilocks and the Three Bears* and its appearance on Harry Potter's breakfast table.

Technological change may also be the cause for the loss of words. *Acutiator* once meant "sharpener of weapons," and *tormentum* once meant "siege engine." Advances in warfare have put these terms out of business. Although one still finds the words *buckboard*, *buggy*, *dogcart*, *hansom*, *surrey*, and *tumbrel* in the dictionary—all of them referring to subtly different kinds of horse-drawn carriages—progress in transportation is likely to render these terms obsolete and eventually they will be lost.

Semantic Change

> The language of this country being always upon the flux, the Struldbruggs of one age do not understand those of another, neither are they able after two hundred years to hold any conversation (farther than by a few general words) with their neighbors the mortals, and thus they lie under the disadvantage of living like foreigners in their own country.
>
> **JONATHAN SWIFT,** *Gulliver's Travels*, 1726

We have seen that a language may gain or lose lexical items. Additionally, the meaning or semantic representation of words may change, by becoming broader or narrower, or by shifting.

Broadening

When the meaning of a word becomes broader, it means everything it used to mean and more. The Middle English word *dogge* referred to a specific breed of dog, but was eventually **broadened** to encompass all members of the species *canis familiaris.* The word *holiday* originally meant a day of religious significance, from "holy day." Today the word refers to any day that we do not have to work. *Picture* used to mean "painted representation," but now you can take a picture with a camera, not to mention a cell phone. *Quarantine* once had the restricted meaning of "forty days' isolation," and *manage* once meant simply to handle a horse.

More recent broadenings, spurred by the computer age, are *computer, mouse, cookie, cache, virus,* and *bundle. Footage* use to refer to a certain length of film or videotape, but nowadays it means any excerpt from the electronic video media such as DVDs, irrespective of whether its length can be measured in feet. *Google* was broadened first from the name of a company to a verb meaning "to use that company's search engine on the Internet," and from there further broadened to simply "search the Internet."

Narrowing

In the King James Version of the Bible (1611 C.E.), God says of the herbs and trees, "to you they shall be for meat" (Genesis 1:29). To a speaker of seventeenth-century English, *meat* meant "food," and *flesh* meant "meat." Since that time, semantic change has narrowed the meaning of *meat* to what it is in Modern English. The word *deer* once meant "beast" or "animal," as its German cognate *Tier* still does. The meaning of *deer* has been narrowed to a particular kind of animal. Similarly, the word *hound* used to be the general term for "dog," like German *Hund.* Today *hound* means a special kind of dog, one used for hunting. *Skyline* once meant "horizon" but has been narrowed to mean "the outline of a city at the horizon."

Meaning Shifts

The third kind of semantic change that a lexical item may undergo is a shift in meaning. The word *knight* once meant "youth" but shifted to "mounted man-at-arms." *Lust* used to mean simply "pleasure," with no negative or sexual overtones. *Lewd* was merely "ignorant," and *immoral* meant "not customary." *Silly* used to mean "happy" in Old English. By the Middle English period it had come to mean "naive," and only in Modern English does it mean "foolish." The overworked Modern English word *nice* meant "ignorant" a thousand years ago. When Juliet tells Romeo, "I am too *fond,*" she is not claiming she likes Romeo too much. She means "I am too *foolish.*"

Reconstructing "Dead" Languages

The living languages, as they were called by the Harvard fellows, were little more than cheap imitations, low distortions. Italian, like Spanish and German, particularly represented the loose political passions, bodily appetites, and absent morals of decadent Europe.

MATTHEW PEARL, *The Dante Club,* 2003

None of your living languages for Miss Blimber. They must be dead—stone dead—and then Miss Blimber dug them up like a Ghoul.

CHARLES DICKENS, *Dombey and Son,* 1848

"Shoe" by Gary Brookins/Chris Cassatt. Copyright 1989 Tribune Media Services. Reprinted with permission.

Despite the disdain for the modern languages expressed in Matthew Pearl's book and by Miss Blimber, it is through the comparative study of the living languages that linguists are able to learn about older languages that left no written record, and the changes that occurred over time.

The Nineteenth-Century Comparativists

When agreement is found in words in two languages, and so frequently that rules may be drawn up for the shift in letters from one to the other, then there is a fundamental relationship between the two languages.

RASMUS RASK (1787–1832)

The chief goal of the nineteenth-century historical and comparative linguists was to develop and elucidate the genetic relationships that exist among the world's languages. They aimed to establish the major language families of the world and to define principles for the classification of languages. They based their theories on observations of regular sound correspondences among certain languages. They proposed that languages displaying systematic similarities and differences must have descended from a common source language—that is, were genetically related. Their work grew out of earlier research.

As a child, Sir William Jones had an astounding propensity for learning languages, including so-called dead ones such as Ancient Greek and Latin. While residing in India he added Sanskrit to his studies and observed that Sanskrit bore to Greek and Latin "a stronger affinity . . . than could possibly have been produced by accident." Jones suggested that these three languages had "sprung from a common source" and that probably Germanic and Celtic had the same origin.

Earlier stage:[a]	bh	dh	gh	b	d	g	p	t	k
	↓	↓	↓	↓	↓	↓	↓	↓	↓
Later stage:	b	d	g	p	t	k	f	θ	x (or h)

FIGURE 11.2 | Grimm's Law, an early Germanic sound shift. Grimm's Law can be expressed in terms of natural classes of speech sounds: Voiced aspirates become unaspirated; voiced stops become voiceless; voiceless stops become fricatives.

[a]This "earlier stage" is Indo-European. The symbols bh, dh, and gh are breathy voiced stop consonants. These phonemes are often called "voiced aspirates."

Following up on Jones's research, the German linguist Franz Bopp pointed out relationships among Sanskrit, Latin, Greek, Persian, and Germanic. At the same time, a young Danish scholar named Rasmus Rask corroborated these results, and brought Lithuanian and Armenian into the relationship as well. Rask was the first scholar to describe formally the regularity of certain phonological differences of related languages.

Rask's work inspired the German linguist Jakob Grimm (of fairy-tale fame), who published a four-volume treatise (1819–1822) that specified the regular sound correspondences among Sanskrit, Greek, Latin, and the Germanic languages. Not only did the *similarities* intrigue Grimm, but also the systematic nature of the *differences*. Where Latin has a [p], English often has an [f]; where Latin has a [t], English often has a [θ]; where Latin has a [k], English often has an [h].

Grimm posited a far earlier language (which we now refer to as Indo-European) from which all these languages evolved. He explained the sound correspondences by means of rules of phonological change (which historical linguists called **sound shift**, or **sound change**). Grimm's major discovery was that certain rules of sound change that applied to the Germanic family of languages, including the ancestors of English, did not apply to Sanskrit, Greek, and Latin. This accounted very nicely for many of the regular differences between the Germanic languages and the others. Because the sound changes discovered by Grimm were so strikingly regular, they became known as **Grimm's Law**, illustrated in Figure 11.2.

Cognates

Cognates are words in related languages that developed from the same ancestral root, such as English *horn* and Latin *cornū*. Cognates often, but not always, have the same meaning in the different languages. From cognates we can observe sound correspondences and from them deduce sound changes. In Figure 11.3 the regular correspondence *p-p-f* of cognates from Sanskrit, Latin, and Germanic (represented by English) indicates that the languages are genetically related. Indo-European **p* is posited as the origin of the *p-p-f* correspondence.[3]

---

[3]The asterisk before a letter indicates a reconstructed sound, not an unacceptable form. This use of the asterisk occurs only in this chapter.

"Shouldn't a unicorn be
called a uniHORN?"

"Family Circus" © Bil Keane, Inc. Reprinted with permission of King Features Syndicate.

Indo-European	Sanskrit	Latin	English
*p	p	p	f
	pitar-	pater	father
	pad-	ped-	foot
	No cognate	piscis	fish
	paśu[a]	pecu	fee

FIGURE 11.3 | Cognates of Indo-European *p.

[a] *ś* is a sibilant pronounced differently from *s*.

Figure 11.4 is a more detailed chart of correspondences, showing an example of each regular correspondence. For each line in the chart linguists can identify many further correspondences such as Sanskrit *pād-*, Latin *ped-*, and English *foot* for p-p-f, thereby showing the consistent and systematic relationships that lead to the reconstruction of the Indo-European sound shown in the first column.

Sanskrit underwent the fewest consonant changes (has more sounds in common with Indo-European), Latin somewhat more, and Germanic (under Grimm's Law) underwent almost a complete restructuring. The changes we observe are changes to the phonemes and phonological rules, and all words with those phonemes will reflect those changes (but see the "caveat" in the following paragraph). If we imagine that the changes happened independently to individual words, rather than individual sounds, we could not explain why so many words

Indo-European	Sanskrit		Latin		English	
*p	p	pitar-	p	pater	f	father
*t	t	trayas	t	trēs	θ	three
*k	ś	śun	k	canis	h	hound
*b	b	No cognate	b	labium	p	lip
*d	d	dva-	d	duo	t	two
*g	j	ajras	g	ager	k	acre
*bh	bh	bhrātar-	f	frāter	b	brother
*dh	dh	dhā	f	fē-ci	d	do
*gh	h	vah-	h	veh-ō	g	wagon

FIGURE 11.4 | Some Indo-European sound correspondences.

beginning with /p/ in Sanskrit and Latin just happen to begin with /f/ in Germanic, and so on. It would far exceed the possibilities of coincidence. It is the fact that the changes are in the phonology of the languages that has resulted in the remarkably regular, pervasive correspondences that allow us to reconstruct much of the Indo-European sound system.

Grimm noted that there were exceptions to the regular correspondences he observed. He stated: "The sound shift is a general tendency; it is not followed in every case." Several decades later, in 1875, Karl Verner explained some of the exceptions to Grimm's Law. He formulated **Verner's Law** to show why Indo-European *p*, *t*, and *k* failed to correspond to *f*, *θ*, and *x* in certain cases:

> *Verner's Law:* When the preceding vowel was unstressed *f*, *θ*, and *x* underwent a further change to *b*, *d*, and *g*.

Encouraged by the regularity of sound change, a group of young nineteenth-century linguists proposed the **Neo-Grammarian hypothesis**, which says that sound shifts are not merely tendencies (as Grimm claimed), but apply in *all* words that meet their environment. If exceptions were nevertheless observed, it was trusted that further laws would be discovered to explain them, just as Verner's Law explained the exceptions to Grimm's Law. The **Neogrammarians** viewed linguistics as a natural science and therefore believed that laws of sound change were unexceptionable natural laws. The "laws" they put forth often did have exceptions, however, which could not always be explained as dramatically as Verner's Law explained the exceptions to Grimm's Law. Still, the work of these linguists provides important data and insights into language change and why such changes occur.

The linguistic work that we have been discussing had some influence on Charles Darwin, and in turn, Darwin's theory of evolution had a profound influence on linguistics and on all science. Some linguists thought that languages had a "life cycle" and developed according to evolutionary laws. In addition, it was believed that every language could be traced to a common ancestor. This theory of biological naturalism has an element of truth to it, but it is an oversimplification of how languages change and evolve into other languages.

Comparative Reconstruction

... Philologists who chase
A panting syllable through time and space
Start it at home, and hunt it in the dark,
To Gaul, to Greece, and into Noah's Ark.

WILLIAM COWPER, "Retirement," 1782

When languages resemble one another in ways not attributable to chance or borrowing or to general principles of Universal Grammar, we may conclude they are descended from a common source. That is, they evolved via linguistic change from an ancestral protolanguage.

The similarity of the basic vocabulary of languages such as English, German, Danish, Dutch, Norwegian, and Swedish is too pervasive for chance or borrowing. We therefore conclude that these languages have a common parent, Proto-Germanic. There are no written records of Proto-Germanic, and certainly no native speakers alive today. Proto-Germanic is a partially reconstructed language whose properties have been deduced based on its descendants. In addition to related vocabulary, the Germanic languages share grammatical properties such as similar sets of irregular verbs, particularly the verb *to be*, and syntactic rules such as the verb (or auxiliary) movement rule discussed earlier in this chapter, further supporting their relatedness.

Once we know or suspect that several languages are related, their protolanguage may be partially determined by **comparative reconstruction**. One proceeds by applying the **comparative method**, which we illustrate with the following brief example.

Restricting ourselves to English, German, and Swedish, we find the word for "man" is *man* [mæn], *Mann* [man], and *man* [man], respectively. This is one of many word sets in which we can observe the regular sound correspondence [m]-[m]-[m] and [n]-[n]-[n] in the three languages. Based on this evidence, the comparative method has us reconstruct *mVn* as the word for "man" in Proto-Germanic. The V indicates a vowel whose quality we are unsure of because, despite the similar spelling, the vowel is phonetically different in the various Germanic languages, and it is unclear how to reconstruct it without further evidence.

Although we are confident that we can reconstruct much of Proto-Germanic with relative accuracy, we can never be sure, and many details remain obscure. To build confidence in the comparative method, we can apply it to Romance languages such as French, Italian, Spanish, and Portuguese. Their protolanguage is the well-known Latin, so we can verify the method by testing it against written records of Latin. Consider the following data, focusing on the initial consonant of each word. In these data, *ch* in French is [ʃ], and *c* in the other languages is [k].

French	Italian	Spanish	Portuguese	English
cher	caro	caro	caro	"dear"
champ	campo	campo	campo	"field"
chandelle	candela	candela	candeia	"candle"

The French [ʃ] corresponds to [k] in the three other languages. This regular sound correspondence, [ʃ]-[k]-[k]-[k], supports the view that French, Italian, Spanish, and Portuguese descended from a common language. The comparative method leads to the reconstruction of [k] in "dear," "field," and "candle" of the parent language, and shows that [k] underwent a change to [ʃ] in French, but not in Italian, Spanish, or Portuguese, which retained the original [k] of the parent language, Latin.

To use the comparative method, analysts identify regular sound correspondences in the cognates of potentially related languages. For each correspondence, they deduce the most likely sound in the parent language. In this way, much of the sound system of the parent may be reconstructed. The various phonological changes in the development of each daughter language as it descended and changed from the parent are then identified. Sometimes the sound that analysts choose in their reconstruction of the parent language is the one that appears most frequently in the correspondence. This is the "majority rules" principle, which we illustrated with the four Romance languages.

Other considerations may outweigh the majority rules principle. The likelihood of certain phonological changes may persuade the analyst to reconstruct a less frequently occurring sound, or even a sound that does not occur in the correspondence. Consider the data in these four hypothetical languages:

Language A	Language B	Language C	Language D
hono	hono	fono	vono
hari	hari	fari	veli
rahima	rahima	rafima	levima
hor	hor	for	vol

Wherever Languages A and B have an *h*, Language C has an *f* and Language D has a *v*. Therefore, we have the sound correspondence *h-h-f-v*. Using the majority rule principle, we might first consider reconstructing the sound *h* in the parent language, but from other data on historical change, and from phonetic research, we know that *h* seldom becomes *v*. The reverse, /f/ and /v/ becoming [h], occurs both historically and as a phonological rule and has an acoustic explanation. Therefore, linguists reconstruct an **f* in the parent, and posit the sound change "*f* becomes *h*" in Languages A and B, and "*f* becomes *v*" in Language D. One obviously needs experience and knowledge to conclude this.

The other correspondences are not problematic as far as these data are concerned:

o-o-o-o   n-n-n-n   a-a-a-e   r-r-r-l   m-m-m-m

They lead to the reconstructed forms **o*, **n*, **a*, **r*, and **m* for the parent language, and the sound changes "*a* becomes *e*" and "*r* becomes *l*" in Language D. These are natural sound changes found in many of the world's languages.

It is now possible to reconstruct the words of the protolanguage. They are **fono*, **fari*, **rafima*, and **for*. In this example, Language D is the most innovative of the three languages, because it has undergone three sound changes.

Language C is the most conservative in that it is identical to the protolanguage insofar as these data are concerned.

The sound changes seen in the previous illustrations are examples of **unconditioned sound change**. The changes occurred irrespective of phonetic context. Following is an example of **conditioned sound change**, taken from three dialects of Italian:

Standard	Northern	Lombard	
fisːo	fiso	fis	"fixed"
kasːa	kasa	kasə	"cabinet"

The correspondence sets are:

f-f-f   i-i-i   sː-s-s   o-o-<>[4]   k-k-k   a-a-a   a-a-ə

It is straightforward to reconstruct *f, *i, and *k. Knowing that a long consonant like sː commonly becomes s (recall Old English fː became f), we reconstruct *sː for the sː-s-s correspondence. A shortening change took place in the Northern and Lombard dialects.

There is evidence in these (very limited) data for a weakening of word-final vowels, again a change we discussed earlier for English. We reconstruct *o for o-o-<> and *a for a-a-ə. In Lombard, a conditioned sound change took place. The sound o was deleted in word-final position, but remained o elsewhere. The sound a became ə in word-final position and remained a elsewhere. As far as we can tell from the data presented, the conditioning factor is word-final position. Vowels in other positions do not undergo change.

We reconstruct the protodialect as having had the words *fisːo meaning "fixed" and *kasːa meaning "cabinet."

It is by means of the comparative method that nineteenth-century linguists were able to initiate the reconstruction of Indo-European, the long-lost ancestral language so aptly conceived by Jones, Bopp, Rask, and Grimm, a language that flourished about 6,000 years ago.

Historical Evidence

You know my method. It is founded upon the observance of trifles.

SIR ARTHUR CONAN DOYLE, "The Boscombe Valley Mystery," in *The Memoirs of Sherlock Holmes,* 1891

The comparative method is not the only way to explore the history of a language or language family, and it may prove unable to answer certain questions because data are lacking or because reconstructions are untenable. For example, how do we know positively how Shakespeare or Chaucer or the author of *Beowulf* pronounced their versions of English? The comparative method leaves many details in doubt, and we have no recordings that give us direct knowledge.

---

[4] The empty angled brackets indicate a loss of the sound.

For many languages, written records go back more than a thousand years. Linguists study these records to find out how languages were once pronounced. The spelling in early manuscripts tells us a great deal about the sound systems of older forms of modern languages. Two words spelled differently were probably pronounced differently. Once several orthographic contrasts are identified, good guesses can be made as to actual pronunciation. For example, because we spell *Mary, merry,* and *marry* differently, we may conclude that at one time most speakers pronounced them differently, probably [meri], [mɛri], and [mæri]. For at least one modern American dialect, only /ɛ/ can occur before /r/, so the three words are all pronounced [mɛri]. That dialect is the result of a sound shift in which both /e/ and /æ/ shifted to /ɛ/ when followed immediately by /r/. This is another instance of a conditioned sound change.

Various documents from the past can be examined for evidence. Private letters are an excellent source of data. Linguists prefer letters written by naive spellers, who will misspell words according to the way they pronounce them. For instance, at one point in English history, all words spelled with *er* in their stems were pronounced as if they were spelled with *ar,* just as in modern British English *clerk* and *derby* are pronounced "clark" and "darby." Some poor speller kept writing *parfet* for *perfect,* which helped linguists discover the older pronunciation.

Clues are also provided by the writings of the prescriptive grammarians of the period. Between 1550 and 1750 scholars known as orthoepists attempted to preserve the "purity" of English. In prescribing how people should speak, they told us how people actually spoke. An orthoepist alive in the United States today might write in a manual: "It is incorrect to pronounce *Cuba* with a final *r.*" Future scholars would know that some speakers of English pronounced it that way.

Some of the best clues to earlier pronunciation are provided by puns and rhymes in literature. Two words rhyme if the vowels and final consonants are the same. When a poet rhymes the verb *found* with the noun *wound,* it strongly suggests that the vowels of these two words were identical:

BENVOLIO: . . . 'tis in vain to seek him here that means not to be found.
ROMEO: He jests at scars that never felt a wound.

Shakespeare's rhymes are helpful in reconstructing the sound system of Elizabethan English. The rhyming of *convert* with *depart* in Sonnet XI strengthens the conclusion that *er* was pronounced as *ar.*

Most powerfully, the above techniques may be combined with the comparative method. Dialect differences discovered through written records may permit comparison of the pronunciation of various words in several dialects. On that basis we can draw conclusions about earlier forms and see what changes took place in the inventory of sounds and in the phonological rules. We illustrated one such case with three Italian dialects on the preceding page.

The historical comparativists working on languages with written records have a challenging job, but not nearly as challenging as that of scholars who are attempting to discover genetic relationships among languages with no written history. Linguists must first transcribe large amounts of language data from all the languages; analyze them phonologically, morphologically, and syntactically;

and establish a basis for relatedness such as similarities in basic vocabulary and regular sound correspondences not resulting from chance or borrowing. Only then can the comparative method be applied to reconstruct the extinct protolanguage.

Proceeding in this manner, linguists have discovered many relationships among Native American languages and have successfully reconstructed Amerindian protolanguages. Similar achievements have been made with the numerous languages spoken in Africa. The large number of African languages have been grouped into four overarching families: Afroasiatic, Nilo-Saharan, Niger-Congo, and Khoisan. For example, Somali is in the Afroasiatic family; Zulu is in the Niger-Congo family; and Hottentot, spoken in South Africa, is in the Khoisan family. These familial divisions are subject to revision if new discoveries or analyses deem it necessary.

Extinct and Endangered Languages

Any language is the supreme achievement of a uniquely human collective genius, as divine and unfathomable a mystery as a living organism.

MICHAEL KRAUSS, in a speech to the Linguistic Society of America, 1991

I am always sorry when any language is lost, because languages are the pedigree of nations.

SAMUEL JOHNSON (1709–1784)

A language dies and becomes extinct when no children learn it. Linguists have identified several ways in which a language might cease to exist, leastwise in its spoken form.

A language may die out more or less suddenly when all of the speakers of the language themselves die or are killed. Such was the case with Tasmanian languages, once spoken on the island of Tasmania, and Nicoleño, a Native American Indian language once spoken in California.

Similarly, a language may cease to exist relatively abruptly when its speakers all stop speaking the language for the duration of their lifetimes. Often the reason for this radical change is survival under the threat of political repression or even genocide. Indigenous languages embedded in other cultures suffer death this way. In order to avoid being identified as "natives," speakers simply stop speaking their native language. Children are unable to learn a language that is not spoken to them, so when the last speaker dies, the language dies.

Most commonly, languages that become extinct do so gradually, often over several generations. This happens to minority languages that are in contact with a dominant language, much as American Indian languages are in contact with English. In each generation, fewer and fewer children learn the language until there are no new learners. The language is said to be dead when the last generation of speakers dies out. Cornish suffered this fate in Britain in the eighteenth century (though recent attempts at revival have resulted in about three hundred nonnative speakers of the language), as have many Native American languages in both North and South America.

While not common, some languages suffer "partial death" in that they survive only in specific contexts, such as a liturgical language. Latin and (at one time) Hebrew are such languages. Latin evolved into the Romance languages and by the ninth century there were few if any peoples speaking Latin in daily situations. Today its use is confined to scholarly and religious contexts.

Many Native American languages are experiencing a reduction in the number of native speakers over time. Only 20 percent of the remaining indigenous languages in the United States are being acquired by children. Hundreds have already ceased to be written or spoken. In the 1500s, at the time of the first European contact, there were over 1,000 indigenous languages spoken throughout the Americas. Once widely spoken American Indian languages such as Comanche, Apache, and Cherokee have fewer native speakers every generation.

Doomed languages have existed throughout time. The Indo-European languages Hittite and Tocharian no longer exist. Hittite disappeared 3,500 years ago, and both dialects of Tocharian gave up the ghost around 1000 C.E.

Dialects, too, may become extinct. Many dialects spoken in the United States are considered endangered by linguists. For example, the sociolinguist Walt Wolfram is studying the dialect spoken on Ocracoke Island off the coast of North Carolina. One reason for the study is to preserve the dialect, which is in danger of extinction because so many young Ocracokers leave the island and raise their children elsewhere, a case of gradual *dialect* death. Vacationers and retirees are diluting the dialect-speaking population, because they are attracted to the island by its unique character, including, ironically, the quaint speech of the islanders.

Linguists have placed many languages on an endangered list. They attempt to preserve these languages by studying and documenting their grammars—the phonetics, phonology, and so on—and by recording for posterity the speech of the last few speakers. Each language provides new evidence on the nature of human cognition through its grammar. In its literature, poetry, ritual speech, and word structure, each language stores the collective intellectual achievements of a culture, offering unique perspectives on the human condition. The disappearance of a language is tragic; not only are these insights lost, but the major medium through which a culture maintains and renews itself is gone as well.

Linguists are not alone in their preservation efforts. Under the sponsorship of language clubs, and occasionally even governments, adults and children learn an endangered language as a symbol of the culture. Gael Linn is a private organization in Ireland that runs language classes in Irish (Gaelic) for adults. Hundreds of public schools in Ireland and Northern Ireland are conducted entirely in Gaelic. In the U.S. state of Hawaii, a movement is under way to preserve and teach Hawaiian, the native language of the islands.

This attempt to slow down or reverse the dying out of a language is also illustrated by the French in Quebec. In 1961, the Quebec Office of the French Language was formed to standardize the dialect of French spoken in Quebec, but ironically refuses to do so for fear of reducing the interintelligibility with other French-speaking communities. It is believed that standardization would linguistically isolate Quebecers and lead to the extinction of French in Canada.

Instead, the office uses its powers to promote the use of French, irrespective of dialect.

A stunning example of the revival of a dormant language occurred in Israel. For centuries, classical Hebrew was used only in religious ceremonies, but today, with some modernization, it has become the national language of Israel. The Academy of the Hebrew Language in Israel undertook a task that had never been done in the history of humanity—to awaken an ancient written language to serve the daily colloquial needs of the people. Twenty-three lexicologists worked with the Bible and the Talmud to add new words to the language. While there is some attempt to keep the language "pure," the academy has given way to popular pressure. Thus, a bank check is called a *check* [tʃek] in the singular and pluralized by adding the Hebrew plural suffix *-im* to form *check-im*, although the Hebrew word *hamcha'ah* was proposed. Similarly, *lipstick* has triumphed over *s'faton* and *pajama* over *chalifat-sheinah* (lit. sleeping suit).

The United Nations, too, is concerned about endangered languages. In 1991, the United Nations Educational, Scientific, and Cultural Organization (UNESCO) passed a resolution that states:

> As the disappearance of any one language constitutes an irretrievable loss to mankind, it is for UNESCO a task of great urgency to respond to this situation by promoting . . . the description—in the form of grammars, dictionaries, and texts—of endangered and dying languages.

The documentation and preservation of dying languages is not only important for social and cultural reasons. There is also a scientific reason for studying these languages. Through examining a wide array of different types of languages, linguists can develop a comprehensive theory of language that accounts for both its universal and language-specific properties.

The Genetic Classification of Languages

The Sanskrit language, whatever be its antiquity, is of a wonderful structure, more perfect than the Greek, more copious than the Latin, and more exquisitely refined than either, yet bearing to both of them a stronger affinity, both in the roots of verbs and in the forms of grammar, than could possibly have been produced by accident; so strong, indeed, that no philologer could examine all three, without believing that they have sprung from some common source, which, perhaps, no longer exists. . . .

SIR WILLIAM JONES (1746–1794)

We have discussed how different languages evolve from one language and how historical and comparative linguists classify languages into families such as Germanic or Romance and reconstruct earlier forms of the ancestral language. When we examine the languages of the world, we perceive similarities and differences among them that provide evidence for degrees of relatedness or for nonrelatedness.

Counting to five in English, German, and Vietnamese shows similarities between English and German not shared by Vietnamese (shown with tones omitted):

English	German	Vietnamese
one	eins	mot
two	zwei	hai
three	drei	ba
four	vier	bon
five	fünf	nam

The similarity between English and German is pervasive. Sometimes it is extremely obvious (*man/Mann*), but at other times a little less obvious (*child/Kind*). No regular similarities or differences apart from those resulting from chance are found between them and Vietnamese.

Pursuing the metaphor of human genealogy, we say that English, German, Norwegian, Danish, Swedish, Icelandic, and so on are sisters in that they descended from one parent and are more closely related to one another than any of them are to non-Germanic languages such as French or Russian.

The Romance languages are also sister languages whose parent is Latin. If we carry the family metaphor to an extreme, we might describe the Germanic languages and the Romance languages as cousins, because their respective parents, Proto-Germanic and early forms of Latin, were siblings.

As anyone from a large family knows, there are cousins, and then there are distant cousins, encompassing nearly anyone with a claim to family bloodlines. This is true of the Indo-European family of languages. If the Germanic and Romance languages are truly cousins, then languages such as Greek, Armenian, Albanian, and even the extinct Hittite and Tocharian are distant cousins. So are Irish, Scots Gaelic, Welsh, and Breton, whose protolanguage, Celtic, was once spoken widely throughout Europe and the British Isles. Breton is spoken in Brittany in the northwest coastal regions of France. It was brought there by Celts fleeing from Britain in the seventh century.

Russian is also a distant cousin, as are its sisters, Bulgarian, Serbo-Croatian, Polish, Czech, and Slovak. The Baltic language Lithuanian is related to English, as is its sister language, Latvian. A neighboring language, Estonian, however, is not a relative. Sanskrit, although far removed geographically, is nonetheless a relative, as pointed out by Sir William Jones. Its offspring, Hindi and Bengali, spoken primarily in South Asia, are distantly related to English. Persian (or Farsi), spoken in modern Iran, is a distant cousin of English, as is Kurdish, which is spoken in Iran, Iraq, and Turkey, and Pashto, which is spoken in Afghanistan and Pakistan. All these languages, except for Estonian, are related, more or less distantly, to one another because they all descended from Indo-European.

Figure 11.5 is an abbreviated family tree of the Indo-European languages that gives a genealogical and historical classification of the languages shown. This diagram is somewhat simplified. For example, it appears that all the Slavic

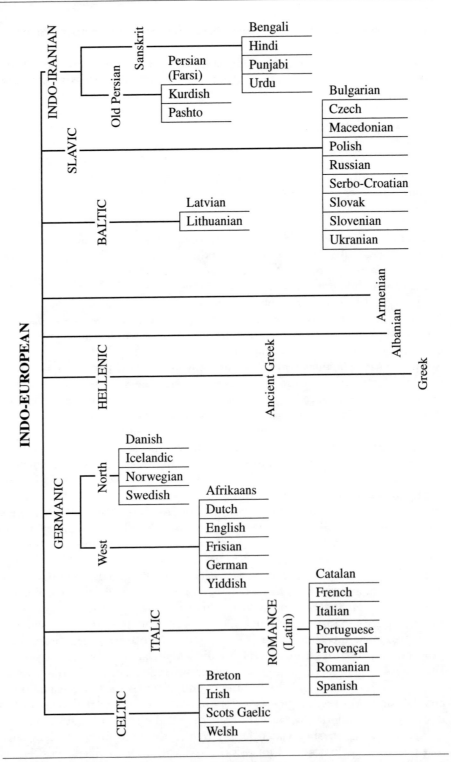

FIGURE 11.5 | The Indo-European family of languages.

languages are sisters. In fact, the nine languages shown can be organized hierarchically, showing some more closely related than others. In other words, the various separations that resulted in the nine Slavic languages we see today occurred several times over a long stretch of time. Similar remarks apply to the other families, including Indo-European.

Another simplification is that the "dead ends"—languages that evolved and died leaving no offspring—are not included. We have already mentioned Hittite and Tocharian as two such Indo-European languages. The family tree also fails to show several intermediate stages that must have existed in the evolution of modern languages. Languages do not evolve abruptly, which is why comparisons with the genealogical trees of biology have limited usefulness. Finally, the diagram fails to show some Indo-European languages because of lack of space.

Languages of the World

And the whole earth was of one language, and of one speech.

GENESIS 11:1, *The Bible,* King James Version

Let us go down, and there confound their language, that they may not understand one another's speech.

GENESIS 11:7, *The Bible,* King James Version

Most of the world's languages do not belong to the Indo-European family. Linguists have also attempted to classify the non-Indo-European languages according to their genetic relationships. The task is to identify the languages that constitute a family and the relationships that exist among them.

The two most common questions asked of linguists are: "How many languages do you speak?" and "How many languages are there in the world?" Both questions are difficult to answer precisely. Most linguists have varying degrees of familiarity with several languages, and many are **polyglots**, persons who speak and understand several languages. Charles V, the Holy Roman Emperor from 1519 to 1558, was a polyglot, for he proclaimed: "I speak Spanish to God, Italian to women, French to men, and German to my horse."

As to the second question, it's difficult to ascertain the precise number of languages in the world because there are no clear criteria to decide what is a language and what is a dialect, as discussed in chapter 10.

With this caveat in mind, recent estimates place the number of spoken languages in the world today (2010) at somewhat less than 7,000, according to the encyclopedia Ethnologue: Languages of the World (see http://www.ethnologue.com/web.asp for more detail). The Ethnologue lists 124 sign languages, from every continent where languages are spoken, though this number is in dispute and may be very much larger. In the city of Los Angeles alone, more than 80 languages are spoken. Students at Hollywood High School go home to hear their parents speak Amharic, Armenian, Arabic, Marshallese, Urdu, Sinhalese, Ibo, Gujarati, Hmong, Afrikaans, Khmer, Ukrainian, Cambodian, Spanish, Tagalog, and Russian, among others.

It is often surprising to discover which languages are genetically related and which ones are not. Nepali, the language of remote Nepal, is an Indo-European language, whereas Hungarian, surrounded on all sides by Indo-European languages, is not.

Some languages have no demonstrable genealogical relationship with other living languages. They are called **language isolates**. Basque, spoken in the Pyrenees Mountains between Spain and France, and Ainu, spoken on the island of Hokkaido, Japan, are among the forty or so isolates mentioned in the Ethnologue. Many sign languages, insofar as it can be determined, are isolates.

It is not possible in an introductory text to give an exhaustive table of families, subfamilies, and individual languages. Besides, some genetic relationships have not yet been firmly established. For example, linguists are divided as to whether Japanese and Turkish are related. We simply mention several language families in the following paragraphs with a few of their members. These language families do not appear to be related to one another or to Indo-European. This, however, may be an artifact of being unable to delve into the past far enough to see common features that time has erased. We cannot eliminate the possibility that the entire world's languages spring ultimately from a single source, an "ur-language" that some have termed **Nostratic**, which is buried, if not concealed, in the depths of the past. Readers interested in this fascinating topic may wish to read the writings of Professor Johanna Nichols of the University of California at Berkeley. And of course more can be found by googling *nostratic*.

Uralic is the other major family of languages, besides Indo-European, that is spoken on the European continent. Hungarian, Finnish, and Estonian are the major representatives of this group.

Afro-Asiatic is a large family of languages spoken in northern Africa and the Middle East. It includes the modern *Semitic* languages of Hebrew and Arabic, as well as languages spoken in biblical times such as Aramaic, Babylonian, Canaanite, and Moabite.

The *Sino-Tibetan* family includes Mandarin, the most populous language in the world, spoken by more than one billion Chinese. This family also includes all of the Chinese languages, as well as Burmese and Tibetan.

Most of the languages of Africa belong to the *Niger-Congo* family, a huge family comprising more than one-fifth of the world's languages (about fifteen hundred). These include more than nine hundred languages grouped into subfamilies such as Kordofanian and Atlantic-Congo. The latter includes individual languages such as Swahili and Zulu.

Nearly as numerous, the *Austronesian* family contains about thirteen hundred languages, spoken over a wide expanse of the globe, from Madagascar, off the coast of Africa, to Hawaii. Hawaiian is an Austronesian language, as are Maori, spoken in New Zealand; Tagalog, spoken in the Philippine Islands; and Malay, spoken in Malaysia and Singapore, to mention just a few.

Surprisingly, the next most numerous family, called *Trans-New Guinea*, is crowded into the relatively small geographic area of New Guinea and neighboring islands, and contains nearly six hundred languages, most of them being Papuan languages. Thus three language families alone make up half of the languages spoken in the world.

Dozens of families and hundreds of languages are, or were, spoken in North and South America. Knowledge of the genetic relationships among these families of languages is often tenuous, and because so many of the languages are approaching extinction, there may be little hope for as thorough an understanding of the Amerindian language families as linguists have achieved for Indo-European.

Types of Languages

All the Oriental nations jam tongue and words together in the throat, like the Hebrews and Syrians. All the Mediterranean peoples push their enunciation forward to the palate, like the Greeks and the Asians. All the Occidentals break their words on the teeth, like the Italians and Spaniards. . . .

ISIDORE OF SEVILLE, 7th century c.e.

There are many ways to classify languages. One way already discussed in this chapter is according to the language family—the genetic classification. This method would be like classifying people according to whether they were related by blood. Another way of classifying languages is by certain linguistic traits, regardless of family. With people, this method would be like classifying them according to height and weight, political preference, religion, degree of wealth, and so on.

So far in this book we have hinted at the different ways that languages might be classified. From a phonological point of view, we have tone languages versus intonation languages—Thai versus English. We have languages with varying numbers of vowel phonemes, from as few as three to as high as a dozen or more. Languages may be classified according the number and kinds of consonants they have and also in terms of what combinations of consonants and vowels may form syllables. Japanese and Hawaiian allow few syllable types (CV and V, mostly), whereas English and most Indo-European languages allow a much wider variety. Languages may use stress phonemically (English), or not (French).

From a morphological standpoint, languages may be classified according to the richness of verb and noun morphology. For example, Vietnamese has little if any word morphology, so its words are monomorphemic; there are no plural affixes on nouns or agreement affixes on verbs. Such languages are referred to as **isolating** or **analytic**. Languages like English have a middling amount of morphology, much less than Old English or Latin once had, or than Russian has today. Languages with more than one morpheme per word are called **synthetic**.

Some synthetic languages are **agglutinative**: words may be formed by a root and multiple affixes where the affixes are easily separated and always retain the same meaning. Swahili is such a language (see exercise 9, chapter 3). The word *ninafika* is *ni* + *na* + *fika*, meaning "I-present-arrive"; *ni* + *ta* + *fika* means "I-will-arrive"; *wa* + *li* + *fika* means "we-past-arrive"; and so on. Each morpheme is unchanging in form and meaning from one word to the next. Turkish is also an agglutinative language, as illustrated in exercise 17 in chapter 3.

In a **fusional** synthetic language the morphemes are, well, fused together, so it is hard to identify their basic shape. Many Indo-European languages are of this type, such as Spanish. In *hablo, hablan, hablé*, meaning "I speak, they speak, I spoke," the affixes carry a fusion of the meanings "person" and "number" and "tense" so that *-o* means "first person, singular, present," *-an* means "third person, plural, present" and *-e* means "first person, past, singular." The affixes themselves cannot be decomposed into the individual meanings that they bear.

Yet other languages—termed **polysynthetic** by linguists—have extraordinarily rich morphologies in which a single word may have ten or more affixes and carry the semantic load of an entire English sentence. Many native languages of North America are polysynthetic, including Mohawk, Cherokee, and Menominee. For example, the Menominee word *paehtāwāēwesew* means "He is heard by higher powers."

From a lexical standpoint, languages are classifiable as to whether they have articles like *the* and *a* in English; as to their system of pronouns and what distinctions are made regarding person, number, and gender; as to their vocabulary for describing family members; as to whether they have noun classes such as the masculine, feminine, and neuter nouns of German, or the multiple noun classes present in Swahili that we observed in chapter 3, and so on.

Every language has sentences that include a subject (S), an object (O), and a verb (V), although individual sentences may not contain all three elements. From the point of view of syntax, languages have been classified according to the basic or most common order in which these elements occur in sentences. There are six possible orders—SVO (subject, verb, object), SOV, VSO, VOS, OVS, and OSV—permitting, in theory, six possible language types. Of these, SVO and SOV languages make up nearly 90 percent of investigated languages in roughly equal proportions. English, Spanish, and Thai are SVO; German, Dutch, and Japanese illustrate SOV languages.

In SVO languages, auxiliary verbs precede main verbs, adverbs follow main verbs, and prepositions precede their head noun. Here are English examples:

They are eating. (Aux-V)
They sing beautifully. (V-Adv) (Cf. *They beautifully sing.)
They are from Tokyo. (Prep-V)

In SOV languages, the opposite tendencies are true. Auxiliary verbs follow the main verb, adverbs precede main verbs, and "prepositions," now called *postpositions*, follow their head noun. Here are Japanese examples:

Akiko	wa	sakana	o	tabete	iru (V-Aux)
Akiko	*topic marker*	fish	*object marker*	eating	is

"Akiko is eating fish."

Akiko	wa	hayaku	tabemasu	(Adv-V)
Akiko	*topic marker*	quickly	eats	

"Akiko eats quickly."

Akiko	wa	Tokyo	kara	desu	(V-PostP)
Akiko	*topic marker*	Tokyo	from	is	

"Akiko is from Tokyo."

These differences, and many more like them, stem from a single underlying parameter choice: the placement of the head of phrase. SVO languages are head-final; SOV languages are head-initial.

The question of why SVO and SOV languages are dominant is not completely understood, but linguists have observed that two principles or constraints are favored:

(1) Subjects precede objects.
(2) The verb V is adjacent to the object O.

SVO and SOV are the only two types that obey both principles. The next most common type in appearance is VSO, here illustrated by Tagalog, which is widely spoken in the Philippine Islands:

Sumagot siya sa propesor
answered he the professor
"He answered the professor."

VSO languages account for nearly 10 percent of languages investigated—the lion's share of what's left over after SVO and SOV languages. It is possible, however, that the VSO order is derived from an underlying order in which the verb and object are adjacent, so there is no violation of principle (2).

Malagasy, spoken on the island of Madagascar, has sentences that on the surface translate literally as the VOS sentence *put—the book on the table—the woman*, meaning "The woman put the book on the table." This would violate principle (1). However, linguists have shown that such sentences are derived from a deeper SVO order that is then transformed by a rule that postposes the S. Apparent OVS and OSV languages may also be derived from underlying orders that are either SVO or SOV and conform to the two principles, though this remains a subject for linguistic research.

That a language is SVO does not mean that SVO is the only possible word order in surface structure. The correlations between language type and the word order of syntactic categories in sentences are *preferred* word orders, and for the most part are violable tendencies. Different languages follow them to a greater or lesser degree. Thus, when a famous comedian said "Believe you me" on network TV, he was understood and imitated despite the VSO word order. Yoda, the Jedi Master of *Star Wars* fame, speaks a strange but perfectly understandable style of English that achieves its eccentricity by being OSV. (Objects may be complements other than Noun Phrases.) Some of Yoda's utterances are:

Sick I've become.
Around the survivors a perimeter create.
Strong with The Force you are.
Impossible to see the future is.
When nine hundred years you reach, look as good you will not.

For linguists, the many languages and language families provide essential data for the study of universal grammar. Although these languages are diverse in many ways, they are also remarkably similar in many ways. We find that languages from northern Greenland to southern New Zealand, from the Far East to the Far West, all have similar sounds, similar phonological and syntactic rules, and similar semantic systems.

Why Do Languages Change?

Some method should be thought on for ascertaining and fixing our language forever. . . .
I see no absolute necessity why any language should be perpetually changing.

JONATHAN SWIFT (1667–1745)

Stability in language is synonymous with rigor mortis.

ERNEST WEEKLEY (1865–1954)

No one knows exactly how or why languages change. As we have shown, linguistic changes do not happen suddenly. Speakers of English did not wake up one morning and decide to use the word *beef* for "ox meat," nor do all the children of one particular generation grow up to adopt a new word. Changes are more gradual, particularly changes in the phonological and syntactic system.

For any one speaker, certain changes may occur instantaneously. When someone acquires a new word, it is not acquired gradually, although full appreciation for all of its possible uses may come slowly. When a new rule enters a speaker's grammar, it is either in or not in the grammar. It may at first be an optional rule, so that sometimes it is used and sometimes it is not, possibly determined by social context or other external factors, but the rule is either there and available for use or not. What is gradual about language change is the spread of certain changes through an entire speech community.

A basic cause of change is the way children acquire the language. No one teaches a child the rules of the grammar. Each child constructs the grammar of her language alone, generalizing rules from the linguistic input she receives. As discussed in chapter 8, the child's language develops in stages until it approximates the adult grammar. The child's grammar is never exactly like that of the adult community because children receive diverse linguistic input. Certain rules may be simplified or overgeneralized, and vocabularies may show small differences that accumulate over several generations.

The older generation may be using certain rules optionally. For example, at certain times they may say "It's I" and at other times "It's me." The less formal style is usually used with children, who, as the next generation, may use only the "me" form of the pronoun in this construction. In such cases the grammar will have changed.

The reasons for some changes are relatively easy to understand. Before television there was no such word as *television*. It soon became a common lexical item. Borrowed words, too, generally serve a useful purpose, and their entry into the language is not mysterious. Other changes are more difficult to explain, such as the Great Vowel Shift in English.

One plausible source of sound change is *assimilation,* an *ease of articulation* process in which one sound influences the pronunciation of an adjacent or nearby sound. For example, vowels are frequently nasalized before nasal consonants because it is easiest to lower the velum to produce nasality in advance of the actual consonant articulation. Once the vowel is nasalized, the contrast that the nasal consonant provided can be equally well provided by the nasalized vowel alone, and the redundant consonant may no longer be pronounced. The contrast between oral and nasal vowels that exists in many languages of the world today (such as French) resulted from just such a historical sound change.

In reconstructing older versions of French, it has been hypothesized that *bol,* "basin," *botte,* "high boot," *bog,* "a card game," *bock,* "Bock beer," and *bon,* "good," were pronounced [bɔl], [bɔt], [bɔg], [bɔk], and [bɔ̃n], respectively. The nasalized vowel in *bon* resulted from the final nasal consonant. Because of a conditioned sound change that deleted nasal consonants in word-final position, *bon* is pronounced [bɔ̃] in modern French. The nasal vowel alone maintains the contrast with the other words.

Another example from English illustrates how such assimilative processes can change a language. In Old English, word initial [kʲ] (like the initial sound of *cute*), when followed by /i/, was further palatalized to become our modern palatal affricate /tʃ/, as illustrated by the following words:

Old English (c = [kʲ])	Modern English (ch = [tʃ])
ciese	cheese
cinn	chin
cild	child

The process of palatalization is found in the history of many languages. In Twi, the word meaning "to hate" was once pronounced [ki]. The [k] became first [kʲ] and then finally [tʃ], so that today "to hate" is [tʃi].

Ease of articulation processes, which make sounds more alike, are countered by the need to maintain contrast. Thus sound change also occurs when two sounds are so acoustically similar that there is a risk of confusion. We saw a sound change of /f/ to /h/ in an earlier example that can be explained by the acoustic similarity of [f] to other sounds.

Analogic change is a generalization of rules that reduces the number of exceptional or irregular morphemes. It was by analogy to *plow/plows* and *vow/vows* that speakers started saying *cows* as the plural of *cow* instead of the earlier plural *kine*. In effect, the plural rule became more general.

The generalization of the plural rule continues today with forms such as *yous* (plural of you) used by many speakers in place of the homophonous *you* for singular and plural.

Plural marking continues to undergo analogic change, as exemplified by the regularization of exceptional plural forms. The plural forms of borrowed words like *datum/data, agendum/agenda, curriculum/curricula, memorandum/memoranda, medium/media, criterion/criteria,* and *virtuoso/virtuosi* are being replaced by regular plurals by many speakers: *agendas, curriculums, memorandums, criterias,* and *virtuosos.* In some cases the borrowed original plural forms were considered to be the singular (as in *agenda* and *criteria*), and the new plural (e.g., *agendas*) is therefore a "plural-plural." In addition, many speakers now regard *data* and *media* as nouns that do not have plural forms, like *information*. All these changes are "economy of memory" changes and lessen the number of irregular forms that must be remembered.

The past-tense rule is also undergoing generalization. By analogy to *bake/baked* and *ignite/ignited*, many children and adults now say *I waked last night* (instead of *woke*) and *She lighted the bonfire* (instead of *lit*). These regular past-tense forms are found in today's dictionaries next to the irregular forms, with which they currently coexist.

Assimilation and analogic change account for some linguistic changes, but they cannot account for others. Simplification and regularization of grammars occur, but so does elaboration or complication. Old English rules of syntax became more complex, imposing a stricter word order on the language, at the same time that case endings were being simplified. A tendency toward simplification is counteracted by the need to limit potential ambiguity. Much of language change is a balance between the two.

Language contact is also a vehicle of language change, particularly with respect to lexical changes due to borrowing, and also phonological changes such as the introduction of new phonemes. As we saw earlier, /v/ came into English owing to its intimate contact with French following the Norman invasion.

Many factors contribute to linguistic change: simplification of grammars, elaboration to maintain intelligibility, borrowing, and so on. Changes are actualized by children learning the language, who incorporate them into their grammar. The exact reasons for linguistic change are still elusive, although it is clear that the imperfect learning of the adult languages by children is a contributing factor. Perhaps language changes for the same reason all things change: it is the nature of things to change. As Heraclitus pointed out centuries ago, "All is flux, nothing stays still. Nothing endures but change."

Summary

All living languages change. Linguistic change such as **sound shift** is found in the history of all languages, as evidenced by the **regular sound correspondences** that exist between different stages of the same language, different dialects of the same language, and different languages. Languages that evolve from a common source are **genetically related**. Genetically related languages were once dialects of the same language. For example, English, German, and Swedish were dialects of an earlier form of Germanic called **Proto-Germanic**, whereas earlier forms of Romance languages, such as Spanish, French, and Italian, were dialects of Latin. Going back even further in time, earlier forms of Proto-Germanic, Latin, and other languages were dialects of **Indo-European**.

All components of the grammar may change. Phonological, morphological, syntactic, lexical, and semantic changes occur. Words, morphemes, phonemes, and rules of all types may be added, lost, or altered. The meaning of words and morphemes may **broaden**, **narrow**, or shift. The lexicon may expand by **borrowing**, which results in **loan words** in the vocabulary. This is very common in **language contact** situations. It also grows through word coinage, blends, compounding, acronyms, and other processes of word formation. On the other hand, the lexicon may shrink as certain words like *typewriter* and *phone booth* are no longer used and become obsolete.

The study of linguistic change is called **historical and comparative linguistics**. Linguists use the **comparative method** to identify regular sound correspondences among the **cognates** of related languages and systematically reconstruct an earlier **protolanguage**. This **comparative reconstruction** allows linguists to peer backward in time and determine the linguistic history of a language family, which may then be represented in a tree diagram similar to Figure 11.5.

Recent estimates place the number of languages in the world today (2010) at somewhat less than 7,000 plus a hundred or more sign languages. These languages are grouped into families, subfamilies, and so on, based on their genetic relationships. A vast number of these languages are dying out because in each generation fewer children learn them. However, attempts are being made to preserve dying languages and dialects for the knowledge they bring to the study of Universal Grammar and the culture in which they are spoken.

Languages may also be classified according to certain characteristics such as a rich versus an impoverished morphology (**analytic** versus **synthetic**), or according to whether their basic word order is Subject-Verb-Object (SVO) like English, or Subject-Object-Verb (SOV) like Japanese, or possibly some other order.

No one knows all the causes of linguistic change. Some sound changes result from assimilation, a fundamentally physiological process of ease of articulation. Others, like the **Great Vowel Shift**, are more difficult to explain. Some grammatical changes are **analogic changes**, generalizations that lead to more regularity, such as *cows* instead of *kine* and *waked* instead of *woke*.

Change comes about through the restructuring of the grammar and lexicon by children learning the language. Grammars may appear to change in the direction of simplicity and regularity, as in the loss of the Indo-European case morphology, but such simplifications may be compensated for by other complexities, such as stricter word order. A balance is always present between simplicity—languages must be learnable—and complexity—languages must be expressive and relatively unambiguous.

References for Further Reading

Aitchison, J. 2001. *Language change: Progress or decay?*, 3rd edn. Cambridge, New York, Melbourne: Cambridge University Press.

Anttila, R. 1989. *Historical and comparative linguistics*. New York: John Benjamins.

Baugh, A. C., and T. Cable. 2002. *A history of the English language*, 5th edn. Upper Saddle River, NJ: Pearson Education.

Campbell, L. 2004. *Historical linguistics: An introduction*, 2nd edn. Cambridge, MA: MIT Press.

Comrie, B. (ed.). 1990. *The world's major languages*. New York: Oxford University Press.

Hock, H. H., and B. D. Joseph. 1996. *Language history, language change, and language relationship: An introduction to historical and comparative linguistics*. New York: Mouton de Gruyter.

Lehmann, W. P. 1992. *Historical linguistics: An introduction*, 3rd edn. London, New York: Routledge.

Lightfoot, D. 1984. *The language lottery*. Cambridge, MA: MIT Press.

Pyles, T., and J. Algeo. 2005. *The origins and development of the English language*, 5th edn. New York: Thomson/Wadsworth.

Wolfram, W. 2001. Language death and dying. In Chambers, J. K., Trudgill, P., and Schilling-Estes, N. (eds.), *The handbook on language variation and change*. Oxford, UK: Basil Blackwell.

Exercises

1. Many changes in the phonological system have occurred in English since 449 C.E. Below are some Old English words (given in their spelling and phonetic forms) and the same words as we pronounce them today. They are typical of regular sound changes that took place in English. What sound changes have occurred in each case?

   Example: OE hlud [xluːd] →   Mod. Eng. loud

   Changes: (1) The [x] was lost.

   (2) The long vowel [uː] became [aʊ].

OE		Mod E
a. crabba [kraba]	→	crab
Changes:		
b. fisc [fɪsk]	→	fish
Changes:		
c. fūl [fuːl]	→	foul
Changes:		
d. gāt [gaːt]	→	goat
Changes:		
e. lǣfan [læːvan]	→	leave
Changes:		
f. tēþ [teːθ]	→	teeth
Changes:		

2. The Great Vowel Shift left its traces in Modern English in such meaning-related pairs as:

   (1) serene/serenity [i]/[ɛ]
   (2) divine/divinity [aɪ]/[ɪ]
   (3) sane/sanity [e]/[æ]

   List five such meaning-related pairs that relate [i] and [ɛ] as in example (1), five that relate [aɪ] and [ɪ] as in example (2), and five that relate [e] and [æ] as in example (3).

	[i]/[ɛ]	[aɪ]/[ɪ]	[e]/[æ]
a.			
b.			
c.			
d.			
e.			

3. Below are given some sentences taken from Old English, Middle English, and early Modern English texts, illustrating some changes that have occurred in the syntactic rules of English grammar. (*Note*: In the sentences, the earlier spelling forms and words have been changed to conform to Modern English. That is, the OE sentence *His suna twegen mon brohte to þæm cynige* would be written as *His sons two one brought to that king*, which in Modern English would be *His two sons were brought to the king*.) Underline the parts of each sentence that differ from Modern English. Rewrite the sentence in Modern English. State what changes must have occurred.

Example: It <u>not</u> belongs to you. (Shakespeare, *Henry IV*)

Mod. Eng.: It does not belong to you.

Change: At one time a negative sentence simply had a *not* before the verb. Today, the word *do*, in its proper morphological form, must appear before the *not*.

a. It nothing pleased his master.
b. He hath said that we would lift them whom that him please.
c. I have a brother is condemned to die.
d. I bade them take away you.
e. I wish you was still more a Tartar.
f. Christ slept and his apostles.
g. Me was told.

4. Yearbooks and almanacs (including ones online) often publish a new-words list. In 2009 several new words, such as *earmark* and *vlog*, entered the English language. Before that, new words such as *byte* and *modem* arrived together with the computer age. Other words have been expanded in meaning, such as *memory* to refer to the storage part of a computer and *crack* meaning a form of cocaine. Sports-related new words include *threepeat* and *skybox*; Harry Potter's world has donated *apparate* and *muggle*, among others. Some fairly recent arrivals came with the new millennium and include *viagra*, *botox*, *waterboarding*, *sudoku*, and *sambuca* (an aniseed liqueur served with a flaming coffee bean).

a. Find five other words or compound words that have entered the language in the last ten years. Describe briefly the source of the word.
b. Think of three words that might be on the way out. (*Hint*: Consider *flapper*, *groovy*, and *slay/slew*. Dictionary entries that say "archaic" are a good source.)
c. Think of three words whose dictionary entries do not say they are verbs, but which you've heard or seen used as verbs. *Example*: "He went to piano over at the club," meaning (we guess) "He went to play the piano at the club."
d. Think of three words that have become, or are becoming, obsolete as a result of changes in technology. *Example*: *Mimeograph*, a method of reproduction, is on the way out because of advances in xerography.

e. One of the trendy words of the current millennium is *power* as used prolifically, if not productively, in new compounds such as *power walk* and *power lunch*. Find five or ten such usages and document a reference where you observed the usage, such as a magazine article or a news report on the radio, Internet, or television.

5. Here is a table showing, in phonemic form, the Latin ancestors of ten words in modern French (given in phonetic form):

Latin	French	Gloss
kor	kœr[5]	heart
kantāre	ʃãte	to sing
klārus	klɛr	clear
kervus	sɛr	deer
karbō	ʃarbõ	coal
kwandō	kã	when
kentum	sã	hundred
kawsa	ʃoz	thing
kinis	sãdrə	ashes
kawda/koda[6]	kø[5]	tail

Are the following statements true or false? Justify your answer.

	True	False
a. The modern French word for "thing" shows that a /k/, which occurred before the vowel /o/ in Latin, became [ʃ] in French.	_____	_____
b. The French word for "tail" probably derived from the Latin word /koda/ rather than from /kawda/.	_____	_____
c. One historical change illustrated by these data is that [s] became an allophone of the phoneme /k/ in French.	_____	_____
d. If there were a Latin word *kertus*, the modern French word would probably be [sɛr]. (Consider only the initial consonant.)	_____	_____

6. Here is how to count to five in a dozen languages, using standard Roman alphabet transcriptions. Six of these languages are Indo-European and six are not. Which are Indo-European? (Just for fun, how many of the languages can you identify? If you get all twelve correct, we'll mention your school in the next edition. You may e-mail your answer and institutional affiliation to either author Rodman or Hyams.)[7]

---

[5]œ and ø are front, rounded vowels.

[6]/kawda/ and /koda/ are the word for "tail" in two Latin dialects.

[7]In the previous edition nobody was completely correct; however, Tugba Rona, a student at the Istanbul International Community School (IICS) in Turkey, deserves an honorable mention.

	L1	L2	L3	L4	L5	L6
a.	en	jedyn	yi	eka	ichi	echad
b.	twene	dwaj	er	dvau	ni	shnayim
c.	thria	tři	san	trayas	san	shlosha
d.	fiuwar	štyri	ssu	catur	shi	arba?a
e.	fif	pjeć	wu	pañca	go	chamishsha

	L7	L8	L9	L10	L11	L12
a.	mot	ün	hana	yaw	uno	nigen
b.	hai	duos	tul	daw	dos	khoyar
c.	ba	trais	set	dree	tres	ghorban
d.	bon	quatter	net	tsaloor	cuatro	durben
e.	nam	tschinch	tasŏt	pindze	cinco	tabon

7. The vocabulary of English consists of native words as well as thousands of loan words. Look up the following words in a dictionary that provides etymologies. Speculate how each word came to be borrowed from the particular language.

   Example: *Skunk* was a Native American term for an animal unfamiliar to the European colonists, so they borrowed that word into their vocabulary so they could refer to the creature.

a.	size	h.	robot	o.	skunk	v.	pagoda
b.	royal	i.	check	p.	catfish	w.	khaki
c.	aquatic	j.	banana	q.	hoodlum	x.	shampoo
d.	heavenly	k.	keel	r.	filibuster	y.	kangaroo
e.	skill	l.	fact	s.	astronaut	z.	bulldoze
f.	ranch	m.	potato	t.	emerald		
g.	blouse	n.	muskrat	u.	sugar		

8. Analogic change refers to a tendency to generalize the rules of language, a major cause of language change. We mentioned two instances, the generalization of the plural rule (*cow/kine* becoming *cow/cows*) and the generalization of the past-tense formation rule (*light/lit* becoming *light/lighted*). Think of at least three other instances of nonstandard usage that are analogic; they are indicators of possible future changes in the language. (*Hint*: Consider fairly general rules and see if you know of dialects or styles that overgeneralize them, for example, comparative formation by adding *-er*.)

9. Linguists have noted the "paradox" that *sound change is regular, but produces irregularity*, and *analogic change is irregular, but produces regularity*. Explain what this means, and illustrate your explanation with specific examples. (*Hint*: Revisit exercises 2 and 8.)

10. Study the following passage from Shakespeare's *Hamlet*, Act IV, Scene iii, and identify every difference in expression between Elizabethan and current Modern English that is evident (e.g., in line 3, *thou* is now *you*).

    HAMLET: A man may fish with the worm that hath eat of a king, and eat of the fish that hath fed of that worm.

KING: What dost thou mean by this?

HAMLET: Nothing but to show you how a king may go a progress through the guts of a beggar.

KING: Where is Polonius?

HAMLET: In heaven. Send thither to see. If your messenger find him not there, seek him i' the other place yourself. But indeed, if you find him not within this month, you shall nose him as you go up the stairs into the lobby.

11. Travelers to Spain who know a little Latin American Spanish are often surprised to encounter speakers who appear to have a lisp. That is, they pronounce an expected [s] as [θ], and moreover they pronounce an expected [j] as an "ly" or palatal lateral whose IPA symbol is [ʎ]. Of course if you've read this book you know that this is a dialectal variation. Consider the following data from two dialects of Spanish:

Dialect 1	Dialect 2	Gloss	Earlier Form (to be completed)
[kasa]	[kaθa]	hunt (noun)	*
[si]	[si]	yes	*
[gajo]	[gaʎo]	rooster	*
[dies]	[dieθ]	ten	*
[pojo]	[pojo]	kind of bench	*
[kaje]	[kaʎe]	street	*
[majo]	[majo]	May	*
[kasa]	[kasa]	house	*
[siŋko]	[θiŋko]	five	*
[dos]	[dos]	two	*
[pojo]	[poʎo]	chicken	*

a. Find the correspondence sets—there are fourteen of them, for example p-p.

b. Reconstruct each of the fourteen protosounds, for example *p.

c. What, if any, are the sound changes that took place in the two dialects?
Dialect 1:
Dialect 2:

d. Complete the table by filling in the reconstructed earlier form.

12. Here are some data from four Polynesian languages:

Maori	Hawaiian	Samoan	Fijian	Gloss	Proto-Polynesian (to be completed)
pou	pou	pou	bou	post	*
tapu	kapu	tapu	tabu	forbidden	*
taŋi	kani	taŋi	taŋi	cry	*
takere	kaʔele	taʔele	takele	keel	*
hono	hono	fono	vono	stay, sit	*
marama	malama	malama	malama	light, moon	*
kaho	ʔaho	ʔaso	kaso	thatch	*

   a. Find the correspondence sets. (*Hint*: There are fourteen. For example: o-o-o-o, p-p-p-b.)

   b. For each correspondence set, reconstruct a protosound. Mention any sound changes that you observe. For example:

      o-o-o-o *o

      p-p-p-b *p   p → b in Fijian.

   c. Complete the table by filling in the reconstructed words in Proto-Polynesian.

13. Consider these data from two American Indian languages:

Yerington Paviotso = YP	Northfork Monachi = NM	Gloss
mupi	mupi	nose
tama	tawa	tooth
piwɨ	piwɨ	heart
sawaʔpono	sawaʔpono	(a feminine name)
nɨmɨ	nɨwɨ	liver
tamano	tawano	springtime
pahwa	pahwa	aunt
kuma	kuwa	husband
wowaʔa	wowaʔa	indians living to the west
mɨhɨ	mɨhɨ	porcupine
noto	noto	throat
tapa	tape	sun
ʔatapɨ	ʔatapɨ	jaw
papiʔi	papiʔi	older brother
patɨ	petɨ	daughter
nana	nana	man
ʔatɨ	ʔetɨ	bow, gun

   a. Identify each sound correspondence. (*Hint*: There are ten correspondence sets of consonants and six correspondence sets of vowels: for example, p-p, m-w, a-a, and a-e.)

   b. (1) For each correspondence you identified in (a) not containing an *m* or *w*, reconstruct a protosound (e.g., for h-h, *h; o-o, *o).

      (2) If the protosound underwent a change, indicate what the change is and in which language it took place.

   c. (1) Whenever a *w* appears in YP, what appears in the corresponding position in NM?

      (2) Whenever an *m* occurs in YP, what two sounds may correspond to it in NM?

      (3) On the basis of the position of *m* in YP words, can you predict which sound it will correspond to in NM words? How?

   d. (1) For the three correspondences you discovered in (a) involving *m* and *w*, should you reconstruct two or three protosounds?

      (2) If you chose three protosounds, what are they and what did they become in the two daughter languages, YP and NM?

(3) If you chose two protosounds, what are they and what did they become in the daughter languages? What further statement do you need to make about the sound changes? (*Hint*: One protosound will become two different pairs, depending on its phonetic environment. It is an example of a conditioned sound change.)

e. Based on the above, reconstruct all the words given in the common ancestor from which both YP and NM descended (e.g., "porcupine" is reconstructed as *mɨhɨ).

14. The people of the Isle of Eggland once lived in harmony on a diet of soft-boiled eggs. They spoke proto-Egglish. Contention arose over which end of the egg should be opened first for eating, the big end or the little end. Each side retreated to its end of the island, and spoke no more to the other. Today, Big-End Egglish and Little-End Egglish are spoken in Eggland. Below are data from these languages.

a. Find the correspondence sets for each pair of cognates, and reconstruct the proto-Egglish word from which the cognates descended.

b. Identify the sound changes that have affected each language. Use *classes* of sounds to express the change when possible. (*Hint*: There are three conditioned sounds changes.)

Big-End Egglish	Little-End Egglish	Gloss	Proto-Egglish (to be completed)
ʃur	kul	omelet	*
ve	vet	yolk	*
rɔ	rɔk	egg	*
ver	vel	eggshell	*
ʒu	gup	soufflé	*
vel	vel	egg white	*
pe	pe	hard-boiled (obscene)	*

15. Consider the following Latin and Greek words. Each of them has provided a root for many English words. Give three examples of English words derived from each of the Latin and Greek roots below (the root is in bold-face). (*Note*: The English word need not begin with the root, e.g., *depose* is derived from the Latin *positus*.)

Example: Latin *pater* "father": English *paternal*, *patricide*, *expatriate*. Note that *paternalistic*, *paternalistically*, and other morphological derivations of *paternal* <u>do not count</u>.

Greek

pente	"five"
anthropos	"man"
arche	"beginning"
pathos	"feeling"
morphe	"shape"
exo	"outside"
sophos	"wise"
gamos	"marriage"
logy	"word"
gigas	"huge, enormous"

Latin

acer	"sharp"
mater	"mother"
bellum	"war"
arbor	"tree"
positus	"put, place"
par	"equal"
nepos	"grandson"
tacere	"to be silent"
scribere	"to write"
lingua	"tongue, language"

12

Writing: The ABCs of Language

The Moving Finger writes; and, having writ,
Moves on: nor all thy Piety nor Wit
Shall lure it back to cancel half a Line,
Nor all thy Tears wash out a Word of it.

OMAR KHAYYÁM, *Rubáiyát*, c. 1080 (trans. Edward FitzGerald, 1859)

The palest ink is better than the sharpest memory.

CHINESE PROVERB

Throughout this book we have emphasized the spoken form of language. The grammar, which represents one's linguistic knowledge, is viewed as a system for relating sound (sign) and meaning. The ability to acquire and use language represents a vital evolutionary development. No individual or peoples discovered or created language. The human language faculty appears to be biologically and genetically determined.

This is not true of the written form of human languages. Children learn to speak naturally through exposure to language, without formal teaching. To become literate—to learn to read and write—one must make a conscious effort and receive instruction.

Before the invention of writing, useful knowledge had to be memorized. Messengers carried information in their heads. Crucial lore passed from the older to the newer generation through speaking. Even in today's world, many spoken languages lack a writing system, and oral literature still abounds. However, human memory is short-lived, and the brain's storage capacity is limited.

Writing overcomes such problems and allows communication across space and through time. Writing permits a society to permanently record its literature, its history and science, and its technology. The creation and development of writing systems is therefore one of the greatest of human achievements.

By *writing* we mean a visual system for representing language, including handwriting, printing, and electronic displays of these written forms. (Braille "writing" is a *tactile* system for the visually impaired.) It might be argued that today we have electronic means of recording sound and images, so writing is becoming obsolete. If writing became extinct, however, there would be no knowledge of electronics for engineers to study; there would be, in fact, little technology in years to come. There would be no e-messaging, no literature, no books, no mail, no newspapers. There would be some advantages—no spam, no poison-pen letters, no "fine print"—but the losses would far outweigh the gains.

The History of Writing

An Egyptian legend relates that when the god Thoth revealed his discovery of the art of writing to King Thamos, the good King denounced it as an enemy of civilization. "Children and young people," protested the monarch, "who had hitherto been forced to apply themselves diligently to learn and retain whatever was taught them, would cease to apply themselves, and would neglect to exercise their memories."

WILL DURANT, *The Story of Civilization* vol. 1, 1935

There are many legends and stories about the invention of writing. Greek legend has it that Cadmus, Prince of Phoenicia and founder of the city of Thebes, invented the alphabet and brought it with him to Greece. In one Chinese fable, the four-eyed dragon-god Cang Jie invented writing, but in another, writing first appeared as markings on the back of the chi-lin, a white unicorn of Chinese legend. In other myths, the Babylonian god Nebo and the Egyptian god Thoth gave writing as well as speech to humans. The Talmudic scholar Rabbi Akiba believed that the alphabet existed before humans were created, and according to Hindu tradition the Goddess Saraswati, wife of Brahma, invented writing.

Although these are delightful stories, it is evident that before a single word was written, uncountable billions were spoken. The invention of writing comes relatively late in human history, and its development was gradual. It is highly unlikely that a particularly gifted ancestor awoke one morning and decided, "Today I'll invent a writing system."

Pictograms and Ideograms

One picture is worth a thousand words.

CHINESE PROVERB

The roots of writing were the early drawings made by ancient humans. Cave art, called **petroglyphs**, such as those found in the Altamira cave in northern Spain, created by humans living more than 20,000 years ago, can be "read" today. They are literal portrayals of life at that time. We don't know why they were

FIGURE 12.1 | Six of seventy-seven symbols developed by the National Park Service for use as signs indicating activities and facilities in parks and recreation areas. These symbols denote, from left to right: environmental study area, grocery store, men's restroom, women's restroom, fishing, and amphitheater. Certain symbols are available with a prohibiting slash—a diagonal red bar across the symbol that means that the activity is forbidden.

National Park Service, U.S. Department of the Interior

produced; they may be aesthetic expressions rather than pictorial communications. Later drawings, however, are clearly "picture writings," or **pictograms**. Unlike modern writing systems, each picture or pictogram is a direct image of the object it represents. There is a nonarbitrary relationship between the form and meaning of the symbol. Comic strips minus captions are pictographic—literal representations of the ideas to be communicated. This early form of writing represented objects in the world directly rather than through the linguistic names given to these objects. Thus they did not represent the words and sounds of spoken language.

Pictographic writing has been found throughout the world, ancient and modern: among Africans, Native Americans including the Inuits of Alaska and Canada, the Incas of Peru, the Yukagirians of Siberia, and the people of Oceania. Pictograms are used today in international road signs, where the native language of the region might not be understood by all travelers. Such symbols do not depend on words. For example, a traveler does not need to know English to understand the signs used by the U.S. National Park Service (Figure 12.1).

Once a pictogram was accepted as the representation of an object, its meaning was extended to attributes of that object, or concepts associated with it. A picture of the sun could represent warmth, heat, light, daytime, and so on. Pictograms began to represent ideas rather than objects. Such generalized pictograms are called **ideograms** ("idea pictures" or "idea writing").

The difference between pictograms and ideograms is not always clear. Ideograms tend to be less direct representations, and one may have to learn what a particular ideogram means. Pictograms tend to be more literal. For example, the no parking symbol consisting of a black letter P inside a red circle with a slanting red line through it is an ideogram. It represents the idea of no parking abstractly. A no parking symbol showing an automobile being towed away is more literal, more like a pictogram.

Inevitably, pictograms and ideograms became highly stylized and difficult to interpret without knowing the system. To learn the system, one learned the words of the language that the ideograms represented. Thus the ideograms became linguistic symbols. They stood for the words, both meaning and sounds, that represented the ideas. This stage was a revolutionary step in the development of writing systems.

Cuneiform Writing

Bridegroom, let me caress you,
My precious caress is more savory than honey,
In the bed chamber, honey-filled,
Let me enjoy your goodly beauty,
Lion let me caress you

TRANSLATION OF A SUMERIAN POEM WRITTEN IN CUNEIFORM

Much of what we know about writing stems from the records left by the Sumerians, an ancient people of unknown origin, who built a civilization in southern Mesopotamia (modern Iraq) more than 6,000 years ago. They left innumerable clay tablets containing business documents, epics, prayers, poems, proverbs, and so on. So copious are these written records that the Pennsylvania Sumerian Dictionary Project has been able to publish electronically an eighteen-volume online dictionary of their written language. It has been available since June 2006.

The writing system of the Sumerians is the oldest one known. They were a commercially oriented people, and as their business deals became increasingly complex, the need for permanent records arose. An elaborate pictography was developed, along with a system of tallies. Some examples are shown here:

| star, sky, God | hand | corn | 5 | oxen[1] | 13 | fish |

Over the centuries the Sumerians simplified and conventionalized their pictography. They began to produce the symbols of their written language by using a wedge-shaped stylus that was pressed into soft clay tablets. The tablets hardened in the desert sun to produce permanent records that were far hardier than modern paper or electronic documents. Had the original American Declaration of Independence been written this way, it would not be in need of restoration and preservation. This form of writing is called **cuneiform**—literally, "wedge-shaped" (from Latin *cuneus*, "wedge"). Here is an illustration of the evolution of Sumerian pictograms to cuneiform:

became ... became ... star

became ... hand

became ... fish

---

[1]The pictograph for "ox" evolved, much later, into the letter *A*.

The cuneiform symbols in the third column do little to remind us (or the Sumerians) of the meaning represented. As cuneiform evolved, its users began to think of the symbols more in terms of the name of the things represented than of the things themselves. Eventually cuneiform script came to represent words of the language. Such a system is called **logographic**, or **word writing**. In this oldest type of writing system, the symbol stands for both the word and the concept, which it may still resemble, however abstractly. Thus **logograms**, the symbols of a word-writing system, are ideograms that represent in addition to the concept, the word or morpheme in the language for that concept.

The cuneiform writing system spread throughout the Middle East and Asia Minor. The Babylonians, Assyrians, and Persians borrowed it. In adopting cuneiform characters, the borrowers often used them to represent the sounds of the syllables in their own languages. In this way cuneiform evolved into a **syllabic writing** system.

In a syllabic writing system, each syllable in the language is represented by its own symbol, and words are written syllable by syllable. Cuneiform writing was never purely syllabic. A large residue of symbols remained that stood for whole words. The Assyrians retained many word symbols, even though every word in their language could be written out syllabically if it were desired. Thus they could write ⟨symbol⟩ *mātu* "country" as:

ma + a + tu

The Persians (ca. 600–400 B.C.E.) devised a greatly simplified syllabic alphabet for their language, which made little use of word symbols. By the reign of Darius I (521–486 B.C.E.), this writing system was in wide use. The following characters illustrate it:

da

di

fa

ma

tu

Emoticons are strings of text characters that, when viewed sideways, form a face expressing a particular emotion. (Some are fixed symbols such as ☺). They are used mostly in e-mail and text messaging to express a feeling. They are a modern, pictographic system similar to cuneiform in that the same symbols are combined in different manners to convey different concepts. Most everyone who uses e-mail recognizes the smiley face :-) to mean "not serious" or "just joking." Several less common emoticons, and their generally accepted meanings, are shown here:

:'–(	"crying"
:–S	"bizarre"
|:*)	"drunk"
:–)~	"drooling"
@}>——	"a rose"

The invention, use, and acceptance of emoticons reflect on a small scale how a writing system such as cuneiform might have spread throughout a country.

The Rebus Principle

2 🐝, ⟍ 🐝 2 🐝

WILLIAM SHAKESPEARE, *Hamlet*, c. 1600

When a graphic sign no longer has a visual relationship to the word it represents, it becomes a **phonographic symbol**, standing for the sounds that represent the word. A single sign can then be used to represent all words with the same sounds—the homophones of the language. If, for example, the symbol ☉ stood for *sun* in English, it could then be used in a sentence like *My ☉ is a doctor*. This sentence is an example of the **rebus principle**.

A rebus is a representation of words by pictures of objects whose names sound like the word. Thus 👁 might represent *eye* or the pronoun *I*. The sounds of the two words are identical, even though the meanings are not. Similarly, 🐝🍃 could represent *belief* (be + lief = bee + leaf = /bi/ + /lif/), and 🐝🍃🍃 could be *believes*.

Proper names can also be written in such a way. If the symbol *l* is used to represent *rod* and the symbol 人 represents *man*, then *l* 人 could represent *Rodman*, although nowadays the name is unrelated to either rods or men. Such combinations often become stylized or shortened so as to be more easily written. *Rodman*, for example, might be written in such a system as *l*人 or even 人.

Jokes, riddles, and advertising use the rebus principle. A popular ice cream company advertises "31derful flavors."

This is not an efficient system because in many languages words cannot be divided into sequences of sounds that have meaning by themselves. It would be difficult, for example, to represent the word *English* (/ɪŋ/ + /glɪʃ/) in English according to the rebus principle. *Eng* by itself does not mean anything, nor does *glish*.

From Hieroglyphics to the Alphabet

"You'd better phrase that more politely.
We no longer use the 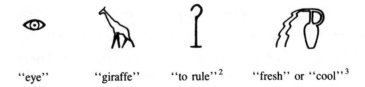 *word."*

At the time that Sumerian pictography was flourishing (around 4000 B.C.E.), the Egyptians were using a similar system, which the Greeks later called hieroglyphics (*hiero*, "sacred," + *glyphikos*, "carvings"). These sacred carvings originated as pictography as shown by the following:

"eye"	"giraffe"	"to rule"[2]	"fresh" or "cool"[3]

---

[2]The symbol portrays the Pharaoh's staff.
[3]Water trickling out of a vase.

Eventually, these pictograms came to represent both the concept and the word for the concept. Once this happened, hieroglyphics became a bona fide logographic writing system. Through the rebus principle, hieroglyphics also became a syllabic writing system.

The Phoenicians, a Semitic people who lived in what is today Lebanon, were aware of hieroglyphics as well as the offshoots of Sumerian writing. By 1500 B.C.E., they had developed a writing system of twenty-two characters, the West Semitic Syllabary. Mostly, the characters stood for consonants alone. The reader provided the vowels, and hence the rest of the syllable, through knowledge of the language. (Cn y rd ths?) Thus the West Semitic Syllabary was both a **syllabary** and a **consonantal alphabet** (also called **abjad**).

The ancient Greeks tried to borrow the Phoenician writing system, but it was unsatisfactory as a syllabary because Greek has too complex a syllable structure. In Greek, unlike Phoenician, vowels cannot be determined by context, so a writing system for Greek required that vowels be specifically written. Fortuitously, Phoenician had more consonants than Greek, so when the Greeks borrowed the system, they used the leftover consonant symbols to represent vowel sounds. The result was **alphabetic writing**, a system in which both consonants and vowels are symbolized. (The word *alphabet* is derived from *alpha* and *beta*, the first two letters of the Greek alphabet.)

Most alphabetic systems in use today derive from the Greek system. The Etruscans knew this alphabet and through them it became known to the Romans, who used it for Latin. The alphabet spread with Western civilization, and eventually most nations of the world had the opportunity to use alphabetic writing.

According to one view, the alphabet was not invented, it was discovered. If language did not include discrete individual sounds, no one could have invented alphabetic letters to represent them. When humans started to use one symbol for one phoneme, they were making more salient their intuitive knowledge of the phonological system of the language.

Modern Writing Systems

... but their manner of writing is very peculiar, being neither from the left to the right, like the Europeans; nor from the right to the left, like the Arabians; nor from up to down, like the Chinese; nor from down to up, like the Cascagians, but aslant from one corner of the paper to the other, like ladies in England.

JONATHAN SWIFT, *Gulliver's Travels,* 1726

We have already mentioned the various types of writing systems used in the world: word or logographic writing, syllabic writing, consonantal alphabet writing, and alphabetic writing. Most of the world's written languages use alphabetic writing. Even Chinese and Japanese, whose native writing systems are not alphabetic, have adopted alphabetic transcription systems for special purposes such as street signs for foreigners and input for computers.

Word Writing

"Peanuts" copyright © United Feature Syndicate, Inc. Reprinted by permission.

In a word-writing or logographic writing system, a written character represents both the meaning and pronunciation of each word or morpheme. Such systems are cumbersome, containing thousands of different characters. By contrast, all of the 450,000 entries in *Webster's Third New International Dictionary* may be written using only twenty-six alphabetic symbols and a handful of punctuation marks and other characters. It is understandable why word writing gave way to alphabetic systems in most places in the world.

The major exceptions are the writing systems used in China and Japan. The Chinese writing system has an uninterrupted history of 3,500 years. For the most part it is a word-writing system, each character representing an individual word or morpheme. Longer words are formed by combining two words or morphemes, as shown by the word meaning "business," *măimai*, which is formed by combining the words meaning "buy" and "sell." This is similar to compounding in English.

A word-writing system would be awkward for English and other Indo-European languages because of the pervasiveness of inflected verb forms such as *take, takes, taken, took,* and *taking,* and inflected noun forms such as *cat, cats, cat's,* and *cats'.* These are difficult to represent without a huge proliferation of characters. The Chinese languages, on the other hand, have little inflection.

Even without the need to represent inflectional forms, Chinese dictionaries contain tens of thousands of characters. A person need know "only" about 5,000, however, to read a newspaper. To promote literacy, the Chinese government has undertaken character simplification programs from time to time. This process was first tried in 213 B.C.E., when the scholar Li Si published an official list of over 3,000 characters whose written forms he had simplified by omitting unneeded strokes. This would be analogous to dictionary writers simplifying *amoeba* to *ameba,* eliminating the superfluous *o*. Since that time, successive generations of Chinese scholars have added new characters and modified old ones, creating redundancy, ambiguity, and complexity. Recent character-simplification efforts continue the ages-old tradition of trying to make the system learnable and usable, while retaining its basic form.

The Chinese government has adopted a spelling system using the Roman alphabet called **Pinyin**, which is now used alongside the regular system of characters. By the time of the Summer Olympics of 2008, nearly all public information signs in Beijing, such as the names of streets, parks, restaurants, hotels, and shopping centers, were printed in both systems for the convenience of foreign visitors. It is not the government's intent to replace the traditional writing, which is an integral part of Chinese culture. To the Chinese, writing is an art—**calligraphy**—and thousands of years of poetry, literature, and history are preserved in the old system.

An additional reason for keeping the traditional system is that it permits all literate Chinese to communicate even though their spoken languages are not mutually intelligible. Thus writing has served as a unifying factor throughout Chinese history, in an area where hundreds of languages and dialects coexist. A Chinese proverb states "people separated by a blade of grass cannot understand each other." The unified writing system is a scythe that cuts across linguistic differences and allows the people to communicate.

This use of written Chinese characters is similar to the use of Arabic numerals, which mean the same thing in many countries. For example, the character 5 (or $\underline{V}$ for that matter) stands for a different sequence of sounds in English, French, and Finnish. It is *five* /faɪv/ in English, *cinq* /sæk/ in French, and *viisi* /viːsi/ in Finnish, but in all these languages 5 means "five" however it is pronounced. Similarly, the spoken word for "rice" is different in the various Chinese languages, but the written character is the same. If the writing system in China were to become alphabetic, each language would be as different in writing as in speaking, and written communication would no longer be possible among the various language communities.

Syllabic Writing

Syllabic writing systems are more efficient than word-writing systems, and they are certainly less taxing on the memory. However, languages with a rich structure of syllables containing many consonant clusters (such as *tr* or *spl*) cannot be efficiently written with a syllabary. To see this difficulty, consider the syllable structures of English:

I	/aɪ/	V	ant	/ænt/	VCC
key	/ki/	CV	pant	/pænt/	CVCC
ski	/ski/	CCV	stump	/stʌmp/	CCVCC
spree	/spri/	CCCV	striped	/straɪpt/	CCCVCC
an	/æn/	VC	ants	/ænts/	VCCC
seek	/sik/	CVC	pants	/pænts/	CVCCC
speak	/spik/	CCVC	sports	/spɔrts/	CCVCCC
scram	/skræm/	CCCVC	splints	/splɪnts/	CCCVCCC

Even this table is not exhaustive; there are syllables whose codas may contain four consonants, such as *strengths* /strɛnkθs/ and *triumphs* /traɪəmpfs/. With more than thirty consonants and over twelve vowels, the number of different possible syllables is astronomical, which is why English, and Indo-European languages in general, are unsuitable for syllabic writing systems.

The Japanese language, on the other hand, is more suited for syllabic writing, because all words in Japanese can be phonologically represented by about one hundred syllables, mostly of the consonant-vowel (CV) type, and there are no underlying consonant clusters. To write these syllables, the Japanese have two syllabaries, each containing forty-six characters, called **kana**. The entire Japanese language can be written using kana. One syllabary, **katakana**, is used for loan words and for special effects similar to italics in European writing. The other syllabary, **hiragana**, is used for native words. Hiragana characters may occur in the same word as ideographic characters, which are called **kanji**, and are borrowed Chinese characters. Thus Japanese writing is part word writing, part syllable writing.

During the first millennium, the Japanese tried to use Chinese characters to write their language. However, spoken Japanese is unlike spoken Chinese. (They are genetically unrelated languages.) A word-writing system alone was not suitable for Japanese, which is a highly inflected language in which verbs may occur in thirty or more different forms. Scholars devised syllabic characters, based on modified Chinese characters, to represent the inflectional endings and other grammatical morphemes. Thus, in Japanese writing, kanji is commonly used for the verb roots, and hiragana symbols for the inflectional markings.

For example, 行 is the character meaning "go," pronounced [i]. The word for "went" in formal speech is *ikimashita*, written 行きました, where the hiragana symbols きました represent the syllables *ki, ma, shi, ta*. Nouns, on the other hand, are not inflected in Japanese, and they can generally be written using Chinese characters alone.

In theory, all of Japanese could be written in hiragana. However, in Japanese, there are many homographs (like *lead* in "lead pipe" or "lead astray"), and the use of kanji disambiguates a word that might be ambiguous if written syllabically, similar to the ambiguity of *can* in "He saw that gasoline can explode." In addition, kanji writing is an integral part of Japanese culture, and it is unlikely to be abandoned.

In America in 1821, the Cherokee Sequoyah invented a syllabic writing system for his native language. Sequoyah's script, which survives today essentially unchanged, proved useful to the Cherokee people and is justifiably a point of great pride for them. The syllabary contains eighty-five symbols, many of them derived from Latin characters, which efficiently transcribe spoken Cherokee. A few symbols are shown here:

J	gu
Ⴖ	hu
ℓℓ	we
W	ta
Н	mi

In some languages, an alphabetic character can be used in certain words to write a syllable. In a word such as bar-b-q, the single letters represent syllables (*b* for [bi] or [bə], *q* for [kju]).

Consonantal Alphabet Writing

Semitic languages, such as Hebrew and Arabic, are written with alphabets that consist only of consonants. Such an alphabet works for these languages because consonants form the root of most words. For example, the consonants *ktb* in Arabic form the root of words associated with "write." Thus *katab* means "to write," *aktib* means "I write," *kitab* means "a book," and so on. Inflectional and derivational processes can be expressed by different vowels inserted into the triconsonantal roots.

Because of this structure, vowels can sometimes be figured out by a person who knows the spoken language, jst lk y cn rd ths phrs, prvdng y knw nglsh. English, however, is unrelated to the Semitic languages like Arabic and Hebrew, and its structure is such that vowels are usually crucial for reading and writing. The English phrase *I like to eat out* would be incomprehensible without vowels, viz. *lk t t t.*

Semitic alphabets provide a way to use diacritic marks to express vowels. This is partly out of the desire to preserve the true pronunciations of religious writings, and partly out of deference to children and foreigners learning to read and write. In Hebrew, dots or other small figures are placed under, above, or even in the center of the consonantal letter to indicate the accompanying vowel. For example, ל represents an l-sound in Hebrew writing. Unadorned, the vowel that follows would be determined by context. However, לֶ (with a tiny triangle of dots below it) indicates that the vowel that follows is [ɛ], so in effect לֶ represents the syllable [lɛ].

These systems are called consonantal alphabets because only the consonants are fully developed symbols. Sometimes they are considered syllabaries because once the reader or writer perceives the vowel, the consonantal letter *seems* to stand for a syllable. With a true syllabary, however, a person need know only the phonetic value of each symbol to pronounce it correctly and unambiguously. Once you learn a Japanese syllabary, you can read Japanese in a (more or less) phonetically correct way without any idea of what you are saying. (The syllabic text doesn't always show word boundaries, and there is no indication of prosodic features such as intonation.) This would be impossible for Arabic or Hebrew.

Alphabetic Writing

Alphabetic writing systems are easy to learn, convenient to use, and maximally efficient for transcribing any human language.

The term **sound writing** is sometimes used in place of *alphabetic writing*, but it does not truly represent the principle involved in the use of alphabets. One-sound ↔ one-letter is inefficient and unintuitive, because we do not need to represent the [pʰ] in *pit* and the [p] in *spit* by two different letters. It is confusing to represent nonphonemic differences in writing because the sounds are seldom perceptible to speakers. Except for the phonetic alphabets, whose function is to record the sounds of all languages for descriptive purposes, most, if not all, alphabets have been devised on the **phonemic principle**.

In the twelfth century, an Icelandic scholar developed an orthography derived from the Latin alphabet for the writing of the Icelandic language of his day. Other scholars in this period were also interested in orthographic reform, but the Icelander, who came to be known as "the First Grammarian" (because his anonymous paper was the first entry in a collection of grammatical essays), was the only one of the time who left a record of his principles. The orthography he developed was clearly based on the phonemic principle. He used minimal pairs to show the distinctive contrasts. He did not suggest different symbols for voiced and unvoiced [θ] and [ð], nor for [f] or [v], nor for velar [k] and palatal [tʃ], because these pairs, according to him, represented allophones of the phonemes /θ/, /f/, and /k/, respectively. He did not use these modern technical terms, but the letters of this alphabet represent the distinctive phonemes of Icelandic of that century.

King Seijong of Korea (1397–1450) realized that the same principles held true for Korean when, with the assistance of scholars, he designed a phonemic alphabet. The king was an avid reader and realized that the more than 30,000 Chinese characters used to write Korean discouraged literacy. The fruit of the king's labor was the Korean alphabet called **Hangul**, which had seventeen consonants and eleven vowels.

The Hangul alphabet was designed on the phonemic principle. Although Korean has the sounds [l] and [r], Seijong represented them by a single letter because they are allophonic variants of the same phoneme. (See exercise 3, chapter 7.) The same is true for the sounds [s] and [ʃ], and [ts] and [tʃ].

Seijong showed further ingenuity in the design of the characters themselves. The consonants are drawn so as to depict the place and manner of articulation. Thus the letter for /g/ is ㄱ to suggest the raising of the back of the tongue to the velum. The letter for /m/ is the closed figure ☐ to suggest the closing of the lips. Vowels are drawn as long vertical or horizontal lines, sometimes with smaller marks attached to them. Thus I represents /i/, ㅜ represents /u/, and ㅏ represents /a/. They are easily distinguishable from the blockier consonants.

In Korean writing, the Hangul characters are grouped into squarish blocks, each corresponding to a syllable. The syllabic blocks, though they consist of alphabetic characters, make Korean look as if it were written in a syllabary. If English were written that way, "Now is the winter of our discontent" would have this appearance:

No	i	th	wi te	o	ou	di co te
w	s	e	n r	f	r	s n nt

The space between letters is less than the space between syllables, which is less than the space between words. An example of Korean writing can be found in exercise 9, item 10 at the end of the chapter, or on the Internet.

These characteristics make Korean writing unique in the world, unlike that of the Europeans, the Arabians, the Chinese, the Cascagians, or even "ladies in England."

Many languages have their own alphabet, and each has developed certain conventions for converting strings of alphabetic characters into sequences of sound (reading), and converting sequences of sounds into strings of alphabetic characters (writing). As we have illustrated with English, Icelandic, and Korean, the rules governing the sound system of the language play an important role in the relation between sound and character.

Most European alphabets use Latin (Roman) letters, adding diacritic marks to accommodate individual characteristics of a particular language. For example, Spanish uses ñ to represent the palatalized nasal phoneme of *señor*, and German has added an umlaut for certain of its vowel sounds that did not exist in Latin (e.g., in *über*). Diacritic marks supplement the forty-six kana of the Japanese syllabaries to enable them to represent the more than 100 syllables of the language. Diacritic marks are also used in writing systems of tone languages such as Thai to indicate the tone of a syllable.

Some languages use two letters together—called a **digraph**—to represent a single sound. English has many digraphs, such as *sh* /ʃ/ as in *she*, *ch* /tʃ/ as in *chop*, *ng* as in *sing* (/sɪŋ/), and *oa* as in *loaf* /lof/.

Besides the European languages, languages such as Turkish, Indonesian, Swahili, and Vietnamese have adopted the Latin alphabet. Other languages that have more recently developed a writing system use some of the IPA phonetic symbols in their alphabet. Twi, for example, uses ɔ, ɛ, and ŋ.

Many Slavic languages, including Russian, use the Cyrillic alphabet, named in honor of St. Cyril, who brought Christianity to the Slavs in the ninth century C.E. It is derived directly from the Greek alphabet without Latin mediation.

Many contemporary alphabets, such as those used for Arabic, Farsi (spoken in Iran), Urdu (spoken in Pakistan), and many languages of the Indian subcontinent are ultimately derived from the ancient Semitic syllabaries.

Figure 12.2 shows a coarse time line of the development of the Roman alphabet.

15000 B.C.E.	—	Cave drawings as pictograms
.		
.		
.		
4000 B.C.E.	—	Sumerian cuneiform
3000 B.C.E.	—	Hieroglyphics
1500 B.C.E.	—	West Semitic Syllabary of the Phoenicians
1000 B.C.E.	—	Ancient Greeks borrow the Phoenician consonantal alphabet
750 B.C.E.	—	Etruscans borrow the Greek alphabet
500 B.C.E.	—	Romans adapt the Etruscan/Greco alphabet to Latin

FIGURE 12.2 | Timeline of the development of the Roman alphabet.

Writing and Speech

ALGERNON: But, my own sweet Cecily, I have never written you any letters.

CECILY: You need hardly remind me of that, Ernest. I remember only too well that I was forced to write your letters for you. I wrote always three times a week, and sometimes oftener.

ALGERNON: Oh, do let me read them, Cecily?

CECILY: Oh, I couldn't possibly. They would make you far too conceited. The three you wrote me after I had broken off the engagement are so beautiful, and so badly spelled, that even now I can hardly read them without crying a little.

OSCAR WILDE, *The Importance of Being Earnest*, 1895

The development of writing freed us from the limitations of time and geography, but spoken language still has primacy and is the principal concern of most linguists. Nevertheless, writing systems are of interest for their own sake.

The written language reflects, to a certain extent, the elements and rules that together constitute the grammar of the language. The letters of the alphabet represent the system of phonemes, although not necessarily in a direct way. The independence of words is revealed by the spaces between them in most writing systems. However, written Japanese and Thai do not require spaces between words, although speakers and writers are aware of the individual words. On the other hand, no writing system shows the individual morphemes within a word in this way, even though speakers know what they are. (The hyphen occasionally serves this purpose in English, as in *ten-speed* or *bone-dry*.)

Languages vary in regard to how much punctuation is used in writing. Some have little or none, such as Chinese. German uses capitalization, a form of punctuation, for all nouns. English uses punctuation to set apart sentences and phrases and to indicate questions, intonation, stress, and contrast.

Consider the difference in meaning between sentences 1 and 2:

1. I don't think I know.
2. I don't think, I know.

In (1), the speaker doesn't know; in (2), the speaker knows. The comma fills in for the pause that would make the meaning clear if spoken.

Similarly, by using an exclamation point or a question mark, the intention of the writer can be made clearer.

3. The children are going to bed at eight o'clock. (a simple statement)
4. The children are going to bed at eight o'clock! (an order)
5. The children are going to bed at eight o'clock? (a question)

In sentences 6 and 7, the use of the comma and quotation marks affects the syntax. In 6 *he* may refer either to John or to someone else, but in sentence 7 the pronoun must refer to someone other than John:

6. John said he's going.
7. John said, "He's going."

The apostrophe used in contractions and possessives also provides syntactic information not always available in the spoken utterance.

8. My cousin's friends (one cousin)
9. My cousins' friends (two or more cousins)

Writing, then, somewhat reflects the spoken language, and punctuation may even distinguish between two meanings not revealed in the spoken forms, as shown in sentences 8 and 9. However, often the spoken language conveys meaning that the written language does not.

In the normal written version of sentence 10,

10. John whispered the message to Bill and then he whispered it to Mary.

he can refer to either John or Bill. In the spoken sentence, if *he* receives extra stress (called **contrastive stress**), it must refer to Bill; if *he* receives normal stress, it refers to John.

A speaker can usually emphasize any word in a sentence by using contrastive stress. Writers sometimes attempt to show emphasis by using all capital letters, italics, or underlining the emphasized word. This is nicely illustrated by the "Garfield" cartoon.

In the first panel we understand Garfield as meaning, "I didn't do it, someone else did." In the second panel the meaning is "I didn't do it, even though you think I did." In the third, the contrastive stress conveys the meaning "I didn't do it, it just happened somehow." In the fourth panel Garfield means, "I didn't do it, though I may be guilty of other things." In each case the boldfaced word is contrasted with something else.

Although such visual devices can help in English, it is not clear that they can be used in a language such as Chinese. In Japanese, however, this kind of emphasis can be achieved by writing a word in katakana.

The use of italics has many functions in written language. One use is to indicate reference to the italicized word, as in "*sheep* is a noun." A children's riddle, which is sung aloud, plays on this distinction:

Railroad crossing, watch out for cars
How do you spell it without any *r*'s?

The answer is "i-t." The joke is that the second line, were it written, would be:

How do you spell *it* without any *r*'s?

Written language is more conservative than spoken language. Once a word is spelled and written down, that spelling remains intact, although the word's pronunciation may change over time. When we write we are more apt to obey the prescriptive rules taught in school than when we speak. We may write "it is I" but we say "it's me." Such informalities abound in spoken language, but in written language may be "corrected" by copy editors, diligent English teachers, and careful writers. A linguist wishing to describe the language that people regularly use therefore cannot depend on written records alone, except when nothing else is available, as in the study of dead languages (see chapter 11).

Spelling

"Do you spell it with a 'v' or a 'w'?" inquired the judge.
"That depends upon the taste and fancy of the speller, my Lord," replied Sam.

CHARLES DICKENS, *The Pickwick Papers*, 1837

If writing represented the spoken language perfectly, spelling reforms would never have arisen. In chapter 6 we discussed some of the problems in the English orthographic system. These problems prompted George Bernard Shaw to observe that:

[I]t was as a reading and writing animal that Man achieved his human eminence above those who are called beasts. Well, it is I and my like who have to do the writing. I have done it professionally for the last sixty years as well as it can be done with a hopelessly inadequate alphabet devised centuries before the English language existed to record another and very different language. Even this alphabet is reduced to absurdity by a foolish orthography based on the notion that the business of spelling is to represent the origin and history of a word instead of its sound and meaning. Thus an intelligent child who is bidden to spell *debt*, and very properly spells it d-e-t, is caned for not spelling it with a b because Julius Caesar spelt the Latin word for it with a b.[4]

[4]Shaw, G. B. 1948. Preface to R. A. Wilson, *The miraculous birth of language*. New York: Philosophical Library.

The irregularities between graphemes (letters) and phonemes have been cited as one reason "why Johnny can't read." Homographs such as *lead* /lid/ and *lead* /lɛd/ have fueled the flames of spelling reform movements. Different spellings for the same sound, silent letters, and missing letters also are cited as reasons that English needs a new orthographic system. The following examples illustrate the discrepancies between spelling and sounds in English:

Same Sound Different Spelling	Different Sound Same Spelling		Silent Letters	Missing Letters	
/aɪ/	thought	/θ/	listen	use	/juz/
	though	/ð/	debt	fuse	/fjuz/
aye	Thomas	/t/	gnome		
buy			know		
by	ate	/e/	psychology		
die	at	/æ/	right		
hi	father	/a/	mnemonic		
Thai	many	/ɛ/	science		
height			talk		
guide			honest		
			sword		
			bomb		
			clue		
			Wednesday		

The spelling of most English words today is based on English as spoken in the fourteenth, fifteenth, and sixteenth centuries. Spellers in those times saw no need to spell the same word consistently. Shakespeare spelled his own name in several ways. In his plays, he spelled the first person singular pronoun variously as *I, ay,* and *aye.*

After Johannes Gutenberg invented the printing press in the mid-fifteenth century, archaic and idiosyncratic spellings became widespread and more permanent. Words in print were frequently misspelled outright because many of the early printers were not native speakers of English.

Spelling reformers saw the need for consistent spelling that correctly reflected the pronunciation of words. To that extent, spelling reform was necessary, but many scholars became overzealous. Because of their reverence for Classical Greek and Latin, these scholars changed the spelling of English words to conform to their etymologies. Where Latin had a *b*, they added a *b* even if it was not pronounced. Where the original spelling had a *c* or *p* or *h*, these letters were added, as shown by these few examples:

Middle English Spelling		Reformed Spelling
indite	→	indict
dette	→	debt
receit	→	receipt
oure	→	hour

Such spelling habits inspired Robert N. Feinstein to compose the following poem, entitled *Gnormal Pspelling:*[5]

Gnus and gnomes and gnats and such
Gnouns with just one G too much.
Pseudonym and psychedelic
P becomes a psurplus relic.
Knit and knack and knife and knocked
Kneedless Ks are overstocked.
Rhubarb, rhetoric and rhyme
Should lose an H from thyme to time.

Many languages have been the subject of **spelling reforms** in the past hundred years, including Dutch, French, Norwegian, and Russian. The motivation is generally to make spelling easier for children or immigrants, and for the convenience of international communications. As recently as 1996 some German-speaking countries imposed spelling reforms that make spelling less archaic (replacing the traditional ß with ss) and more regular (*rauh → rau* (rough) because of *blau, grau, genau*). As is so often the case, there is much resistance to the imposed changes, which continues to this day.

Text messaging, and its offspring twittering, is having a growing effect on spelling. Owing to limited space, the words in a text message are often spelled as tersely as comprehension allows. For example, "wat uz tnk of da wy da englsh lang iz evolvn thru da eva incresin yus of txt msges" (82 keystrokes) for "what do you (all) think of the way the English language is evolving through the ever increasing use of text messages?" (117 keystrokes). Text message spelling is far from standardized. Each person has his own peculiar habits. The need to be understood is paramount, though, and a trick once known only to reading experts has been discovered by the folks who text message: When the letters of a word are scrambled or omitted, retaining the first and last letters is the most important. Try this:

fi yuo cna raed tihs, you porbblay hvae a snees fo txet mssegnig

The rebus principle also pops up in text messaging: *cre8* for "create" or *1der* for "wonder." There is much phonetic spelling: *yusfl* for "useful" or *thru* for "through," and a plethora of acronyms: LOL for "laugh out loud," among thousands of others. And even the most tradition-bound spellers may want to step aside and wink at the keystroke-saving *nite* for "knight," *Wensday* for "Wednesday," and so on.

Although some say—these "some" are always saying—that texting and twittering are wrecking the language, in truth the adaptation to the mobile phone is yet another example of the enormous creativity that is part of our language competence. And truly, there is nothing in texting that hasn't been done before in the history of writing, from rebuses to logographs to syllabic spelling to acronyms to abbreviations to secret code words (used to deceive eavesdropping parents)

---

[5]"Gnormal Pspelling" by Robert N. Feinstein from "Son of an Oyster." Copyright © 1986 by Robert N. Feinstein. Reprinted by permission of Roger Lathbury DBA Orchises Press as representative for the estate of Robert N. Feinstein.

and so on. An excellent treatment of the subject is to be found in David Crystal's book *Txtng: The Gr8 Db8*.

The current English spelling system is based primarily on the earlier pronunciations of words. The many changes that have occurred in the sound system of English since then are not reflected in the current spelling, which was frozen due to widespread printed material and scholastic conservatism.

For these reasons, modern English orthography does not always represent what we know about the phonology of the language. The disadvantage is partially offset by the fact that the writing system allows us to read and understand what people wrote hundreds of years ago without the need for translations. If there were a one-to-one correspondence between our spelling and the sounds of our language, we would have difficulty reading the works of Shakespeare and Dickens.

Languages change. It is not possible to maintain a perfect correspondence between pronunciation and spelling, nor is it totally desirable. For instance, in the case of homophones, it is helpful at times to have different spellings for the same sounds, as in the following pair:

The book was red. The book was read.

Lewis Carroll makes the point with humor:

> "And how many hours a day did you do lessons?" said Alice.
> "Ten hours the first day," said the Mock Turtle, "nine the next, and so on."
> "What a curious plan!" exclaimed Alice.
> "That's the reason they're called lessons," the Gryphon remarked, "because they lessen from day to day."

There are also reasons for using the same spelling for different pronunciations. A morpheme may be pronounced differently when it occurs in different contexts. The identical spelling reflects the fact that the different pronunciations represent the same morpheme. This is the case with the plural morpheme. It is always spelled with an *s* despite being pronounced [s] in *cats* and [z] in *dogs*. The sound of the morpheme is determined by rules, in this case and elsewhere.

Similarly, the phonetic realizations of the underlined vowels in the following forms follow a regular pattern:

aɪ/ɪ	i/ɛ	e/æ
div<u>i</u>ne/div<u>i</u>nity	ser<u>e</u>ne/ser<u>e</u>nity	s<u>a</u>ne/s<u>a</u>nity
ch<u>i</u>ld/ch<u>i</u>ldren	obsc<u>e</u>ne/obsc<u>e</u>nity	prof<u>a</u>ne/prof<u>a</u>nity
s<u>i</u>gn/s<u>i</u>gnature	cl<u>ea</u>n/cl<u>ea</u>nse	hum<u>a</u>ne/hum<u>a</u>nity

These considerations have led some scholars to suggest that in addition to being phonemic, English has a **morphophonemic orthography**. To read English correctly, morphophonemic knowledge is required. This contrasts with a language such as Spanish, whose orthography is almost purely phonemic.

Other examples provide further motivation for spelling irregularities. The *b* in *debt* may remind us of the related word *debit*, in which the *b* is pronounced.

The same principle is true of pairs such as *sign/signal, bomb/bombardier,* and *gnosis/prognosis/agnostic.*

There are also different spellings that represent the different pronunciations of a morpheme when confusion would arise from using the same spelling. For example, there is a rule in English phonology that changes a /t/ to an /s/ in certain cases:

democrat → democracy

The different spellings have resulted partly because this rule does not apply to all morphemes, so that *art + y* is *arty,* not **arcy.* Regular phoneme-to-grapheme rules determine in many cases when a morpheme is to be spelled identically and when it is to be changed.

Other subregularities are apparent. A *c* always represents the /s/ sound when it is followed by a *y, i,* or *e,* as in *cynic, citizen,* and *censure.* Because it is always pronounced [k] when it is the final letter in a word or when it is followed by any other vowel (*coat, cat, cut,* and so on), no confusion results. The *th* spelling is usually pronounced voiced [ð] between vowels (the result of an historical intervocalic voicing rule), and in function words such as *the, they, this,* and *there.* Elsewhere it is the voiceless [θ].

There is another important reason why spelling should not always be tied to the phonetic pronunciation of words. Different dialects of English have divergent pronunciations. Cockneys drop their "(h)aitches," and Bostonians and Southerners drop their *r*'s; *neither* is pronounced [niðər], [naɪðər], and [niðə] by Americans, [naɪðə] by the British, and [neðər] by the Irish; some Scots pronounce *night* [nɪxt]; people say "Chicago" and "Chicawgo," "hog" and "hawg," "bird" and "boyd"; *four* is pronounced [fɔː] by the British, [fɔr] in the Midwest, and [foə] in the South; *orange* is pronounced in at least two ways in the United States: [arəndʒ] and [ɔrəndʒ].

Although dialectal pronunciations differ, the common spellings indicate the intended word. It is necessary for the written language to transcend local dialects. With a uniform spelling system, a native of Atlanta and a native of Glasgow can communicate through writing. If each dialect were spelled according to its pronunciation, written communication among the English-speaking peoples of the world would suffer.

Spelling Pronunciations

For pronunciation, the best general rule is to consider those as the most elegant speakers who deviate least from written words.

SAMUEL JOHNSON (1707–1784)

Write with the learned, pronounce with the vulgar.

BENJAMIN FRANKLIN, *Poor Richard's Almanack,* mid-eighteenth century

Despite the primacy of the spoken word over the written language, the written word is often regarded with excessive reverence. The stability, permanency, and graphic nature of writing cause some people to favor it over ephemeral and elusive speech. Humpty Dumpty expressed a rather typical attitude when he said, "I'd rather see that done on paper."

Writing has affected speech only marginally, however, most notably in the phenomenon of **spelling pronunciation**. Since the sixteenth century, we find that spelling has to some extent influenced standard pronunciation. The most important of such changes stem from the eighteenth century under the influence and decrees of the dictionary makers and the schoolteachers. The struggle between those who demanded that words be pronounced according to the spelling and those who demanded that words be spelled according to their pronunciation generated great heat in that century. The preferred pronunciations were given in the many dictionaries printed in the eighteenth century, and the "supreme authority" of the dictionaries influenced pronunciation in this way.

Spelling also has influenced pronunciation of words that are used infrequently in daily speech. In many words that were spelled with an initial *h*, the *h* was silent as recently as the eighteenth century. Then, no [h] was pronounced in *honest*, *hour*, *habit*, *heretic*, *hotel*, *hospital*, and *herb*. Common words like *honest* and *hour* continued *h*-less, despite the spelling. The other less frequently used words were given a "spelling pronunciation," and the *h* is sounded today. *Herb* is currently undergoing this change. In British English the *h* is pronounced, whereas in American English it generally is not.

Similarly, the *th* in the spelling of many words was once pronounced like the /t/ in *Thomas*. Later most of these words underwent a change in pronunciation from /t/ to /θ/, as in *anthem*, *author*, and *theater*. Nicknames may reflect the earlier pronunciations: "Kate" for "Ca*th*erine," "Betty" for "Eliza*beth*," "Art" for "Ar*th*ur." *Often* is often pronounced with the *t* sounded, though historically it is silent, and up-to-date dictionaries now indicate this pronunciation as an alternative.

The clear influence of spelling on pronunciation is observable in the way place-names are pronounced. *Berkeley* is pronounced [bɔrkli] in California, although it stems from the British [baːkli]; *Worcester* [wʊstər] or [wʊstə] in Massachusetts is often pronounced [wurtʃɛstər] in other parts of the country. *Salmon* is pronounced [sæmən] in most parts of the United States, but many Southern speakers pronounce the [l] and say [sælmən].

Although the written language has some influence on the spoken, it does not change the basic system—the grammar—of the language. The writing system, conversely, reflects, in a more or less direct way, the grammar that every speaker knows.

Summary

Writing is a basic tool of civilization. Without it, the world as we know it could not exist. The precursor of writing was "picture writing," which used **pictograms** to represent objects directly and literally. Pictograms are called **ideograms** when the drawing becomes less literal, and the meaning extends to concepts associated with the object originally pictured. When ideograms become associated with the words for the concepts they signify, they are called **logograms**. Logographic systems are true writing systems in the sense that the symbols stand for words of a language.

The Sumerians first developed a pictographic writing system to keep track of commercial transactions. It was later expanded for other uses and eventually evolved into the highly stylized (and stylus-ized) **cuneiform** writing. Cuneiform was generalized to other writing systems by application of the **rebus principle**, which uses the symbol of one word or syllable to represent another word or syllable pronounced the same.

The Egyptians also developed a pictographic system known as **hieroglyphics**. This system influenced many peoples, including the Phoenicians, who developed the West Semitic Syllabary. The Greeks borrowed the Phoenician system, and in adapting it to their own language they used the symbols to represent both consonant and vowel sound segments, thus inventing the first alphabet.

There are four types of writing systems: (1) **logographic** (word writing), where every symbol or character represents a word or morpheme (as in Chinese); (2) **syllabic**, where each symbol represents a syllable (as in Japanese hiragana); (3) **consonantal alphabetic**, where each symbol represents a consonant and vowels may be represented by diacritical marks (as in Hebrew); and (4) **alphabetic**, where each symbol represents (for the most part) a vowel or consonant (as in English).

Languages change over time, but writing systems tend to be more conservative. In many languages, including English, spelling may no longer accurately reflect pronunciation. This has led to **spelling reforms** in many countries. Also, when the spoken and written forms of the language diverge, some words may be pronounced as they are spelled, sometimes as a result of the efforts of pronunciation reformers.

There are advantages to a conservative spelling system. A common spelling permits speakers whose dialects have diverged to communicate through writing, as is best exemplified in China, where the "dialects" (languages, really) are mutually unintelligible. People are also able to read and understand their language as it was written centuries ago. In addition, despite a certain lack of correspondences between sound and spelling, the spelling often reflects speakers' morphological and phonological knowledge.

References for Further Reading

Adams, M. J. 1996. *Beginning to read*. Cambridge, MA: MIT Press.

Biber, D. 1988. *Variation across speech and writing*. Cambridge, UK: Cambridge University Press.

Coulmas, F. 1989. *The writing systems of the world*. Cambridge, MA: Blackwell Publishers.

Crystal, David. 2008. *Txtng: The gr8 db8*. London: Oxford University Press.

Cummings, D. W. 1988. *American English spelling*. Baltimore, MD: The Johns Hopkins University Press.

Daniels, P. T., and W. Bright (eds.). 1996. *The world's writing systems*. New York: Oxford University Press.

DeFrancis, J. 1989. *Visible speech: The diverse oneness of writing systems*. Honolulu: University of Hawaii Press.

Gaur, A. 1984. *A history of writing*. London: The British Library.

Rogers, H. 2005. *Writing systems: A linguistic approach*. Malden, MA: Blackwell Publishing.

Sampson, G. 1985. *Writing systems: A linguistic introduction.* Stanford, CA: Stanford University Press.

Senner, W. M. (ed.). 1989. *The origins of writing.* Lincoln: University of Nebraska Press.

Exercises

1. A. "Write" the following words and phrases, using pictograms that you invent:

   a. eye
   b. a boy
   c. two boys
   d. library
   e. tree
   f. forest
   g. war
   h. honesty
   i. ugly
   j. run
   k. Scotch tape
   l. smoke

   B. Which words are most difficult to symbolize in this way? Why?

   C. How does the following statement reveal the problems in pictographic writing? "A grammar represents the unconscious, internalized linguistic competence of a native speaker."

2. A *rebus* is a written representation of words or syllables that uses pictures of objects whose names resemble the sounds of the intended words or syllables. For example, might be the symbol for "eye" or "I" or the first syllable in "idea."

   A. Using the rebus principle, "write" the following words:

   a. tearing
   b. icicle
   c. bareback
   d. cookies

   B. Why would such a system be a difficult system in which to represent all words in English? Illustrate with an example.

3. A. Construct non-Roman alphabetic letters to replace the letters used to represent the following sounds in English:

   [t r s k w tʃ i æ f n]

   B. Use the letters you created plus the regular alphabet symbols for the other sounds to write the following words in your "new" orthography.

   a. character
   b. guest

    c. cough
    d. photo
    e. cheat
    f. rang
    g. psychotic
    h. tree

4. Suppose the English writing system were a *syllabic* system instead of an *alphabetic* system. Use capital letters to symbolize the necessary syllabic units for the following words, and list your "syllabary." *Example*: Given the words *mate*, *inmate*, *intake*, and *elfin*, you might use: A = mate, B = in, C = take, and D = elf. In addition, write the words using your syllabary. *Example*: inmate—BA; *elfin*—DB; *intake*—BC; *mate*—A. (Do not use more syllable symbols than you absolutely need.)

    a. childishness
    b. childlike
    c. Jesuit
    d. lifelessness
    e. likely
    f. zoo
    g. witness
    h. lethal
    i. jealous
    j. witless
    k. lesson

5. In the following pairs of English words, the boldfaced portions are pronounced the same but spelled differently. Can you think of any reason why the spelling should remain distinct? (*Hint*: Reel and *real* are pronounced the same, but *reality* shows the presence of a phonemic /æ/ in *real*.)

	A	B	Reason
a.	I am	iamb	
b.	goose	produce	
c.	fashion	complication	
d.	Newton	organ	
e.	no	know	
f.	hymn	him	

6. In the following pairs of words, the boldfaced portions are spelled the same but pronounced differently. State some reasons why the spelling of the words in column B should not be changed.

	A	B	Reason
a.	mingle	long	The *g* is pronounced in *longer.*
b.	line	children	
c.	sonar	resound	
d.	cent	mystic	

  e. crumble bomb
  f. cats   dogs
  g. stagnant design
  h. serene obscenity

7. Each of the following sentences is ambiguous in the written form. How can these sentences be made unambiguous when they are spoken?

 Example: John hugged Bill and then he kissed him.

 For the meaning "John hugged and kissed Bill," use normal stress (*kissed* receives stress). For the meaning "Bill kissed John," contrastive stress is needed on both *he* and *him*.

 a. What are we having for dinner, Mother?
 b. She's a German language teacher.
 c. They formed a student grievance committee.
 d. Charles kissed his wife and George kissed his wife too.

8. In the written form, the following sentences are not ambiguous, but they would be if spoken. State the devices used in writing that make the meanings explicit.

 a. They're my brothers' keepers.
 b. He said, "He will take the garbage out."
 c. The red book was read.
 d. The flower was on the table.

9. Match the ten samples of writing and the ten languages. There are enough hints in this chapter to get most of them. (The source of these examples, and many others, is *Languages of the World* by Kenneth Katzner, 1975, New York: Funk & Wagnalls.)

 a. ____ Cherokee 1. 仮に勝手に変えるようなことをすれば.

 b. ____ Chinese 2. Κι ὁ νοῦς του ἀγκάλιασε ποιετικὰ τὴν Κρήτη.

 c. ____ German (Gothic style) 3. «Что это? я падаю? у меня ноги подкашиваются»,

 d. ____ Greek 4. וְהָיָה ׀ בְּאַחֲרִית הַיָּמִים נָכוֹן יִהְיֶה הַר

 e. ____ Hebrew 5. Saá sáre yi bèŋ atekyé bí â mpɔ̀torɔ áhyɛ́

 f. ____ Icelandic 6. 既然必须和新的群众的时代相结合.

 g. ____ Japanese 7. *ᎿᏒ ᎠᏝ ᏚᏍᎩ ᏣᏉ ᎫᎠᎢᎴ.*

 h. ____ Korean 8. Þótt þú langförull legðir sérhvert land undir fót,

 i. ____ Russian 9. Pharao's Anblick war wunderbar.

 j. ____ Twi 10. 스위스는 독특한 체제

10. The following appeared on the safety card of a Spanish airline. Identify each language.

 (You will probably have to spend some time in the library, or scouring the Internet, to get this right. You may also want to visit various departments of foreign languages at your school.)

1. **Para su seguridad**
2. **For your safety**
3. **Pour votre sécurité**
4. **Für ihre Sicherheit**
5. **Per la Vostra sicurezza**
6. **Para sua segurança**
7. あなたの安全のために
8. **Для Вашей безогасности**
9. **Dla bezpieczeństwa pasażerów**
10. **Za vašu sigurnost**
11. **Γιά τήν ἀσφάλειά σας**
12. **Kendi emniyetiniz için**
13. من أجـل سـلامتك

11. Diderot and D'Alembert, the French "Encyclopedists," wrote:

> The Chinese have no alphabet; their very language is incompatible with one, since it is made up of an extremely limited number of sounds. It would be impossible to convey the sound of Chinese through our alphabet or any other alphabet.

Comment on this.

12. Here are several emoticons. See if you can assign a meaning to each one. There is no one correct answer because they haven't been in the language long enough to become conventionalized. One possible set of answers is printed upside down in the footnote.[6]

a. >:–(
b. :–#
c. 8:—(
d. :D
e. :-(o)
f. :–(O)
g. |–)
h. :/)

13. Just as words may be synonyms (*sad, unhappy*), so may emoticons. Thus :–> and :–) are both used to mean "just kidding."

6

a. Annoyance. b. My lips are sealed. c. Condescension. d. Ha, ha. e. Surprise. f. I'm yelling. g. See no evil. h. Not that funny.

    A. Try to come up with three instances in which different emoticons have approximately the same meaning.

    B. Emoticons may also be ambiguous, that is, subject to different interpretations. You may have discovered that in the previous exercise. Cite three instances in which a single emoticon may be given two different interpretations.

14. Make up five or ten emoticons along with their meaning. Don't just look for them on the Internet (where you'll find hundreds of them). Be creative! For example, **3:>8** to mean "bull!" or "stubborn."

15. Punctuate the following with periods, commas, semicolons, and capital letters so that it makes sense:

that that is is that that is not is not that that is not is not that that is that that is is not that that is not

16. Think of three (or more) "majority rules" sound-spelling correspondences, and then the several exceptions to each one that make learning to read English difficult. In the text we noted words like *brave, cave, Dave, gave, slave*, etc. in which *a* followed by "silent *e*" is pronounced [e], but *have* is exceptional in that the *a* is pronounced [æ]. Another example might be the *ea* spelling in *beak, leak, peak, weak, teak*, where it is pronounced [i], with exceptions such as *steak* or the president's name *Reagan*, where the *ea* is pronounced [e], or the past tense of *read* where it is pronounced [ɛ].

17. Investigate *nushu* using the time-honored template of answering: *what, who, where, when,* and *why*. Using the Internet, a good library, or any other source, answer the questions:

    a. What is nushu?
    b. Who was involved with nushu?
    c. Where did nushu exist?
    d. When did nushu exist?
    e. Why did nushu exist?
    f. **Speculative:** Can you think of a situation in your own country that might give rise to a nushu-like situation?

18. Research project: Investigate the 1996 spelling reform in German-speaking countries. What are the countries involved? Are there reasons for the reform movement other than ease of learning and international communications? Give three other reforms than those mentioned in this book. What are some of the arguments *against* this spelling reform legislation? Do you think the spelling reform will "take hold" in this century? Or will there be a return to the traditional system?

19. Spelling rhyme occurs when two words with similar spelling but different pronunciations are rhymed. Words like *move* and *love* are considered to rhyme by many poets; however, there must be a common consonant in the final syllable, in this case [v]. Examine your favorite poems, or the lyrics of your favorite songs, and find five instances of spelling rhyme. *Example*: in the late Michael Jackson's highly popular song *Thriller* we find:

Creatures crawl in search of <u>blood</u>
To terrorize your <u>neighborhood</u>

where *blood* and *neighborhood* are spelling rhymes.

Glossary

AAE Abbreviates **African American English**.[1] See **Ebonics**, **AAVE**.

AAVE Abbreviates **African American Vernacular English**. See **Ebonics**, **AAE**.

abbreviation Shortened form of a word, e.g., *prof* from *professor*. See **clipping**.

abjad Consonantal alphabet writing system; the **consonantal alphabet** of such a system.

accent (1) Prominence. See **stressed syllable**; (2) the phonology or pronunciation of a specific **regional dialect**, e.g., Southern accent; (3) the pronunciation of a language by a nonnative speaker, e.g., French accent.

accidental gap Phonological or morphological form that constitutes possible but nonoccurring lexical items, e.g., *blick*, *unsad*.

acoustic Pertaining to physical aspects of sound.

acoustic phonetics The study of the physical characteristics of speech sounds.

acoustic signal The sound waves produced by any sound source, including speech.

acquired dyslexia Loss of ability to read correctly following brain damage in persons who were previously literate.

acronym Word composed of the initials of several words and pronounced as such, e.g., *PET* scan from *positron-emission tomography* scan. See **alphabetic abbreviation**.

active sentence A sentence in which the noun phrase **subject** in d-structure is also the noun phrase subject in s-structure, e.g., *The dog chased the car.* See **passive sentence**.

adjective (Adj) The syntactic category, also lexical category, of words that function as the head of an **adjective phrase**, and that have the semantic effect of qualifying or describing the referents of nouns, e.g., *tall, bright, intelligent*. See **adjective phrase**.

adjective phrase (AP) A syntactic category, also phrasal category, whose head is an adjective possibly accompanied by premodifiers, that occurs inside noun phrases and as complements of the verb *to be*, e.g., *worthy of praise, several miles high, green, more difficult*.

adjunction A movement operation that copies an existing node and creates a new level to which the moved category is appended.

adverb (Adv) The syntactic category, also lexical category, of words that qualify the verb such as manner adverbs like *quickly* and time adverbs like *soon*. The position of the adverb in the sentence depends on its semantic type, e.g., *John will soon eat lunch, John eats lunch quickly*.

affix A **bound morpheme** attached to a stem or root. See **prefix**, **suffix**, **infix**, **circumfix**, **stem**, **root**.

affricate A sound produced by a stop closure followed immediately by a slow release characteristic of a **fricative**; phonetically a sequence of stop + fricative, e.g., the *ch* in *chip*, which is [tʃ] and like [t] + [ʃ].

African American (Vernacular) English (AA(V)E) Dialects of English spoken by some Americans of African descent, or by any person raised from infancy in a place where AAE is spoken. See **Ebonics**.

agent The **thematic role** of the noun phrase whose referent does the action described by the verb, e.g., *George* in *George hugged Martha*.

agglutinative language A type of **synthetic language** in which words may be formed by a root and multiple affixes where the affixes are easily separated and always retain the same meaning.

agrammatic aphasics Persons suffering from **agrammatism**.

---

[1]Bold words in definitions have a separate entry in this glossary, regardless of whether the bold word or term is preceded by the expression *See*.

agrammatism (agrammatic) Language disorder usually resulting from damage to Broca's region in which the patient has difficulty with certain aspects of syntax, especially functional categories. See **Broca's area.**

agreement The process by which one word in a sentence is altered depending on a property of another word in that sentence, such as gender or number, e.g., the addition of *s* to a regular verb when the subject is third-person singular (in English).

allomorph Alternative phonetic form of a **morpheme**, e.g., the [-s], [-z], and [əz] forms of the plural morpheme in *cats*, *dogs*, and *kisses*.

allophone A predictable phonetic realization of a **phoneme**, e.g., [p] and [pʰ] are allophones of the phoneme /p/ in English.

alphabetic abbreviation A word composed of the initials of several words and pronounced letter-by-letter, e.g., *MRI* from *magnetic resonance imaging*. See **acronym.**

alphabetic writing A writing system in which each symbol typically represents one sound segment.

alveolar A sound produced by raising the tongue to the **alveolar ridge**, e.g., [s], [t], [n].

alveolar ridge The part of the hard palate directly behind the upper front teeth.

ambiguous, ambiguity The terms used to describe a word, phrase, or sentence with multiple meanings.

American Sign Language (ASL) The sign language used by the deaf community in the United States. See **sign languages.**

analogic change A language change in which a rule spreads to previously unaffected forms, e.g., the plural of *cow* changed from the earlier *kine* to *cows* by the generalization of the plural formation rule or by **analogy** to regular plural forms. Also called **internal borrowing.**

analogy The use of one form as an exemplar by which other forms can be similarly constructed, e.g., based on *bow/bows, sow/sows*, English speakers began to say *cows* instead of the older *kine*. Analogy also leads speakers to say **brang* as a past tense of *bring* based on *sing/sang/sung, ring/rang/rung*, and so on.

analytic Describes a sentence that is true by virtue of its meaning alone, irrespective of context, e.g., *Kings are male.* See **contradiction.**

analytic language A language in which most words contain a single morpheme, and there is little if any word morphology, e.g., there are no plural affixes on nouns or agreement affixes on verbs. Also called an isolating language. Vietnamese is an example of an analytic language.

anomalous Semantically ill-formed, e.g., *Colorless green ideas sleep furiously.*

anomaly A violation of semantic rules resulting in expressions that seem nonsensical, e.g., *The verb crumpled the milk.*

anomia A form of **aphasia** in which patients have word-finding difficulties.

antecedent A noun phrase with which a pronoun is **coreferential**, e.g., *the man who is eating* is the antecedent of the pronoun *himself* in the sentence *The man who is eating bit himself.*

anterior A phonetic feature of consonants whose place of articulation is in front of the palato-alveolar area, including **labials, interdentals,** and **alveolars.**

antonymic pair Two words that are pronounced the same (i.e., are homonyms) but spelled differently and whose meanings are opposite, e.g., *raise* and *raze.* See **autoantonym.**

antonyms Words that are opposite with respect to one of their semantic properties, e.g., *tall/short* are both alike in that they describe height, but opposite in regard to the extent of the height. See **gradable pair, complementary pair, relational opposites.**

aphasia Language loss or disorder following brain damage.

approximants Sounds in which the articulators have a near frictional closeness, but no actual friction occurs, e.g., [w], [j], [r], and [l] in English, where the first three are central approximants, and [l] is a lateral approximant.

arbitrary Describes the property of language, including sign language, whereby there is no natural or intrinsic relationship between the way a word is pronounced (or signed) and its meaning.

arc Part of the graphical depiction of a transition network represented as an arrow, often labeled, connecting two nodes. See **node, transition network**.

argot The specialized words used by a particular group, such as pilots or linguists, e.g., *morphophonemics* in linguistics.

arguments The various NPs that occur with a verb, e.g., *Jack* and *Jill* are arguments of *loves* in *Jack loves Jill*.

argument structure The various NPs that occur with particular verbs, called its arguments, e.g., **intransitive verbs** take a subject NP only; **transitive verbs** take both a subject and direct object NP.

article (Art) One of several subclasses of determiners, e.g., *the, a*.

articulatory phonetics The study of how the vocal tract produces speech sounds; the physiological characteristics of speech sounds.

aspirated Describes a voiceless stop produced with a puff of air that results when the vocal cords remain open for a brief period after the release of the stop, e.g., the [pʰ] in *pit*. See **unaspirated**.

assimilation rules/assimilation A phonological process that changes feature values of segments to make them more similar, e.g., a vowel becomes [+nasal] when followed by [+nasal] consonant. Also called **feature-spreading rules**.

asterisk The symbol * used to indicate ungrammatical or anomalous examples, e.g., **cried the baby*, **sincerity dances*. Also used in historical and comparative linguistics to represent a reconstructed form.

auditory phonetics The study of the perception of speech sounds.

autoantonym A word that has two opposite meanings, e.g., *cleave*, "to split apart" or "to cling together." See **antonymic pair**.

automatic machine translation The use of computers to translate from one language to another. See **source language, target language**.

Aux A syntactic category containing **auxiliary verbs** and abstract tense morphemes that functions as the **head** of a **sentence (S)**. It is also called **INFL**.

auxiliary verb Verbal elements, traditionally called "helping verbs," that co-occur with, and qualify, the **main verb** in a verb phrase with regard to such properties as tense, e.g., *have, be, will*.

babbling Speech sounds produced in the first few months after birth that gradually come to include only sounds that occur in the language of the household. Deaf children babble with hand gestures.

baby talk A certain **style** of speech that many adults use when speaking to children that includes among other things exaggerated intonation. See **motherese, child-directed speech (CDS)**.

back-formation Creation of a new word by removing an affix from an old word, e.g., *donate* from *donation*; or by removing what is mistakenly considered an affix, e.g., *edit* from *editor*.

backtracking The process of undoing an analysis—usually a top-down analysis—when sensory data indicates it has gone awry, and beginning again at a point where the analysis is consistent with the data, e.g., in the syntactic analysis of *The little orange car sped*, analyzing *orange* as a noun, and later reanalyzing it as an adjective. See **top-down processing**.

base Any **root** or **stem** to which an affix is attached.

bidialectal Persons who know one or more **dialects** and speak the one most appropriate to the sociolinguistic context, often mixing the several dialects. See **codeswitching**.

bilabial A sound articulated by bringing both lips together.

bilingualism The ability to speak two (or more) languages with native or near native proficiency, either by an individual speaker (**individual bilingualism**) or within a society (**societal bilingualism**).

bilingual language acquisition The (more or less) simultaneous acquisition of two or more languages before the age of three years such that each language is acquired with native competency.

bilingual maintenance (BM) Education programs that aim to maintain competence in both languages for the entire educational experience.

birdcall One or more short notes that convey messages associated with the immediate environment, such as danger, feeding, nesting, and flocking.

bird song A complex pattern of notes used to mark territory and to attract mates.

blend A word composed of the parts of more than one word, e.g., *smog* from *smoke* + *fog*.

blocked A derivation that is prevented by a prior application of morphological rules, e.g., when *Commun* + *ist* entered the language, words such as *Commun* + *ite* (as in *Trotsky* + *ite*) or *Commun* + *ian* (as in *grammar* + *ian*) were not needed and were not formed.

borrowing The incorporating of a loan word from one language into another, e.g., English borrowed *buoy* from Dutch. See **loan word**.

bottom-up processing Data-driven analysis of linguistic input that begins with the small units like phones and proceeds stepwise to increasingly larger units like words and phrases until the entire input is processed, often ending in a complete sentence and semantic interpretation. See **top-down processing**.

bound morpheme A morpheme that must be attached to other morphemes, e.g., -*ly*, -*ed*, *non-*. Bound morphemes are **prefixes, suffixes, infixes, circumfixes**, and some **roots** such as *cran* in *cranberry*. See **free morpheme**.

bound pronoun A pronoun (or more generally, a **pro-form**) whose antecedent is explicitly mentioned in the discourse. See **unbound, free pronoun**.

broadening A semantic change in which the meaning of a word changes over time to become more encompassing, e.g., *dog* once meant a particular breed of *dog*.

Broca, Paul A French neurologist of the nineteenth century who identified a particular area of the left side of the brain as a language center.

Broca's aphasia See agrammatism.

Broca's area A front part of the left hemisphere of the brain, damage to which causes agrammatism or Broca's aphasia. Also called Broca's region.

calligraphy The art of writing or drawing Chinese characters.

case A characteristic of nouns and pronouns, and in some languages articles and adjectives, determined by the function in the sentence, and generally indicated by the morphological form of the word, e.g., *I* is in the nominative case of the first-person singular pronoun in English and functions as a subject; *me* is in the accusative case and functions as an object.

case endings Suffixes on the noun based on its grammatical function, such as *'s* of the English genitive case indicating possession, e.g., *Robert's sheepdog*.

case morphology The process of **inflectional morphemes** combining with nouns to indicate the grammatical relation of the noun in its sentence, e.g., in Russian, the inflectional suffix -*a* added to a noun indicates that the noun is an object.

case theory The study of thematic roles or grammatical case in languages of the world.

cause/causative The thematic role of the noun phrase whose referent is a natural force that is responsible for a change, e.g., *the wind* in *The wind damaged the roof*.

cerebral hemispheres The left and right halves of the brain, joined by the **corpus callosum**.

characters (Chinese) The units of Chinese writing, each of which represents a morpheme or word. See **ideogram**, **ideograph**, **logograms**.

Chicano English (ChE) A dialect of English spoken by some bilingual Mexican Americans in the western and southwestern United States.

child-directed speech (CDS) The special intonationally exaggerated speech that some adults sometimes use to speak with small children, sometimes called **baby talk**. See **motherese**.

circumfix A bound morpheme, parts of which occur in a word both before and after the root, e.g., *ge—t* in German *geliebt*, "loved," from the root *lieb*.

classifier A grammatical morpheme that marks the semantic class of a noun, e.g., in Swahili, nouns that refer to human artifacts such as beds and chairs are prefixed with the classifiers *ki* if singular and *vi* if plural; *kiti*, "chair" and *viti*, "chairs."

click A speech sound produced by sucking air into the mouth and forcing it between articulators to produce a sharp sound, e.g., the sound often spelled *tsk*.

clipping The deletion of some part of a longer word to give a shorter word with the same meaning, e.g., *phone* from *telephone*. See **abbreviation**.

closed class A category, generally a **functional category**, that rarely has new words added to it, e.g., prepositions, conjunctions. See **open class**.

coarticulation The transfer of **phonetic features** to adjoining segments to make them more alike, e.g., vowels become [+nasal] when followed by consonants that are [+nasal].

cocktail party effect An informal term that describes the ability to filter out background noise and focus on a particular sound source or on a particular person's speech.

coda One or more phonological segments that follow the **nucleus** of a syllable, e.g., the /st/ in /prist/ *priest*.

codeswitching The movement back and forth between two languages or dialects within the same sentence or discourse.

cognates Words in related languages that developed from the same ancestral root, such as English *man* and German *Mann*.

coinage The construction and/or invention of new words that then become part of the lexicon, e.g., *podcast*.

collocation analysis Textual analysis that reveals the extent to which the presence of one word influences the occurrence of nearby words.

comparative linguistics The branch of historical linguistics that explores language change by comparing related languages.

comparative method The technique linguists use to deduce forms in an ancestral language by examining corresponding forms in several of its descendant languages.

comparative reconstruction The deducing of forms in an ancestral language of genetically related languages by application of the **comparative method**.

competence, linguistic The knowledge of a language represented by the mental grammar that accounts for speakers' linguistic ability and creativity. For the most part, linguistic competence is unconscious knowledge.

complement The constituent(s) in a phrase other than the head that complete(s) the meaning of the phrase and which is **C-selected** by the verb. In the verb phrase *found a puppy*, the noun phrase *a puppy* is a complement of the verb *found*.

complementary distribution The situation in which phones never occur in the same phonetic environment, e.g., [p] and [pʰ] in English. See **allophone**.

complementary pair Two **antonyms** related in such a way that the negation of one is the meaning of the other, e.g., *alive* means *not dead*. See **gradable pair**, **relational opposites**.

complementizer (C) A syntactic category, also functional category, of words, including *that, if, whether*, that introduce an **embedded sentence**, e.g., *his belief that sheepdogs* *can swim*, or, *I wonder if sheepdogs can swim*. The complementizer has the effect of turning a sentence into a complement.

compositional semantics A theory of meaning that calculates the truth value or meaning of larger units by the application of semantic rules to the truth value or meaning of smaller units.

compound A word composed of two or more words, which may be written as a single word or as words separated by spaces or hyphens, e.g., *dogcatcher, dog biscuit, dog-tired*.

computational forensic linguistics A sub-area of **forensic linguistics** that concerns itself with computer applications in matters involving language, the law, and the judicial system.

computational lexicography The building of electronic dictionaries suitable for use by computational linguists.

computational linguistics A subfield of linguistics and computer science that is concerned with the computer processing of human language.

computational morphology The programming of computers to analyze the structure of words.

computational phonetics and phonology The programming of computers to analyze the speech signal into phones and phonemes.

computational pragmatics The programming of computers to take context and situation into account when determining the meaning of expressions.

computational semantics The programming of computers to determine the meaning of words, phrases, sentences, and discourse.

computational syntax The programming of computers to analyze the structure of sentences. See **parse, bottom-up processing, top-down processing**.

concatenative (speech) synthesis The computer production of speech based on assembling prerecorded human pronunciations of basic units such as phones, syllables, morphemes, words, phrases, or sentences.

concordance An alphabetical index of the words in a text that gives the frequency of each word, its location in the text, and its surrounding context.

conditioned sound change Historical phonological change that occurs in specific phonetic contexts, e.g., the voicing of /f/ to [v] when it occurs between vowels.

connectionism Modeling grammars through the use of networks consisting of simple neuron-like units connected in complex ways so that different connections vary in strength, and can be strengthened or weakened through exposure to linguistic data. For example, in phonology there would be stronger connections among /p/, /t/, and /k/ (the voiceless stops and a natural class) than among /p/, /n/, and /i/. In morphology there would be stronger connections between *play/played* and *dance/danced* than between *play* and *danced*. Semantically, there would be stronger connections between *melody* and *music* than between *melody* and *sheepdog*. Syntactically, there would be stronger connections between *John loves Mary* and *Mary is loved by John* than between *John loves Mary* and *Mary knows John*.

connotative meaning/connotation The evocative or affective meaning associated with a word. Two words or expressions may have the same **denotative meaning** but different connotations, e.g., *president* and *commander-in-chief*.

consonant A speech sound produced with some constriction of the air stream. See **vowel**.

consonantal The phonetic feature that distinguishes the class of obstruents, liquids, and nasals, which are [+consonantal], from other sounds (vowels and glides), which are [−consonantal].

consonantal alphabet The symbols of a **consonantal writing** system.

consonantal writing A writing system of symbols that represent only **consonants**; vowels are inferred from context, e.g., Arabic.

constituent A syntactic unit in a **phrase structure tree**, e.g., *the girl* is a noun phrase constituent in the sentence *the boy loves the girl*.

constituent structure The hierarchically arranged syntactic units such as noun phrase and verb phrase that underlie every sentence.

constituent structure tree See **phrase structure tree**.

content words The nouns, verbs, adjectives, and adverbs that constitute the major part of the vocabulary. See **open class**.

context The discourse preceding an utterance together with the real-world knowledge of speakers and listeners. See **linguistic context, situational context**.

continuant A speech sound in which the air stream flows continually through the mouth; all speech sounds except stops and affricates.

contour tones In tone language, tones in which the **pitch** glides from one level to another, e.g., from low to high as in a rising tone.

contradiction Describes a sentence that is false by virtue of its meaning alone, irrespective of context, e.g., *Kings are female*. See **analytic, tautology**.

contradictory Mutual negative entailment: the truth of one sentence necessarily implies the falseness of another sentence, and vice versa, e.g., *The door is open* and *The door is closed* are contradictory sentences. See **entailment**.

contralateral Refers to neural signals that travel between one side of the body (left/right) and the opposite **cerebral hemisphere** (right/left).

contrast Different sounds contrast when their presence alone distinguishes between otherwise identical forms, e.g., [f] and [v] in *fine* and *vine*, but not [p] and [pʰ] in [spik] and [spʰik] (two variant ways of saying *speak*). See **minimal pair**.

contrasting tones In tone languages, different tones that make different words, e.g., in Nupe, *bá* with a high tone and *bà* with a low tone mean "be sour" and "count," respectively.

contrastive stress Additional stress placed on a word to highlight it or to clarify the referent of a pronoun, e.g., in *Joe hired Bill and he hired Sam*, with contrastive stress on *he*, it is usually understood that Bill rather than Joe hired Sam.

convention, conventional The agreed-on, although generally arbitrary, relationship between the form and meaning of words.

cooperative principle A broad principle within whose scope fall the various **maxims of conversation**. It states that in order to communicate effectively, speakers should agree to be informative and relevant.

coordinate structure A syntactic structure in which two or more constituents of the same syntactic category are joined by a conjunction such as *and* and *or*, e.g., *bread and butter, the big dog or the small cat, huffing and puffing*.

coreference The relation between two noun phrases that refer to the same entity.

coreferential Describes noun phrases (including pronouns) that refer to the same entity.

coronals The class of consonants articulated by raising the tip or blade of the tongue, including **alveolars** and **palatals**, e.g., [t], [ʃ].

corpus A collection of language data gathered from spoken or written sources used for linguistic research and analysis.

corpus callosum The nerve fibers connecting the right and left **cerebral hemispheres**.

cortex The approximately ten billion neurons that form the outside surface of the brain; also referred to as gray matter.

count nouns Nouns that can be enumerated, e.g., *one potato, two potatoes*. See **mass nouns**.

cover symbol A symbol that represents a class of sounds, e.g., C for consonants, V for vowels.

creativity of language, creative aspect of linguistic knowledge Speakers' ability to combine the finite number of linguistic units of their language to produce and understand an infinite range of novel sentences.

creole A language that begins as a **pidgin** and eventually becomes the native language of a speech community.

creolization The linguistic *expansion* in the lexicon and grammar, and an increase in the contexts of use, of an existing **pidgin**. See **pidginization**.

critical-age hypothesis The theory that states that there is a window of time between early childhood and puberty for learning a first language, and beyond which first language acquisition is almost always incomplete.

critical period The time between early childhood and puberty during which a child can acquire a native language easily, swiftly, and without external intervention. After this period, the acquisition of the grammar is difficult and, for some individuals, never fully achieved.

C-selection The classifying of verbs and other lexical items in terms of the syntactic category of the complements that they accept (C stands for categorial), sometimes called **subcategorization**, e.g., the verb *find* C-selects, or is subcategorized for, a noun phrase complement.

cuneiform A form of writing in which the characters are produced using a wedge-shaped stylus, and most notably utilized by ancient civilizations of the Middle East such as the Sumerians.

data mining Complex methods of retrieving and using information from immense and varied sources of data through the use of advanced statistical tools.

declarative (sentence) A sentence that asserts that a particular situation exists. See **interrogative**.

declension A list of the inflections or **cases** of nouns, pronouns, adjectives, and determiners in categories such as grammatical relationship, number, and gender.

deep structure See **d-structure**.

definite Describes a noun phrase that refers to a particular object known to the speaker and listener.

deictic/deixis Refers to words or expressions whose reference relies on context and the orientation of the speaker in space and time, e.g., *I, yesterday, there, this cat*.

demonstrative articles, demonstratives Words such as *this, that, those,* and *these* that function syntactically as articles but are semantically **deictic** because context is needed to determine the referent of the noun phrase in which they occur.

denotative meaning The referential meaning of a word or expression. See **connotative meaning**.

dental A place-of-articulation term for consonants articulated with the tongue against, or nearly against, the front teeth. See **interdental**.

derivation The steps in the application of rules to an underlying form that results in a surface representation, e.g., in deriving a syntactic s-structure from a d-structure, or in deriving a phonetic form from a phonemic form.

derivational affix See **derivational morpheme**.

derivational morpheme A morpheme added to a stem or root to form a new stem or word, possibly, but not necessarily, resulting in a change in syntactic category, e.g., *-er* added to a verb like *kick* to give the noun *kicker*.

derived structure Any structure resulting from the application of transformational rules.

derived word The form that results from the addition of a **derivational morpheme**, e.g., *firmly* from *firm + ly*.

descriptive grammar A linguist's description or model of the mental grammar, including the units, structures, and rules. An explicit statement of what speakers know about their language. See **prescriptive grammar, teaching grammar.**

determiner (Det) The syntactic category, also functional category, of words and expressions, which when combined with a noun form a noun phrase. Includes the articles *the* and *a*, **demonstratives** such as *this* and *that*, quantifiers such as *each* and *every*, etc.

diacritics Additional markings on written symbols to specify various phonetic properties such as **length, tone, stress, nasalization;** extra marks on a written character that change its usual value, e.g., the tilde ~ drawn over the letter *ñ* in Spanish to represent a palatalized nasal rather than an alveolar nasal.

dialect A variety of a language whose grammar differs in systematic ways from other varieties. Differences may be lexical, phonological, syntactic, and semantic. See **regional dialect, social dialect, prestige dialect.**

dialect area A geographic area defined by the predominant use of a particular language variety, or a particular characteristic of a language variety, e.g., an area where *bucket* is used rather than *pail*. See **dialect, dialect atlas, isogloss.**

dialect atlas A book of **dialect maps** showing the areas where specific dialectal characteristics occur in the speech of the region.

dialect continuum A geographic range of slightly varying **dialects** occurring between two distinctly different dialects spoken in different regions of a language area.

dialect leveling Movement toward greater uniformity or decrease in variations among dialects.

dialect map A map showing the areas where specific dialectal characteristics occur in the speech of the region.

dichotic listening Experimental methods for brain research in which subjects hear different auditory signals in the left and right ears.

digraph Two letters used to represent a single sound, e.g., *gh* represents [f] in *enough.*

diphthong A sequence of two vowels run together as a single phonological unit, e.g., [aɪ, aʊ, ɔɪ] as in *bite, bout, boy.* See **monophthong.**

direct object The grammatical relation of a noun phrase when it appears immediately below the verb phrase (VP) and next to the verb in deep structure; the noun phrase complement of a transitive verb, e.g., *the puppy* in *the boy found the puppy.*

discontinuous morpheme A morpheme with multiple parts that occur in more than one place in a word or sentence, e.g., *ge* and *t* in German *geliebt,* "loved." See **circumfix.**

discourse A linguistic unit that comprises more than one sentence.

discourse analysis The study of broad speech units comprising multiple sentences.

discreteness A fundamental property of human language in which larger linguistic units are perceived to be composed of smaller linguistic units, e.g., *cat* is perceived as the phonemes /k/, /æ/, /t/; *the cat* is perceived as *the* and *cat.*

dissimilation rules Phonological **rules** that change feature values of segments to make them less similar, e.g., a fricative dissimilation rule: /θ/ is pronounced [t] following another fricative. In English dialects with this rule, *sixth* /sɪks + θ/ is pronounced [sɪkst].

distinctive Describes linguistic elements that contrast, e.g., [f] and [v] are distinctive segments. Voice is a distinctive phonetic feature of consonants.

distinctive features Phonetic properties of phonemes that account for their ability to contrast meanings of words, e.g., *voice, tense.* Also called **phonemic features.**

ditransitive verb A verb that appears to take two noun-phrase objects, e.g., *give* in *he gave Sally his cat.* Ditransitive verb phrases often have an alternative form with a prepositional phrase in place of the first noun phrase, as in *he gave his cat to Sally.*

dominate In a **phrase structure tree,** when a continuous downward path can be traced from a node labeled A to a node labeled B, then A dominates B.

downdrift The gradual lowering of the absolute **pitch** of tones during an utterance in a tone language. During downdrift, tones retain their *relative* values to one another.

d-structure Any **phrase structure tree** generated by the phrase structure rules of a transformational grammar; the basic syntactic structures of the grammar. Also called **deep structure**. See **transformational rule**.

Dual Language Immersion An education program that enrolls English-speaking children and minority-language students in roughly equal numbers, with the intention of making all students bilingual.

dyslexia A cover term for the various types of reading impairment.

ear witnessing The use of human listeners to identify an unknown speaker of an utterance, as opposed to **speaker identification**, which uses computers to achieve that end.

Early Middle English Vowel Shortening A sound change that shortened vowels such as the first *i* in *criminal*. As a result, *criminal* was unaffected by the **Great Vowel Shift**, leading to word pairs such as *crime/criminal*.

ease of articulation The tendency of speakers to adjust their pronunciation to make it easier, or more efficient, to move the articulators. Phonetic and phonological rules are often the result of ease of articulation, e.g., the rule of English that nasalizes vowels when they precede a nasal consonant.

Ebonics An alternative term, first used in 1997, for the various dialects of **African American English**.

embedded sentence A sentence that occurs within a sentence in a **phrase structure tree**, e.g., *You know that sheepdogs cannot read*.

emoticon A string of text characters that, when viewed sideways, forms a face or figure expressing a particular emotion, e.g., [8<\ to express "dismay." Frequently used in e-mail.

entail One sentence entails another if the truth of the first necessarily implies the truth of the second, e.g., *The sun melted the ice* entails *The ice melted* because if the first is true, the second must be true.

entailment The relationship between two sentences, where the truth of one necessitates the truth of the other, e.g., *Corday assassinated Marat* and *Marat is dead*; if the first is true, the second must be true.

epenthesis The insertion of one or more **phones** in a word, e.g., the insertion of [ə] in *children* to produce [tʃɪlədrən] instead of [tʃɪldrən].

eponym A word taken from a proper name, such as *Hertz* for "unit of frequency."

etymology The history of words; the study of the history of words.

euphemism A word or phrase that replaces a **taboo** word or is used to avoid reference to certain acts or subjects, e.g., *powder room* for *toilet*.

euphemism treadmill The process whereby a euphemism takes on the taboo characteristics of the word it replaced, thereby requiring another euphemism, e.g., *cripple—handicapped—disabled—challenged*.

event/eventive A type of sentence that describes activities such as *John kissed Mary*, as opposed to describing states such as *John knows Mary*. See **state/stative**.

event-related brain potentials (ERP) The electrical signals emitted from different areas of the brain in response to different kinds of stimuli.

experiencer The thematic role of the noun phrase whose referent perceives something, e.g., *Helen* in *Helen heard Robert playing the piano*.

extension The referential part of the meaning of an expression; the referent of a noun phrase. See **reference**, **referent**.

feature-changing rules Phonological **rules** that change feature values of segments, either to make them more similar (see **assimilation rules**) or less similar (see **dissimilation rules**).

feature matrix A representation of phonological segments in which the columns represent segments and the rows represent features, each cell being marked with a + or − to designate the presence or absence of the feature for that segment.

feature-spreading rules See assimilation rules.

finger spelling In signing, hand gestures that represent letters of the alphabet used to spell words for which there is no sign.

flap A speech sound in which the tongue touches the alveolar ridge and withdraws. It is often an allophone of /t/ and /d/ in words such as *writer* and *rider*. Also called **tap**.

folk etymology The process whereby the history of a word is derived from nonscientific speculation or false analogy with another word, e.g., *hooker* for "prostitute" is falsely believed to be derived from the name of the U.S. Civil War general Joseph Hooker.

forensic linguistics A subfield of linguistics that applies to language as used in legal and judicial matters.

form The phonological or gestural representation of a morpheme or word.

formant In the frequency analysis of speech, a band of frequencies of higher intensity than surrounding frequencies, which appears as a dark line on a **spectrogram**. Individual vowels display different formant patterns.

formant (speech) synthesis The computer production of sound based on the blending of electronic-based acoustic components; no prerecorded human sounds are used.

fossilization A characteristic of second-language learning in which the learner reaches a plateau and seems unable to acquire some property of the L2 grammar.

free morpheme A single **morpheme** that constitutes a word, e.g., *dog*.

free pronoun A pronoun that refers to some object not explicitly mentioned in the sentence, e.g., *it* in *Everyone saw it*. Also called **unbound**. See **bound pronoun**.

free variation Alternative pronunciations of a word in which one sound is substituted for another without changing the word's meaning, e.g., pronunciation of *bottle* as [batəl] or [baʔəl].

fricative A consonant sound produced with so narrow a constriction in the vocal tract as to create sound through friction, e.g., [s], [f].

front vowels Vowel sounds in which the tongue is positioned forward in the mouth, e.g., [i], [æ].

function word A word that does not always have a clear lexical meaning but has a grammatical function; function words include conjunctions, **prepositions**, **articles**, auxiliaries, **complementizers**, and pronouns. See **closed class**.

functional category One of the categories of function words, including **determiner**, **Aux**, **complementizer**, and **preposition**. These categories are not lexical or phrasal categories. See **lexical category**, **phrasal category**.

fundamental difference hypothesis Second language acquisition (L2) differs fundamentally from first language acquisition (L1).

fundamental frequency In speech, the rate at which the vocal cords vibrate, symbolized as F_0, called F-zero, perceived by the listener as **pitch**.

fusional languages Synthetic languages in which several meanings are packed into what appears to be a single affix, such as *-amos* in Spanish *hablamos* meaning "first person, plural, present tense."

gapping The syntactic process of deletion in which subsequent occurrences of a verb are omitted in similar contexts, e.g., *Bill washed the grapes and Mary, the cherries*.

garden path sentences Sentences that appear at first blush to be ungrammatical, but with further syntactic processing turn out to be grammatical, e.g., *The horse raced past the barn fell*.

geminate A sequence of two identical sounds; a long vowel or long consonant denoted either by writing the phonetic symbol twice as in [biiru], [sakki] or by use of a colon-like symbol [bi:ru], [sak:i].

generate To specify precisely, concisely, and in all particulars, e.g., syntactic rules generate the different kinds of sentence structures of a language.

generative grammar A grammar that accounts for linguistic knowledge by means of rules that generate all and only the grammatical sentences of the language.

generic term A word that applies to a whole class, such as *wombat* in *the wombat lives across the seas, among the far Antipodes*. A word that is ordinarily masculine, when used to refer to both sexes, e.g., *mankind* meaning "the human race"; the masculine pronoun when used as a neutral form, as in *Everyone should do* his *duty*.

genetically related Describes two or more languages that developed from a common, earlier language, e.g., French, Italian, and Spanish, which all developed from Latin.

glide A speech sound produced with little or no obstruction of the air stream that is always preceded or followed by a vowel, e.g., [w] in *we*, [j] in *you*.

gloss A word in one language given to express the meaning of a word in another language, e.g., "house" is the English gloss for the French word *maison*.

glottal/glottal stop A speech sound produced with constriction at the **glottis**; when the air is stopped completely at the glottis by tightly closed vocal cords, a glottal stop is produced.

glottis The vocal cords themselves and/or the opening between the vocal cords.

goal The thematic role of the noun phrase toward whose referent the action of the verb is directed, e.g., *the theater* in *The kids went to the theater*.

gradable pair Two antonyms related in such a way that more of one is less of the other, e.g., *warm* and *cool*; more warm is less cool, and vice versa. See **complementary pair**, **relational opposites**.

grammar The mental representation of a speaker's linguistic competence; what a speaker knows about a language, including its phonology, morphology, syntax, semantics, and lexicon. A linguistic description of a speaker's mental grammar.

grammar translation A method of second-language learning in which the student memorizes words and syntactic rules and translates them between the native language and target language.

grammatical, grammaticality Describes a well-formed sequence of words, one conforming to rules of **syntax**.

grammatical case See case.

grammatical categories Traditionally called "parts of speech"; also called **syntactic categories**; expressions of the same grammatical category can generally substitute for one another without loss of grammaticality, e.g., **noun phrase, verb phrase, adjective, auxiliary verb**.

grammatical morpheme A function word or bound morpheme required by the syntactic rules, e.g., *to* and *s* in *he wants to go*. See **inflectional morpheme**.

grammatical relation Any of several structural positions that a noun phrase may assume in a sentence. See **subject, direct object**.

graphemes The symbols of an alphabetic writing system; the letters of an alphabet.

Great Vowel Shift A sound change that took place in English some time between 1400 and 1600 C.E. in which seven long vowel phonemes were changed.

Grimm's Law The description of a phonological change in the sound system of an early ancestor of the Germanic languages formulated by Jakob Grimm.

Hangul An alphabet based on the phonemic principle for writing the Korean language designed in the fifteenth century.

head (of a compound) The rightmost word, e.g., *house* in *doghouse*. It generally indicates the category and general meaning of the compound.

head (of a phrase) The central word of a phrase whose lexical category defines the type of phrase, e.g., the noun *man* is the head of the noun phrase *the man who came to* *dinner*; the verb *wrote* is the head of the verb phrase *wrote a letter to his mother*; the adjective *red* is the head of the adjective phrase *very bright red*.

hemiplegic An individual (child or adult) with acquired unilateral lesions of the brain who retains both hemispheres (one normal and one diseased).

hemispherectomy The surgical removal of a hemisphere of the brain.

heteronyms Different words spelled the same (i.e., **homographs**) but pronounced differently, e.g., *bass*, meaning either "low tone" [bes] or "a kind of fish" [bæs].

hierarchical structure The groupings and subgroupings of the parts of a sentence into syntactic categories, e.g., *the bird sang* [[[the] [bird]] [sang]]; the groupings and subgroupings of morphemes in a word, e.g., *unlockable* [[un] [[lock][able]]]. Hierarchical structure is generally depicted in a **tree diagram**.

hieroglyphics A writing system used by the Egyptians around 4000 B.C.E. that began as a **pictographic writing** system and evolved over time into a **logographic writing** and **syllabic writing** system.

hiragana A Japanese **syllabary** used to write native words of the language, most often together with ideographic characters. See **kanji**.

historical and comparative linguistics The branch of linguistics that deals with how languages change, what kinds of changes occur, and why they occur.

historical linguistics See **historical and comparative linguistics**.

holophrastic The stage of child language acquisition in which one word conveys a complex message similar to that of a phrase or sentence.

homographs Words spelled identically, and possibly pronounced the same, e.g., *bear* meaning "to tolerate," and *bear* the animal; or *lead* the metal and *lead*, what leaders do.

homonyms/homophones Words pronounced, and possibly spelled, the same, e.g., *to, too, two*; or *bat* the animal, *bat* the stick, and *bat* meaning "to flutter" as in "bat the eyelashes."

homorganic consonants Two sounds produced at the same place of articulation, e.g., [m] and [p]; [t], [d], [n]. See **assimilation rules**.

homorganic nasal rule A phonological assimilation rule that changes the place of articulation feature of a nasal consonant to agree with that of a following consonant, e.g., /n/ becomes [m] when preceding /p/ as in *impossible*.

hypercorrection Deviations from the "norm" thought by speakers to be "more correct," such as saying *between he and she* instead of *between him and her*.

hyponyms Words whose meanings are specific instances of a more general word, e.g., *red, white*, and *blue* are hyponyms of the word *color*; *triangle* is a hyponym of *polygon*.

iambic Stress on the second syllable of a two-syllable word, e.g., *giráffe*.

iconic, iconicity A nonarbitrary relationship between form and meaning in which the form bears a resemblance to its meaning, e.g., the male and female symbols on (some) restroom doors.

ideogram, ideograph A character of a word-writing system, often highly stylized, that represents a concept, or the pronunciation of the word representing that concept.

idiolect An individual's way of speaking, reflecting that person's grammar.

idiom/idiomatic phrase An expression whose meaning does not conform to the **principle of compositionality**, that is, may be unrelated to the meaning of its parts, e.g., *kick the bucket* meaning "to die."

ill-formed Describes an ungrammatical or anomalous sequence of words.

illocutionary force The intended effect of a speech act, such as a warning, a promise, a threat, and a bet, e.g., the illocutionary force of *I resign!* is the act of resignation.

imitation A proposed mechanism of child language acquisition, according to which children learn their language by imitating adult speech.

immediately dominate If a node labeled A is directly above a node labeled B in a phrase structure tree, then A immediately dominates B.

implicature An inference based not only on an utterance, but also on assumptions about what the speaker is trying to achieve, e.g., *Are you using the ketchup?* to mean "Please pass the ketchup" while dining in a café.

impoverished data Refers to the incomplete, noisy, and unstructured utterances that children hear, including slips of the tongue, false starts, and ungrammatical and incomplete sentences, together with a lack of concrete evidence about abstract grammatical rules and structure.

individual bilingualism The ability of an individual speaker to speak two (or more) languages with native or near native proficiency. See **bilingualism, societal bilingualism.**

Indo-European The descriptive name given to the ancestor language of many modern language families, including Germanic, Slavic, and Romance. Also called **Proto-Indo-European.**

infinitive An uninflected form of a verb, e.g., (to) *swim.*

infinitive sentence An **embedded sentence** that does not have a tense and therefore is a "to" form, e.g., *sheepdogs to be fast readers* in the sentence *He believes sheepdogs to be fast readers.*

infix A bound morpheme that is inserted in the middle of another morpheme, e.g., Tagalog *sulat* "writing" but *sumulat* "to write" after insertion of the infix *um.*

INFL Abbreviates "inflection," a term sometimes used in place of **Aux**; the head of a sentence (S).

inflectional affix See inflectional morpheme.

inflectional morpheme A bound grammatical morpheme that is affixed to a word according to rules of syntax, e.g., third-person singular verbal suffix -*s.*

information retrieval The process of using a computer to search a database for items on a particular topic. See **data mining.**

innateness hypothesis The theory that the human species is genetically equipped with a Universal Grammar, which provides the basic design for all human languages.

instrument The thematic role of the noun phrase whose referent is the means by which an action is performed, e.g., *a paper clip* in *Houdini picked the lock with a paper clip.*

intension The inherent, nonreferential part of the meaning of an expression, also called sense. See **sense, extension.**

intensity The magnitude of an acoustic signal, which is perceived as loudness.

interdental A sound produced by inserting the tip of the tongue between the upper and lower teeth, e.g., the initial sounds of *thought* and *those.*

interlanguage grammars The intermediate grammars that second-language learners create on their way to acquiring the (more or less) complete grammar of the target language.

internal borrowing See analogic change.

International Phonetic Alphabet (IPA) The phonetic alphabet designed by the International Phonetic Association to be used to represent the sounds found in all human languages.

International Phonetic Association (IPA) The organization founded in 1888 to further phonetic research and to develop the International Phonetic Alphabet.

interrogative (sentence) A sentence that questions whether a particular situation exists. See **declarative.**

intonation The pitch contour of a phrase or sentence.

intransitive verb A verb that must not have (does not C-select for) a direct object complement, e.g., *sleep, rise.*

IP Inflection Phrase. A term sometimes used in place of **sentence** (S). A phrasal category whose head is **Aux**.

ipsilateral Refers to neural signals that travel between one side of the body (left/right) and the same cerebral hemisphere (left/right). See **contralateral**.

isogloss A geographic boundary that separates areas with **dialect** differences, e.g., a line on a map on one side of which most people say *faucet* and on the other side of which most people say *spigot*.

isolating language A language in which most words contain a single morpheme, and there is little if any word morphology, e.g., no plural affixes on nouns or agreement affixes on verbs. Also called an analytic language, e.g., Vietnamese.

jargon Special words peculiar to the members of a profession or group, e.g., *glottis* for phoneticians. See **argot**. Also, the nonsense words sometimes used by Wernicke's aphasics.

jargon aphasia Form of aphasia in which phonemes are substituted, resulting in non-sense words; often produced by people who have severe **Wernicke's aphasia**.

kana The characters of either of the two Japanese syllabaries, **katakana** and **hiragana**.

kanji The Japanese term for the Chinese characters used in Japanese writing.

katakana A Japanese **syllabary** generally used for writing loan words and to achieve the effect of italics.

L2 acquisition See second language acquisition.

labial A sound articulated at the lips, e.g., [b], [f].

labiodental A sound produced by touching the bottom lip to the upper teeth, e.g., [v].

labio-velar A sound articulated by simultaneously raising the back of the tongue toward the velum and rounding the lips. The [w] of English is a labio-velar glide.

language contact The situation in which speakers of different languages regularly inter-act with one another, and especially where there are many bilingual or multilingual speakers.

language isolate A natural language with no demonstrable genealogical relationship with other living languages.

larynx The structure of muscles and cartilage in the throat that contains the vocal cords and **glottis**; often called the "voice box."

late closure principle A psycholinguistic principle of language comprehension that states: Attach incoming material to the phrase that was most recently processed, e.g., *he said that he slept yesterday* associates *yesterday* with *he slept* rather than with *he said*.

lateral A sound produced with air flowing past one or both sides of the tongue, e.g., [l].

lateralization, lateralized Terms used to refer to cognitive functions localized to one or the other hemisphere of the brain.

lax vowel A vowel produced with relatively less tension in the vocal cords and little ten-dency to diphthongize, e.g., [ʊ] in *put*, [pʊt]. Most lax vowels do not occur at the ends of syllables, that is, [bʊ] is not a possible English word. See **tense**.

length A prosodic feature referring to the duration of a segment. Two sounds may con-trast in length, e.g., in Japanese the first vowel is [+long] in /biːru/ "beer" but [−long], therefore short, in /biru/ "building."

level tones Relatively stable (nongliding) **pitch** on syllables of tone languages. Also called register tones.

lexical access The process of searching the mental **lexicon** for a phonological string to determine if it is an actual word.

lexical ambiguity Multiple meanings of sentences due to words that have multiple mean-ings, e.g., *He blew up the pictures of his ex-girlfriend.*

lexical category A general term for the word-level syntactic categories of noun, verb, adjective, and adverb. These are the categories of content words like *man, run, large,* and *rapidly*, as opposed to functional category words such as *the* and *and*. See **functional category**, **phrasal category**, **open class**.

lexical decision Task of subjects in psycholinguistic experiments who on presentation of a spoken or printed stimulus must decide whether it is a word or not.

lexical gap Possible but nonoccurring words; forms that obey the **phonotactic constraints** of a language yet have no meaning, e.g., *blick* in English.

lexical paraphrases Sentences that have the same meaning due to synonyms, e.g., *She lost her purse* and *She lost her handbag*.

lexical semantics The subfield of semantics concerned with the meanings of words and the meaning relationships among words.

lexicographer One who edits or works on a dictionary.

lexicography The editing or making of a dictionary.

lexicon The component of the grammar containing speakers' knowledge about morphemes and words; a speaker's mental dictionary.

lexifier language The dominant language of a **pidgin** (and **creole**) that provides the basis for the majority of the lexical items in the language.

lingua franca A language common to speakers of diverse languages that can be used for communication and commerce, e.g., English is the lingua franca of international airline pilots.

linguistic competence See **competence, linguistic**.

linguistic context The discourse that precedes a phrase or sentence that helps clarify meaning.

linguistic determinism The strongest form of the **Sapir-Whorf hypothesis**, which holds that the language we speak establishes how we perceive and think about the world.

linguistic performance See **performance, linguistic**.

linguistic relativism A weaker form of the **Sapir-Whorf hypothesis**, which holds that different languages encode different categories, and that speakers of different languages therefore think about the world in different ways. For example, speakers of languages that have fewer color words will be less sensitive to gradations of color.

linguistic sign Sounds or gestures, typically morphemes in spoken languages and signs in sign languages, that have a form bound to a meaning in a single unit, e.g., *dog* is a linguistic sign whose form is its pronunciation [dag] and whose meaning is *Canis familiaris* (or however we define "dog").

linguistic theory A theory of the principles that characterize all human languages. See **Universal Grammar**.

liquids A class of consonants including /l/ and /r/ and their variants that share vowel-like acoustic properties and may function as syllabic nuclei.

loan translations Compound words or expressions whose parts are translated literally into the borrowing language, e.g., *marriage of convenience* from French *mariage de convenance*.

loan word Word in one language whose origins are in another language, e.g., in Japanese, *besiboru*, "baseball," is a loan word from English. See **borrowing**.

localization The hypothesis that different areas of the brain are responsible for distinct cognitive systems. See **lateralization**.

location The thematic role of the noun phrase whose referent is the place where the action of the verb occurs, e.g., *Oslo* in *It snows in Oslo*.

logograms The symbols of a **word-writing** or **logographic writing** system.

logographic writing See **word writing**.

machine translation See **automatic machine translation**.

magnetic resonance imaging (MRI) A technique to investigate the molecular structures in human organs including the brain, which may be used to identify sites of brain lesions.

main verb The verb that functions as the head in the highest verb phrase of a sentence, e.g., *save* in *They save money to travel.* See **head of a phrase**.

manner of articulation The way the air stream is obstructed as it travels through the vocal tract. **Stop, nasal, affricate,** and **fricative** are some manners of articulation. See **place of articulation**.

marked In a gradable pair of antonyms, the word that is *not* used in questions of degree, e.g., *low* is the marked member of the pair *high/low* because we ordinarily ask *How high is the mountain?* not **How low is the mountain?*; in a masculine/feminine pair, the word that contains a derivational morpheme, usually the feminine word, e.g., *princess* is marked, whereas *prince* is unmarked. See **unmarked**.

mass nouns Nouns that cannot ordinarily be enumerated, e.g., *milk, water; *two milks* is ungrammatical except when interpreted to mean "two kinds of milk," "two containers of milk," and so on. See **count nouns**.

maxim of manner A conversational convention that a speaker's discourse should be brief and orderly, and should avoid ambiguity and obscurity.

maxim of quality A conversational convention that a speaker should not lie or make unsupported claims.

maxim of quantity A conversational convention that a speaker's contribution to the discourse should be as informative as is required, neither more nor less.

maxim of relevance A conversational convention that a speaker's contribution to a discourse should always have a bearing on, and a connection with, the matter under discussion.

maxims of conversation Conversational conventions such as the **maxim of quantity** that people appear to obey to give coherence and sincerity to discourse.

mean length of utterances (MLU) The average number of words or morphemes in a child's utterance. It is a more accurate measure of the acquisition stage of language than chronological age.

meaning The conceptual or semantic aspect of a sign or utterance that permits us to comprehend the message being conveyed. Expressions in language generally have both form—pronunciation or gesture—and meaning. See **extension, intension, sense, reference**.

mental grammar The internalized grammar that a descriptive grammar attempts to model. See **linguistic competence**.

metalinguistic awareness A speaker's conscious awareness *about* language and the use of language, as opposed to linguistic *knowledge*, which is largely unconscious. This book is very much about metalinguistic awareness.

metaphor Nonliteral, suggestive meaning in which an expression that designates one thing is used implicitly to mean something else, e.g., *The night has a thousand eyes*, to mean "One may be unknowingly observed at night."

metathesis The phonological process that reorders segments, often by transposing two sequential sounds, e.g., the pronunciation of *ask* /æsk/ in some English dialects as [æks].

metonym, metonymy A word substituted for another word or expression with which it is closely associated, e.g., *gridiron* to refer to the game of American football.

mimetic Similar to imitating, acting out, or miming.

minimal attachment principle The principle that in comprehending language, listeners create the simplest structure consistent with the grammar, e.g., *the horse raced past the barn* is interpreted as a complete sentence rather than a noun phrase containing a relative clause, as if it were *the horse* (that was) *raced past the barn.*

minimal pair (or set) Two (or more) words that are identical except for one phoneme that occurs in the same position in each word, e.g., *pain* /pen/, *bane* /ben/, *main* /men/.

modal An auxiliary verb other than *be, have,* and *do,* such as *can, could, will, would,* and *must.*

modularity (modular) The organization of the brain and mind into distinct, independent, and autonomous parts that interact with each other.

monogenetic theory of language origin The belief that all languages originated from a single language. See **Nostratic**.

monomorphemic word A word that consists of one morpheme.

monophthong Simple vowel, e.g., [ɛ] in [bɛd]. See **diphthong**.

monosyllabic Having one syllable, e.g., *boy*, *through*.

morpheme Smallest unit of linguistic meaning or function, e.g., *sheepdogs* contains three morphemes, *sheep*, *dog*, and the function morpheme for plural, *s*.

morphological parser A process, often a computer program, that uses rules of word formation to decompose words into their component morphemes.

morphological rules Rules for combining morphemes to form stems and words.

morphology The study of the structure of words; the component of the grammar that includes the rules of word formation.

morphophonemic orthography A writing system, such as that for English, in which morphological knowledge is needed to read correctly, e.g., in *please/pleasant* the *ea* represents [i]/[ɛ].

morphophonemic rules Rules that specify the pronunciation of morphemes; a morpheme may have more than one pronunciation determined by such rules, e.g., the plural morpheme /z/ in English is regularly pronounced [s], [z], or [əz].

motherese See **child-directed speech (CDS)**.

naming task An experimental technique that measures the response time between seeing a printed word and saying that word aloud.

narrowing A semantic change in which the meaning of a word changes in time to become less encompassing, e.g., *deer* once meant "animal."

nasal (nasalized) sound Speech sound produced with an open nasal passage (lowered velum), permitting air to pass through the nose as well as the mouth, e.g., /m/. See **oral sound**.

nasal cavity The passageways between the throat and the nose through which air passes during speech if the velum is open (lowered). See **oral cavity**.

natural class A class of sounds characterized by a phonetic property or feature that pertains to all members of the set, e.g., the class of stops. A natural class may be defined with a smaller feature set than that of any individual member of the class.

negative polarity item (NPI) An expression that is grammatical in the presence of negation, but ungrammatical in simple affirmative sentences, e.g., *any* in *James does not have any money* but **James has any money*.

Neo-Grammarians A group of nineteenth-century linguists who claimed that sound shifts (i.e., changes in phonological systems) took place without exceptions.

Neo-Grammarian hypothesis The claim that sound shifts (i.e., changes in phonological systems) take place without exceptions.

neurolinguistics The branch of linguistics concerned with the brain mechanisms that underlie the acquisition and use of human language; the study of the neurobiology of language.

neutralization Phonological processes or rules that obliterate the contrast between two phonemes in certain environments, e.g., in some dialects of English /t/ and /d/ are both pronounced as voiced flaps between vowels, as in *writer* and *rider*, thus neutralizing the voicing distinction so that the two words sound alike.

node A labeled branch point in a phrase structure tree; part of the graphical depiction of a transition network represented as a circle, pairs of which are connected by arcs. See **arc, phrase structure tree, transition network**.

noncontinuant A sound in which air is blocked momentarily in the oral cavity as it passes through the vocal tract. See **stops, affricate**.

nondistinctive features Phonetic features of phones that are predictable by rule, e.g., aspiration in English.

nonphonemic features See nondistinctive features.

nonredundant A phonetic feature that is distinctive, e.g., stop, voice, but not aspiration in English.

nonsense word A permissible phonological form without meaning, e.g., *slithy*.

Nostratic A hypothetical language that is postulated as the first human language.

noun (N) The syntactic category, also lexical category, of words that can function as the head of a noun phrase, such as *book, Jean, sincerity*. In many languages nouns have grammatical alternations for number, case, and gender and occur with determiners.

noun phrase (NP) The syntactic category, also phrasal category, of expressions containing some form of a noun or pronoun as its head, and which functions as the subject or as various objects in a sentence.

nucleus That part of a syllable that has the greatest acoustic energy; the vowel portion of a syllable, e.g., /i/ in /mit/ *meet*.

obstruents The class of sounds consisting of nonnasal stops, fricatives, and affricates. See sonorants.

onomatopoeia/onomatopoeic Refers to words whose pronunciations suggest their meaning, e.g., *meow, buzz*.

onset One or more phonemes that precede the syllable nucleus, e.g., /pr/ in /prist/ *priest*.

open class The class of lexical content words; a category of words that commonly adds new words, e.g., nouns, verbs.

Optimality Theory The hypothesis that a universal set of ranked phonological constraints exists, where the higher the constraint is ranked, the more influence it exerts on the language, e.g., in English, one constraint is the following: *Obstruent sequences may not differ with respect to their voice feature at the end of a word*.

oral cavity The mouth area through which air passes during the production of speech. See nasal cavity.

oral sound A non-nasal speech sound produced by raising the velum to close the nasal passage so that air can escape only through the mouth. See nasal sound.

orthography The written form of a language; spelling.

overextension The broadening of a word's meaning in language acquisition to encompass a more general meaning, e.g., using *dog* for any four-legged animals including cats or horses.

overgeneralization Children's treatment of irregular verbs and nouns as if they were regular, e.g., *bringed, goed, foots, mouses*, for *brought, went, feet, mice*. This shows that the child has acquired the regular rules but has not yet learned that there are exceptions.

palatal A sound produced by raising the front part of the tongue to the palate.

palate The bony section of the roof of the mouth behind the alveolar ridge.

paradigm A set of forms derived from a single root morpheme, e.g., *give, gives, given, gave, giving*; or *woman, women, woman's, women's*.

paradox A sentence to which it is impossible to ascribe a truth value, e.g., *this sentence is false*.

parallel processing The ability of a computer to carry out several tasks simultaneously as a result of the presence of multiple central processors.

parameters The small set of alternatives for a particular phenomenon made available by Universal Grammar. For example, Universal Grammar specifies that a phrase must have a head and possibly complements; a parameter states whether the complement(s) precedes or follows the head.

paraphrases Sentences with the same truth conditions; sentences with the same meaning, except possibly for minor differences in emphasis, e.g., *He ran up a big bill* and *He ran a big bill up*. See **synonymy**.

parse The act of determining the grammaticality of sequences of words according to rules of syntax, and assigning a linguistic structure to the grammatical ones.

parser A computer program that determines the grammaticality of sequences of words according to whatever rules of syntax are stored in the computer's memory, and assigns a linguistic structure to the grammatical ones.

participle The form of a verb that occurs after the auxiliary verbs *be* and *have*, e.g., *kissing* in *John is kissing Mary* is a present participle; *kissed* in *John has kissed many girls* is a past participle; *kissed* in *Mary was kissed by John* is a passive participle.

passive sentence A sentence in which the verbal complex contains a form of *to be* followed by a verb in its participle form, e.g., *The girl was kissed by the boy*; *The robbers must not have been seen*. In a passive sentence, the direct object of a transitive verb in d-structure functions as the subject in s-structure. See **active sentence**.

performance, linguistic The *use* of linguistic competence in the production and comprehension of language; behavior as distinguished from linguistic knowledge, e.g., linguistic competence permits one-million-word sentences, but linguistic performance prevents this from happening.

performative sentence A sentence containing a performative verb used to accomplish some act. Performative sentences are affirmative and declarative, and are in first-person, present tense, e.g., *I now pronounce you husband and wife*, when spoken by a justice of the peace in the appropriate situation, is an act of marrying.

performative verb A verb, certain usages of which result in a **speech act**, e.g., *resign* when the sentence *I resign!* is interpreted as an act of resignation.

person deixis The use of terms to refer to persons whose reference relies entirely on context, e.g., pronouns such as *I, he, you* and expressions such as *this child*. See **deictic, time deixis, place deixis, demonstrative articles**.

petroglyph A drawing on rock made by prehistoric people.

pharynx The tube or cavity in the vocal tract above the glottis through which the air passes during speech production.

phone A phonetic realization of a **phoneme**.

phoneme A contrastive phonological **segment** whose phonetic realizations are predictable by rule.

phonemic features Phonetic properties of phonemes that account for their ability to contrast meanings of words, e.g., *voice, tense*. Also called **distinctive features**.

phonemic principle The principle that underlies alphabetic writing systems in which one symbol typically represents one phoneme.

phonemic representation The phonological representation of words and sentences prior to the application of phonological rules.

phonetic alphabet Alphabetic symbols used to represent the phonetic segments of speech in which there is a one-to-one relationship between each symbol and each speech sound.

phonetic features Phonetic properties of segments (e.g., voice, nasal, alveolar) that distinguish one segment from another.

phonetic representation The representation of words and sentences after the application of phonological rules; symbolic transcription of the pronunciation of words and sentences.

phonetic similarity Refers to sounds that share most phonetic features.

phonetics The study of linguistic speech sounds, how they are produced (**articulatory phonetics**), how they are perceived (**auditory** or perceptual **phonetics**), and their physical aspects (**acoustic phonetics**).

phonetic transcription The "spelling" of a word in terms of the individual phones it contains, using a **phonetic alphabet**, as opposed to ordinary **orthography**, e.g., [fǝnɛrɪk] for *phonetic*.

phonographic symbol A symbol in a writing system that stands for the sounds of a word.

phonological rules Rules that apply to phonemic representations to derive phonetic representations or pronunciation.

phonology The sound system of a language; the component of a grammar that includes the inventory of sounds (phonetic and phonemic units) and rules for their combination and pronunciation; the study of the sound systems of all languages.

phonotactics/phonotactic constraints Rules stating permissible strings of phonemes; within a syllable, e.g., a word-initial nasal consonant may be followed only by a vowel (in English). See **possible word, nonsense word, accidental gap**.

phrasal category The class of syntactic categories that occur on the left side of phrase structure rules, and are therefore composed of other categories, possibly including other phrasal categories, e.g., noun phrase (NP). See **lexical category, functional category**.

phrasal semantics See **sentential semantics**.

phrase structure rules Principles of grammar that specify the constituency of syntactic categories and of phrase structure trees, e.g., VP → V NP.

phrase structure tree A tree diagram with syntactic categories at each node that reveals both the linear and hierarchical structure of phrases and sentences.

phrenology A pseudoscience of examining bumps on the skull to determine personality traits and intellectual ability. Its contribution to neurolinguistics is that its methods were highly suggestive of the modular theory of brain structure.

pictogram A symbol in a writing system that resembles the object represented in a direct way; a nonarbitrary form of writing.

pictographic writing A method of writing that utilizes **pictograms**, or literal representations of the word.

pidgin A simple but rule-governed language developed for communication among speakers of mutually unintelligible languages, often based on one of those languages called the **lexifier language**. See **substrate languages**.

pidginization The process of the creation of a pidgin that involves a simplification of the grammars of the impinging languages and a reduction of the number of domains in which the language is used. See **creolization, pidgin**.

Pinyin An alphabetic writing system for Mandarin Chinese using a Western-style alphabet to represent individual sounds.

pitch The fundamental **frequency** of sound perceived by the listener.

pitch contour The intonation of a sentence.

place deixis The use of terms to refer to places whose reference relies entirely on context, e.g., *here, there, behind, next door*. See **deictic, time deixis, person deixis, demonstrative articles**.

place of articulation The part of the vocal tract at which constriction occurs during the production of consonants. See **manner of articulation**.

plosives Oral, or non-nasal, stop consonants, so called because the air that is stopped explodes with the release of the closure.

polyglot A person who speaks several languages.

polymorphemic word A word that consists of more than one **morpheme**.

polysemous/polysemy Describes a single word with several closely related but slightly different meanings, e.g., *face*, meaning "face of a person," "face of a clock," "face of a building."

polysynthetic language Languages with extraordinarily rich morphologies in which a single word may carry the semantic content of an entire sentence.

positron emission tomography (PET) Method to detect changes in brain activities and relate these changes to localized brain damage and cognitive tasks.

possessor The thematic role of the noun phrase to whose referent something belongs, e.g., *the dog* in *The dog's tail wagged furiously.*

possible word A string of sounds that obeys the **phonotactic constraints** of the language but has no meaning, e.g., *gimble*. Also called a **nonsense word.**

poverty of the stimulus See impoverished data.

pragmatics The study of how context and situation affect meaning.

predictable feature A nondistinctive, noncontrastive, redundant phonetic feature, e.g., aspiration in English voiceless stops, or nasalization in English vowels.

prefix An **affix** that is attached to the beginning of a morpheme or stem, e.g., *in-* in *inoperable.*

preposition (P) The syntactic category, also functional category, that heads a prepositional phrase, e.g., *at, in, on, up.*

prepositional object The grammatical relation of the noun phrase that occurs immediately below a **prepositional phrase (PP)** in d-structure.

prepositional phrase (PP) The syntactic category, also phrasal category, consisting of a prepositional head and a noun phrase complement, e.g., *with a key, into the battle, over the top.*

prescriptive grammar Rules of grammar brought about by grammarians' attempts to legislate what speakers' grammatical rules should be, rather than what they are. See **descriptive grammar, teaching grammar.**

prestige dialect The dialect usually spoken by people in positions of power, and the one deemed correct by prescriptive grammarians, e.g., RP (received *pronunciation*) (British) English, the dialect spoken by the English royal family.

presupposition Implicit assumptions about the world required to make an utterance meaningful or relevant, e.g., "some tea has already been taken" is a presupposition of *Take some more tea!*

primes The basic formal units of sign languages that correspond to phonological elements of spoken language.

priming An experimental procedure that measures the response time between hearing a word and grasping the meaning of that word, as a function of whether the participant has heard a related word previously. See **semantic priming.**

principle of compositionality A principle of semantic interpretation that states that the meaning of a word, phrase, or sentence depends both on the meaning of its components (morphemes, words, phrases) and how they are combined structurally.

productive Refers to **morphological rules** that can be used freely and apply to all forms to create new words, e.g., the addition to an adjective of *-ish* meaning "having somewhat of the quality," such as *newish, tallish, incredible-ish.*

pro-form A word that replaces another word or expression found elsewhere in discourse, or understood from the situational context. Pronouns are the best known pro-forms, but words like *did* may function as "pro-verb phrases" as in *John washed three sheepdogs and Mary did too.*

proper name A word or words that refer to a person, place, or other entity with a unique reference known to the speaker and listener. Usually capitalized in writing, e.g., Nina Hyams, New York, Atlantic Ocean.

prosodic bootstrapping The learning of word or phrase segmentation by infants inferred from the stress pattern of a language.

prosodic feature The duration (length), pitch, or loudness of speech sounds.

Proto-Germanic The name given by linguists to the language that was an ancestor of English, German, and other Germanic languages.

Proto-Indo-European (PIE) See Indo-European.

protolanguage The earliest identifiable language from which genetically related languages developed.

psycholinguistics The branch of linguistics concerned with **linguistic performance**, language acquisition, and speech production and comprehension.

rebus principle In writing, the use of a **pictogram** for its phonetic value, e.g., using a picture of a bee to represent the verb *be* or the sound [b].

recast The repetition with "corrections" of a child's utterance by an adult. E.g., the child says *I holded the rabbit*, and the adult corrects by saying *You mean you held the rabbit.*

recursive rule A **phrase structure rule** that repeats its own category on its right side, e.g., VP → VP PP, hence permitting phrase structures of potentially unlimited length, corresponding to that aspect of speakers' **linguistic competence**.

reduced vowel A vowel that is unstressed and generally pronounced as schwa [ə] in English.

redundant Describes a nondistinctive, nonphonemic feature that is predictable from other feature values of the segment, e.g., [+voice] is redundant for any [+nasal] phoneme in English because all nasals are voiced.

reduplication A morphological process that repeats or copies all or part of a word to produce a new word, e.g., *wishy-washy, teensy-weensy, hurly-burly*. Also used in some languages as an inflectional process, e.g., Samoan *manao/mananao*, "he wishes/they wish."

reference That part of the meaning of a noun phrase that associates it with some entity. That part of the meaning of a declarative sentence that associates it with a **truth value**, either true or false. Also called **extension**. See **referent, sense**.

reference resolution In computational pragmatics, the computer algorithms that determine when two expressions have the same referent, e.g., identifying the referents of pronouns.

referent The entity designated by an expression, e.g., the referent of *John* in *John knows Sue* is the actual person named John; the referent of *Raleigh is the capital of California* is the truth value *false*. Also called **extension**.

reflexive pronoun A pronoun ending with *-self* that generally requires a noun-phrase antecedent within the same S, e.g., *myself, herself, ourselves, itself.*

regional dialect A dialect spoken in a specific geographic area that may arise from, and is reinforced by, that area's integrity. For example, a Boston dialect is maintained because large numbers of Bostonians and their descendants remain in the Boston area. See **social dialect**.

register A stylistic variant of a language appropriate to a particular social setting. Also called **style**.

register tones In tone languages, level tones; high, mid, or low tones.

regular sound correspondence The occurrence of different sounds in the same position of the same word in different languages or dialects, with this parallel holding for a significant number of words, e.g., [aɪ] in non-Southern American English corresponds to [aː] in Southern American English. Also found between newer and older forms of the same language.

relational opposites A pair of **antonyms** in which one describes a relationship between two objects and the other describes the same relationship when the two objects are reversed, e.g., *parent/child, teacher/pupil*; John is the parent of Susie describes the same relationship as Susie is the child of John. See **gradable pair, complementary pair**.

retroflex sound A sound produced by curling the tip of the tongue back behind the alveolar ridge, e.g., the pronunciation of /r/ by many speakers of English.

rime The nucleus + coda of a syllable, e.g., the /en/ of /ren/ *rain.*

root The **morpheme** that remains when all affixes are stripped from a complex word, e.g., *system* from *un + system + atic + ally*.

rounded vowel A vowel sound produced with pursed lips, e.g., [o].

rules of syntax Principles of grammar that account for the grammaticality of sentences, their hierarchical structure, their word order, whether there is structural ambiguity, etc. See **phrase structure rules**, **transformational rules**.

SAE See **Standard American English**.

Sapir-Whorf hypothesis The proposition that the structure of a language influences how its speakers perceive the world around them. It is often presented in its weak form, **linguistic relativism**, and its strong form, **linguistic determinism**.

savant An individual who shows special abilities in one cognitive area while being deficient in others. Linguistic savants have extraordinary language abilities but are deficient in general intelligence.

second language acquisition The acquisition of another language or languages after first language acquisition is under way or completed. Also called **L2 acquisition**.

segment (1) An individual sound that occurs in a language; (2) the act of dividing utterances into sounds, morphemes, words, and phrases.

semantic bootstrapping The learning of word categories inferred from the word's meaning, e.g., a word whose meaning is a person, place or thing would be considered a noun.

semantic features Conceptual elements by which a person understands the meanings of words and sentences, e.g., "female" is a semantic feature of the nouns *girl* and *filly*; "cause" is a semantic feature of the verbs *darken* and *kill*.

semantic network A network of **arcs** and **nodes** used to represent semantic information about sentences.

semantic priming The effect of being able to recognize a word (e.g., *doctor*) more rapidly after exposure to a semantically similar word (e.g., *nurse*) than after exposure to a semantically more distant word. The word *nurse* primes the word *doctor*.

semantic properties See **semantic features**.

semantic representation A symbolic system suitable for the characterization of the meaning of natural language utterances in a computer, e.g., logic-based expressions or **semantic networks**.

semantic rules Principles for determining the meaning of larger units like sentences from the meaning of smaller units like noun phrases and verb phrases.

semantics The study of the linguistic meaning of morphemes, words, phrases, and sentences.

sense The inherent part of an expression's meaning that, together with context, determines its referent. Also called **intension**. For example, knowing the sense or intension of a noun phrase such as *the president of the United States in the year 2010* allows one to determine that Barack Obama is the referent. See **intension**, **reference**.

sentence (S) A syntactic category of expressions consisting minimally of a **noun phrase** (NP) followed by a **verb phrase** (VP) in **d-structure**. Also called a **TP** (tense phrase). The head of S is the category **Aux**.

sentential semantics The subfield of semantics concerned with the meaning of syntactic units larger than the word.

Separate Systems Hypothesis A proposal that a bilingual child builds a distinct lexicon and grammar for each language being acquired.

sequential bilingualism Refers to the acquisition of a second language by someone (adult or child) who has already acquired a first language.

shadowing task An experiment in which subjects are asked to repeat what they hear as rapidly as possible as it is being spoken. During the task, subjects often unconsciously correct "errors" in the input.

sibilants The class of sounds that includes alveolar and palatal **fricatives** and **affricates**, characterized acoustically by an abundance of high frequencies perceived as "hissing," e.g., [s], [tʃ].

sign A single gesture (possibly with complex meaning) in the sign languages used by the deaf.

sign languages The languages used by deaf people in which linguistic units such as morphemes and words as well as grammatical relations are formed by manual and other body movements.

simultaneous bilingualism Refers to the (more or less) simultaneous acquisition of two languages beginning in infancy (or before the age of three years).

sisters In a phrase structure tree, two categories that are directly under the same node, e.g., V and the direct object NP are sisters inside the verb phrase.

situational context Knowledge of who is speaking, who is listening, what objects are being discussed, and general facts about the world we live in, used to aid in the interpretation of meaning.

slang Words and phrases used in casual speech, often invented and spread by close-knit social or age groups, and fast-changing.

slip of the tongue An involuntary deviation of an intended utterance. See **spoonerism**. Also called **speech error**.

social dialect A dialect spoken by members of a group delineated by socioeconomic class, racial background, place of origin, or gender, and perpetuated by the integrity of the social class. See **regional dialect**.

societal bilingualism The mutual abilities of a community to speak two (or more) languages with native or near native proficiency. See **bilingualism, individual bilingualism**.

sociolinguistic variable A linguistic phenomenon such as double negation whose occurrence varies according to the social context of the speaker.

sonorants The class of sounds that includes **vowels, glides, liquids,** and **nasals**; nonobstruents. See **obstruents**.

sound change See **sound shift**.

sound shift Historical phonological change. Also called **sound change**.

sound symbolism The notion that certain sound combinations occur in semantically similar words, e.g., *gl* in *gleam, glisten, glitter*, which all relate to vision.

sound writing A term sometimes used to mean a writing system in which one sound is represented by one letter. Sound-writing systems do not employ the phonemic principle and are similar to phonetic transcriptions.

source The thematic role of the noun phrase whose referent is the place from which an action originates, e.g., *Mars* in *Mr. Wells just arrived from Mars*.

source language In automatic machine translation, the language being translated. See **target language, automatic machine translation**.

speaker identification The use of computers to assist in matching a voice recording by an unknown person to a known person.

specific language impairment (SLI) Difficulty in acquiring language faced by certain children with no other cognitive deficits.

specifier The category of the left sister of X' in **x-bar theory**, e.g., a **determiner** in an NP or an **adverb** in a VP. It is a modifier of the head and is often optional.

spectrogram A visual representation of speech decomposed into component frequencies, with time on the horizontal axis, frequency on the vertical axis, and intensity portrayed on a gray scale—the darker, the more intense. Also called **voiceprint**.

speech act The action or intent that a speaker accomplishes when using language in context, the meaning of which is inferred by hearers, e.g., *There is a bear behind you* may be intended as a warning in certain contexts, or may in other contexts merely be a statement of fact. See **illocutionary force**.

speech error An inadvertent deviation from an intended utterance that often results in ungrammaticality, nonsense words, anomaly, etc. See **slip of the tongue**, **spoonerism**.

speech recognition In computer processing, the ability to analyze speech sounds into phones, phonemes, morphemes, and words; the transcription of speech.

speech synthesis An electronic process that produces speech either from acoustically simulated sounds or from prerecorded units. See **formant synthesis**, **concatenative synthesis**.

speech understanding Computer processing for interpreting speech, one part of which is **speech recognition**.

spelling pronunciation Pronouncing a word as it is spelled, irrespective of its actual pronunciation by native speakers, e.g., pronouncing *Wednesday* as "wed-ness-day."

spelling reform The attempt by governments or academic institutions to change the spelling of words to more accurately reflect their current pronunciation.

spell-out rules Rules that convert abstract inflectional morphemes such as tense, agreement, and possessive into affixes.

split brain The result of an operation for epilepsy in which the **corpus callosum** is severed, thus separating the brain into its two hemispheres; split-brain patients are studied to determine the role of each hemisphere in cognitive and language processing.

spoonerism A speech error in which phonemic segments are reversed or exchanged, e.g., *you have hissed my mystery lecture* for the intended *you have missed my history lecture*; named after the Reverend William Archibald Spooner, a nineteenth-century Oxford don.

S-selection The classifying of verbs and other lexical items in terms of the semantic category of the head and complements that they accept, e.g., the verb *assassinate* S-selects for a human subject and a prestigious, human NP complement.

s-structure The structure that results from applying transformational rules to a d-structure. It is syntactically closest to actual utterances. Also called **surface structure**. See **transformational rule**.

standard The dialect (regional or social) considered to be the norm.

Standard American English (SAE) An idealized dialect of English that some prescriptive grammarians consider the proper form of English.

state/stative A type of sentence that describes states of being such as *Mary likes oysters*, as opposed to describing events such as *Mary ate oysters*. See **event/eventive**.

stem The base to which an affix is attached to create a more complex form that may be another stem or a word. See **root**, **affix**.

stemming In computational morphology, the analysis of words into their component morphemes by the recursive stripping off of affixes.

stops [−continuant] sounds in which the airflow is briefly but completely stopped in the oral cavity, e.g., [p,n,g].

stress, stressed syllable A syllable with relatively greater length, loudness, and/or higher pitch than other syllables in a word, and therefore perceived as prominent. Also called **accent**.

stress-timed language A language in which at least one syllable of a word receives primary stress. English is such a language.

structural ambiguity The phenomenon in which the same sequence of words has two or more meanings that is accounted for by different phrase structure analyses, e.g., *He saw a boy with a telescope*.

structure dependent (1) A principle of Universal Grammar that states that the application of **transformational rules** is determined by phrase structure properties, as opposed to structureless sequences of words or specific sentences; (2) the way children construct rules using their knowledge of syntactic structure irrespective of the specific words in the structure or their meaning.

style A situation dialect, e.g., formal speech, casual speech; also called **register**.

subcategorization See C-selection.

subject The grammatical relation of a noun phrase to a S(entence) when it appears immediately below that S in a phrase structure tree, e.g., *the zebra* in *The zebra has stripes.*

subject-verb agreement The addition of an **inflectional morpheme** to the main verb depending on a property of the noun phrase subject, such as number or gender. In English, it is the addition of *s* to a verb when the subject is third-person singular present tense, e.g., *A greyhound runs fast* versus *Greyhounds run fast.*

substrate languages The language(s) of the indigenous people in a language contact situation that contributes to the lexicon and grammar of a pidgin or creole but in a less obvious way than the **superstrate language**.

suffix An **affix** that is attached to the end of a morpheme or stem, e.g., *-er* in *Lew is taller than Bill.*

summarization The computer scanning of a text and condensation to its most salient points.

superstrate language The language that provides most of the lexical items of a pidgin or creole, typically the language of the socially or economically dominant group. Also called **lexifier language**. See **substrate languages**.

suppletive forms A term used to refer to **inflected morphemes** in which the regular rules do not apply, e.g., *went* as the past tense of *go.*

suprasegmentals Prosodic features, e.g., length, tone.

surface structure See s-structure.

syllabary The symbols of a syllabic writing system.

syllabic A phonetic feature of those sounds that may constitute the nucleus of syllables; all vowels are syllabic, and liquids and nasals may be syllabic in such words as *towel, button, bottom.*

syllabic writing A writing system in which each syllable in the language is represented by its own symbol, e.g., **hiragana** in Japanese.

syllable A phonological unit composed of an **onset**, **nucleus**, and **coda**, e.g., *elevator* has four syllables: *el e va tor*; *man* has one syllable.

syllable-timed language A language in which the syllables have approximately the same loudness, length, and pitch, as opposed to a **stress-timed language**. French, for example, is such a language.

synonyms Words with the same or nearly the same meaning, e.g., *pail* and *bucket.*

synonymy (synonymous) Having the same meaning in all contexts. More technically, in the semantic component of the grammar, two sentences are synonymous if they **entail** each other, e.g., *the cat ate the rat*; *the rat was eaten by the cat.* See **paraphrases**.

syntactic bootstrapping The learning of word meaning inferred from syntax, e.g., when a child hears *John glouted Mary a clibe* he realizes that *glout* is a verb and likely means the transferring of something from one person to another.

syntactic category/class See grammatical categories.

syntax The rules of sentence formation; the component of the mental grammar that represents speakers' knowledge of the structure of phrases and sentences.

synthetic language Languages in which words often contain multiple morphemes, e.g., English and Indo-European languages in general.

T (tense) A term sometimes used in place of **Aux**. The syntactic category that is the head of **TP** (tense phrase) or **sentence (S)**.

taboo Words or activities that are considered inappropriate for "polite society," e.g., *cunt*, *prick*, *fuck* for vagina, penis, and sexual intercourse, respectively.

tap A speech sound in which the tongue quickly touches the alveolar ridge, as in some British pronunciations of /r/. Also called **flap**.

target language In automatic machine translation, the language into which the source language is translated. See **source language**, **automatic machine translation**.

tautology A sentence that is true in all situations; a sentence true from the meaning of its words alone, e.g., *Kings are not female*. Also called **analytic**.

teaching grammar A set of language rules written to help speakers learn a foreign language or a different dialect of their language. See **descriptive grammar**, **prescriptive grammar**.

telegraphic speech Utterances of children that may omit **grammatical morphemes** and/ or **function words**, e.g., *He go out* instead of *He is going out*.

telegraphic stage The period of child language acquisition that follows the two-word stage and consists primarily of **telegraphic speech**.

tense A phonetic feature that distinguishes similar pairs of vowels. Vowels that are [+tense] are somewhat longer in duration and higher in tongue position and pitch than the corresponding [−tense] (lax) vowel, e.g., in English [i] is a high front tense vowel whereas [ɪ] is a high front lax vowel. See **lax vowel**. Also a term sometimes used in place of **Aux**, and usually abbreviated T, it is the syntactic category that is the head of **TP** (tense phrase) or sentence (S).

text-to-speech A computer program that converts written text into the basic units of a speech synthesizer, such as phones for **formant synthesizers**, or diphones, disyllables, etc. for **concatenative synthesizers**.

thematic role The semantic relationship between the verb and the noun phrases of a sentence, such as **agent**, **theme**, **location**, **instrument**, **goal**, **source**.

theme The thematic role of the noun phrase whose referent undergoes the action of the verb, e.g., *Martha* in *George hugged Martha*.

theta assignment The ascribing of thematic roles to the syntactic elements in a sentence.

time deixis The use of terms to refer to time whose reference relies entirely on context, e.g., *now*, *then*, *tomorrow*, *next month*. See **deictic**, **deixis**, **demonstrative articles**, **person deixis**, **place deixis**.

tip of the tongue (TOT) phenomenon The difficulty encountered from time to time in retrieving a particular word or expression from the mental lexicon. Anomic aphasics suffer from an extreme form of this problem. See **anomia**.

tone The contrastive **pitch** of syllables in **tone languages**. Two words may be identical except for such differences in pitch, e.g., in Thai *naa* [naː] with falling pitch means "face," but with a rising pitch means "thick." See **register tones**, **contour tones**.

tone language A language in which the **tone** or **pitch** on a syllable is phonemic, so that words with identical segments but different tones are different words, e.g., Mandarin Chinese, Thai.

top-down processing Expectation-driven analysis of linguistic input that begins with the assumption that a large syntactic unit such as a sentence is present, and then analyzes it into successively smaller constituents (e.g., phrases, words, morphemes), which are ultimately compared with the sensory or acoustic data to validate the analysis. If the analysis is not validated, the procedure backs up to the previously validated point and then resumes. See **bottom-up processing**, **backtracking**.

topicalization A transformation that moves a syntactic element to the front of a sentence, e.g., deriving *Greyhounds I love very much* from *I love greyhounds very much*.

TP (tense phrase) A term sometimes used in place of **sentence (S)**. A phrasal category whose head is **Aux**.

transcription, phonemic The phonemic representation of speech sounds using phonetic symbols, ignoring phonetic details that are predictable by rule, usually given between slashes, e.g., /pæn/, /spæn/ for *pan*, *span* as opposed to the phonetic representation [pʰæn], [spæn].

transcription, phonetic The representation of speech sounds using phonetic symbols between square brackets. They may reflect nondistinctive predictable features such as aspiration and nasality, e.g., [pʰat] for *pot* or [mæn] for *man*.

transfer of grammatical rules The application of rules from one's first language to a second language that one is attempting to acquire. The "accent" that second-language learners have is a result of the transfer of first language phonetic and phonological rules.

transformational rule, transformation A syntactic rule that applies to an underlying phrase structure tree of a sentence (either **d-structure** or an intermediate structure already affected by a transformation) and derives a new structure by moving or inserting elements, e.g., the transformational rules of *wh* movement and *do* insertion relate the deep structure sentence *John saw who* to the surface structure *Who(m) did John see.*

transformationally induced ambiguity This occurs when different **d-structures** are mapped into the same **s-structure** by one or more transformations, e.g., the ambiguous *George loves Laura more than Dick* may be transformationally derived from the d-structures *George loves Laura more than Dick loves Laura*, or *George loves Laura more than George loves Dick*, with the underlined words being deleted under identity by a transformation in either case.

transition network A graphical representation that uses nodes connected by labeled arcs to depict syntactic and semantic relationships. See **node, arc.**

transitional bilingual education (TBE) Educational programs in which students receive instruction in both English and their native language, for example Spanish, and the native language support is gradually phased out over two or three years.

transitive verb A verb that C-selects an obligatory noun-phrase complement, e.g., *find.*

tree diagram A graphical representation of the linear and hierarchical structure of a phrase or sentence. A **phrase structure tree.**

trill A speech sound in which part of the tongue vibrates against part of the roof of the mouth, e.g., the /r/ in Spanish *perro* ("dog") is articulated by vibrating the tongue tip behind the alveolar ridge; the /r/ in French *rouge* ("red") may be articulated by vibrations at the uvula.

trochaic Stress on the first syllable of a two-syllable word, e.g., *páper.*

truth conditions The circumstances that must be known to determine whether a sentence is true, and therefore part of the meaning, or **sense,** of declarative sentences.

truth-conditional semantics A theory of meaning that takes the semantic knowledge of knowing when sentences are true and false as basic.

truth value TRUE or FALSE; used to describe the truth of declarative sentences in context; the **reference** of a declarative sentence in **truth-conditional semantics.**

unaspirated Phonetically voiceless stops in which the vocal cords begin vibrating immediately upon release of the closure, e.g., [p] in *spot*. See **aspirated.**

unbound A pronoun or pro-form whose reference is determined from context rather than linguistic discourse. See **free pronoun, bound pronoun.**

unconditioned sound change Historical phonological change that occurs in all phonetic contexts, e.g., the **Great Vowel Shift** of English in which long vowels were modified wherever they occurred in a word.

underextension The narrowing of a word's meaning in language acquisition to a more restrictive meaning, e.g., using *dog* for only the family pet and not for other dogs.

ungrammatical Describes structures that fail to conform to the rules of grammar.

uniformity of theta assignment A principle of Universal Grammar that states that the various thematic roles are always structurally in the same place in deep structure, e.g., the thematic role of *theme* is always a direct object.

uninterpretable Describes an utterance whose meaning cannot be determined because of nonsense words, e.g., *All mimsy were the borogoves.*

Unitary System Hypothesis A proposal that a bilingual child initially constructs only one lexicon and one grammar for both (or all) languages being acquired.

Universal Grammar (UG) The innate principles and properties that pertain to the grammars of all human languages.

unmarked The term used to refer to that member of a gradable pair of antonyms used in questions of degree, e.g., *high* is the unmarked member of high/low; in a masculine/feminine pair, the word that does not contain a derivational morpheme, usually the masculine word, e.g., *prince* is unmarked, whereas *princess* is marked. See **marked.**

uvula The fleshy appendage hanging down from the end of the **velum** (soft palate).

uvular A sound produced by raising the back of the tongue to the **uvula.**

velar A sound produced by raising the back of the tongue to the soft palate, or **velum.**

velum The soft palate; the part of the roof of the mouth behind the hard palate.

verb (V) The syntactic category, also lexical category, of words that can be the head of a verb phrase. Verbs denote actions, sensations, and states, e.g., *climb, hear, understand.*

verb phrase (VP) The syntactic category of expressions that contains a verb as its head along with its complements such as noun phrases and prepositional phrases, e.g., *gave the book to the child.*

verbal particle A word identical in form to a preposition which, when paired with a verb, has a particular meaning. A particle, as opposed to a preposition, is characterized syntactically by its ability to occur next to the verb, or transposed to the right, e.g., *out,* in *spit out* as in *He spit out his words,* or *He spit his words out.* Compare with *He ran out the door* versus **he ran the door out,* where *out* is a preposition.

Verner's Law The description of a conditioned phonological change in the sound system of certain Indo-European languages wherein voiceless fricatives were changed when the preceding vowel was unstressed. It was formulated by Karl Verner as an explanation to some of the exceptions to **Grimm's Law.**

vocal tract The oral and nasal cavities, together with the vocal cords, glottis, and pharynx, all of which may be involved in the production of speech sounds.

vocalic A phonetic feature that distinguishes vowels and liquids, which are [+vocalic], from other sounds (obstruents, glides, nasals), which are [−vocalic]. The feature is little used in contemporary linguistic literature.

voiced sound A speech sound produced with vibrating vocal cords.

voiceless sound A speech sound produced with open, nonvibrating vocal cords.

voiceprint A common term for a **spectrogram.**

vowel A sound produced without significant constriction of the air flowing through the oral cavity.

well-formed Describes a grammatical sequence of words, one conforming to rules of syntax. See **grammatical, ill-formed.**

Wernicke, Carl Neurologist who showed that damage to specific parts of the left cerebral hemisphere causes specific types of language disorders.

Wernicke's aphasia The type of aphasia resulting from damage to **Wernicke's area.**

Wernicke's area The back (posterior) part of the left brain that if damaged causes a specific type of aphasia. Also called Wernicke's region.

***wh* questions** Interrogative sentences beginning with one or more of the words *who(m)*, *what, where, when,* and *how,* and their equivalents in languages that do not have *wh* words, such as *quién* in Spanish: *Who(m) do you like? ¿A quién le gusta?*

word writing A system of writing in which each character represents a word or morpheme of the language, e.g., Chinese. See **ideograph, logographic writing.**

X-bar theory A universal schema specifying that the internal organization of all phrasal categories (i.e., NP, PP, VP, TP(=S), AdjP, AdvP) can be broken down into three levels, e.g., NP, N', and N.

yes-no question An interrogative sentence that inquires as to whether a certain situation is true or not, e.g., *Is the boy asleep?*

Index

NOTE: Page references in *italics* refer to illustrations and cartoons.

Abbreviated English (AE), 486
abjad, 547
"-able," 83, 95–96
accents, 433. *see also* dialects
accent (word stress), 297–298, 337–338
accidental gaps, 302
acoustic phonetics, 232
acoustic signals
  language processing and, 378
  speech signals, 57–58
acquired dyslexia, 49
acronyms, 504
active-passive sentences, 157
Ade, George, 160
adjectives
  adjective phrases (AdjP), 128
  determiners *vs.,* 140
adjunction, 156
adverb (Adv), 128
adverbial phrase (AdvP), 128
affixes, 83
affricates, 242
African American English (AAE), 15, 442–446
  Chicano English *vs.,* 447
  creoles and, 459–460
  "Ebonics" and, 468–469
African American Vernacular English (AAVE), 15n

African languages
  clicks in, 232, 244
  families of, 518, 524
  phonology and, 271, 279–280, 293
  in society, 459
Afroasiatic languages, 518, 524
agents, 205
agglutinative languages, 525
agrammatic aphasics, 48
agrammatic language, 48
Akan language, 271, 279–280, 293
Akiba, Rabbi, 541
Alice's Adventures in Wonderland (Carroll), 78, 87, 99, 118, 213, 377, 489, 495
allomorphs, 268–272. *see also* morphemes
allophones, 277–278
  of /t/, 274, 274–275
  vowel nasalization and, 272–274
alphabet
  advent of, 546–547
  alphabetic abbreviations, 504
  alphabetic writing, 547, 551–553
  phonetic, 232–234, 233
Alsted, Johann Heinrich, 17
alveolar ridge, 236, 237
alveolars, 236, 237. *see also* phonetics; phonology
(alveo)palatals, 236, 237
Amahl (case study), 340
ambiguity

sentence meaning and, 182–183
structural ambiguity, 121, 149–151
American College Dictionary, The, 474
American English. *see also* English language; phonetics
phonetic symbols for consonants of, 244, 245
phonology, feature specifications, 283–284, 284, 285
regional dialects
  dialect atlases, 436, 437
  lexical differences, 435
  phonological differences, 434–435
  syntactic differences, 436–438
social dialects, 439, 439–452
  African American English, 442–446
  genderlects, 448–451
  Latino (Hispanic) English, 446–448
  sociolinguistic analysis, 451–452
  "standard" for, 439–442
sound change and, 489–491
vowel classification, 248